新美

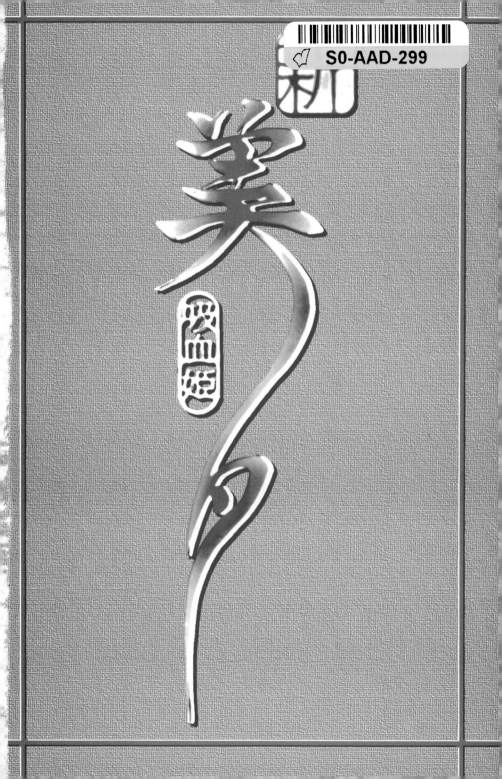

新美句

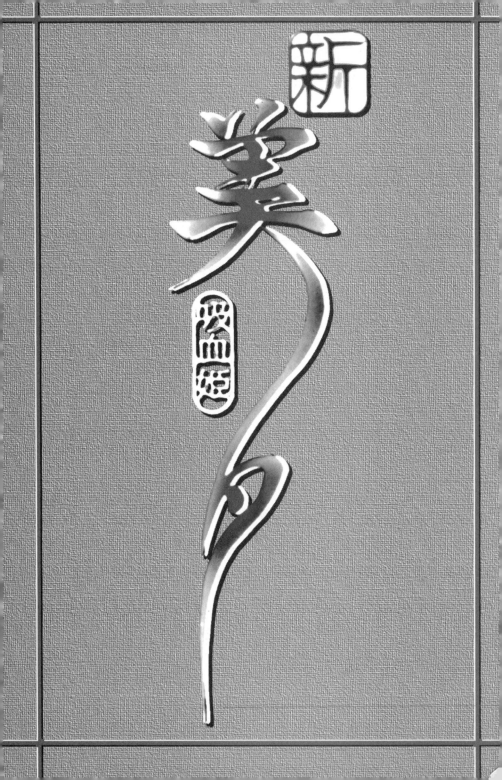

STUDIO IRONCAT GRAPHIC NOVEL

NEW VAMPIRE MIYU

Episode I: The Shinma Menace

STORY AND ART
BY
TOSHIHIRO HIRANO
&
NARUMI KAKINOUCHI

Table of Contents

THIS VOLUME CONTAINS **NEW VAMPIRE MIYU VOLUME I**
IN ITS ENTIRETY

STORY AND ART BY
TOSHIHIRO HIRANO & NARUMI KAKINOUCHI

TRANSLATION BY SACHIKO UCHIDA & KUNI KIMURA
TOUCH-UP ART BY STEPHEN R. BENNETT IV
EDITOR: KEVIN BENNETT
LAYOUT, COVER ASSEMBLY,COPY EDITOR: MARK HOFMANN
COVER DESIGN: HITOSHI USAMI
SPECIAL THANKS TO COL. P. YFF, USMC,
KAYT ROBARTS, CHRIS SEATON,
BRAD KANE, STEPHANIE BROWN
& KAT HOFER

PUBLISHED BY STUDIO IRONCAT
607 WILLIAM STREET, SUITE 213
FREDERICKSBURG, VA 22401

WWW.IRONCAT.COM

SECOND PRINTING

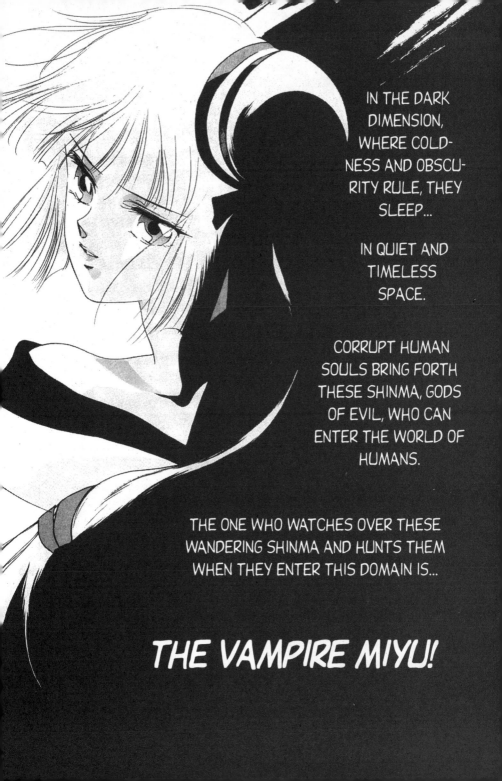

IN THE DARK
DIMENSION,
WHERE COLD-
NESS AND OBSCU-
RITY RULE, THEY
SLEEP...

IN QUIET AND
TIMELESS
SPACE.

CORRUPT HUMAN
SOULS BRING FORTH
THESE SHINMA, GODS
OF EVIL, WHO CAN
ENTER THE WORLD OF
HUMANS.

THE ONE WHO WATCHES OVER THESE
WANDERING SHINMA AND HUNTS THEM
WHEN THEY ENTER THIS DOMAIN IS...

THE VAMPIRE MIYU!

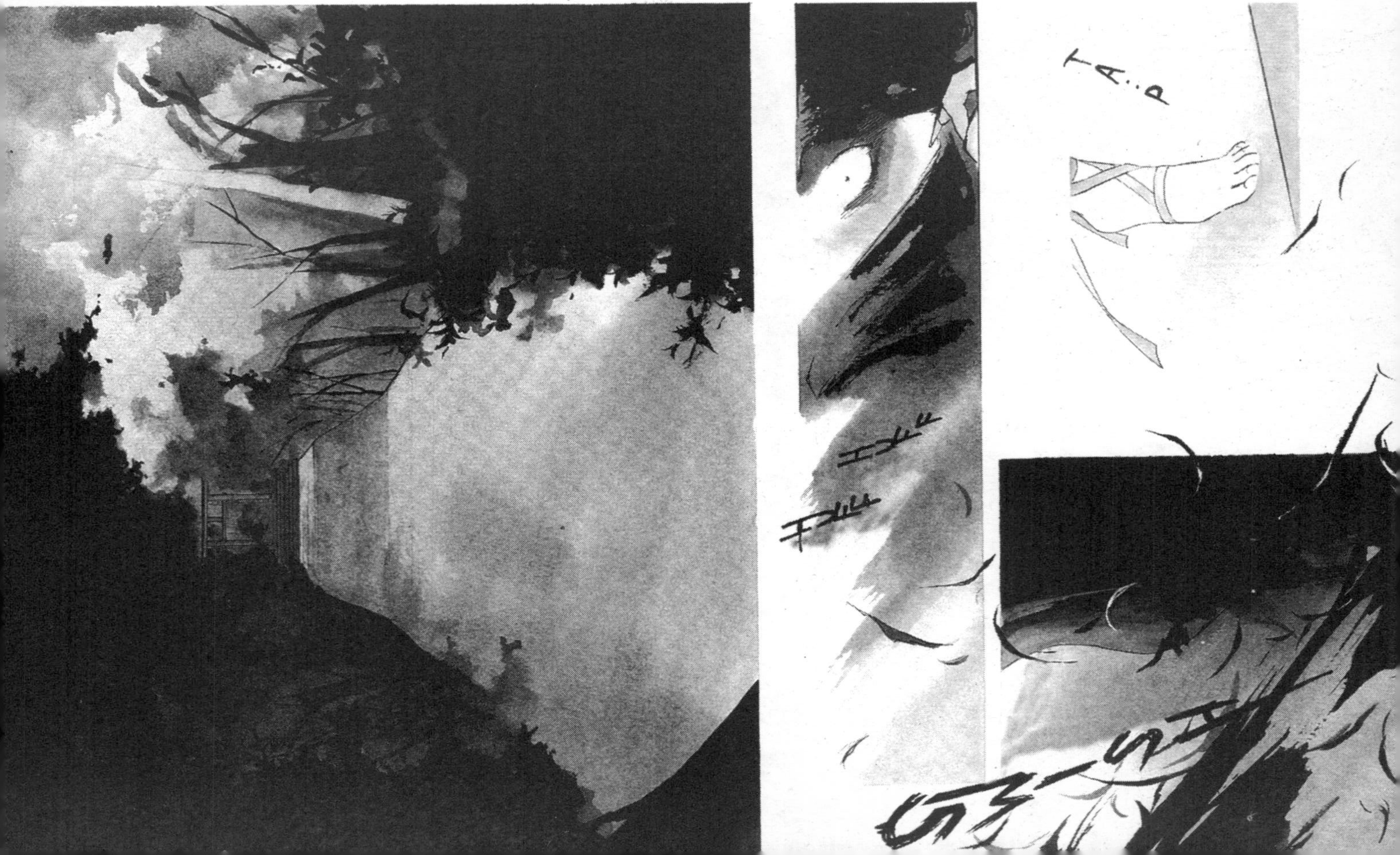
TA..P
HUFF HUFF
SWISH

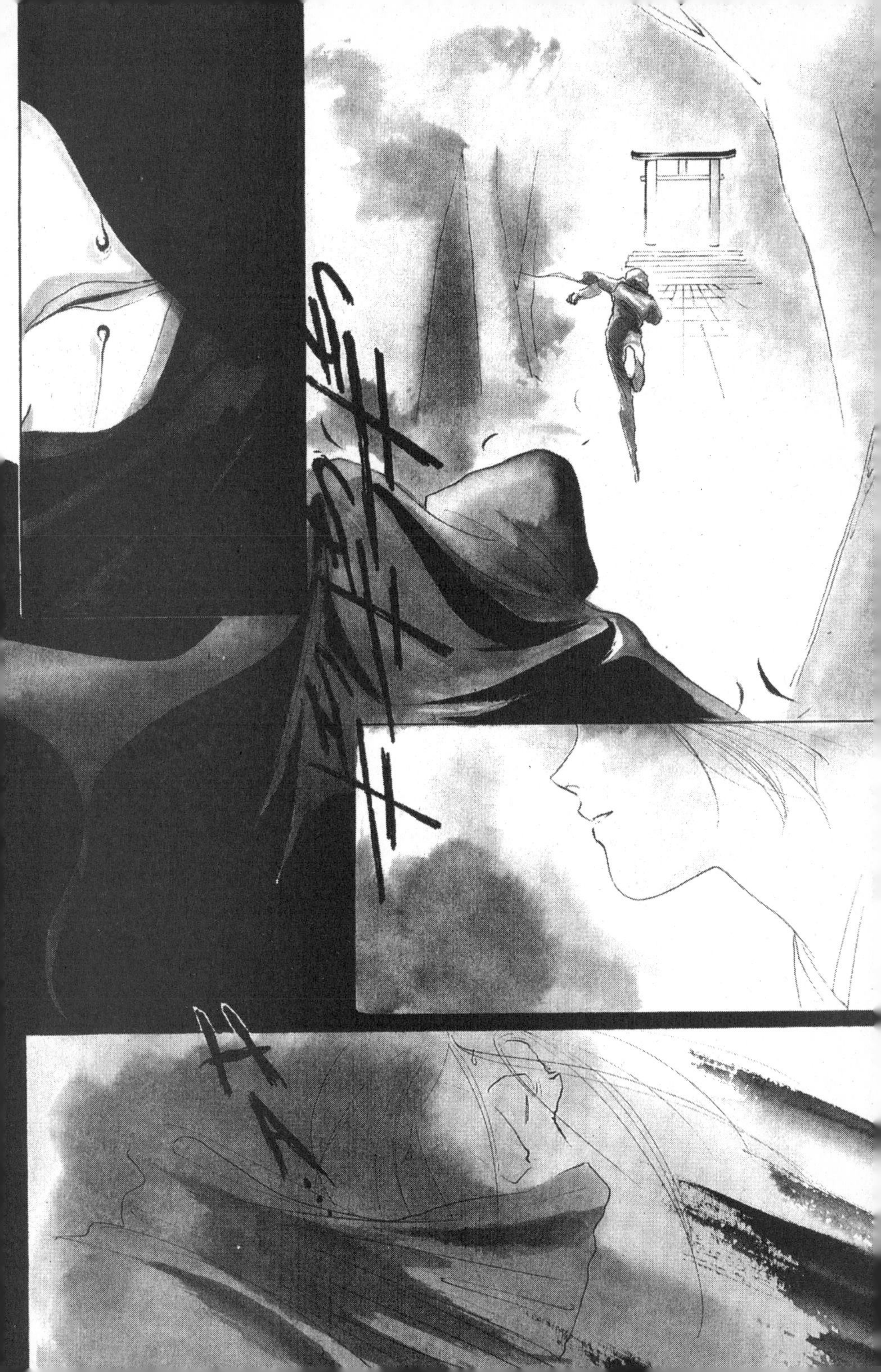
SHSHSH
HA

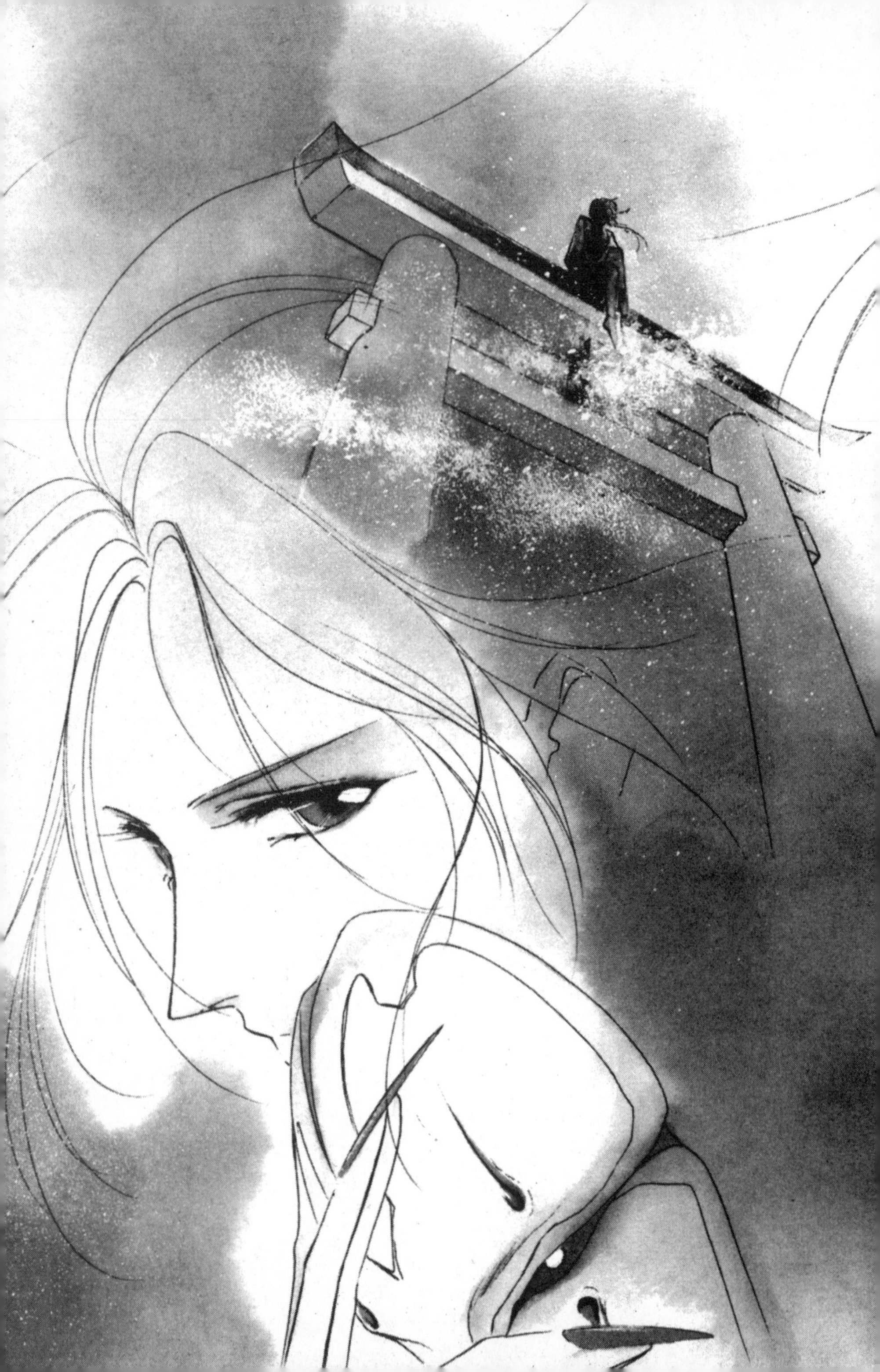

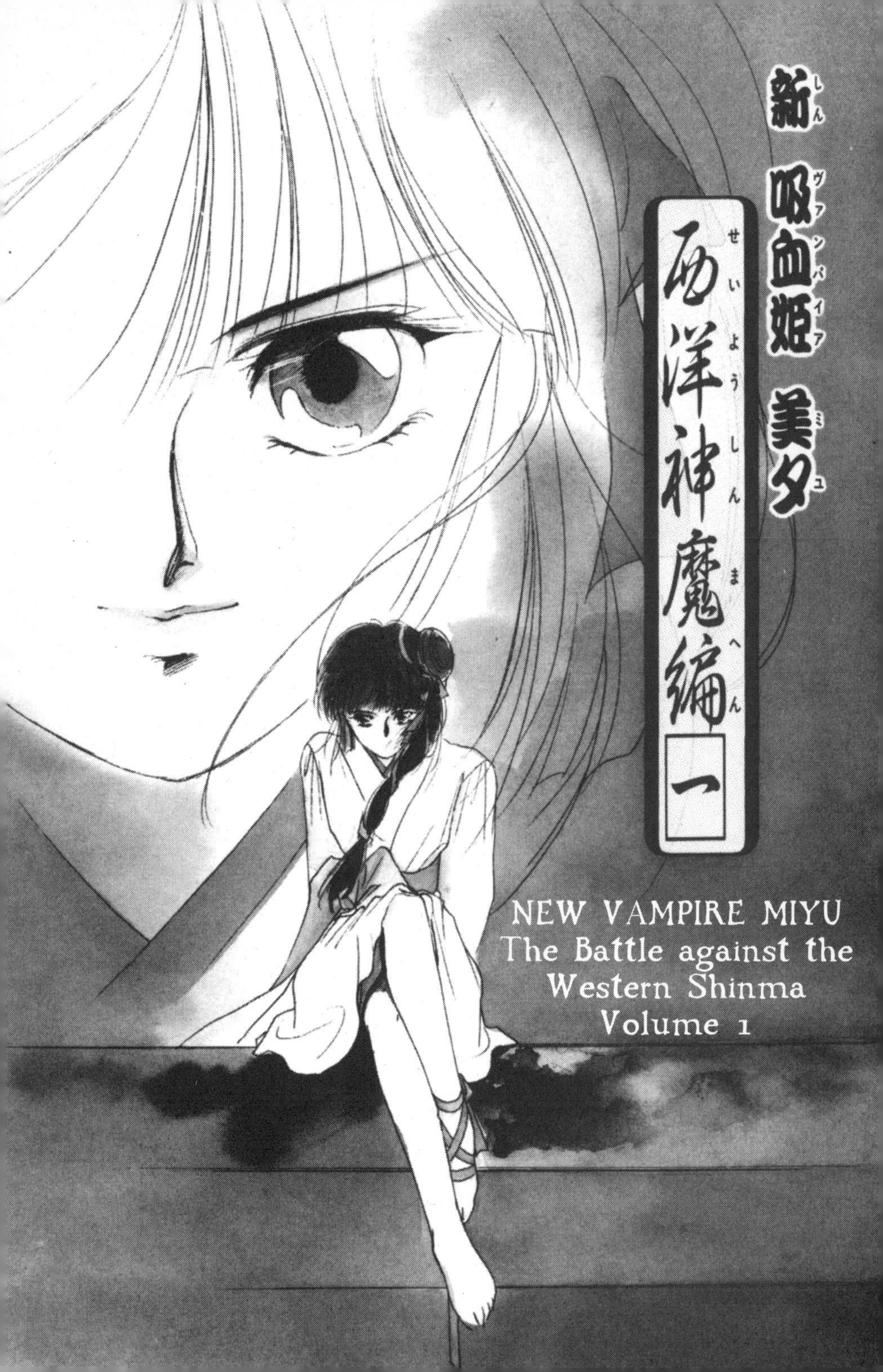
新吸血姫美夕
西洋神魔編
一
NEW VAMPIRE MIYU
The Battle against the
Western Shinma
Volume 1

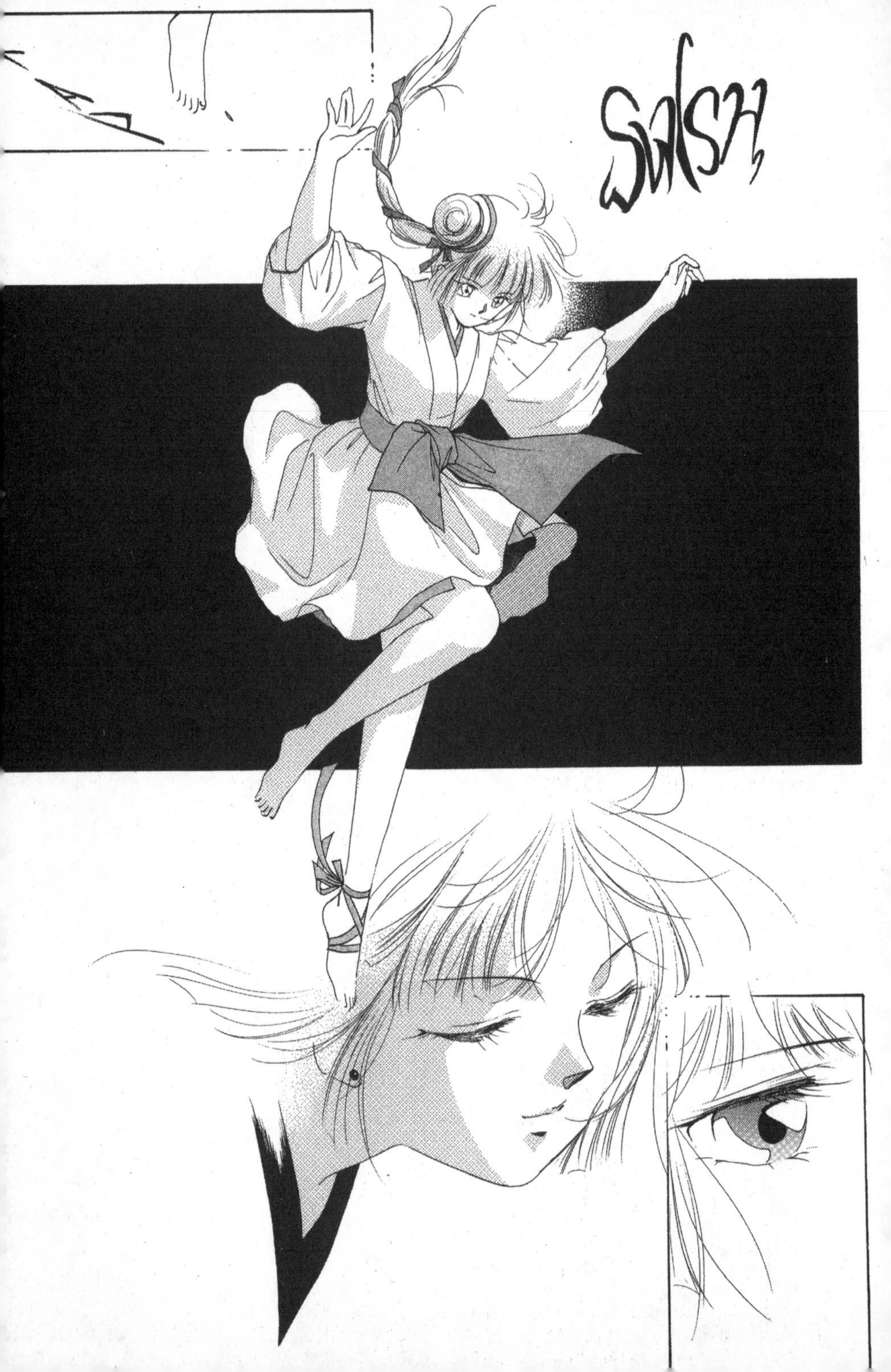
SWISH

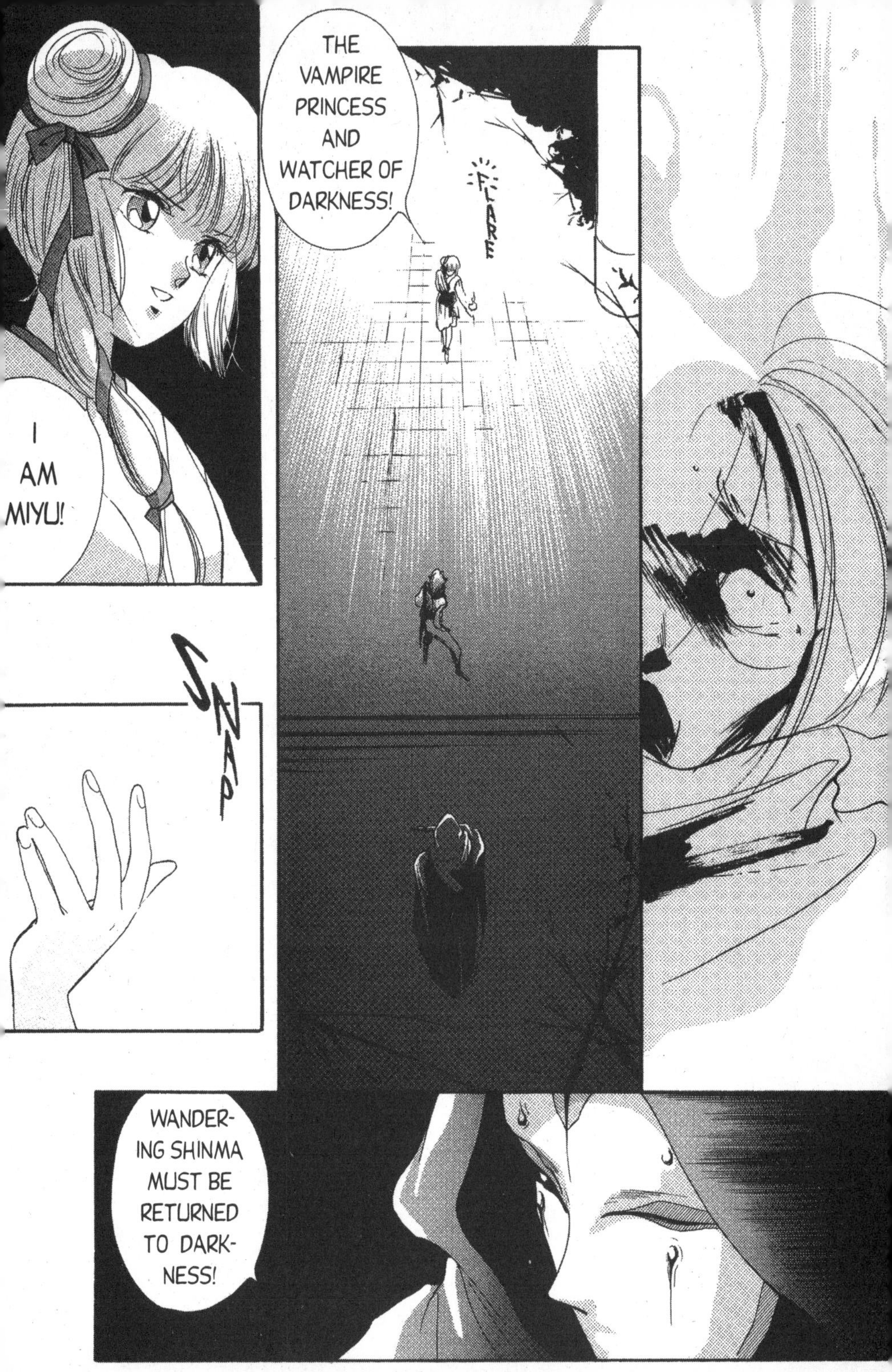
THE VAMPIRE PRINCESS AND WATCHER OF DARKNESS!
FLARE
I AM MIYU!
SNAP
WANDER-ING SHINMA MUST BE RETURNED TO DARK-NESS!

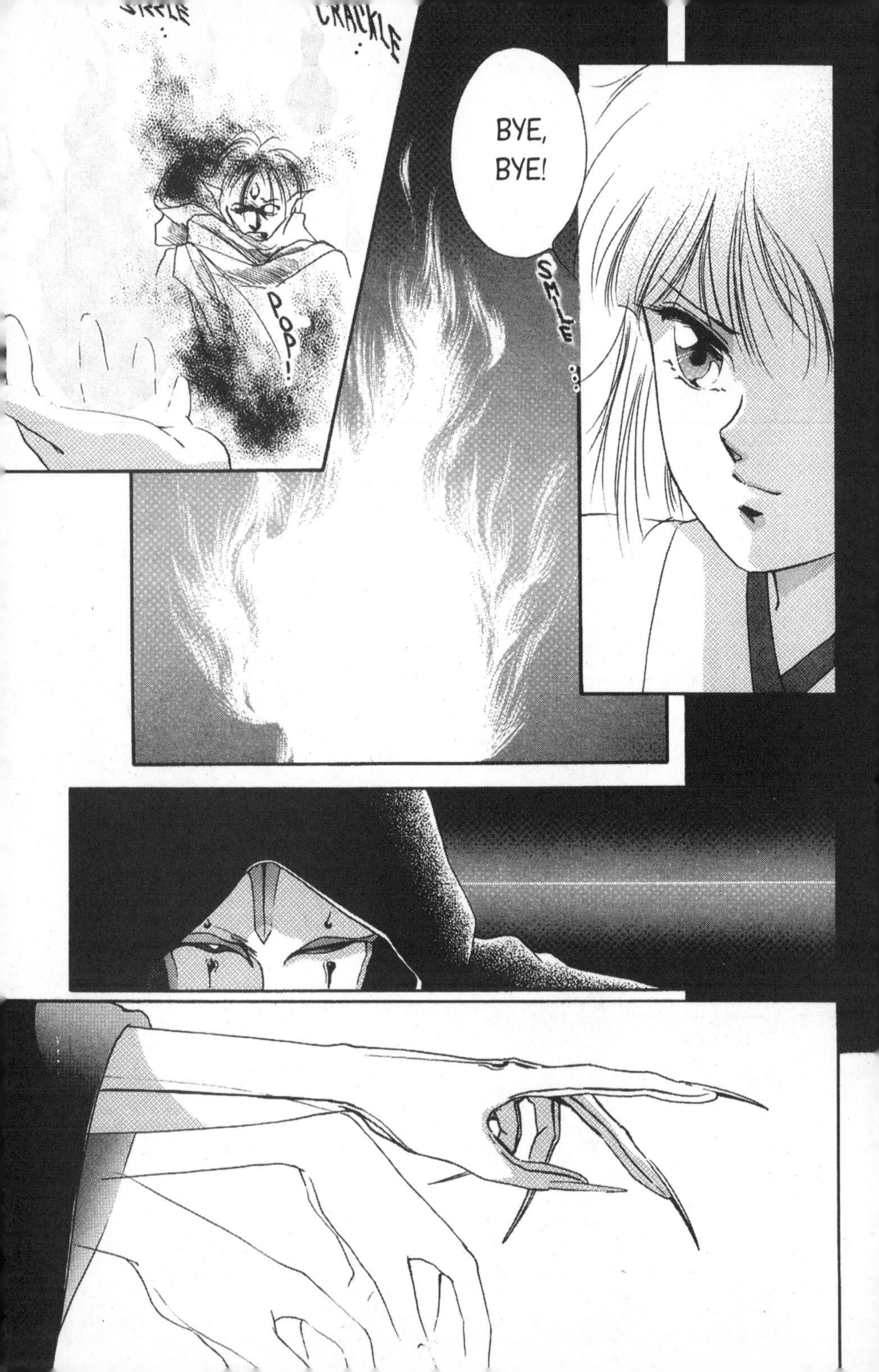
CRACKLE
BYE, BYE!
SMILE...
POP!

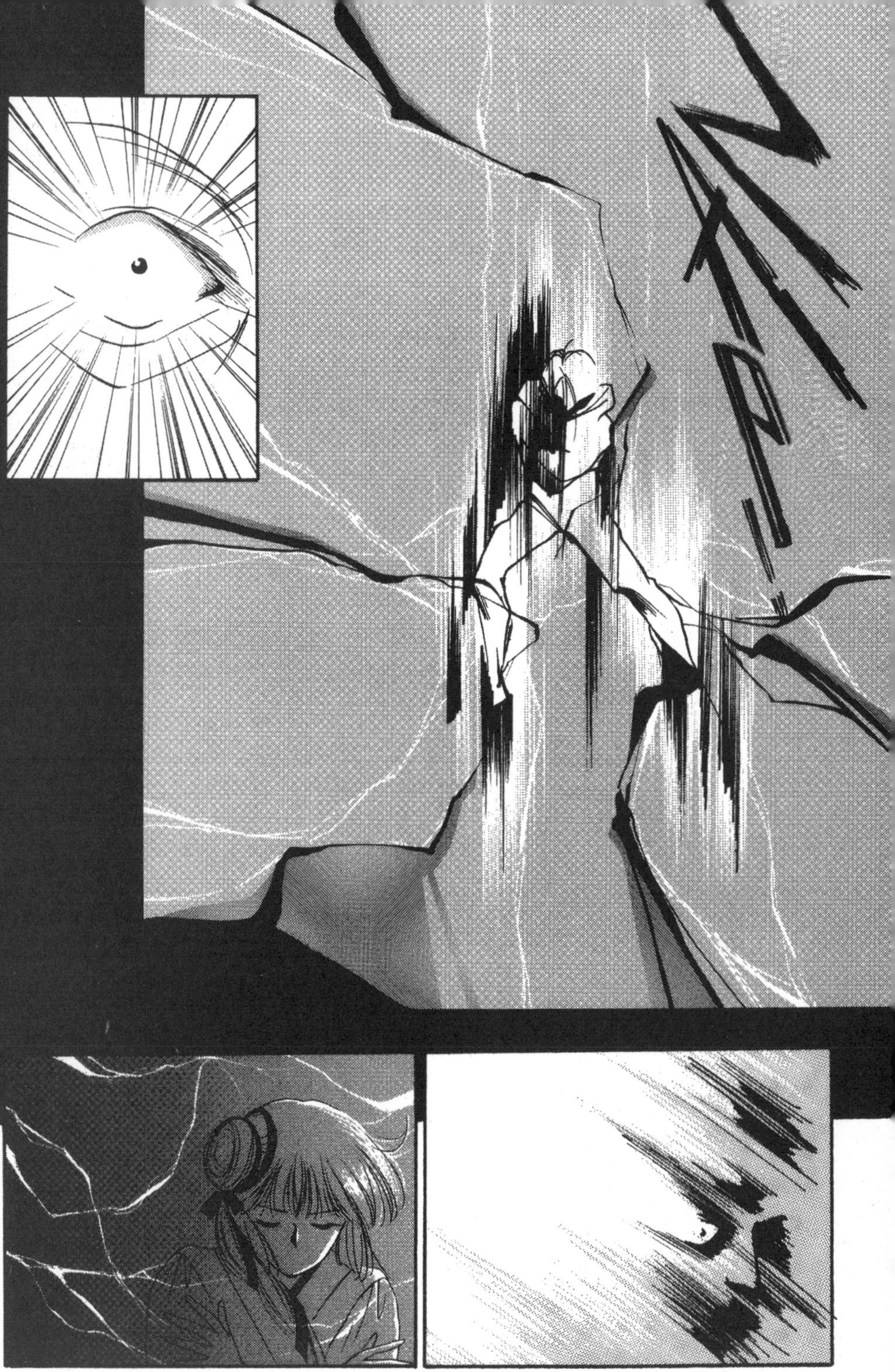

ZAP

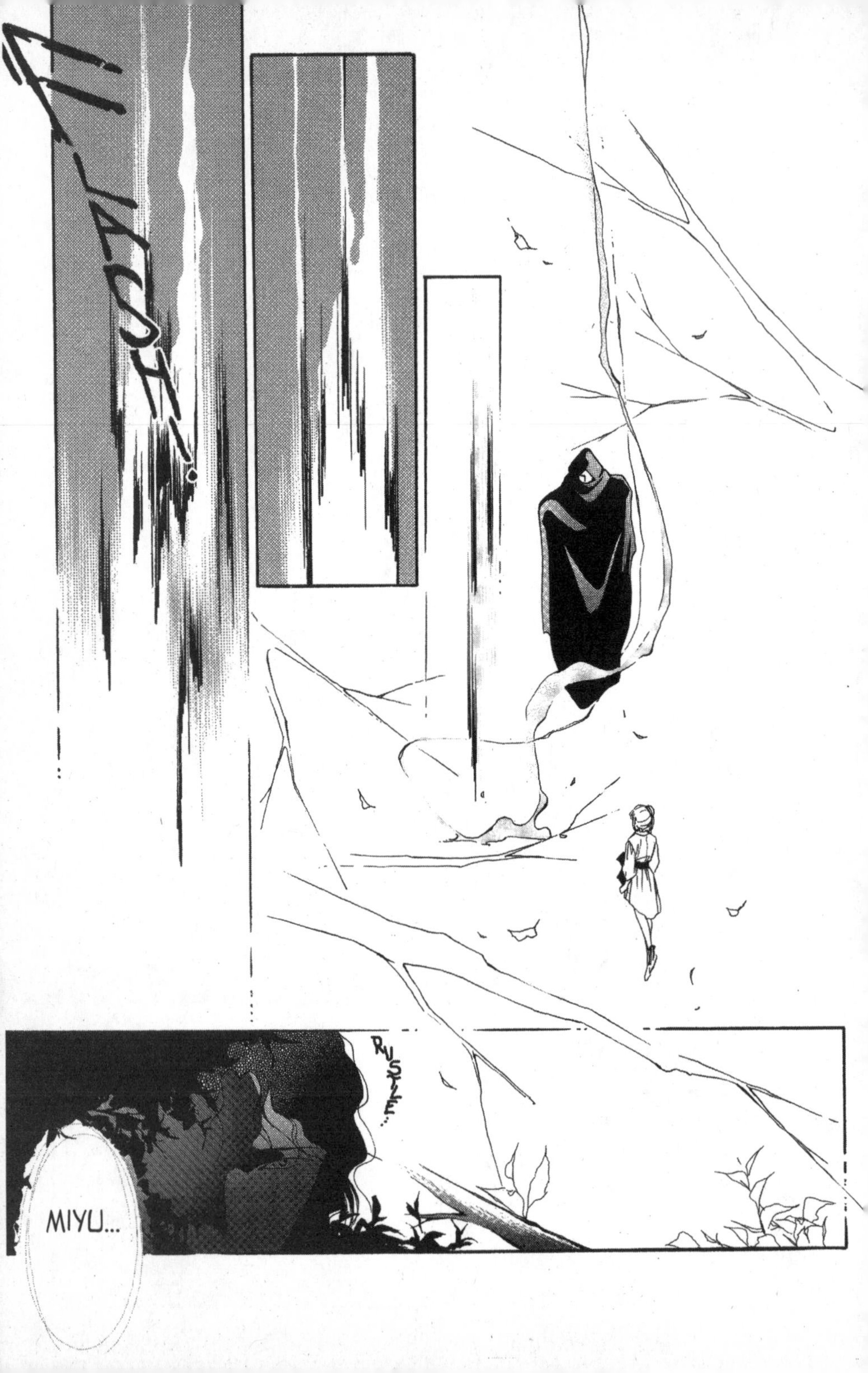
RUSTLE...
MIYU...

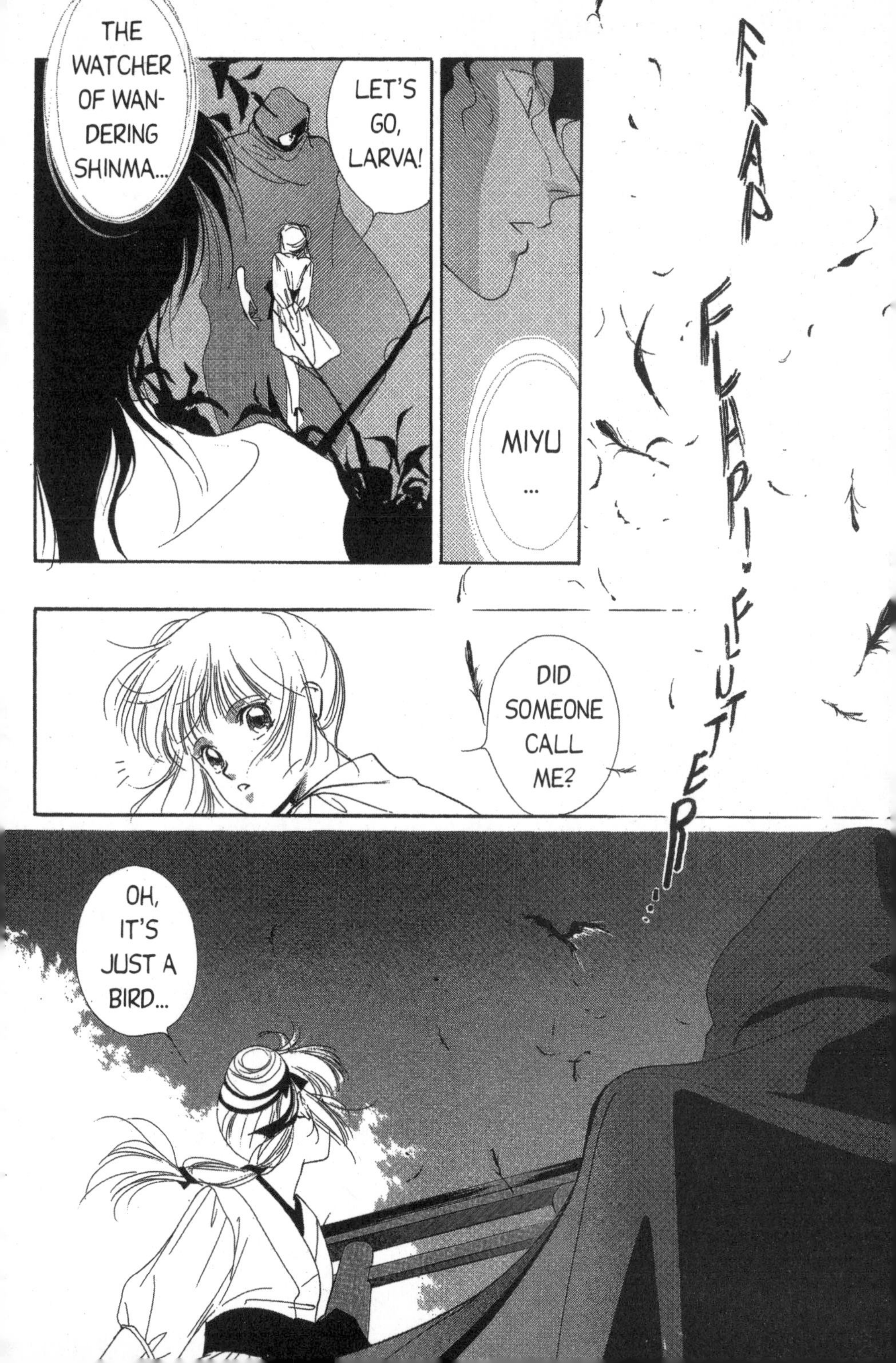
FLAP FLAP! FLUTTER
LET'S GO, LARVA!
THE WATCHER OF WAN-DERING SHINMA...
MIYU ...
DID SOMEONE CALL ME?
OH, IT'S JUST A BIRD...

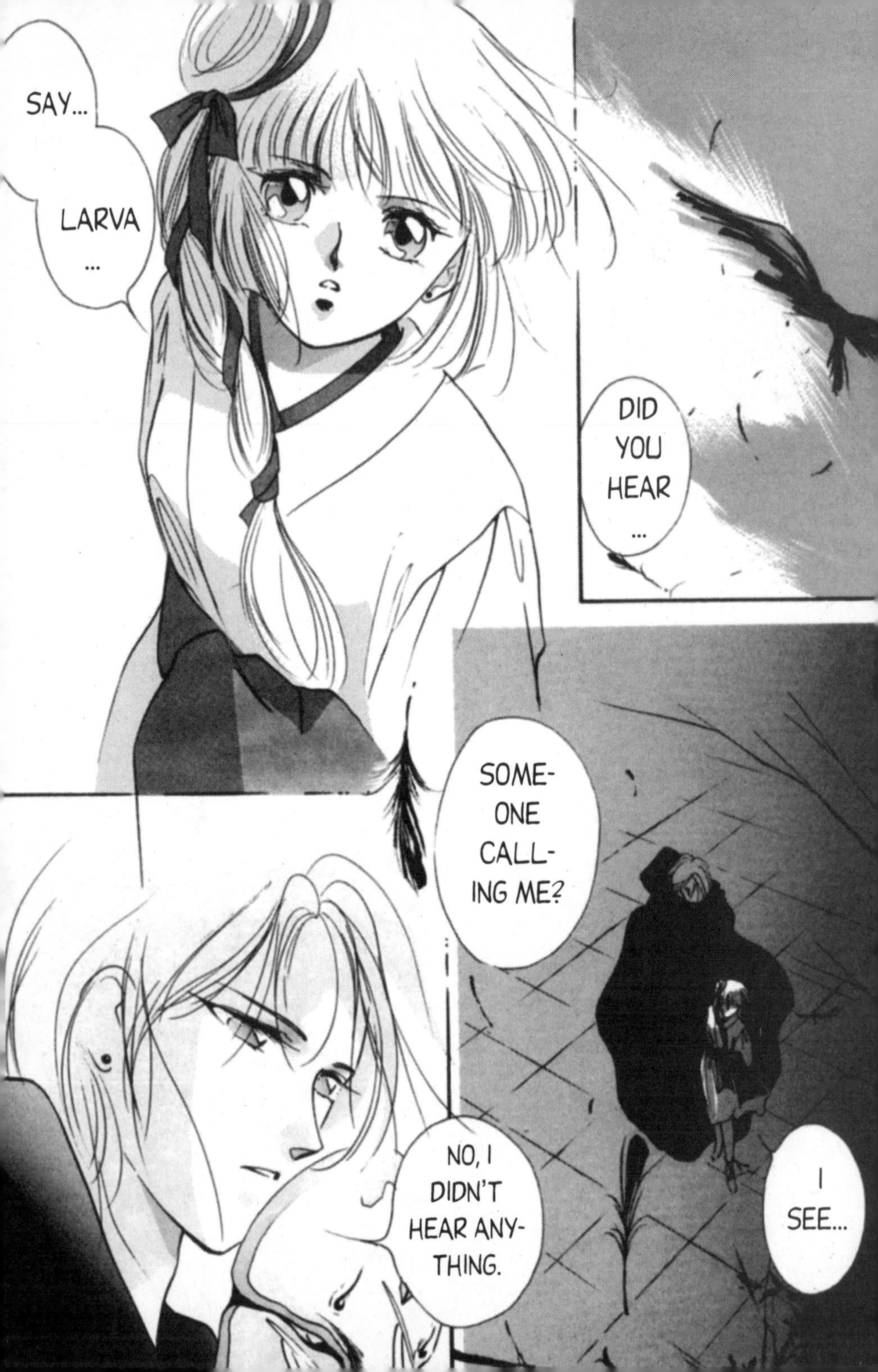
SAY...
LARVA ...
DID YOU HEAR ...
SOME-ONE CALL-ING ME?
NO, I DIDN'T HEAR ANY-THING.
I SEE...

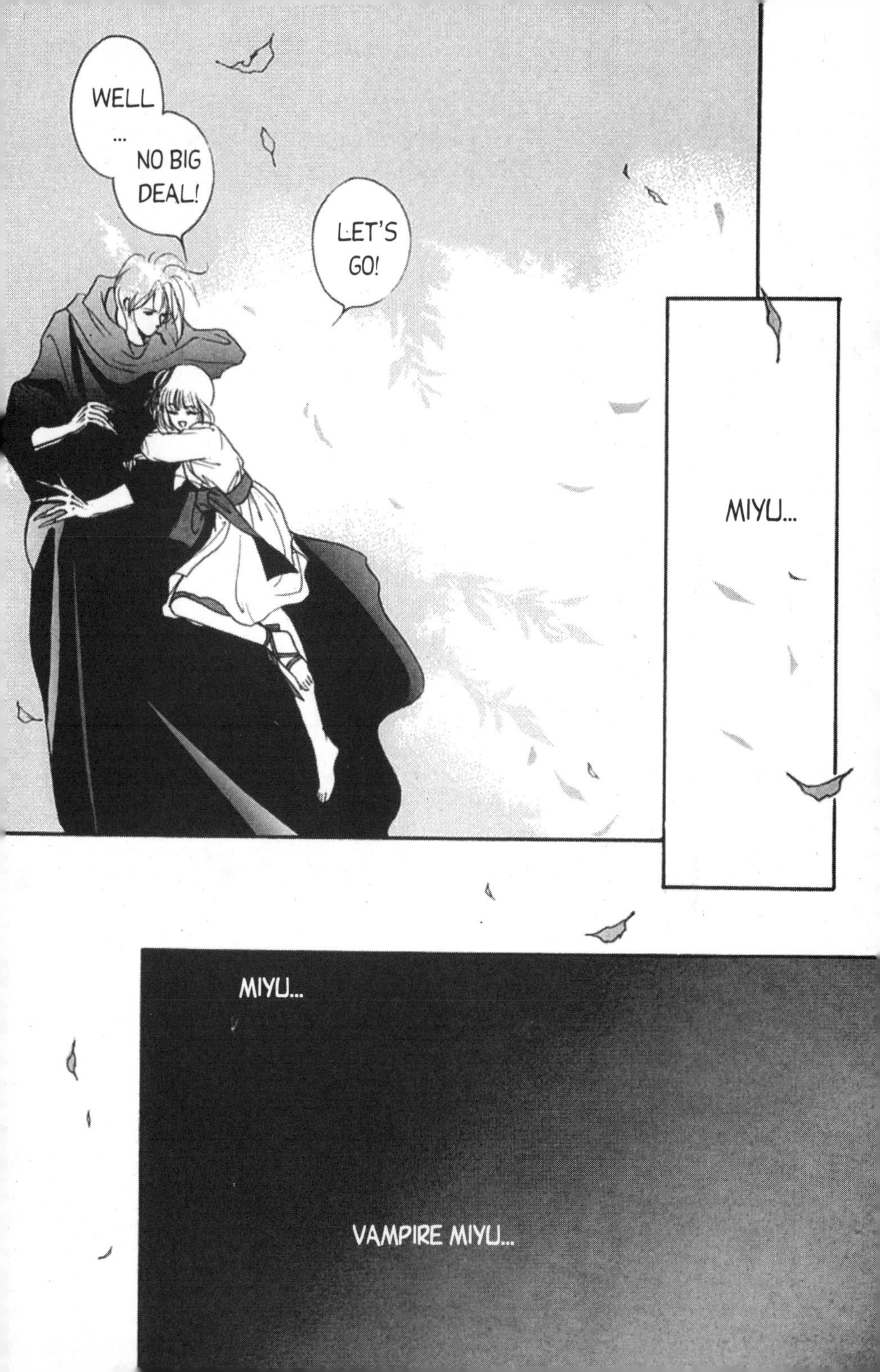
WELL ... NO BIG DEAL!
LET'S GO!
MIYU...
MIYU...
VAMPIRE MIYU...

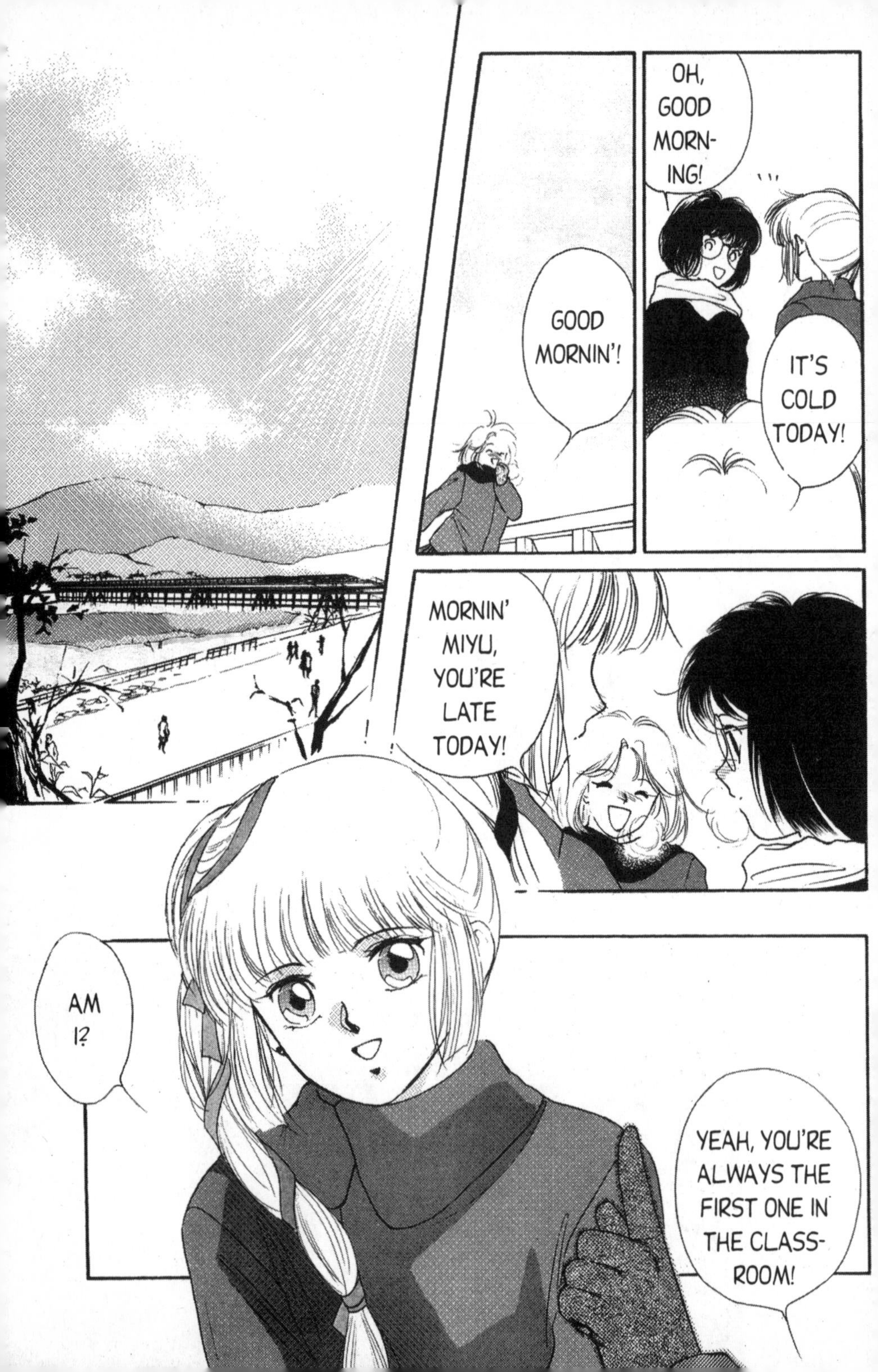
GOOD MORNIN'!
OH, GOOD MORN-ING!
IT'S COLD TODAY!
MORNIN' MIYU, YOU'RE LATE TODAY!
AM I?
YEAH, YOU'RE ALWAYS THE FIRST ONE IN THE CLASS-ROOM!

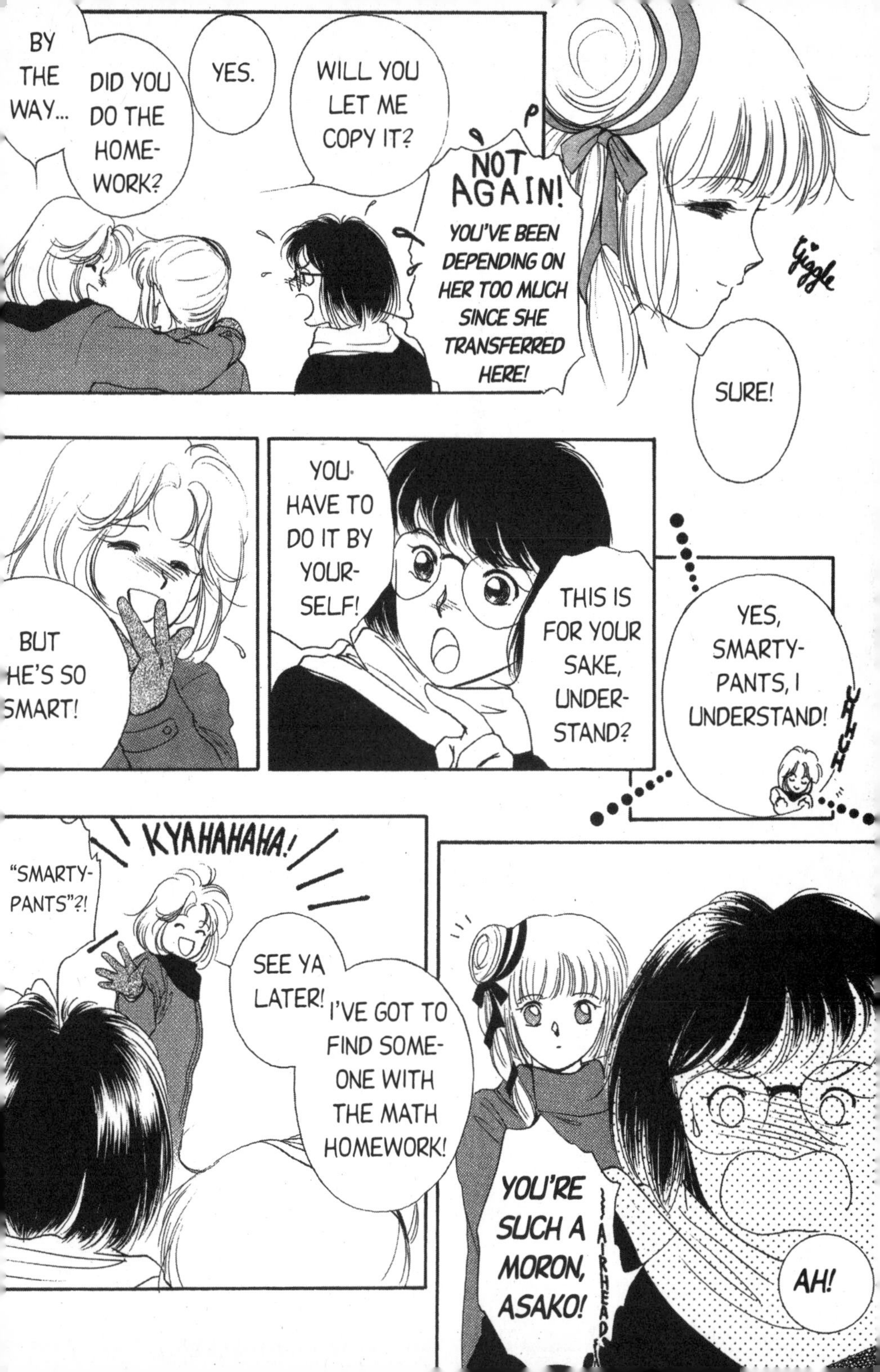
BY THE WAY...
DID YOU DO THE HOMEWORK?
YES.
WILL YOU LET ME COPY IT?
NOT AGAIN!
YOU'VE BEEN DEPENDING ON HER TOO MUCH SINCE SHE TRANSFERRED HERE!
giggle
SURE!
BUT HE'S SO SMART!
YOU HAVE TO DO IT BY YOURSELF!
THIS IS FOR YOUR SAKE, UNDERSTAND?
YES, SMARTY-PANTS, I UNDERSTAND!
KYAHAHAHA!
"SMARTY-PANTS"?!
SEE YA LATER!
I'VE GOT TO FIND SOMEONE WITH THE MATH HOMEWORK!
YOU'RE SUCH A MORON, ASAKO!
AIRHEAD
AH!

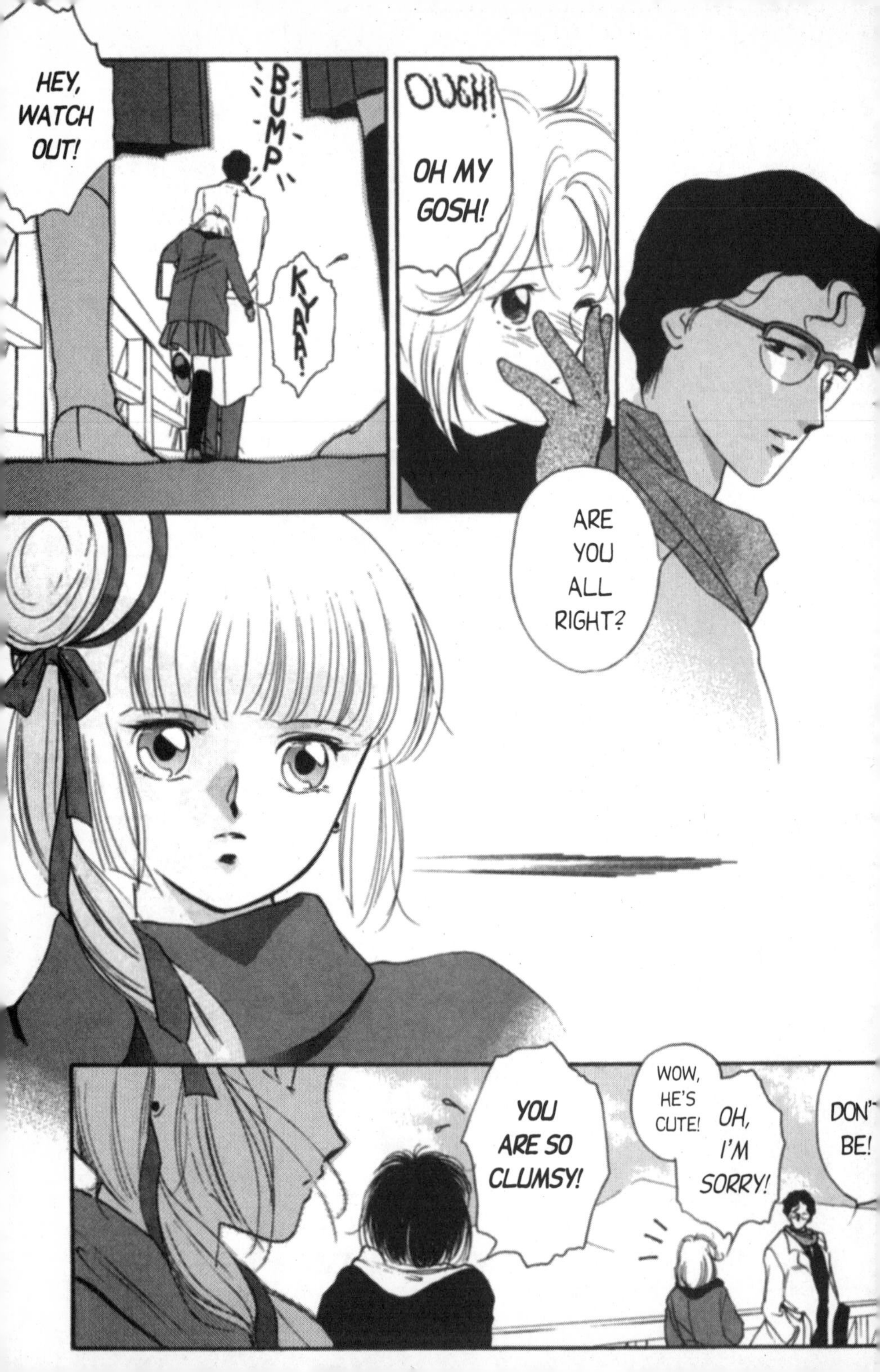
OUCH!
OH MY GOSH!
HEY, WATCH OUT!
BUMP
KYAA!
ARE YOU ALL RIGHT?
DON'T BE!
OH, I'M SORRY!
WOW, HE'S CUTE!
YOU ARE SO CLUMSY!

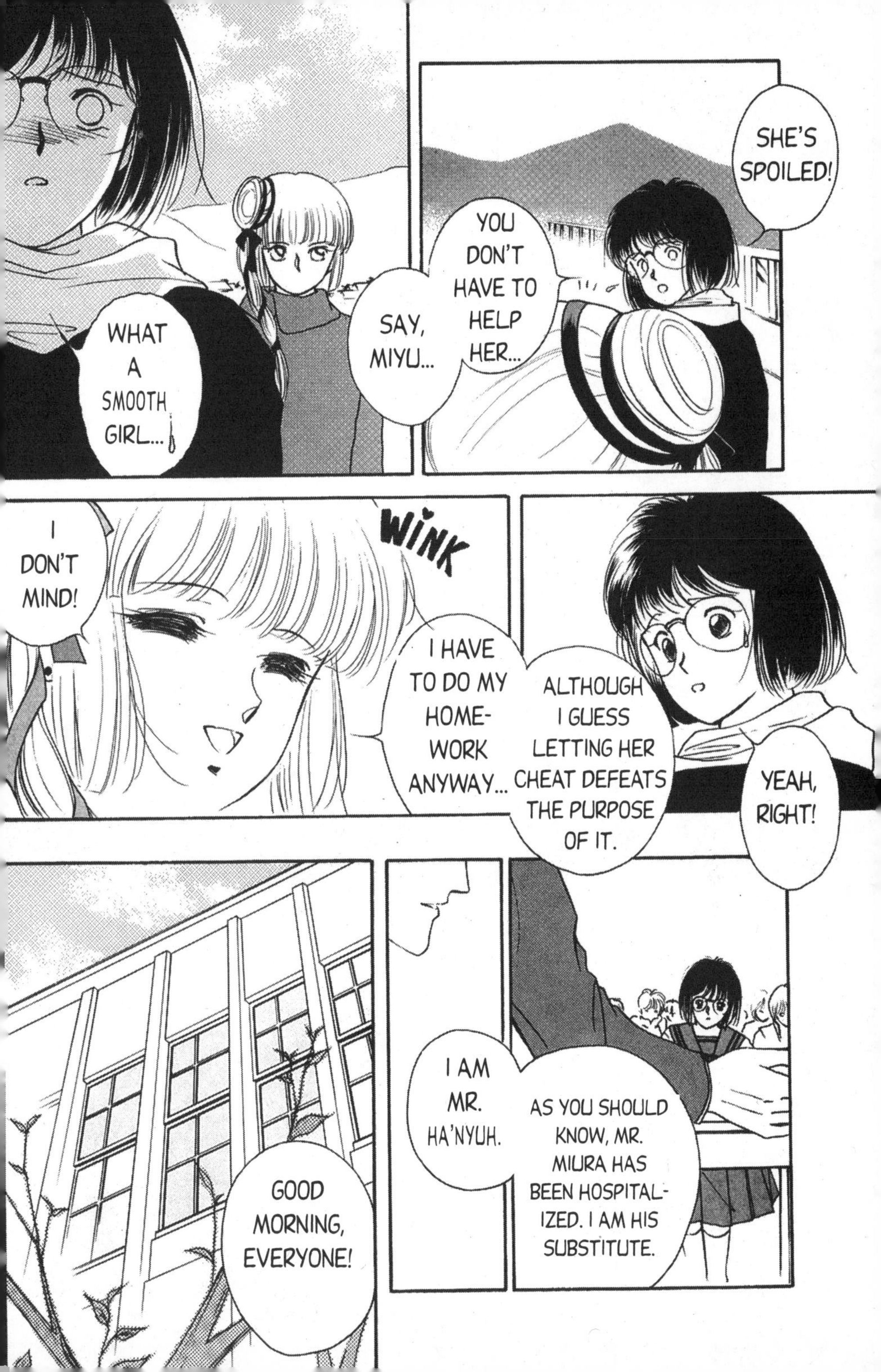
WHAT A SMOOTH GIRL...
SAY, MIYU...
YOU DON'T HAVE TO HELP HER...
SHE'S SPOILED!
I DON'T MIND!
WINK
I HAVE TO DO MY HOME-WORK ANYWAY...
ALTHOUGH I GUESS LETTING HER CHEAT DEFEATS THE PURPOSE OF IT.
YEAH, RIGHT!
GOOD MORNING, EVERYONE!
I AM MR. HA'NYUH.
AS YOU SHOULD KNOW, MR. MIURA HAS BEEN HOSPITAL-IZED. I AM HIS SUBSTITUTE.

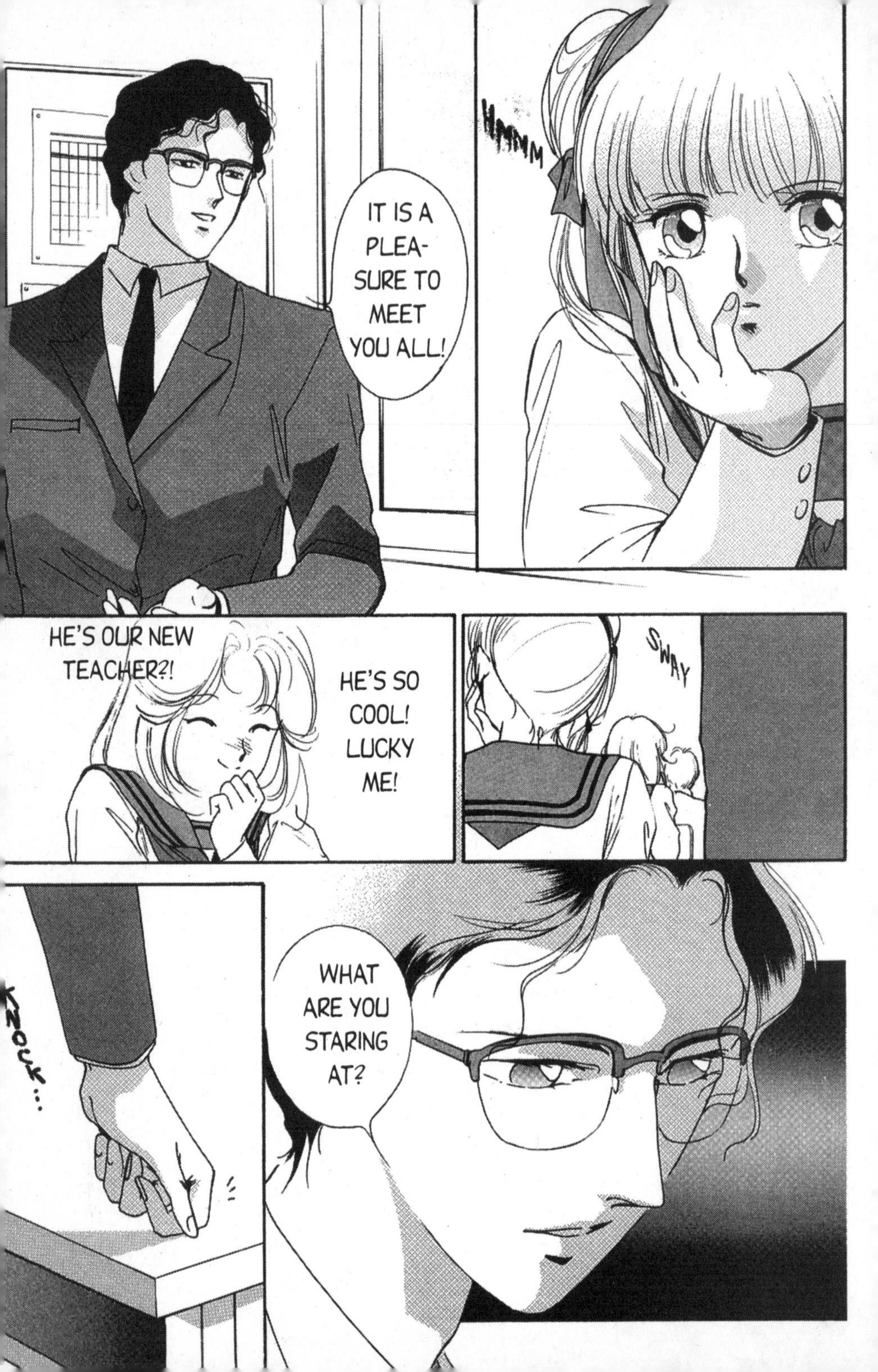
HMMM
IT IS A PLEA-SURE TO MEET YOU ALL!
SWAY
HE'S OUR NEW TEACHER?!
HE'S SO COOL! LUCKY ME!
WHAT ARE YOU STARING AT?
KNOCK...

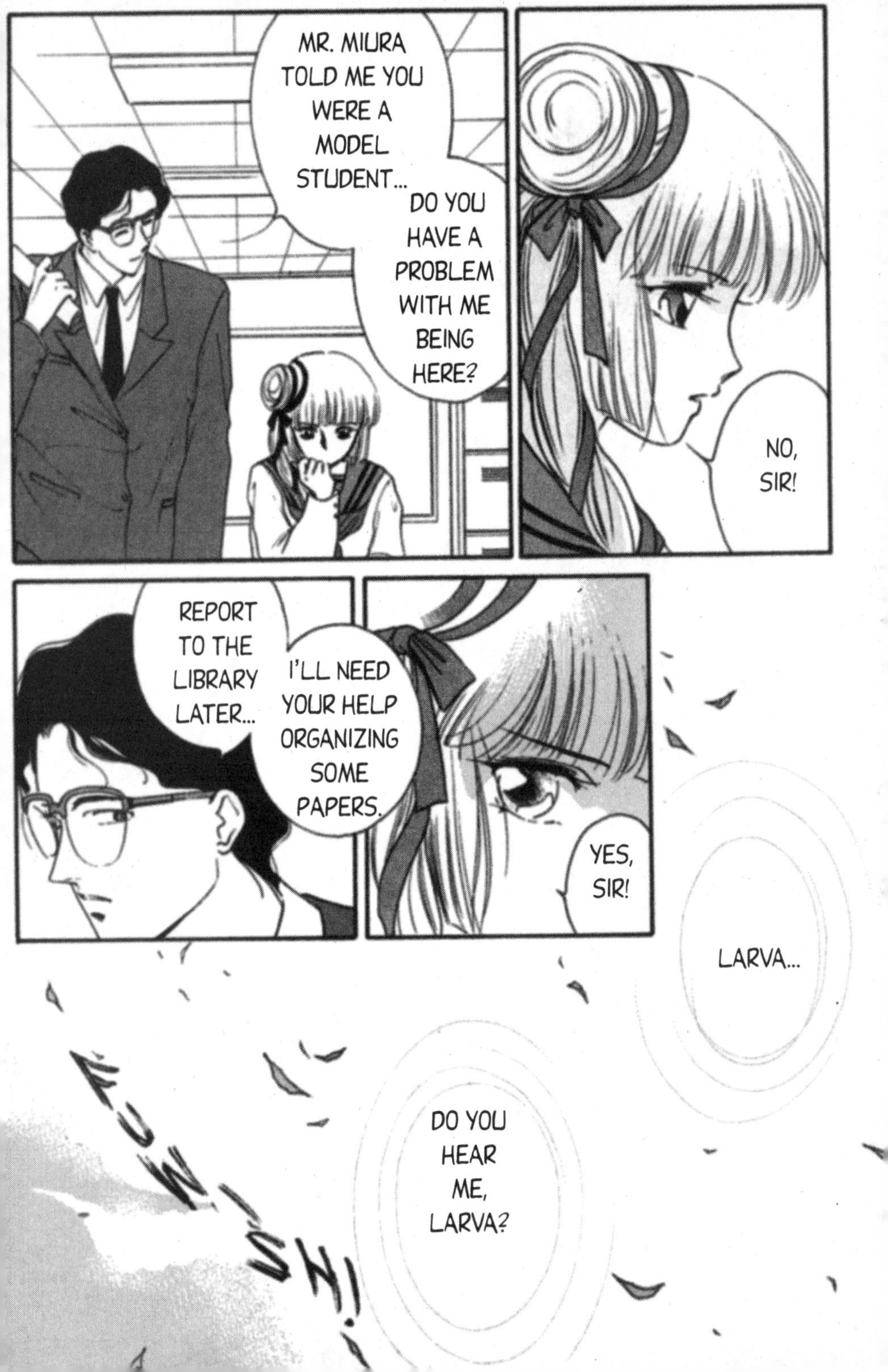
MR. MIURA TOLD ME YOU WERE A MODEL STUDENT...
DO YOU HAVE A PROBLEM WITH ME BEING HERE?
NO, SIR!
REPORT TO THE LIBRARY LATER...
I'LL NEED YOUR HELP ORGANIZING SOME PAPERS.
YES, SIR!
LARVA...
DO YOU HEAR ME, LARVA?
FWISH!

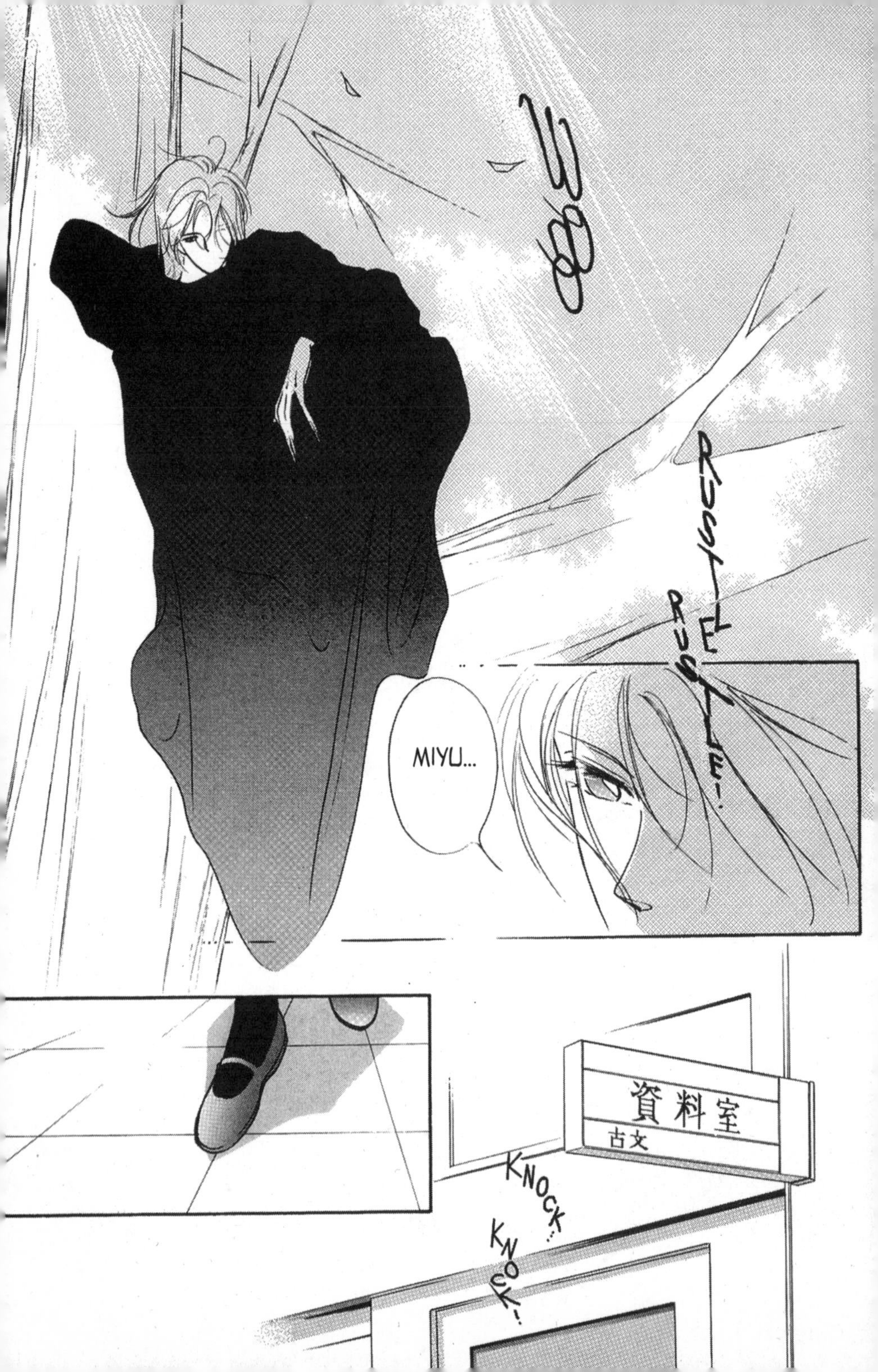
RUSTLE
RUSTLE!
MIYU...
資料室
古文
KNOCK..
KNOCK..

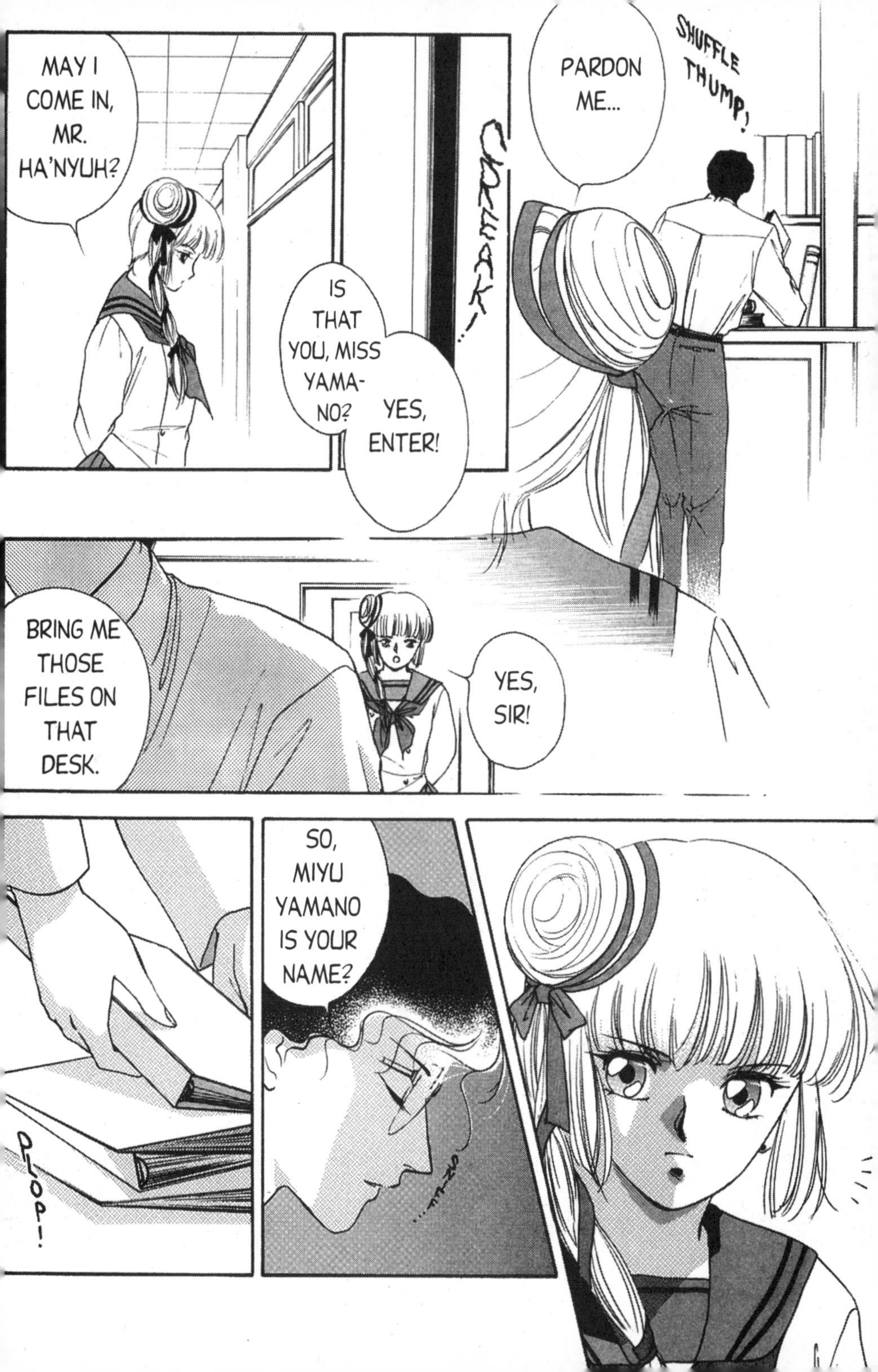
MAY I COME IN, MR. HA'NYUH?
CREEAK...!
IS THAT YOU, MISS YAMA-NO?
YES, ENTER!
PARDON ME...
SHUFFLE THUMP!
BRING ME THOSE FILES ON THAT DESK.
YES, SIR!
PLOP!
SO, MIYU YAMANO IS YOUR NAME?

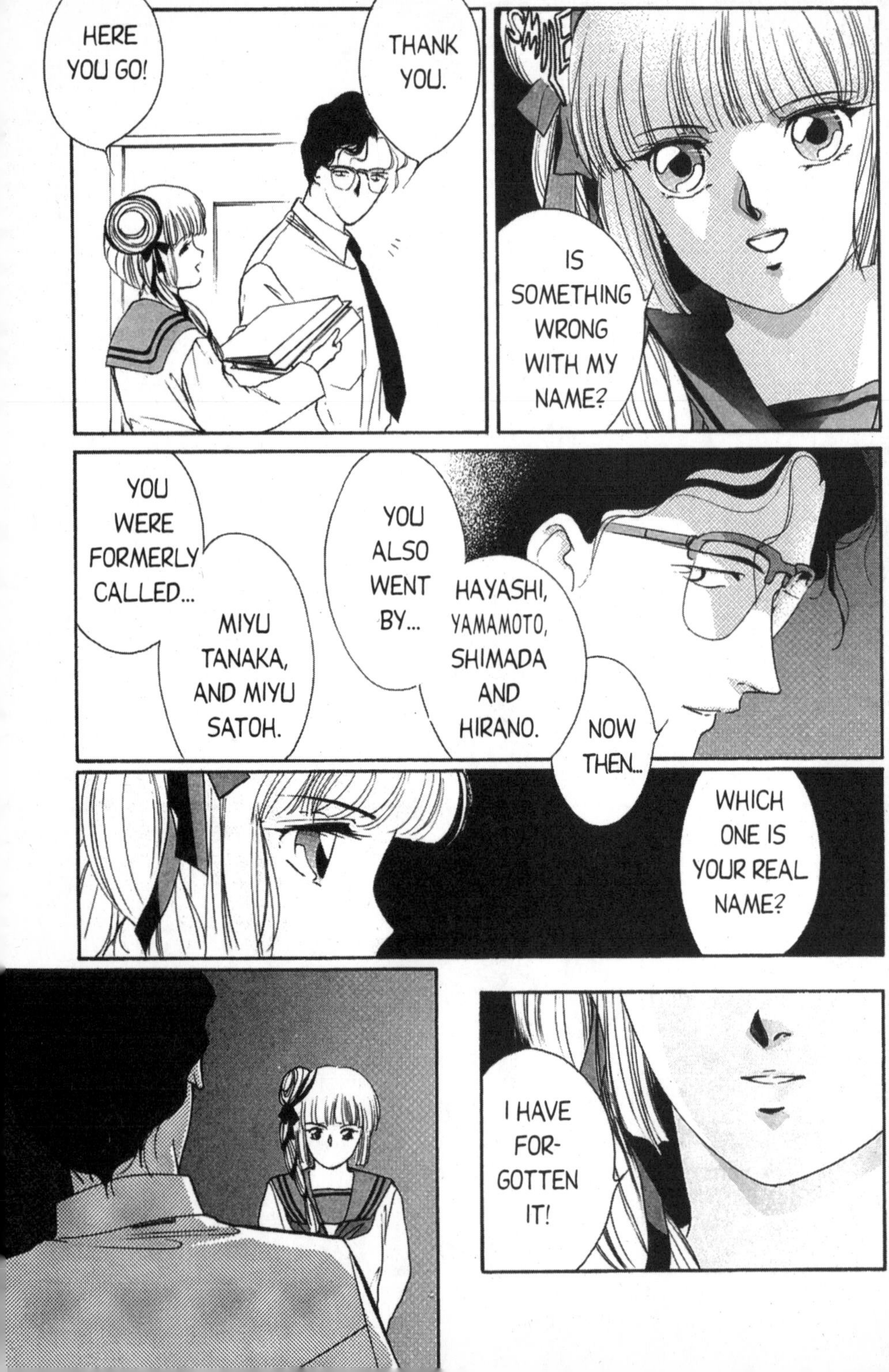
HERE YOU GO!
THANK YOU.
SMILE
IS SOMETHING WRONG WITH MY NAME?
YOU WERE FORMERLY CALLED...
MIYU TANAKA, AND MIYU SATOH.
YOU ALSO WENT BY...
HAYASHI, YAMAMOTO, SHIMADA AND HIRANO.
NOW THEN...
WHICH ONE IS YOUR REAL NAME?
I HAVE FOR-GOTTEN IT!

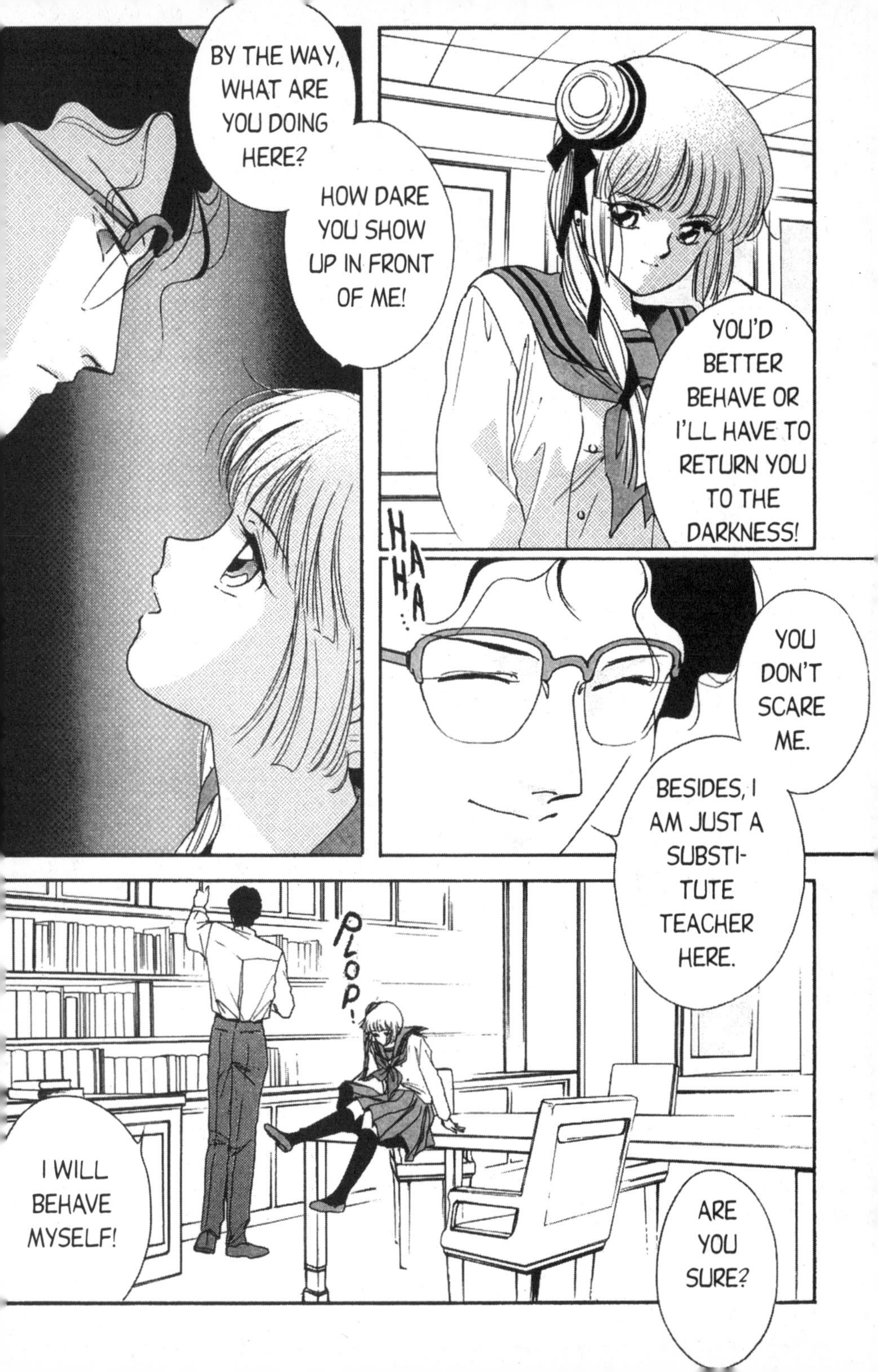
BY THE WAY, WHAT ARE YOU DOING HERE?
HOW DARE YOU SHOW UP IN FRONT OF ME!
YOU'D BETTER BEHAVE OR I'LL HAVE TO RETURN YOU TO THE DARKNESS!
HAHA...
YOU DON'T SCARE ME.
BESIDES, I AM JUST A SUBSTI-TUTE TEACHER HERE.
PLOP!
I WILL BEHAVE MYSELF!
ARE YOU SURE?

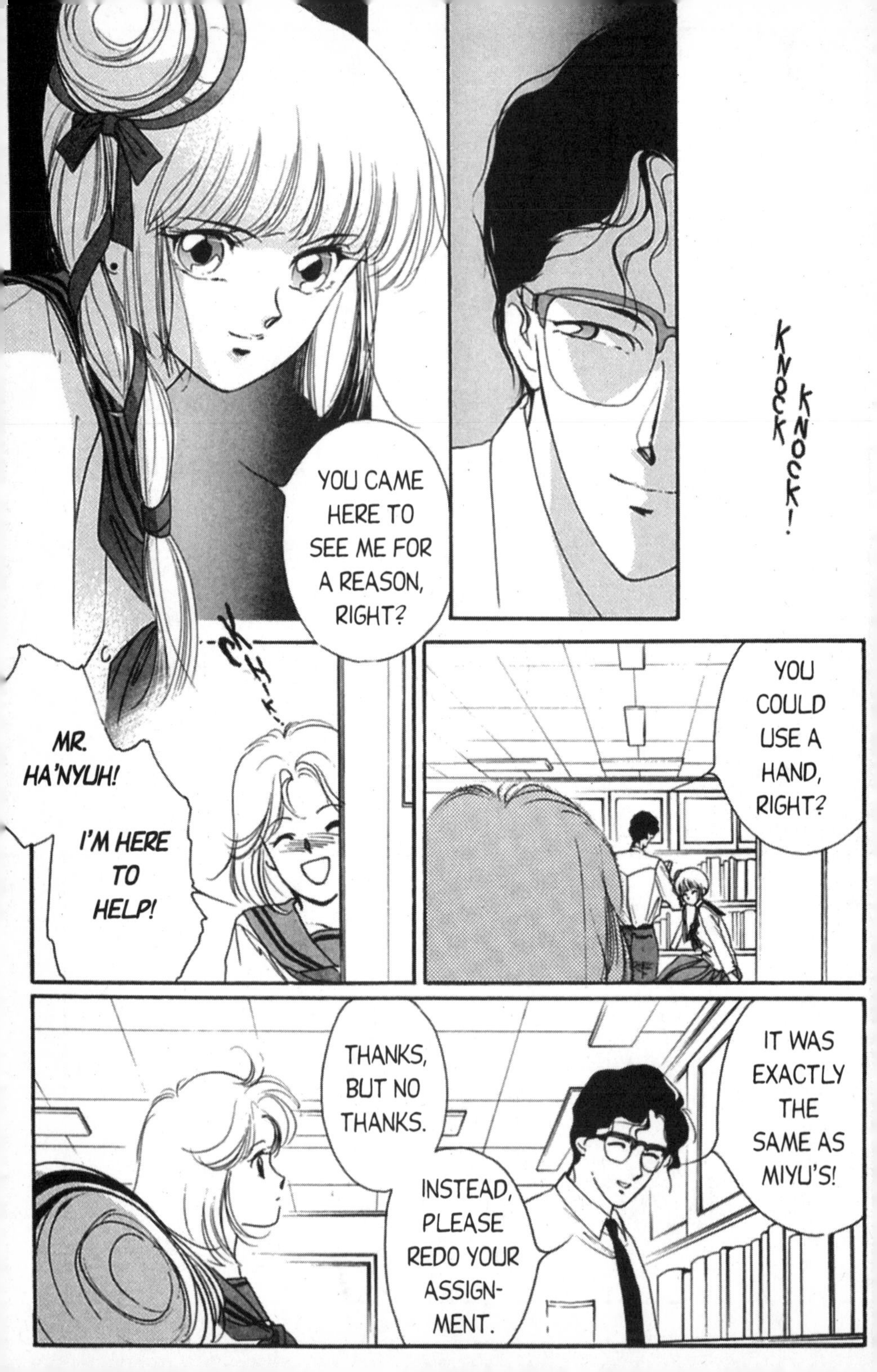
KNOCK KNOCK!
YOU CAME HERE TO SEE ME FOR A REASON, RIGHT?
YOU COULD USE A HAND, RIGHT?
MR. HA'NYUH!
I'M HERE TO HELP!
IT WAS EXACTLY THE SAME AS MIYU'S!
THANKS, BUT NO THANKS.
INSTEAD, PLEASE REDO YOUR ASSIGNMENT.

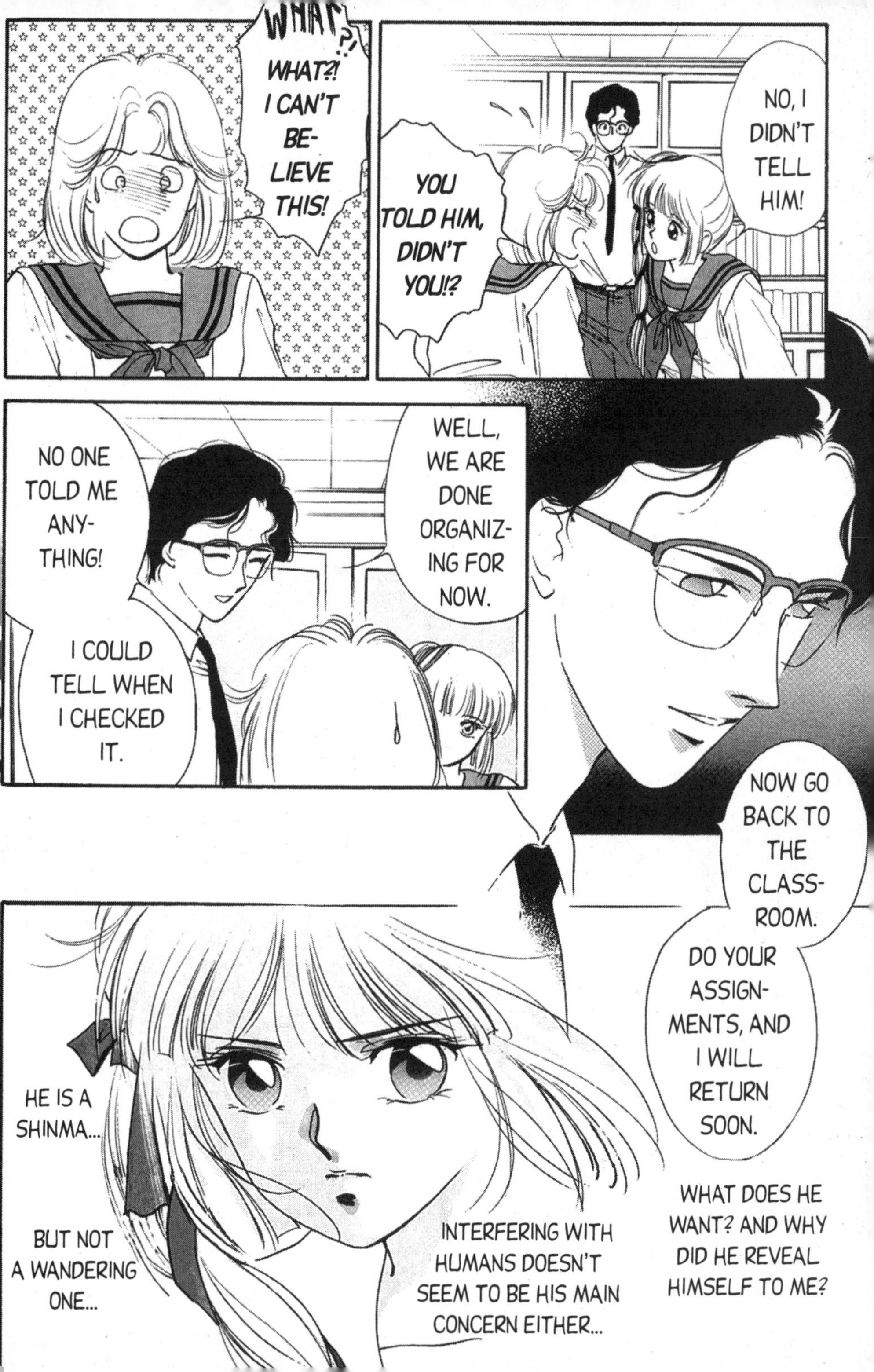
WHAT?!
WHAT?! I CAN'T BE-LIEVE THIS!
YOU TOLD HIM, DIDN'T YOU!?
NO, I DIDN'T TELL HIM!
NO ONE TOLD ME ANY-THING!
I COULD TELL WHEN I CHECKED IT.
WELL, WE ARE DONE ORGANIZ-ING FOR NOW.
NOW GO BACK TO THE CLASS-ROOM.
DO YOUR ASSIGN-MENTS, AND I WILL RETURN SOON.
HE IS A SHINMA...
BUT NOT A WANDERING ONE...
INTERFERING WITH HUMANS DOESN'T SEEM TO BE HIS MAIN CONCERN EITHER...
WHAT DOES HE WANT? AND WHY DID HE REVEAL HIMSELF TO ME?

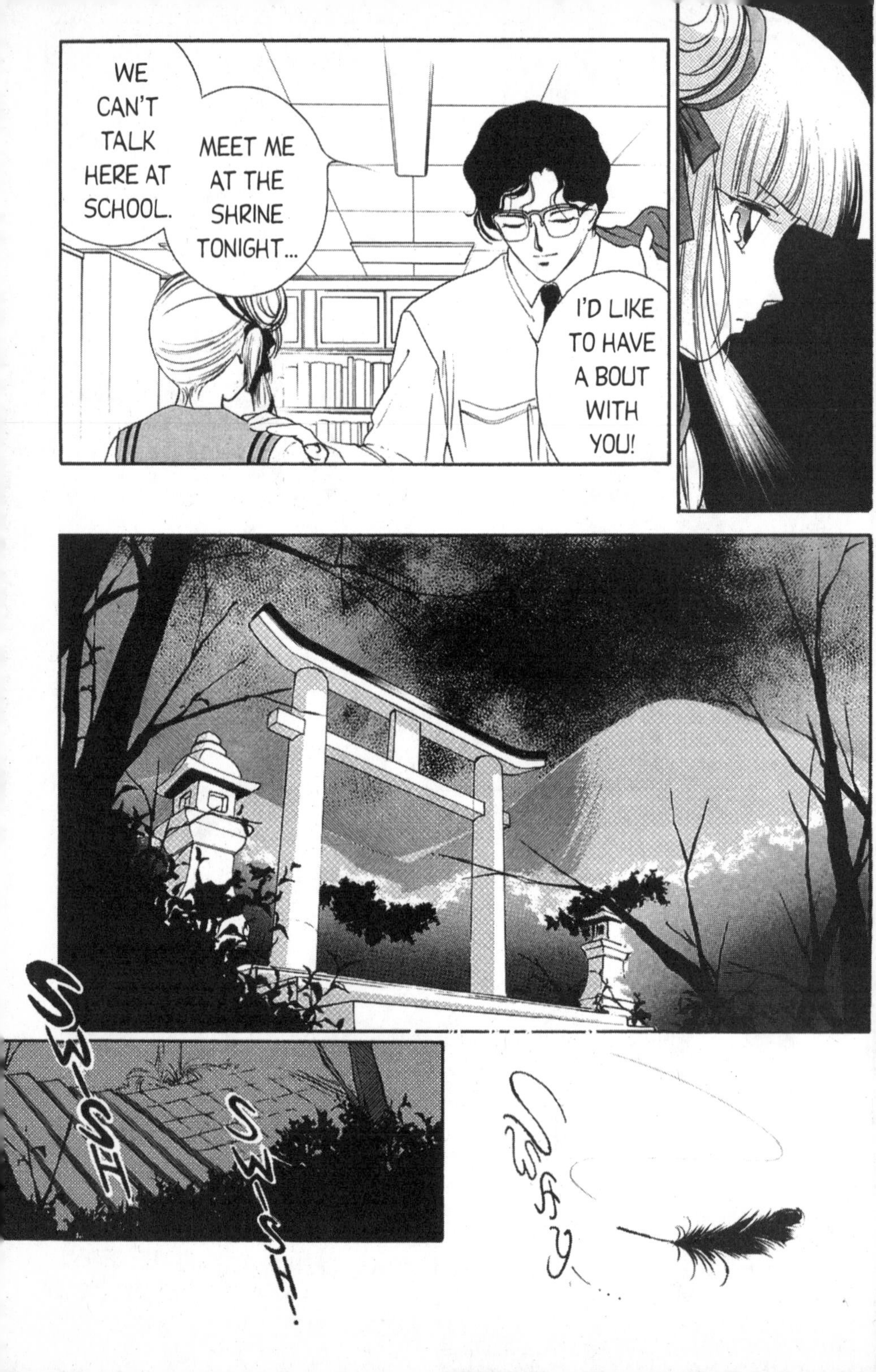
WE CAN'T TALK HERE AT SCHOOL.
MEET ME AT THE SHRINE TONIGHT...
I'D LIKE TO HAVE A BOUT WITH YOU!
SW-SH
SW-SH...
WOOSH...

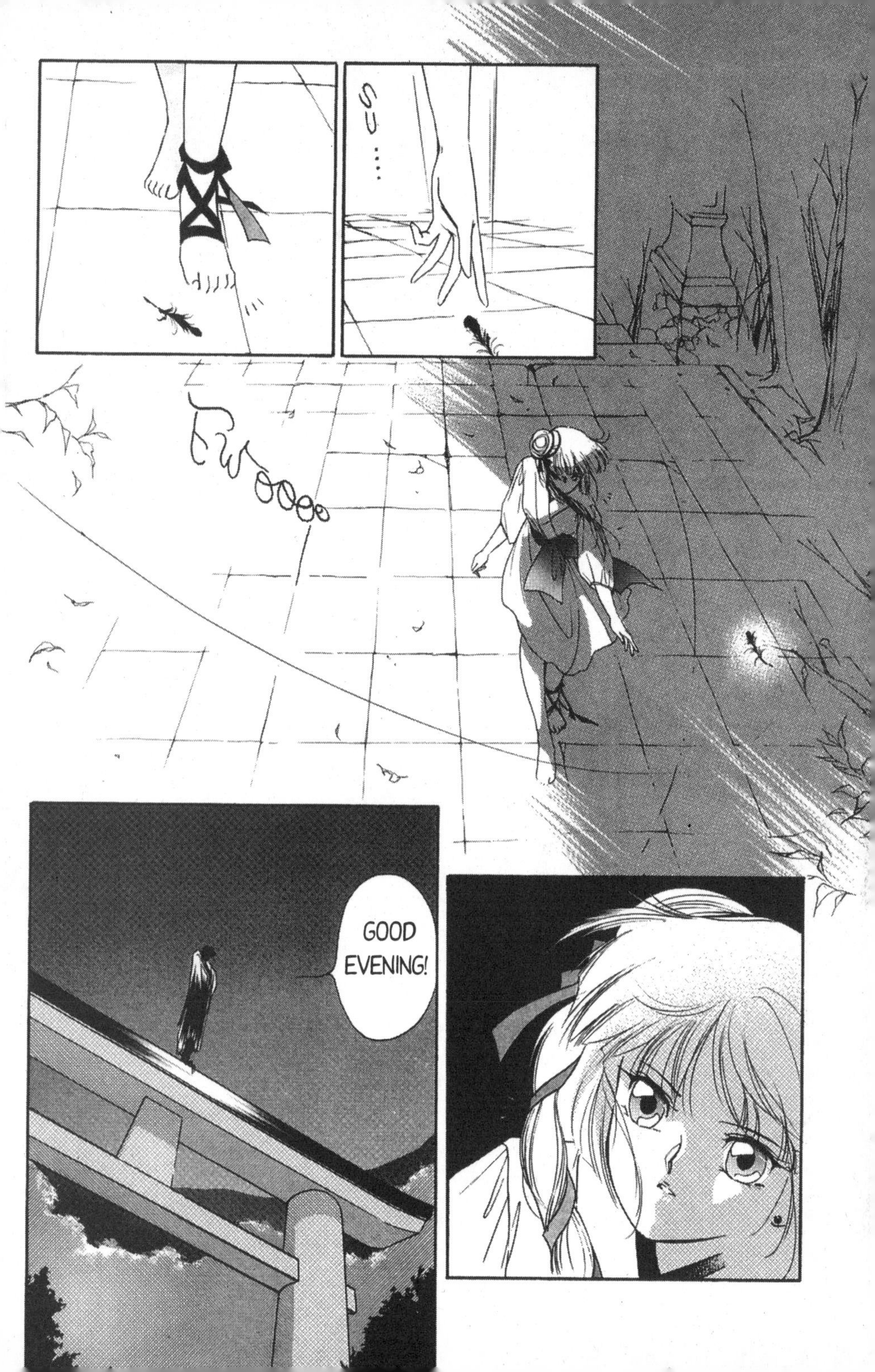
SU....
FWOOOO
GOOD EVENING!

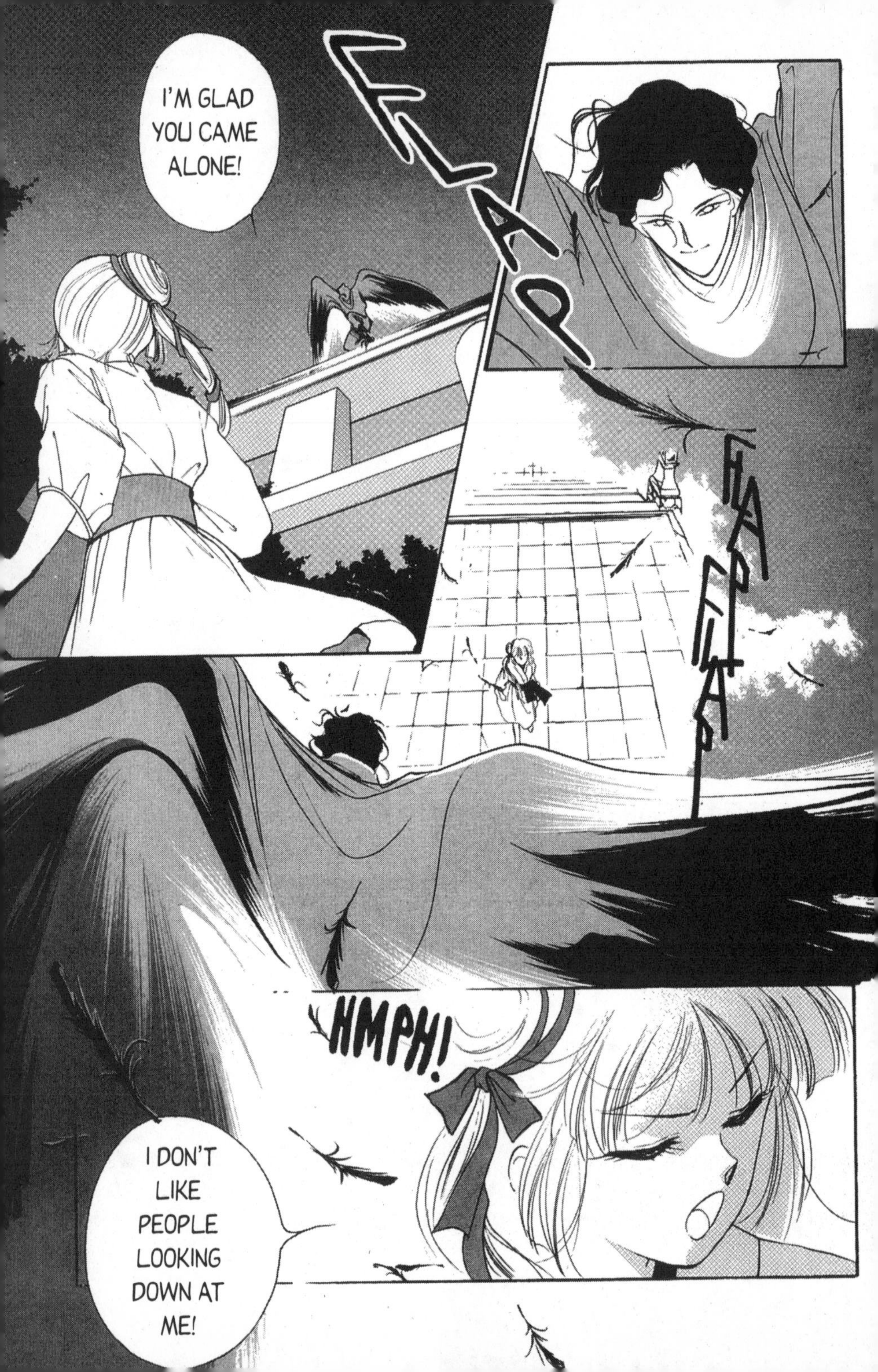

I'M GLAD YOU CAME ALONE!
FLLAP
FLAP FLAP
HMPH!
I DON'T LIKE PEOPLE LOOKING DOWN AT ME!

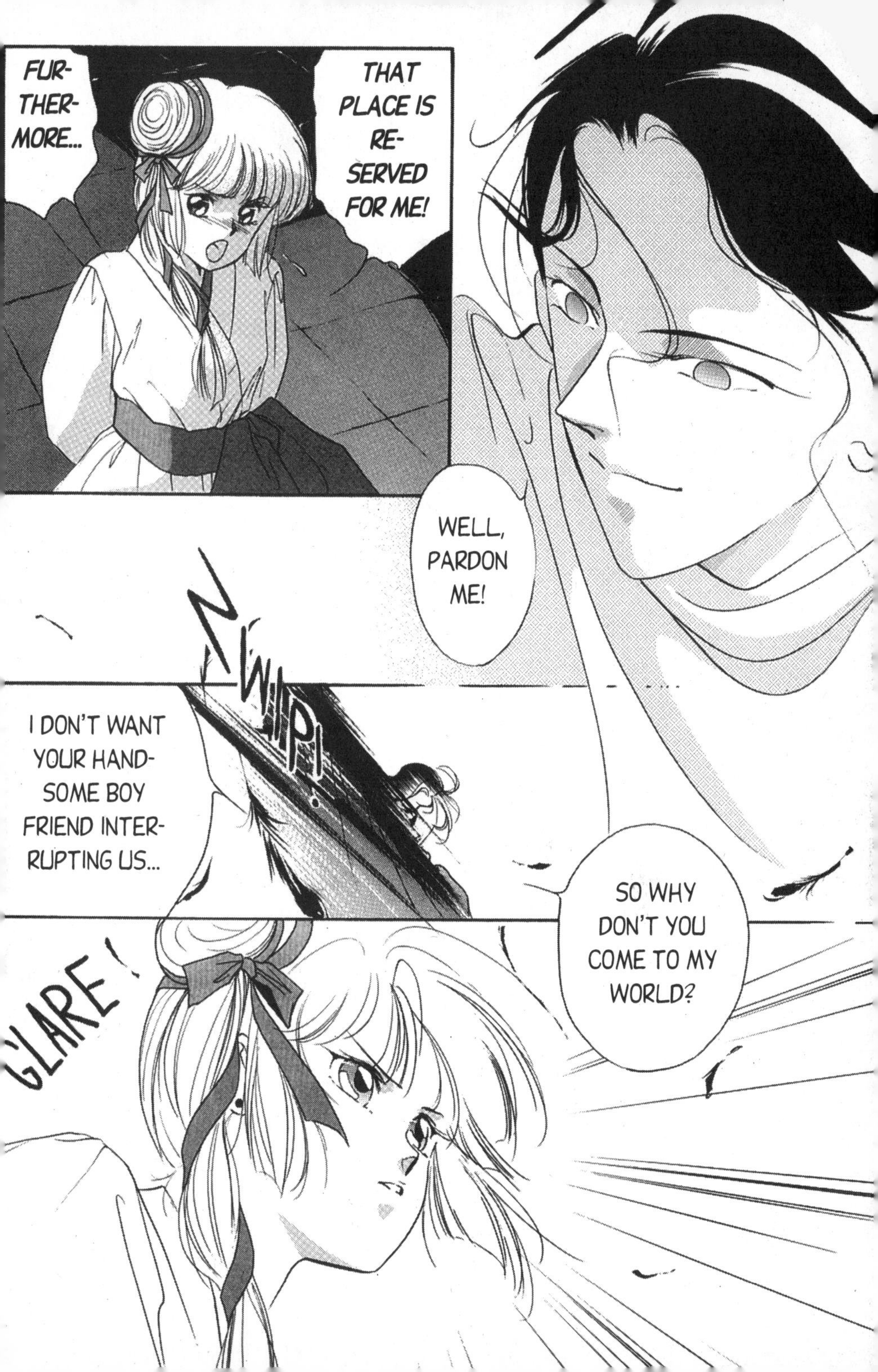
FUR-THER-MORE...
THAT PLACE IS RE-SERVED FOR ME!
WELL, PARDON ME!
ZWIP!
I DON'T WANT YOUR HAND-SOME BOY FRIEND INTER-RUPTING US...
SO WHY DON'T YOU COME TO MY WORLD?
GLARE!

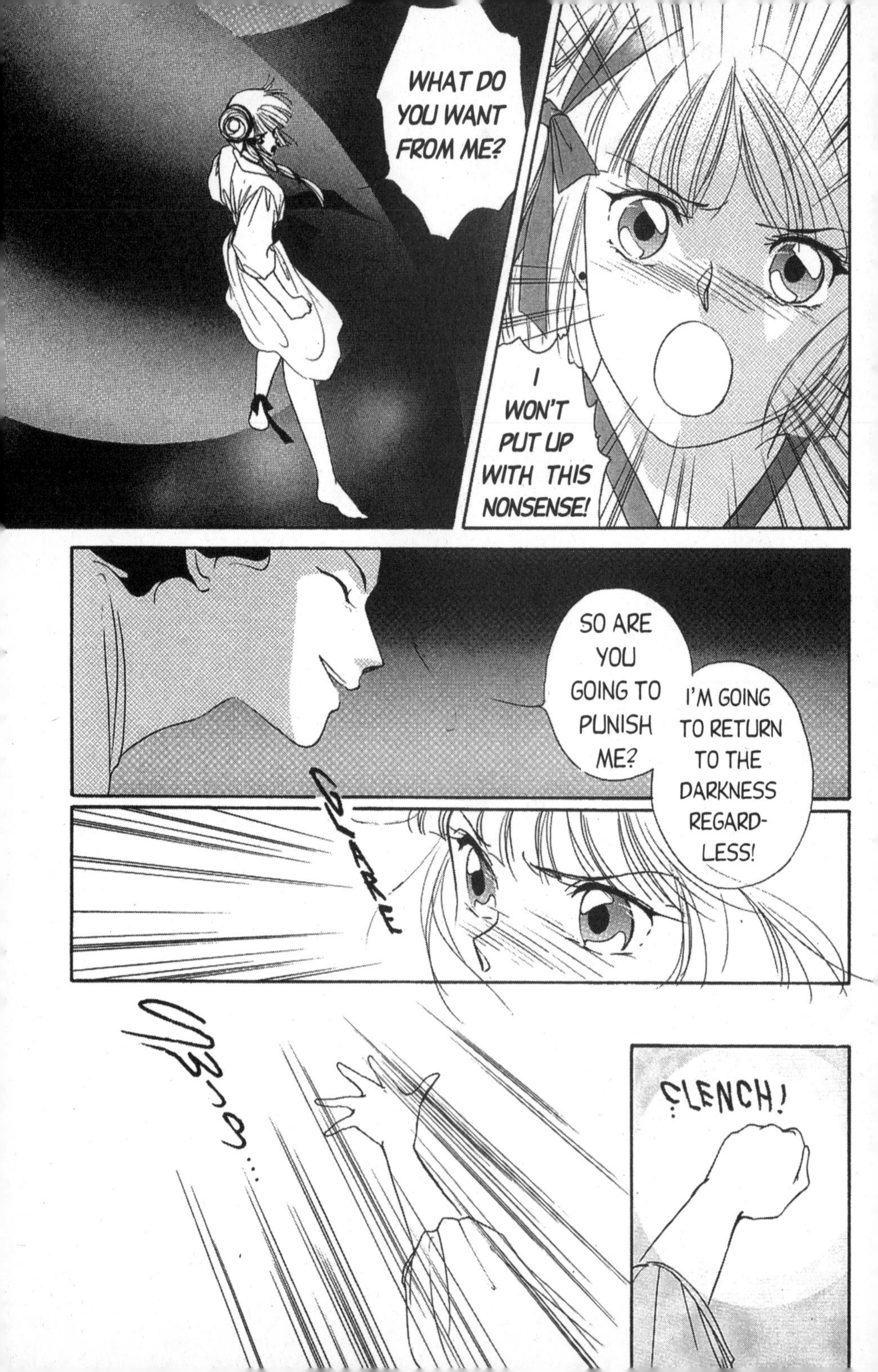
WHAT DO YOU WANT FROM ME?
I WON'T PUT UP WITH THIS NONSENSE!
SO ARE YOU GOING TO PUNISH ME?
I'M GOING TO RETURN TO THE DARKNESS REGARDLESS!
CLENCH!

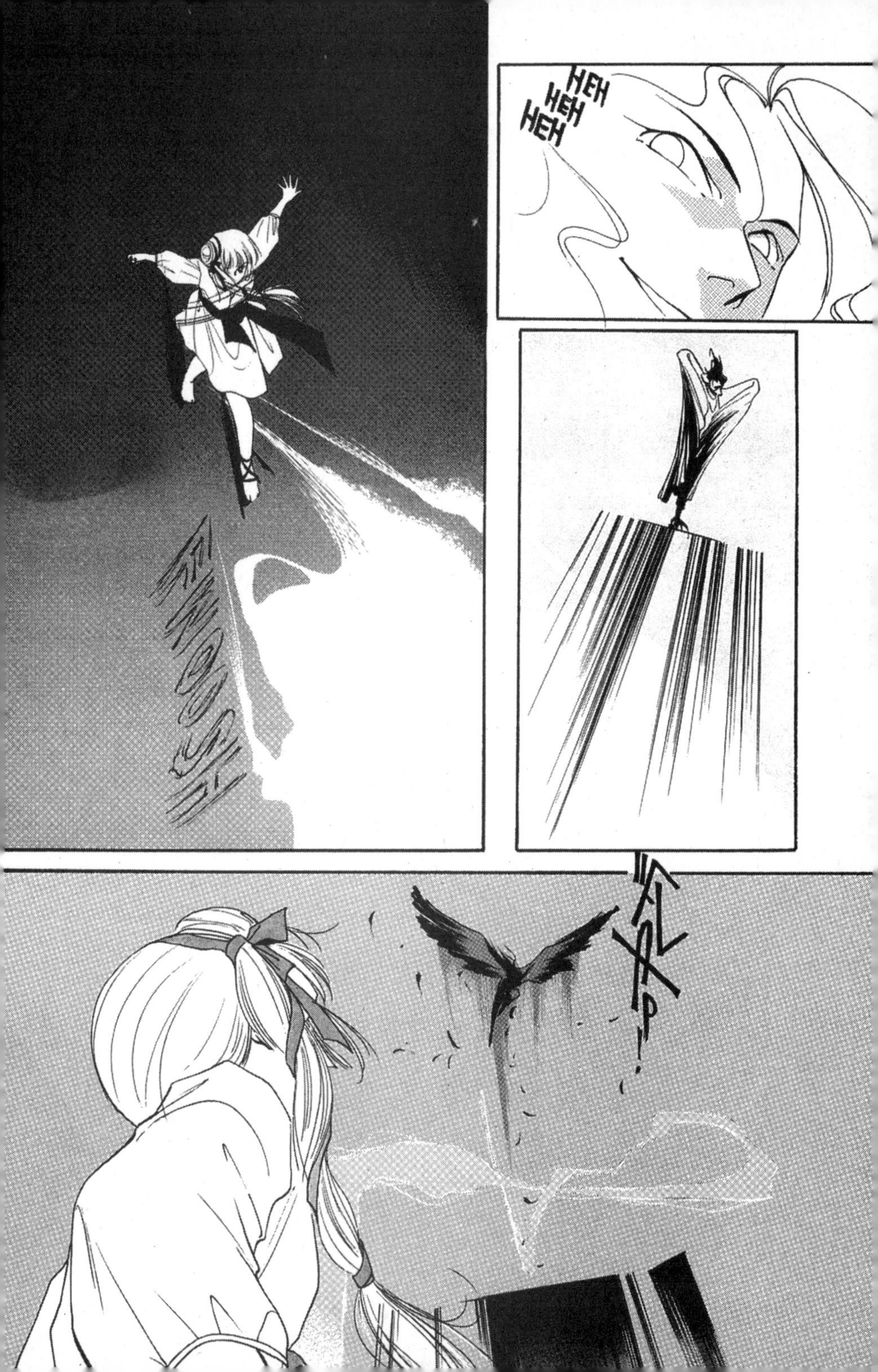
HEH
HEH
HEH
FLAP!

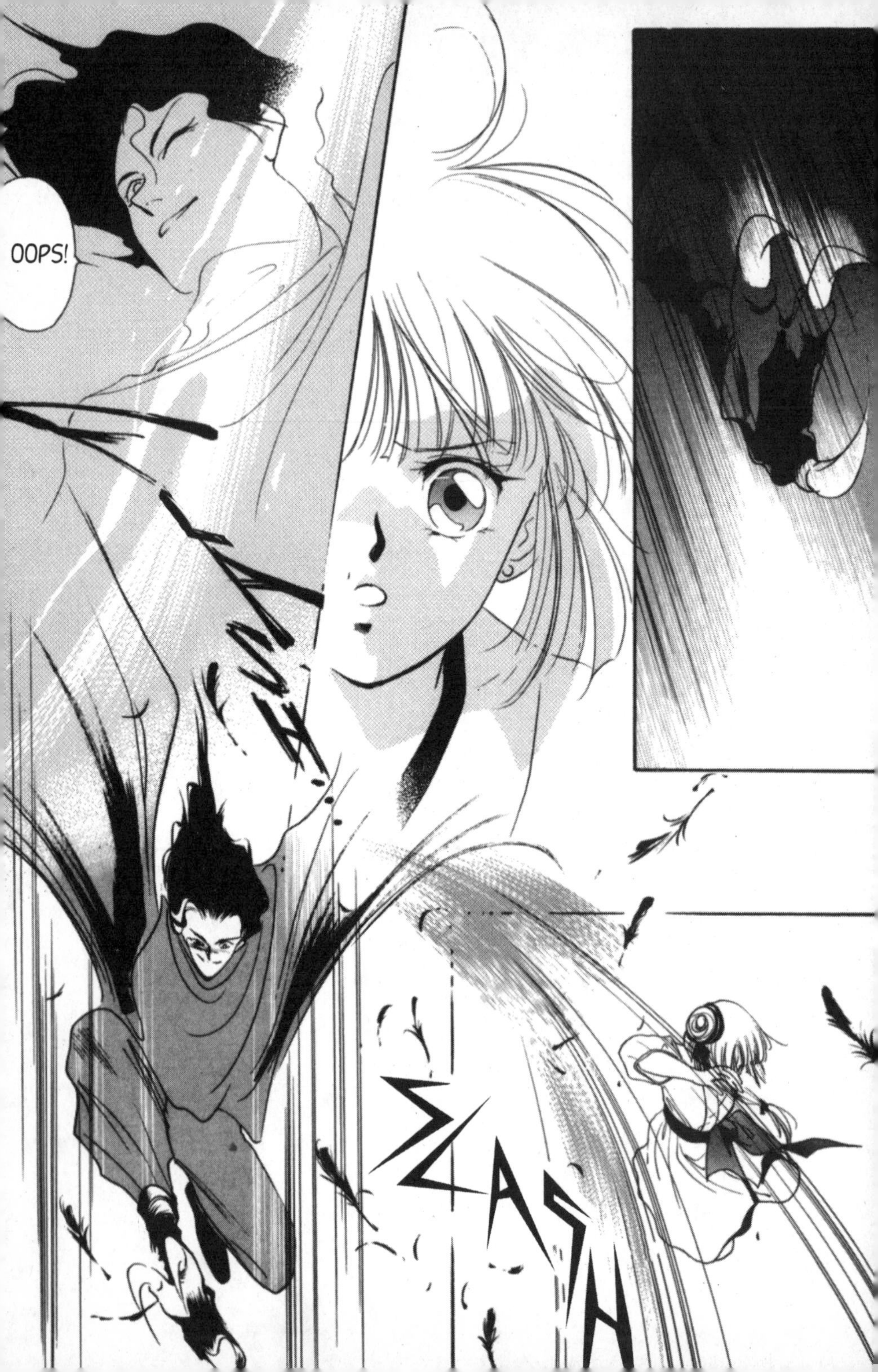

OOPS!
ZASH

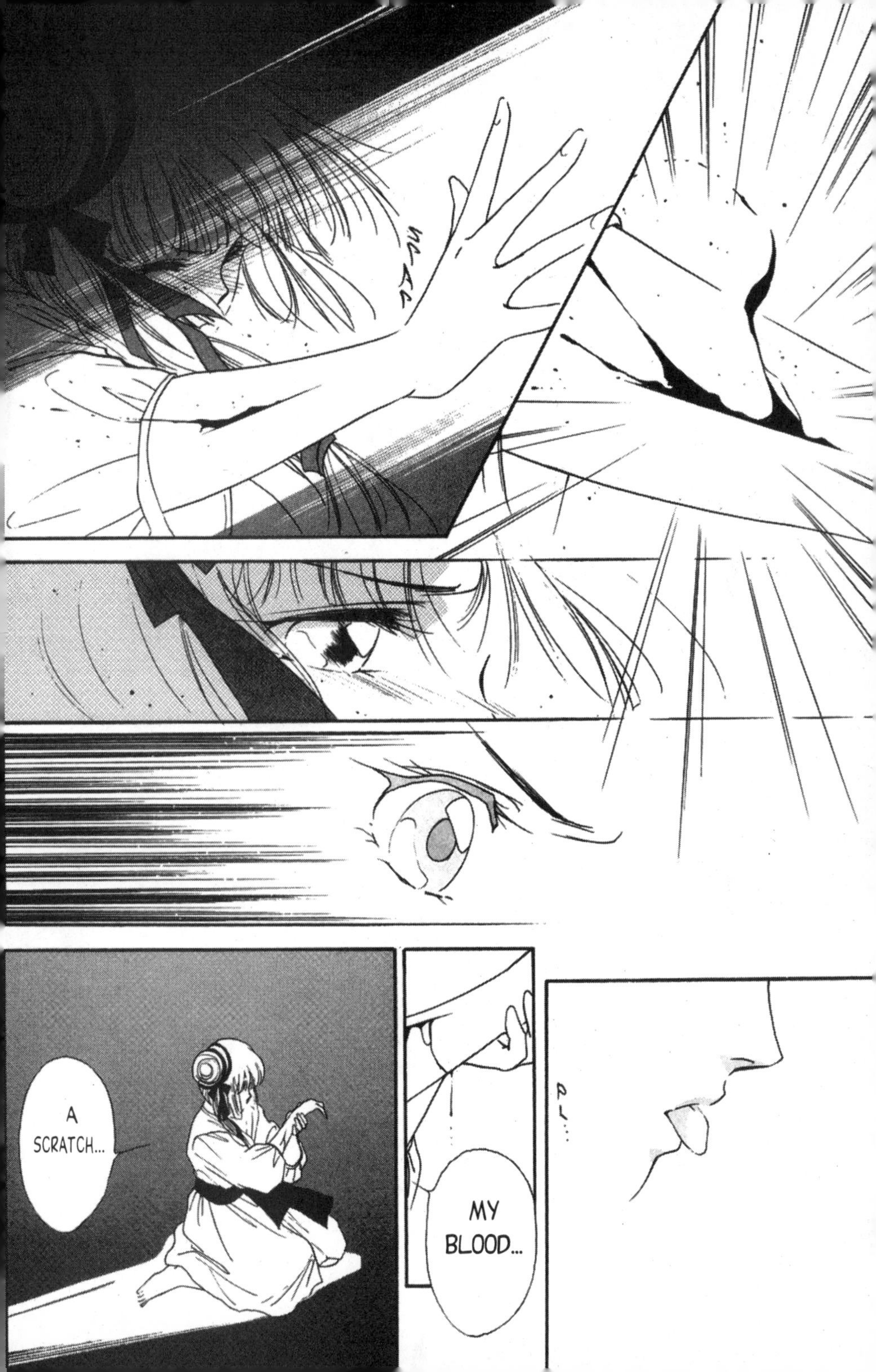
MY BLOOD...
A SCRATCH...

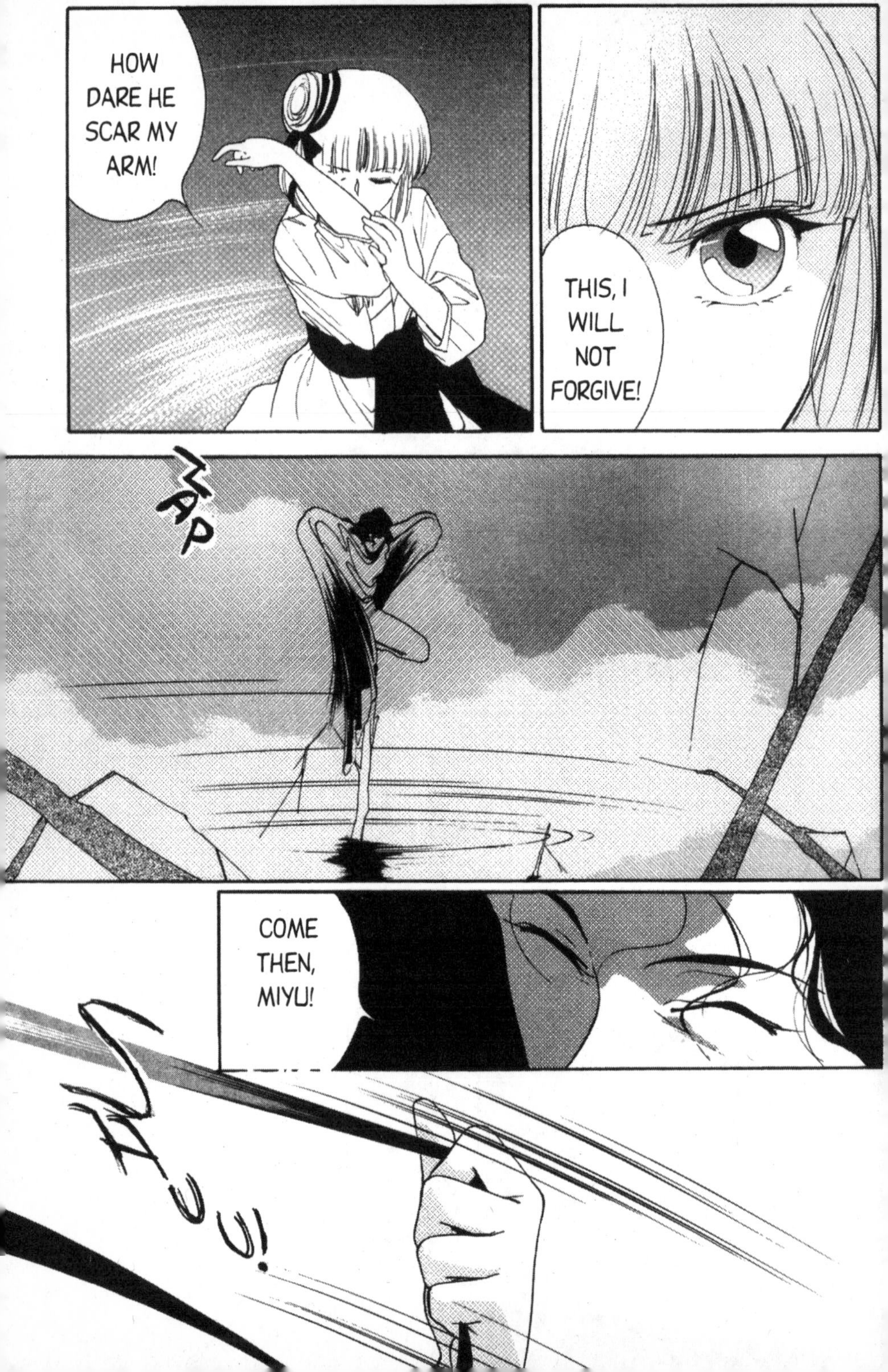
HOW DARE HE SCAR MY ARM!
THIS, I WILL NOT FORGIVE!
ZAP
COME THEN, MIYU!
SHAAUU!

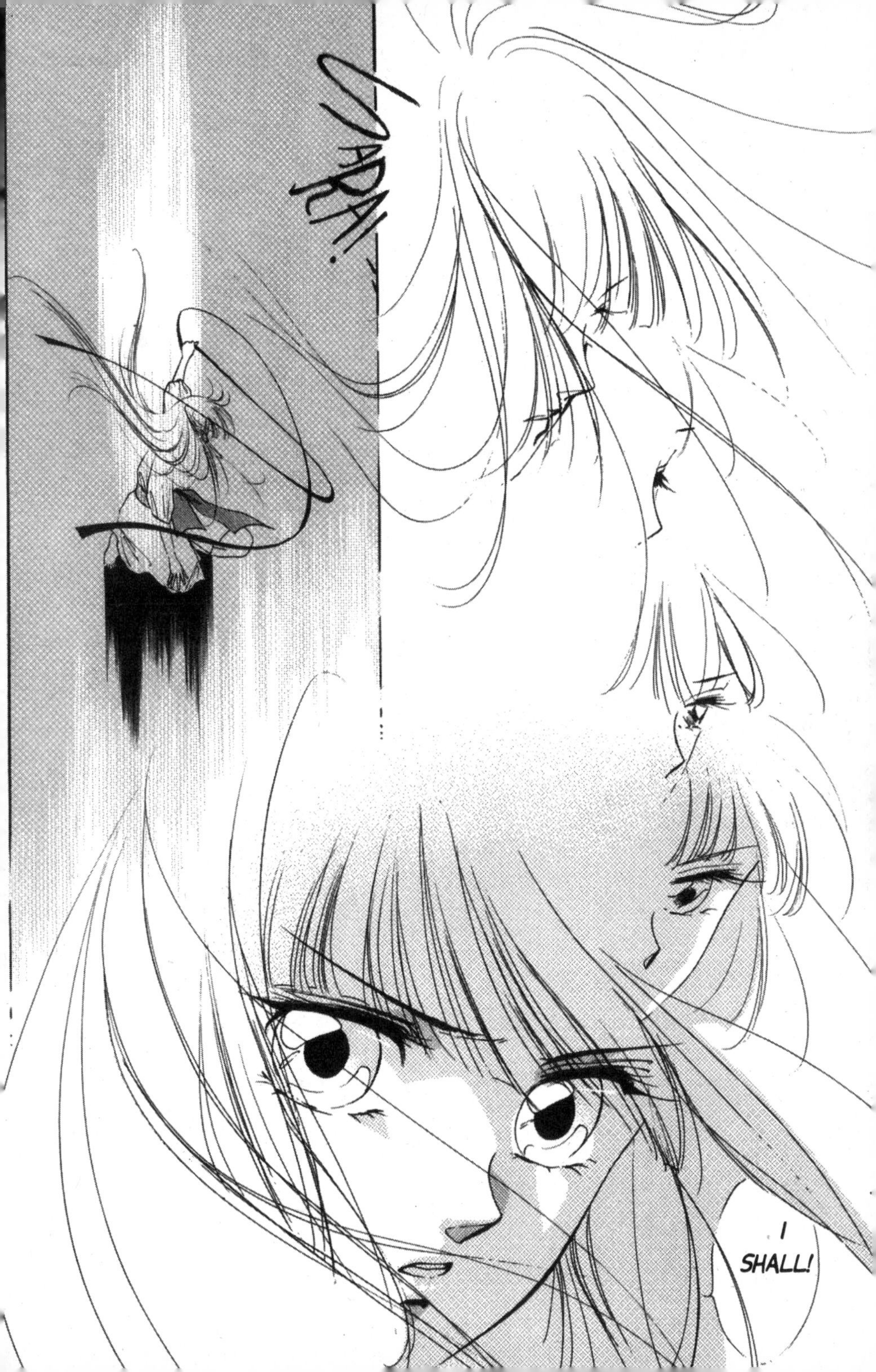

QARAI!!
I SHALL!

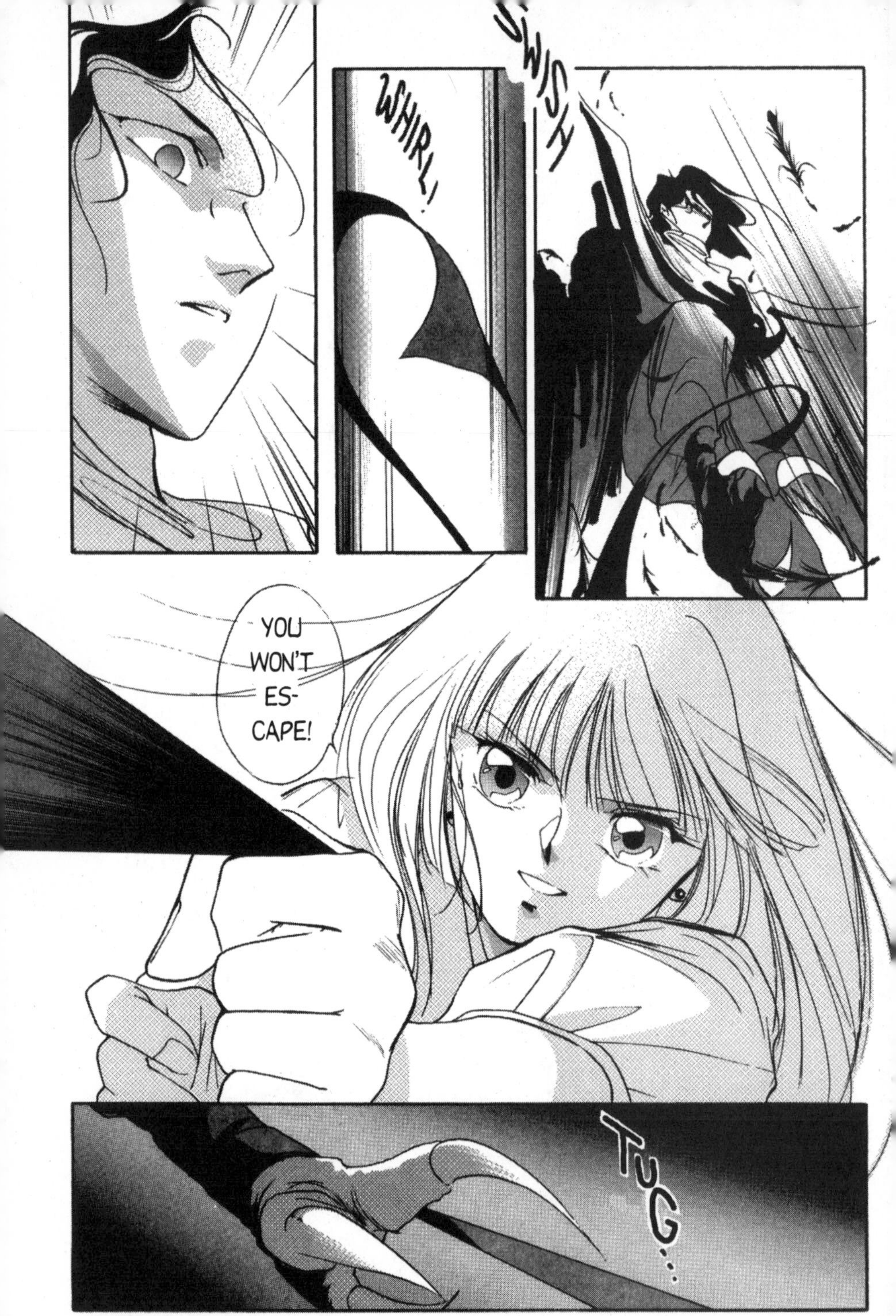
SWISH
WHIRL!
YOU WON'T ES-CAPE!
TUG...

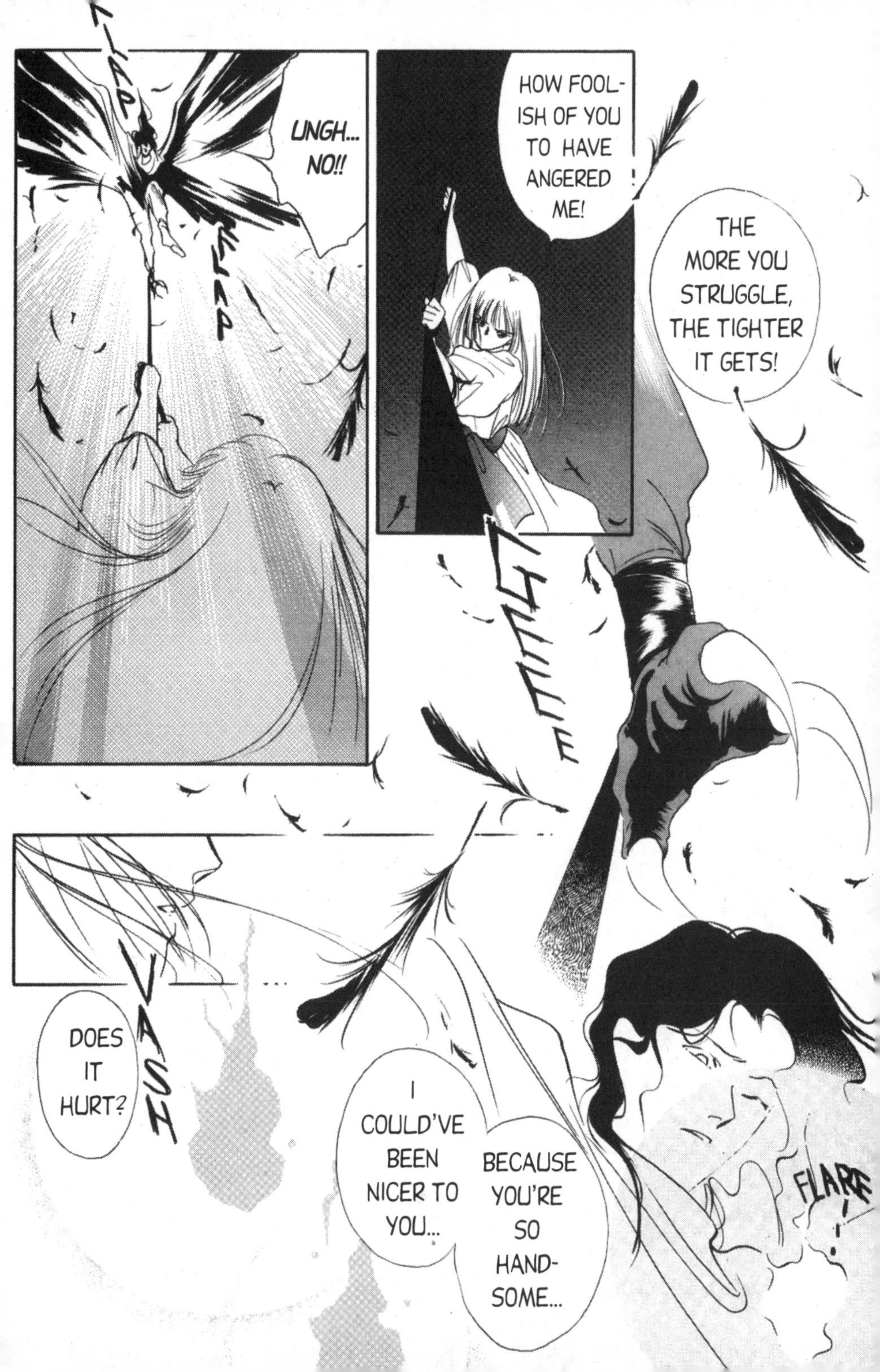

HOW FOOLISH OF YOU TO HAVE ANGERED ME!
THE MORE YOU STRUGGLE, THE TIGHTER IT GETS!
UNGH... NO!!
FLAP
FLAP
I COULD'VE BEEN NICER TO YOU...
BECAUSE YOU'RE SO HANDSOME...
FLARE
DOES IT HURT?
VASH

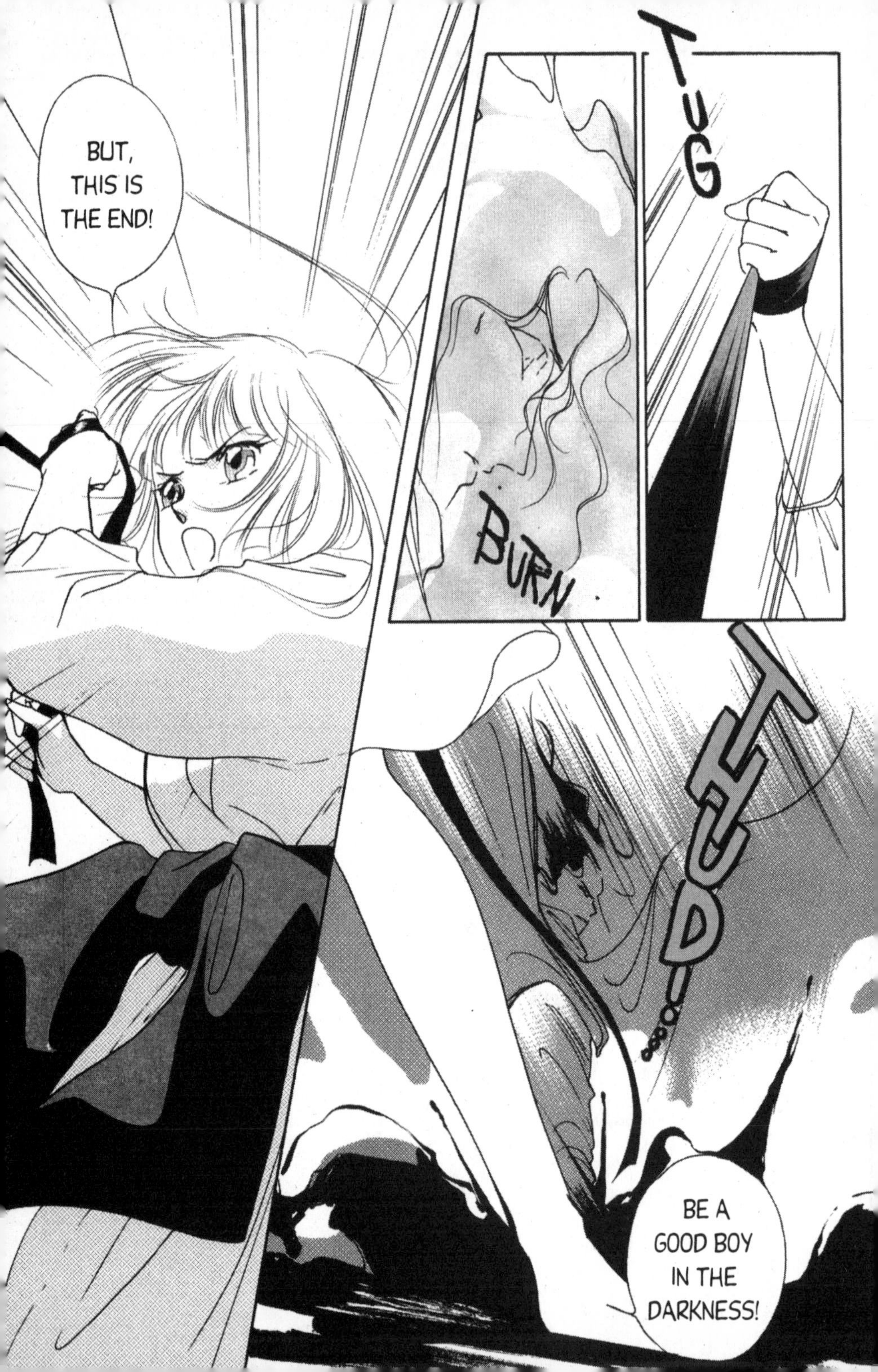
TUG
BURN
BUT, THIS IS THE END!
THUD!
BE A GOOD BOY IN THE DARKNESS!

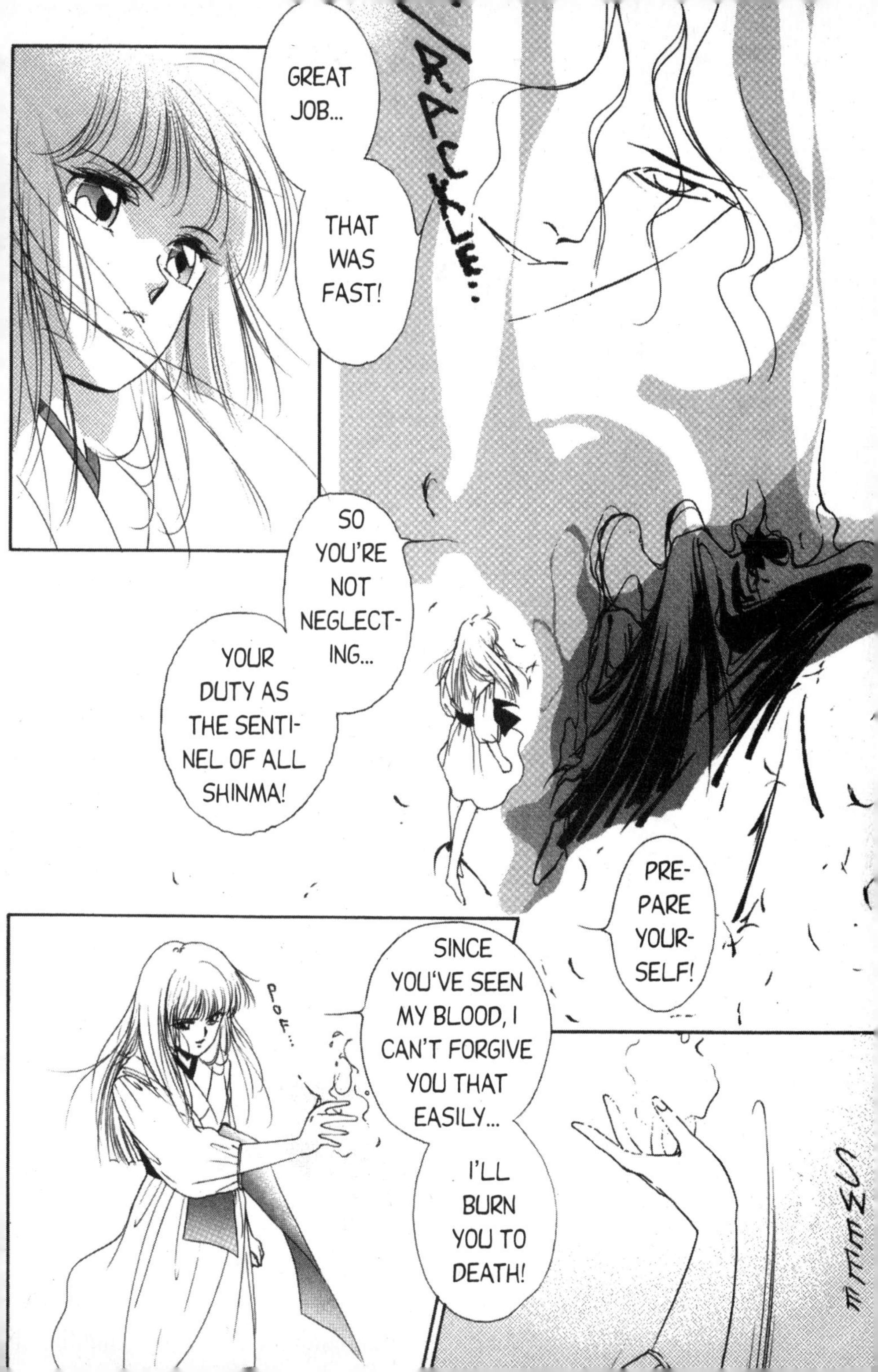
GREAT JOB...
THAT WAS FAST!
SO YOU'RE NOT NEGLECT-ING...
YOUR DUTY AS THE SENTI-NEL OF ALL SHINMA!
PRE-PARE YOUR-SELF!
SINCE YOU'VE SEEN MY BLOOD, I CAN'T FORGIVE YOU THAT EASILY...
I'LL BURN YOU TO DEATH!

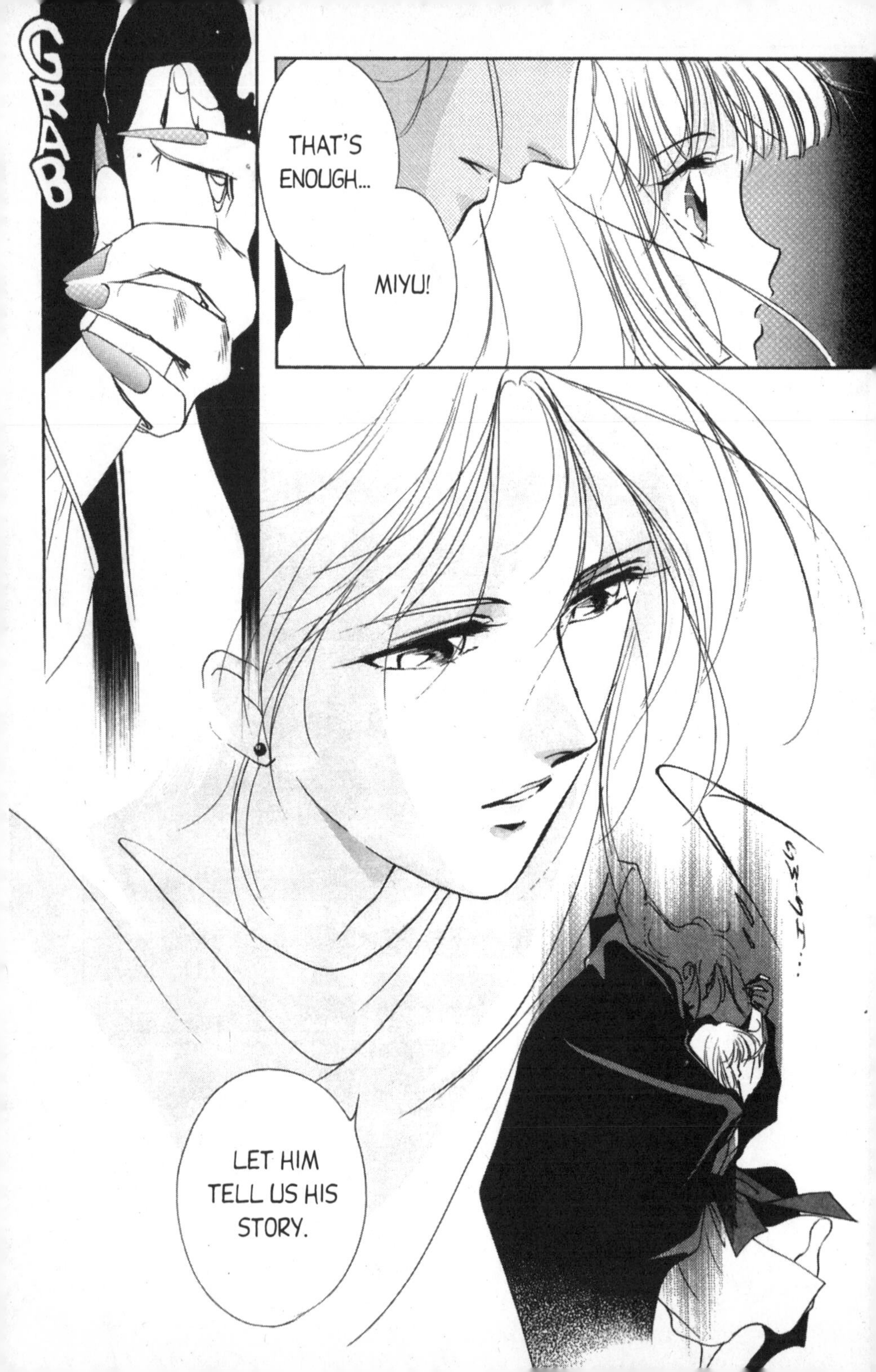
THAT'S ENOUGH...
MIYU!
GRAB
LET HIM TELL US HIS STORY.

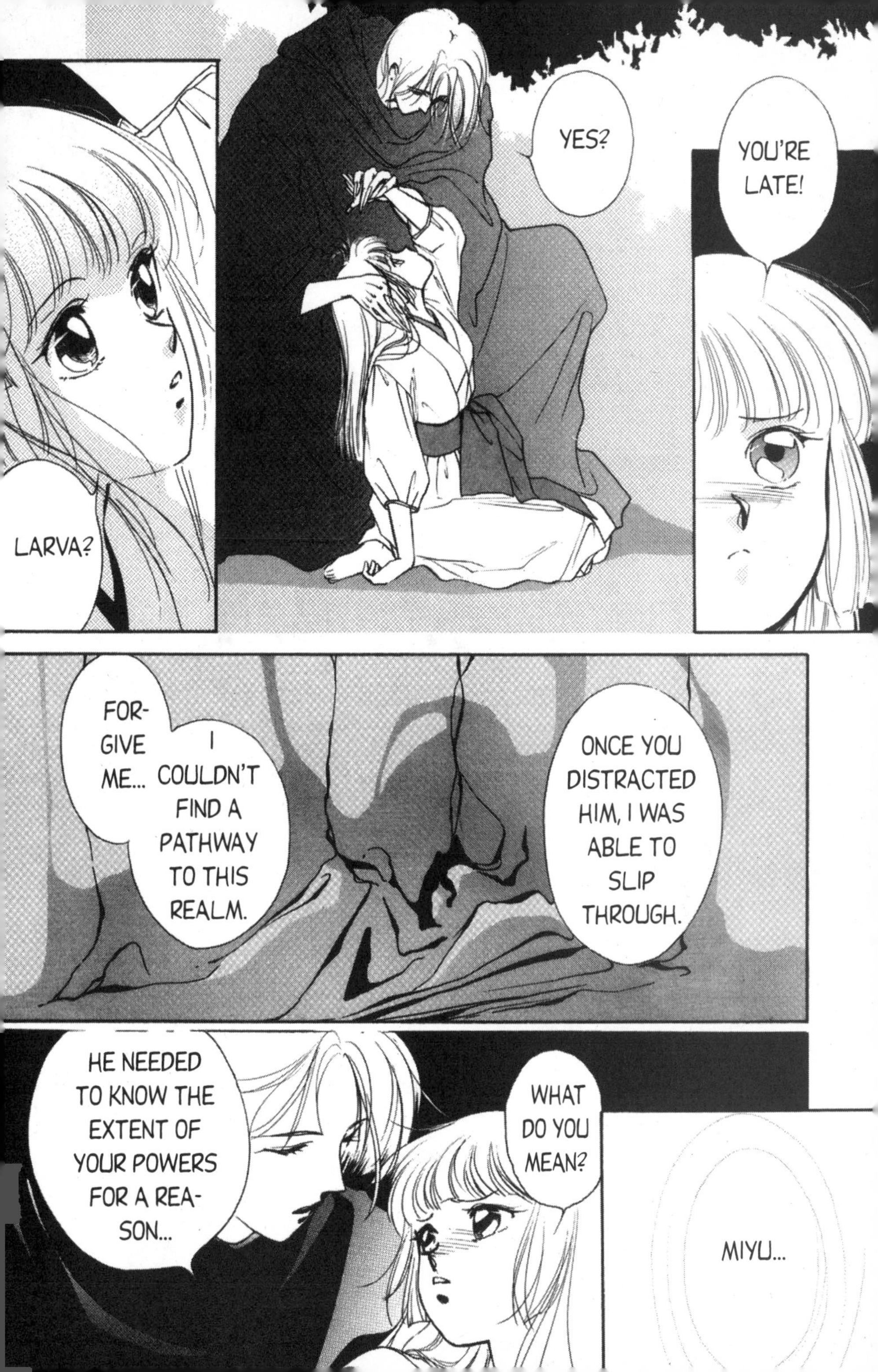
YOU'RE LATE!
YES?
LARVA?
ONCE YOU DISTRACTED HIM, I WAS ABLE TO SLIP THROUGH.
FOR-GIVE ME...
I COULDN'T FIND A PATHWAY TO THIS REALM.
MIYU...
WHAT DO YOU MEAN?
HE NEEDED TO KNOW THE EXTENT OF YOUR POWERS FOR A REA-SON...

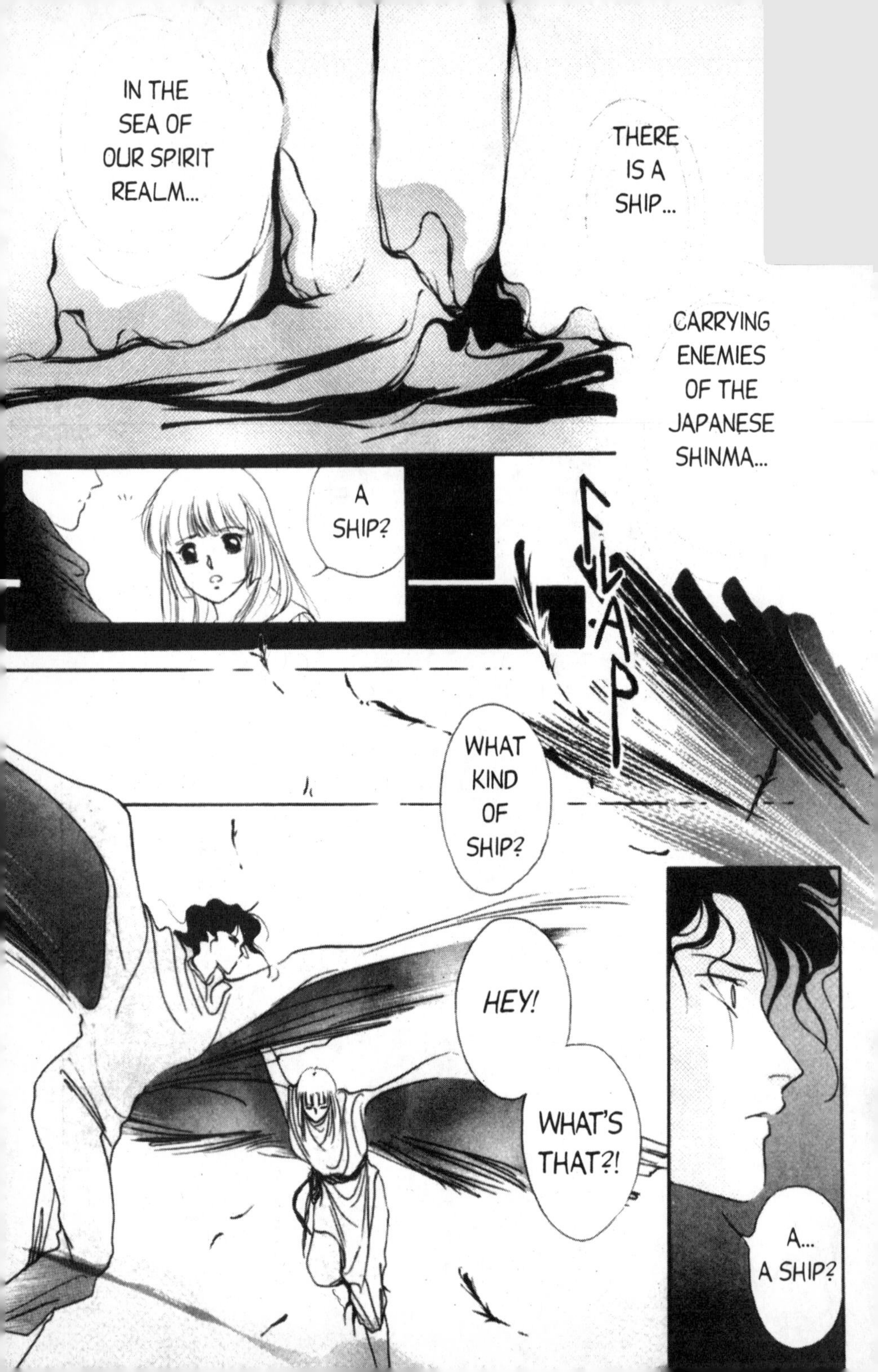
THERE IS A SHIP...
IN THE SEA OF OUR SPIRIT REALM...
CARRYING ENEMIES OF THE JAPANESE SHINMA...
FLAP
A SHIP?
WHAT KIND OF SHIP?
A... A SHIP?
HEY!
WHAT'S THAT?!

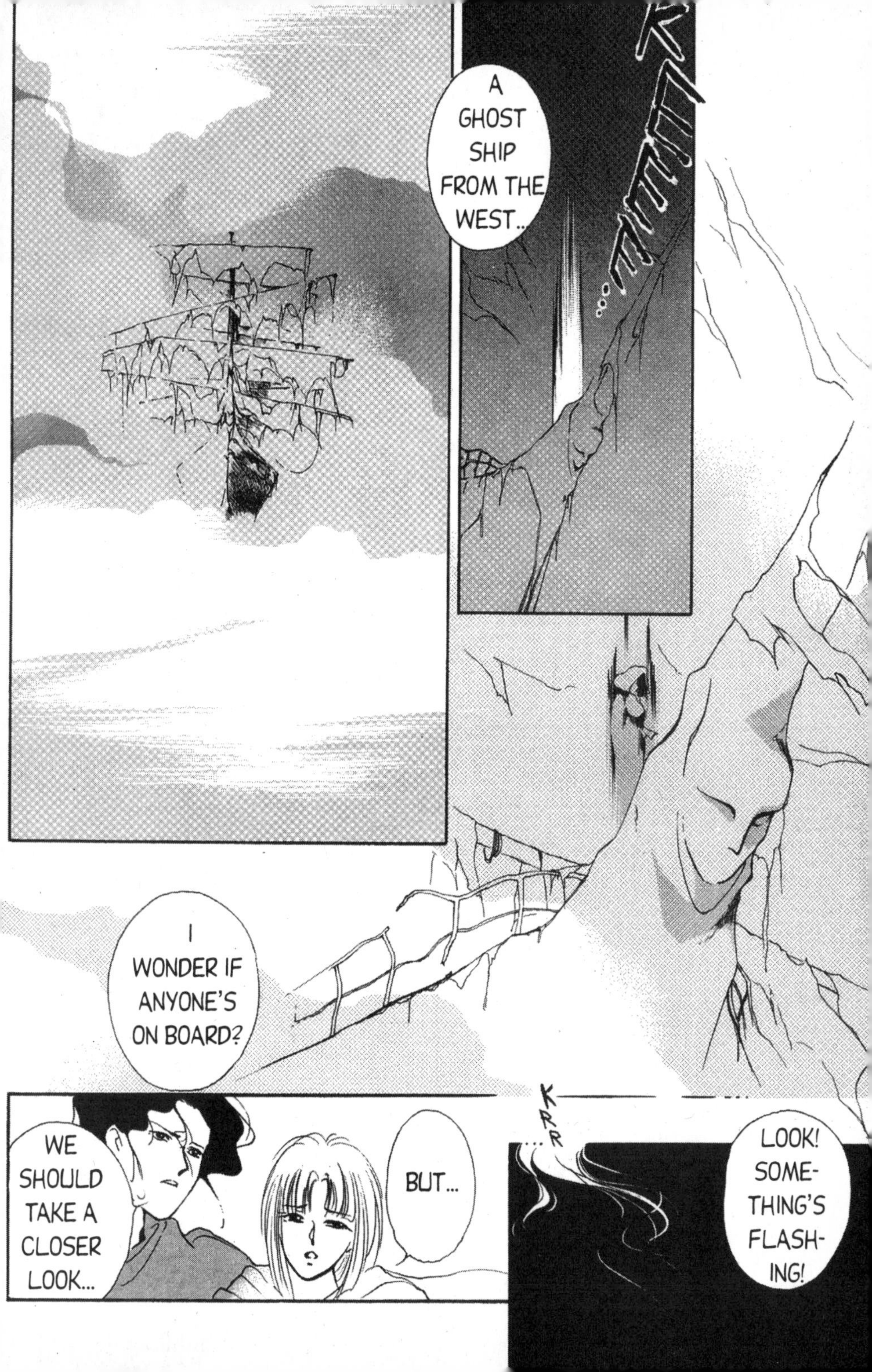
KLUNK...
A GHOST SHIP FROM THE WEST...
I WONDER IF ANYONE'S ON BOARD?
KRR...
LOOK! SOMETHING'S FLASHING!
BUT...
WE SHOULD TAKE A CLOSER LOOK...

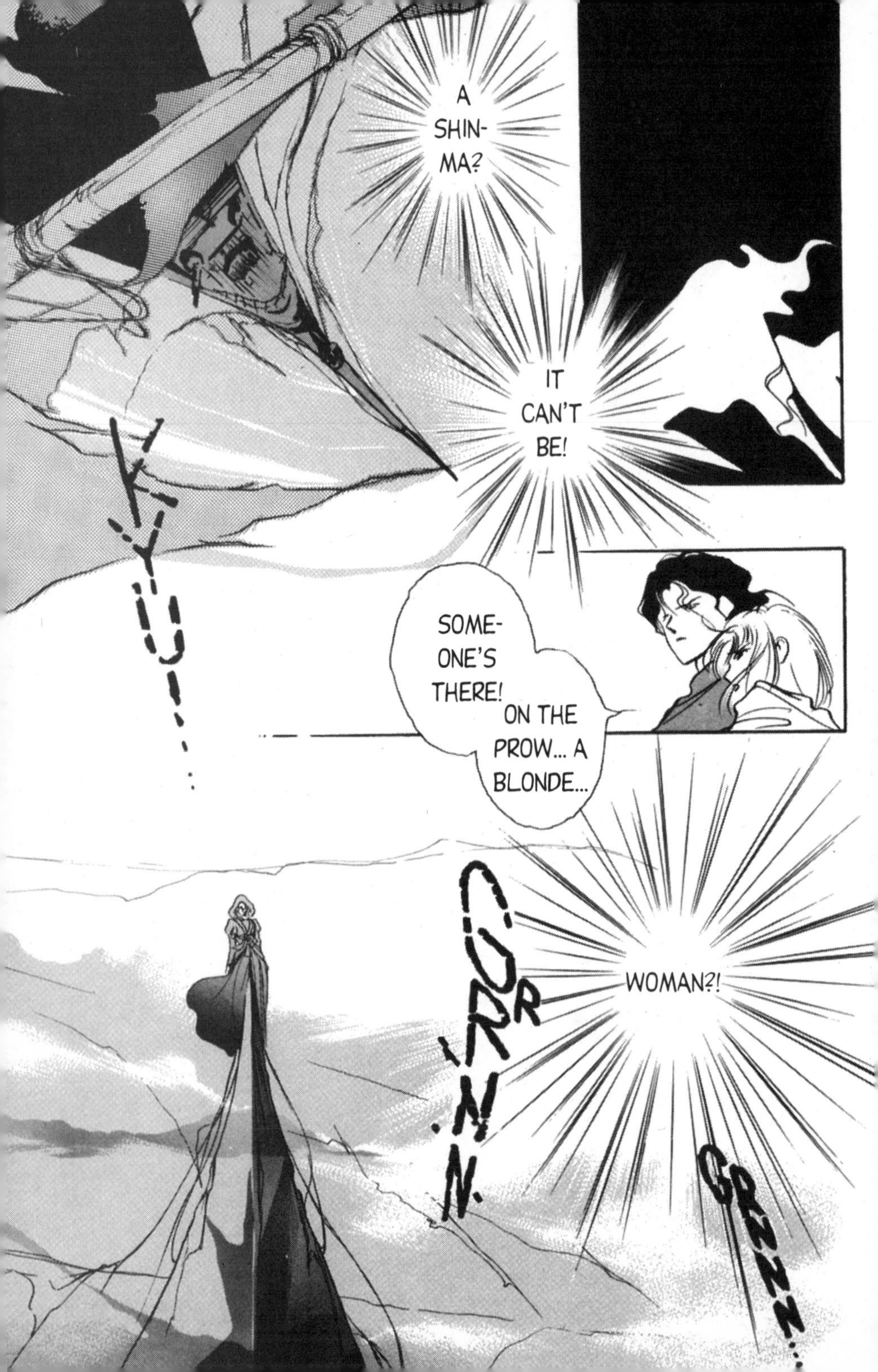
A SHIN-MA?
IT CAN'T BE!
KYU!...
SOME-ONE'S THERE!
ON THE PROW... A BLONDE...
WOMAN?!
GORRNNN.
GRNNN...

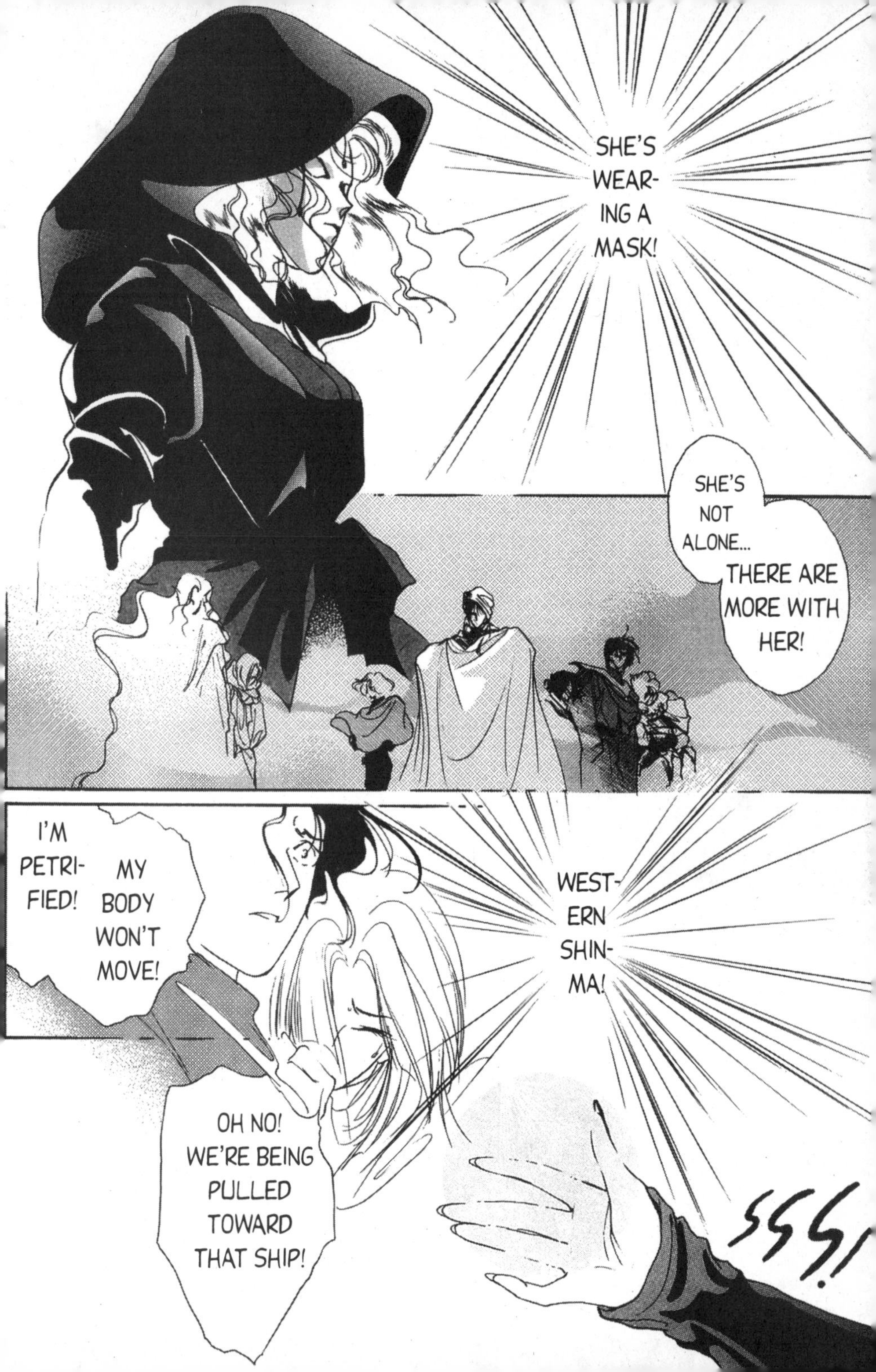
SHE'S WEAR-ING A MASK!
SHE'S NOT ALONE...
THERE ARE MORE WITH HER!
WEST-ERN SHIN-MA!
MY BODY WON'T MOVE!
I'M PETRI-FIED!
OH NO! WE'RE BEING PULLED TOWARD THAT SHIP!
SSS!

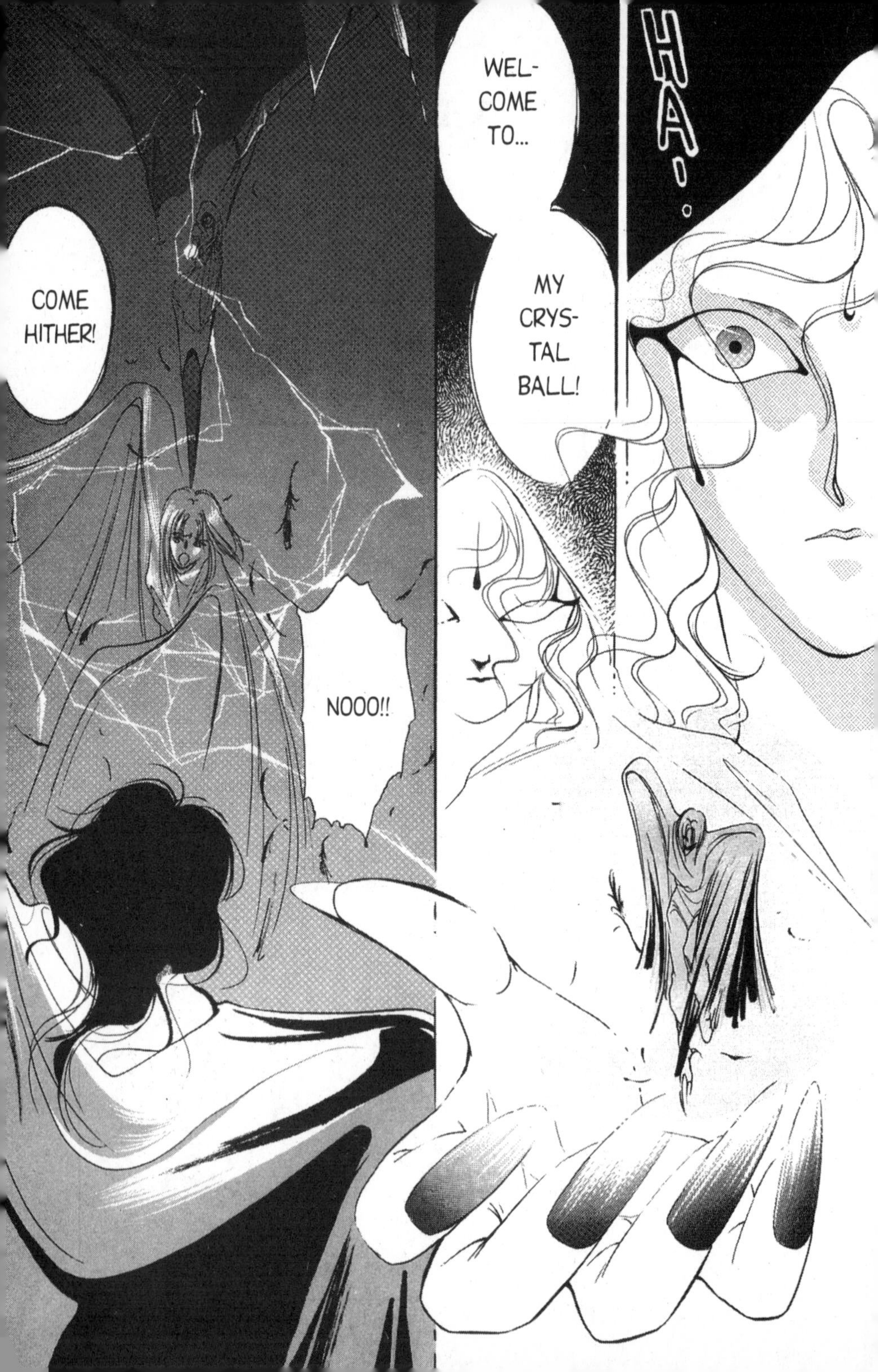
HA!
WEL-COME TO...
MY CRYS-TAL BALL!
COME HITHER!
NOOO!!

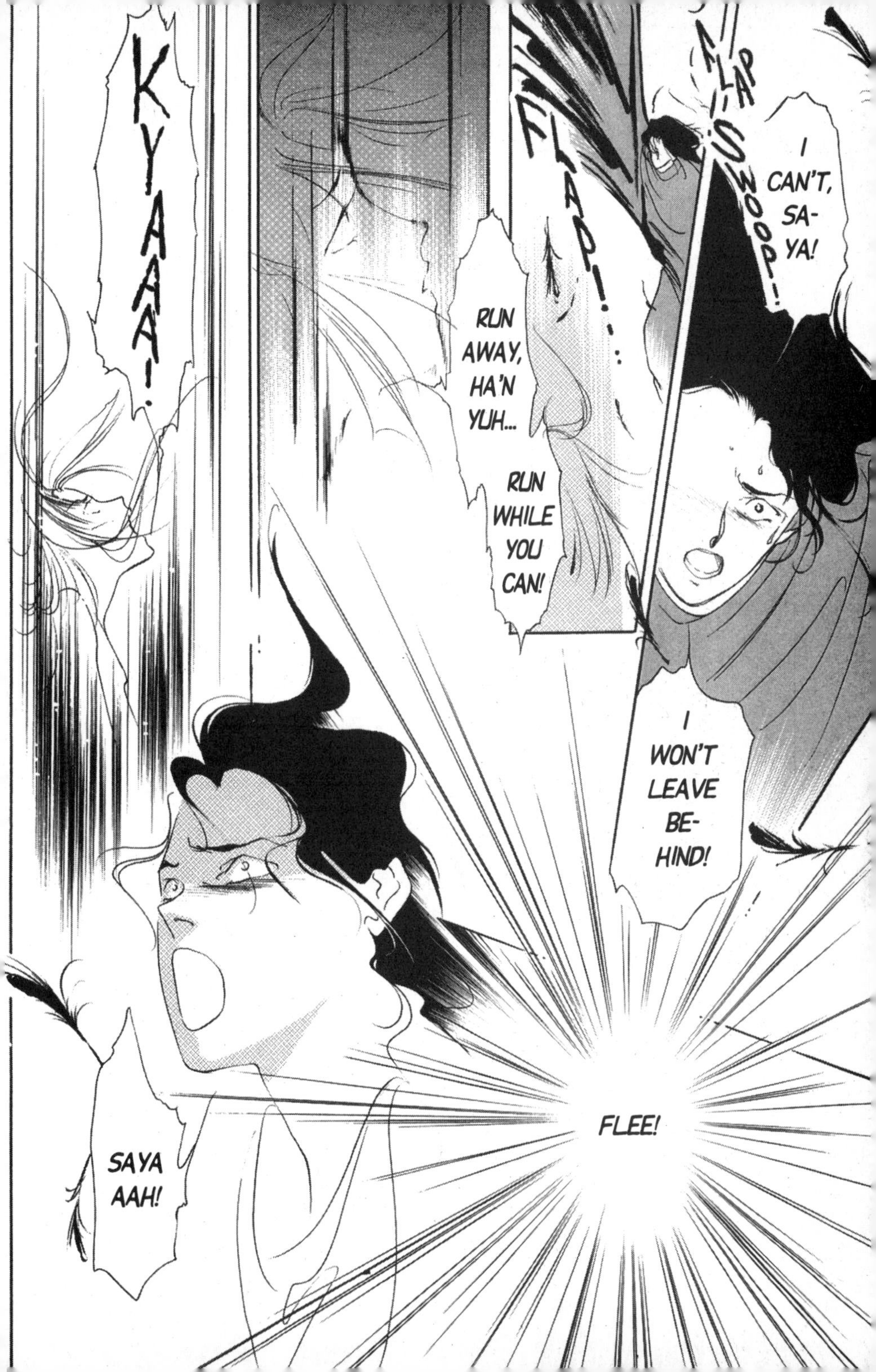
I CAN'T, SA-YA!
FLAP FLAP
SWOOP!
FLAP!...
RUN AWAY, HA'N YUH...
RUN WHILE YOU CAN!
KYAAAA!
I WON'T LEAVE BE-HIND!
FLEE!
SAYA AAH!

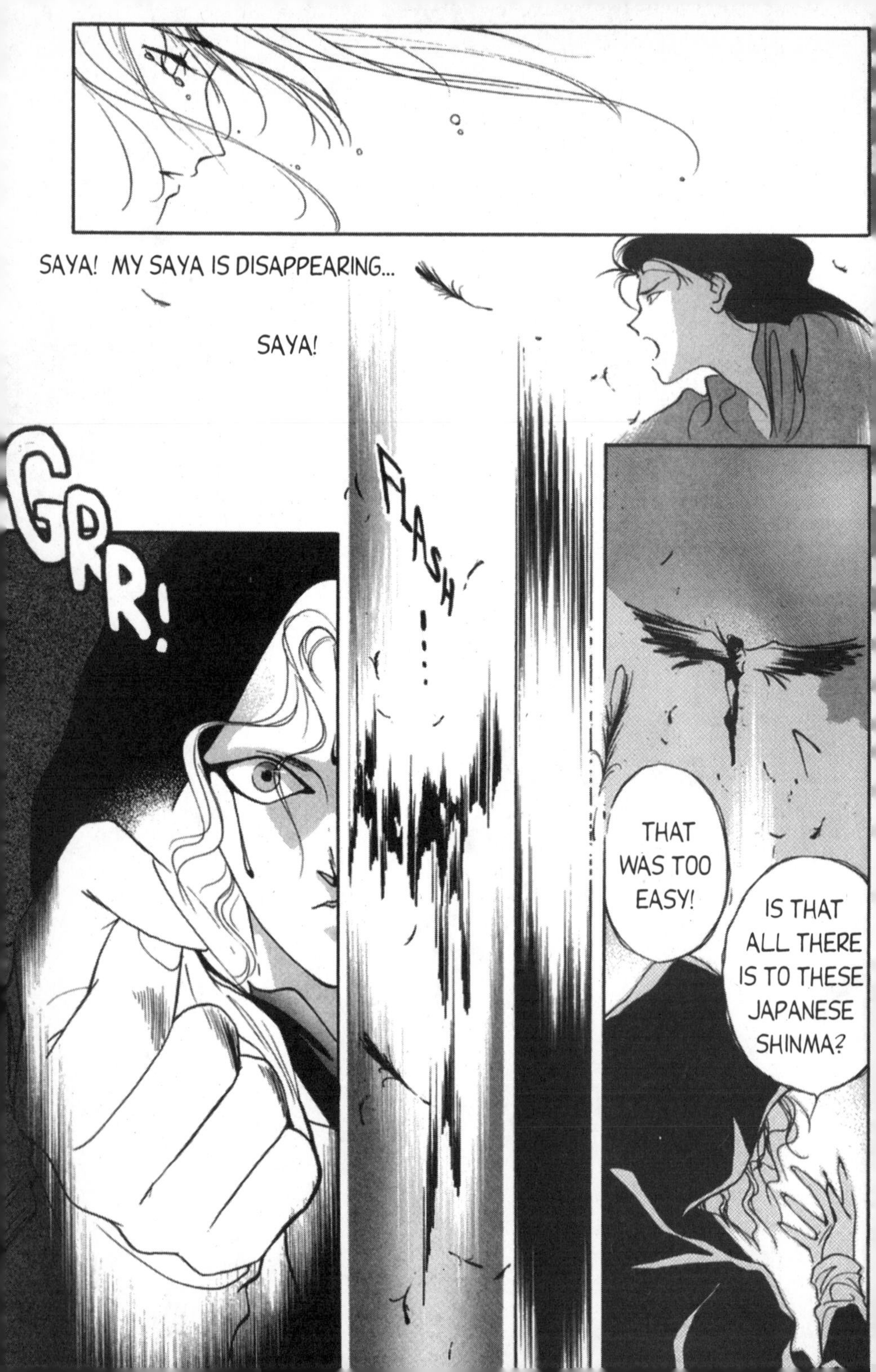
SAYA! MY SAYA IS DISAPPEARING...
SAYA!
GRR!
FLASH...
THAT WAS TOO EASY!
IS THAT ALL THERE IS TO THESE JAPANESE SHINMA?

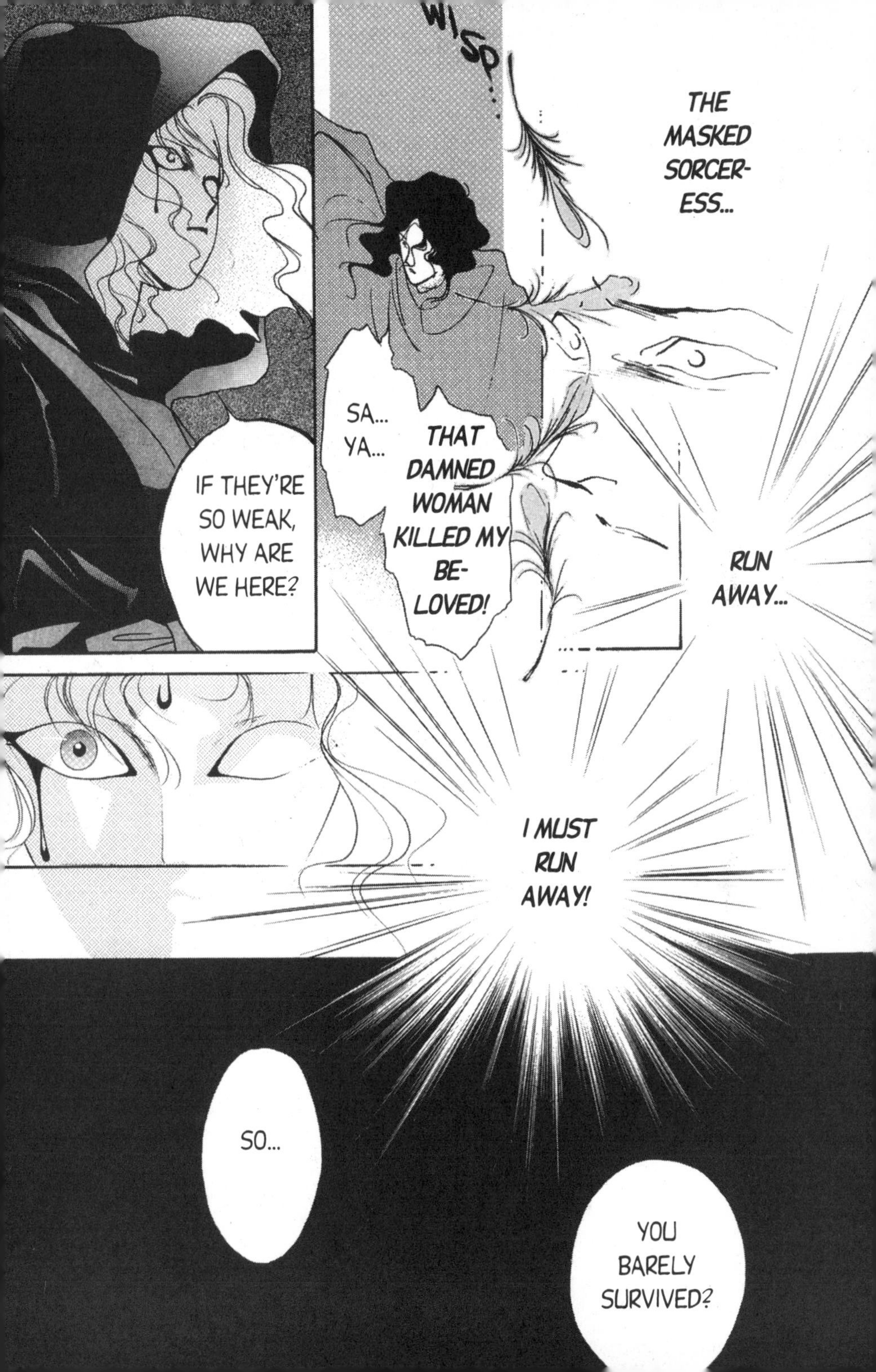
WISP...
THE MASKED SORCERESS...
SA... YA...
THAT DAMNED WOMAN KILLED MY BELOVED!
IF THEY'RE SO WEAK, WHY ARE WE HERE?
RUN AWAY...
I MUST RUN AWAY!
SO...
YOU BARELY SURVIVED?

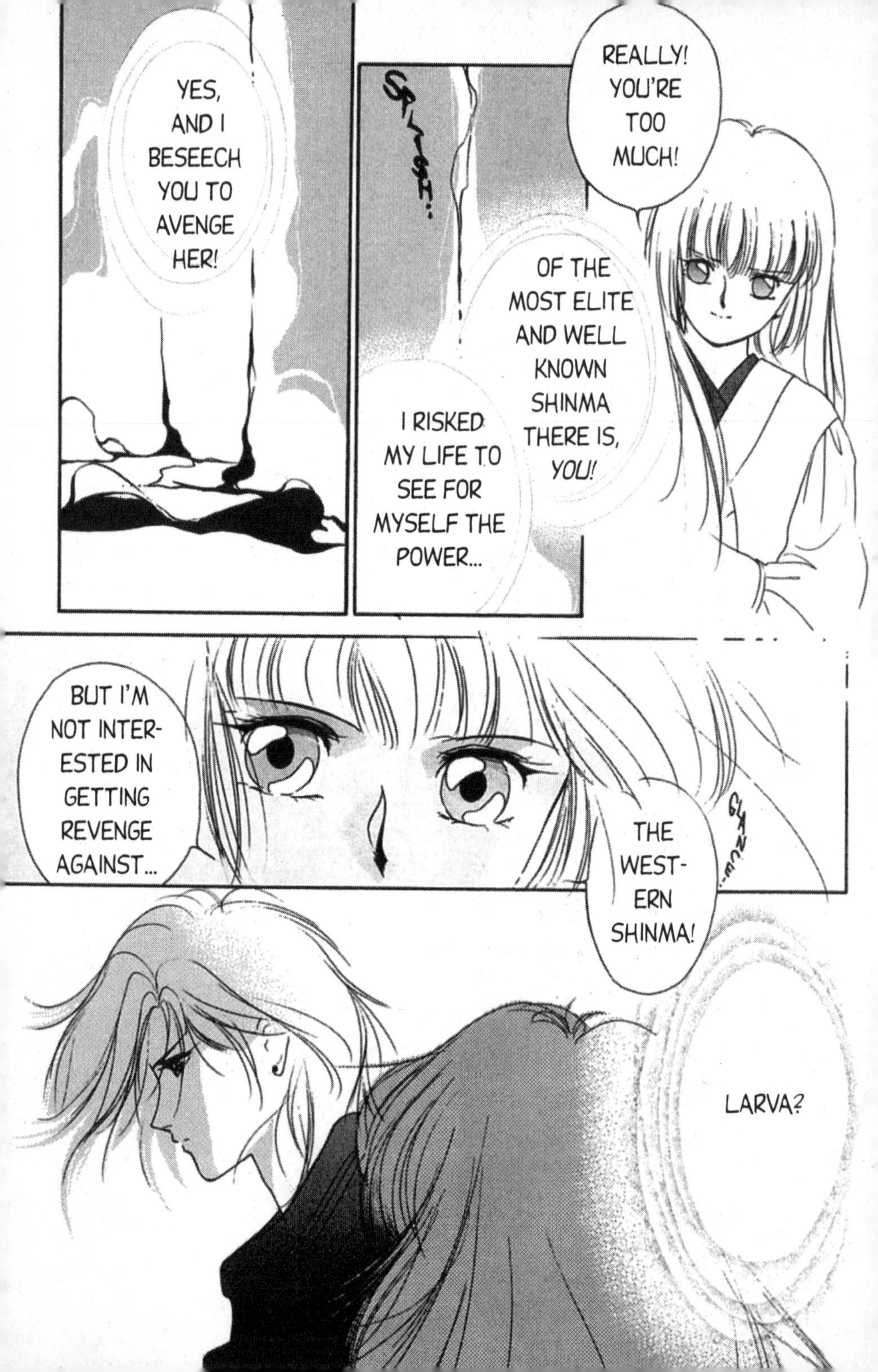
I RISKED MY LIFE TO SEE FOR MYSELF THE POWER...
OF THE MOST ELITE AND WELL KNOWN SHINMA THERE IS, *YOU!*
REALLY! YOU'RE TOO MUCH!
YES, AND I BESEECH YOU TO AVENGE HER!
BUT I'M NOT INTER-ESTED IN GETTING REVENGE AGAINST...
THE WEST-ERN SHINMA!
LARVA?

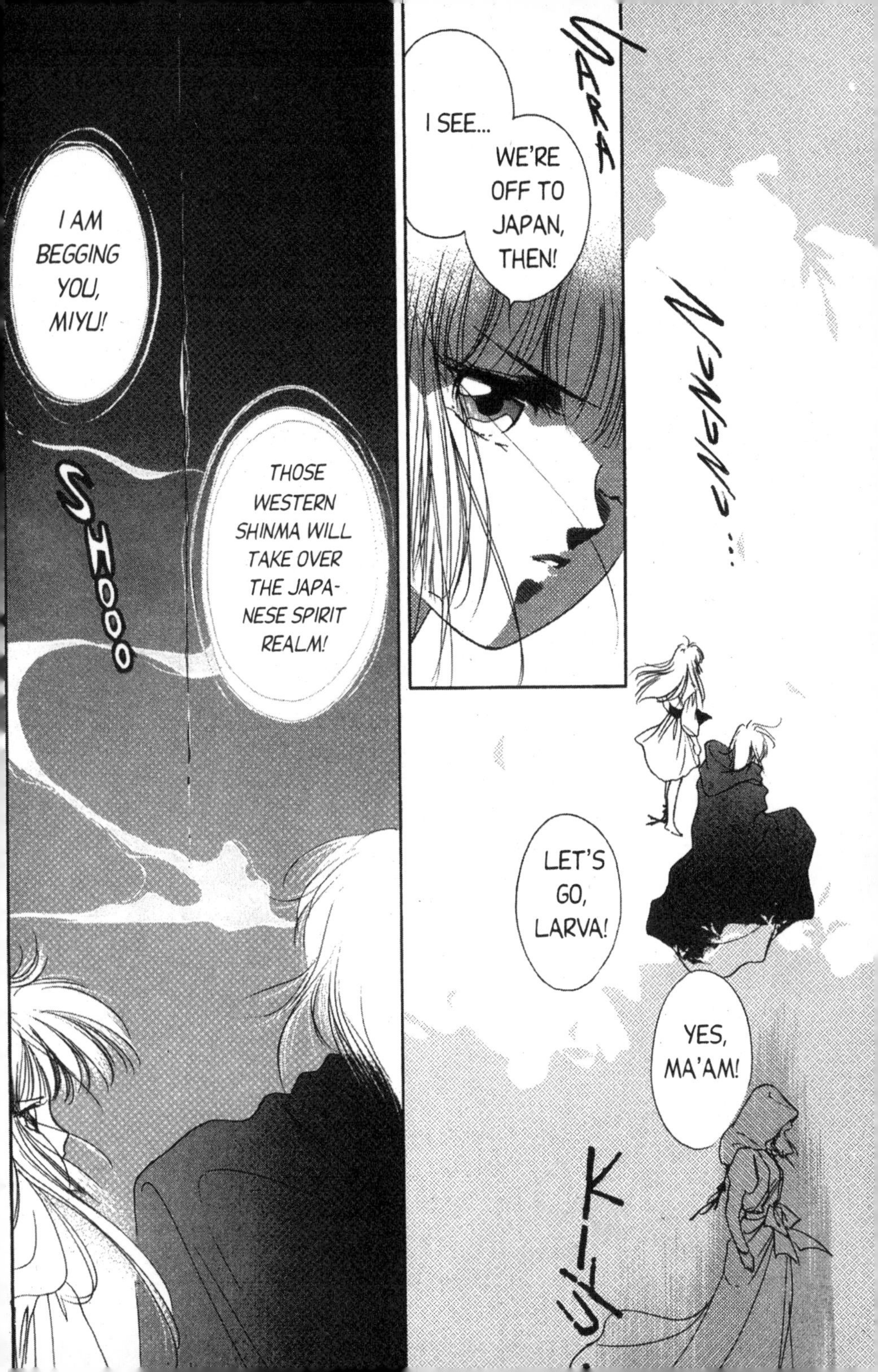
SARA
I SEE... WE'RE OFF TO JAPAN, THEN!
NNNN...
LET'S GO, LARVA!
YES, MA'AM!
KIII
I AM BEGGING YOU, MIYU!
THOSE WESTERN SHINMA WILL TAKE OVER THE JAPANESE SPIRIT REALM!
SHOOOO

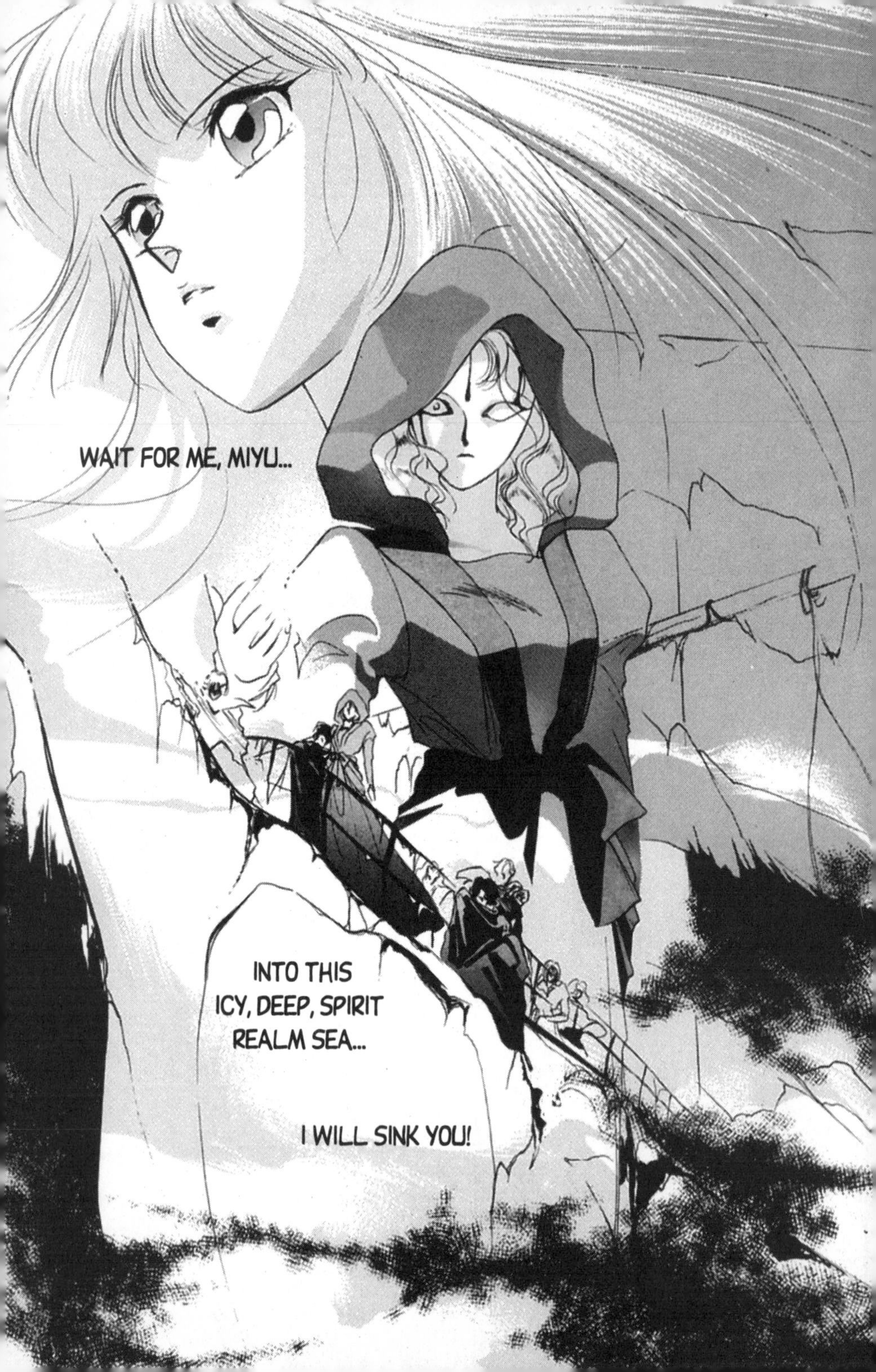
WAIT FOR ME, MIYU...
INTO THIS ICY, DEEP, SPIRIT REALM SEA...
I WILL SINK YOU!

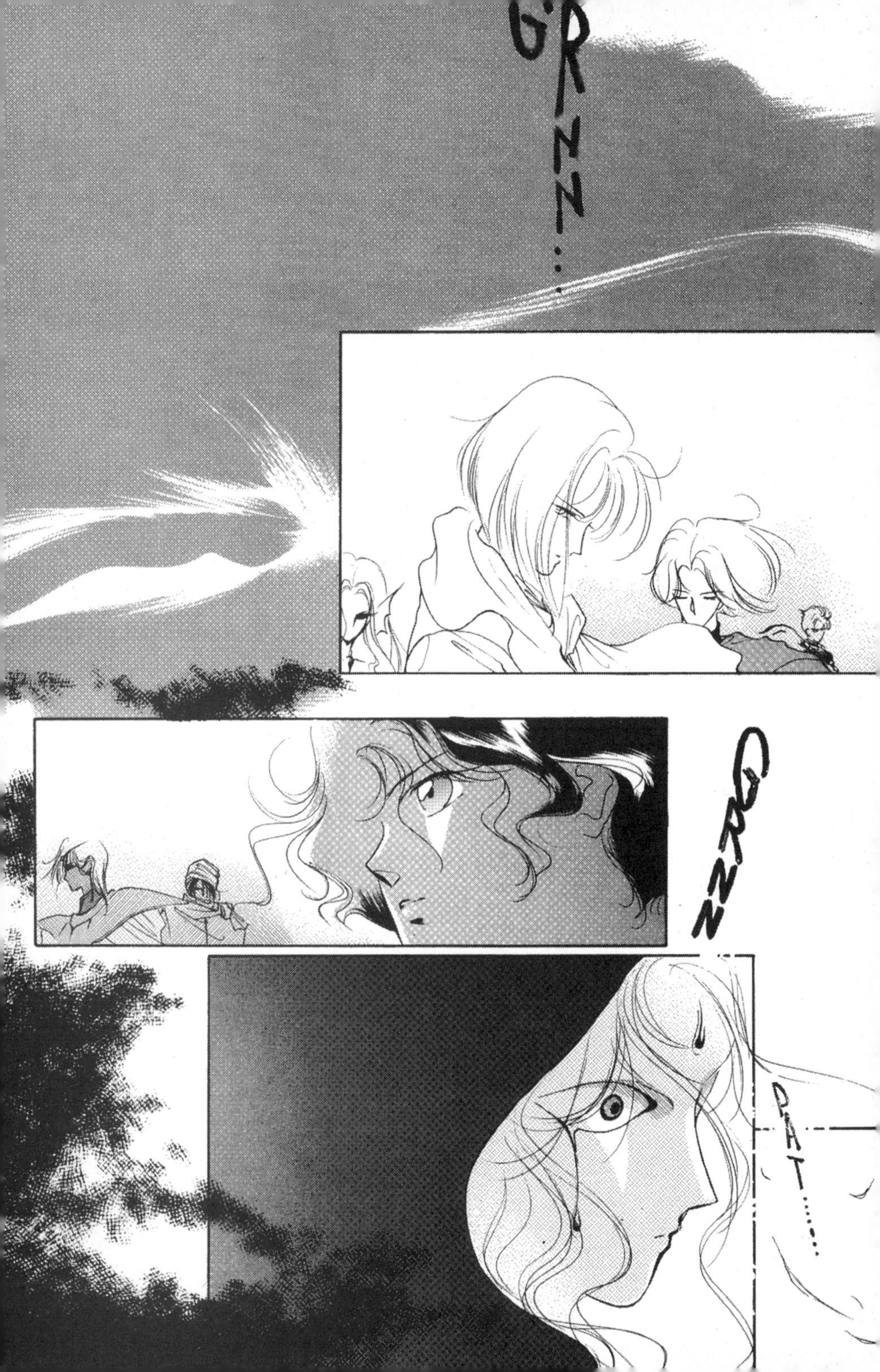
G'RNN...
G'RNN
DAT......

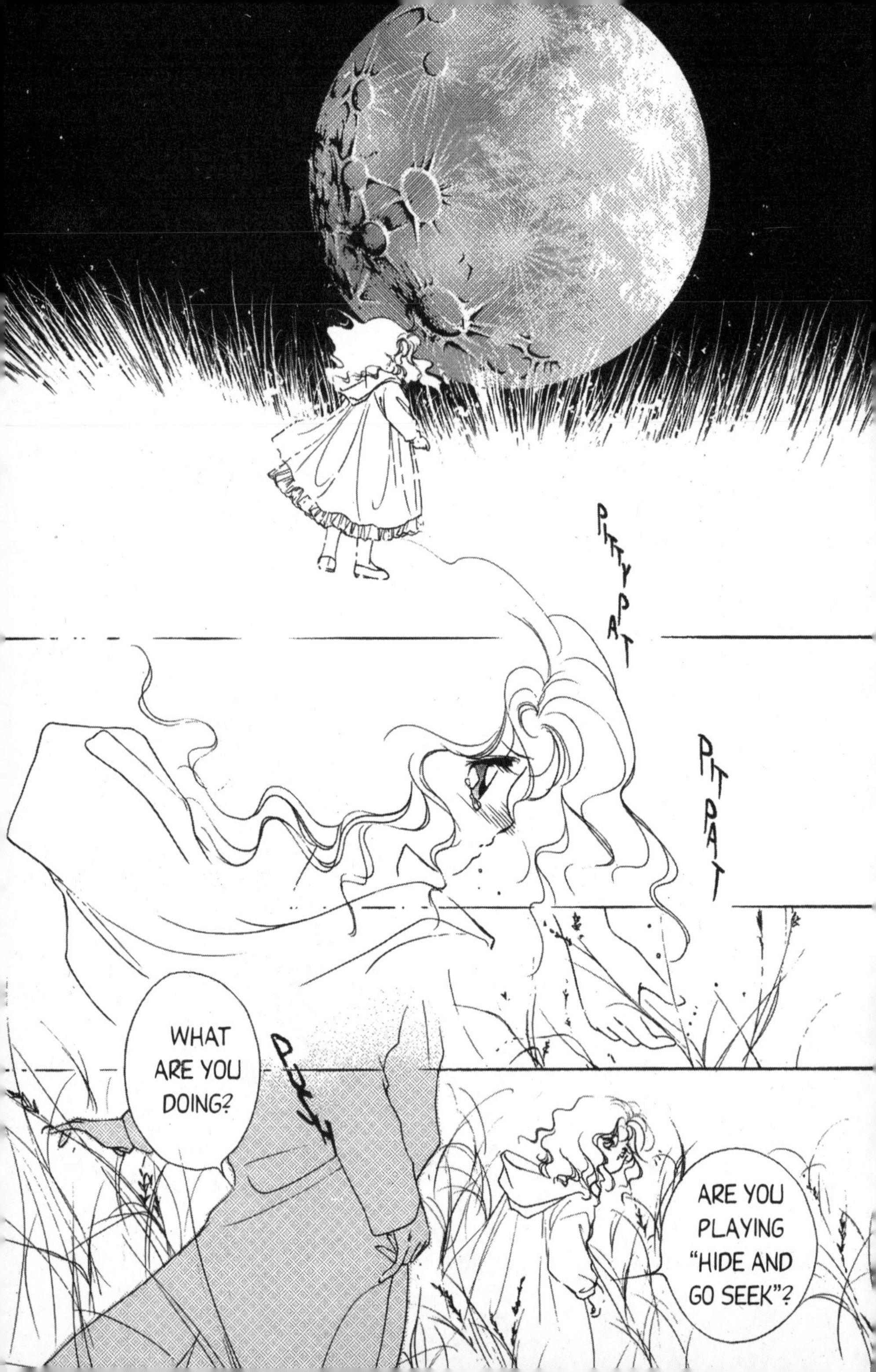
PITTY PAT
PIT PAT
WHAT ARE YOU DOING?
ARE YOU PLAYING "HIDE AND GO SEEK"?

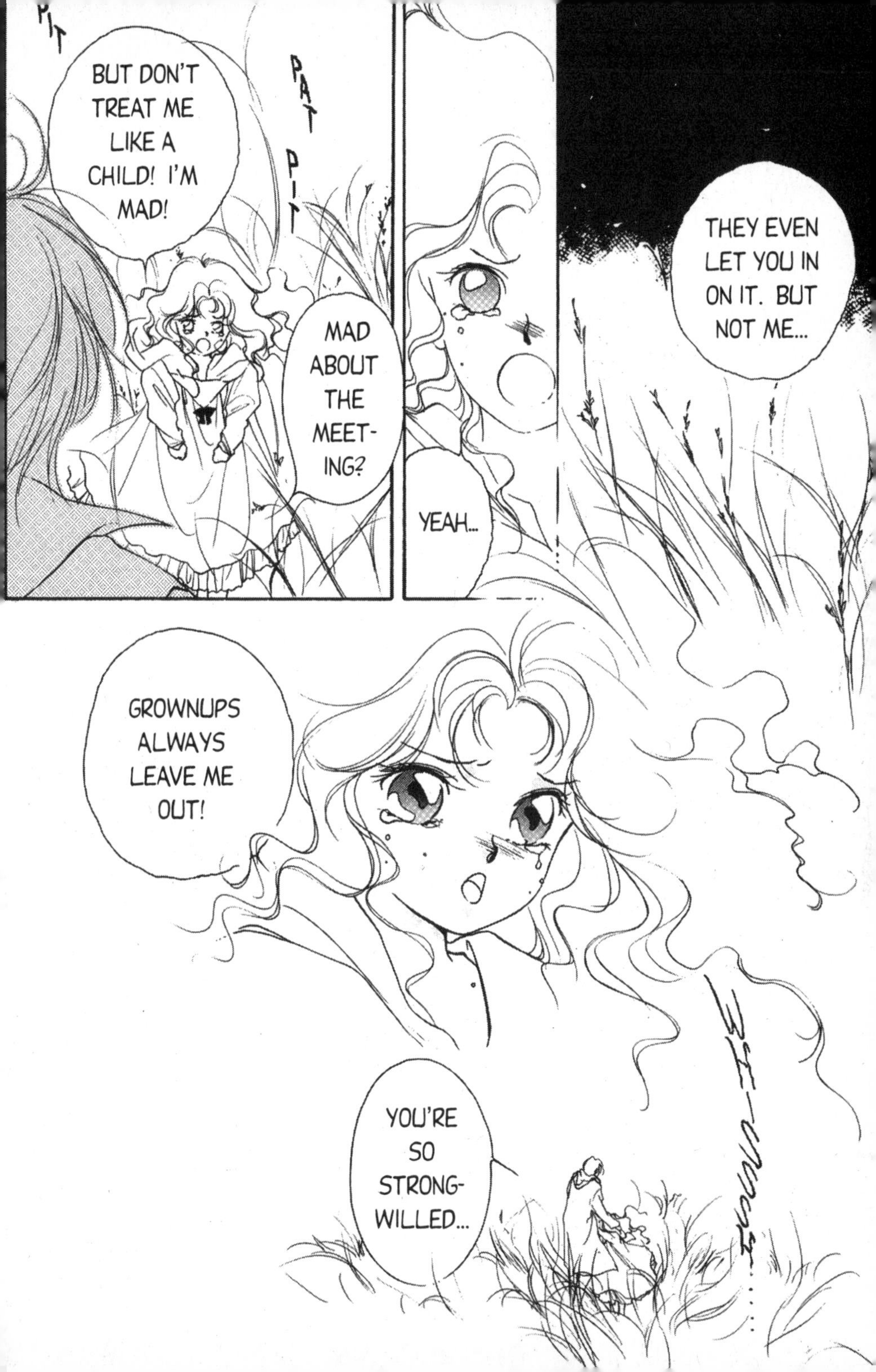
PIT
BUT DON'T TREAT ME LIKE A CHILD! I'M MAD!
PAT PIT
MAD ABOUT THE MEET-ING?
YEAH...
THEY EVEN LET YOU IN ON IT. BUT NOT ME...
GROWNUPS ALWAYS LEAVE ME OUT!
YOU'RE SO STRONG-WILLED...

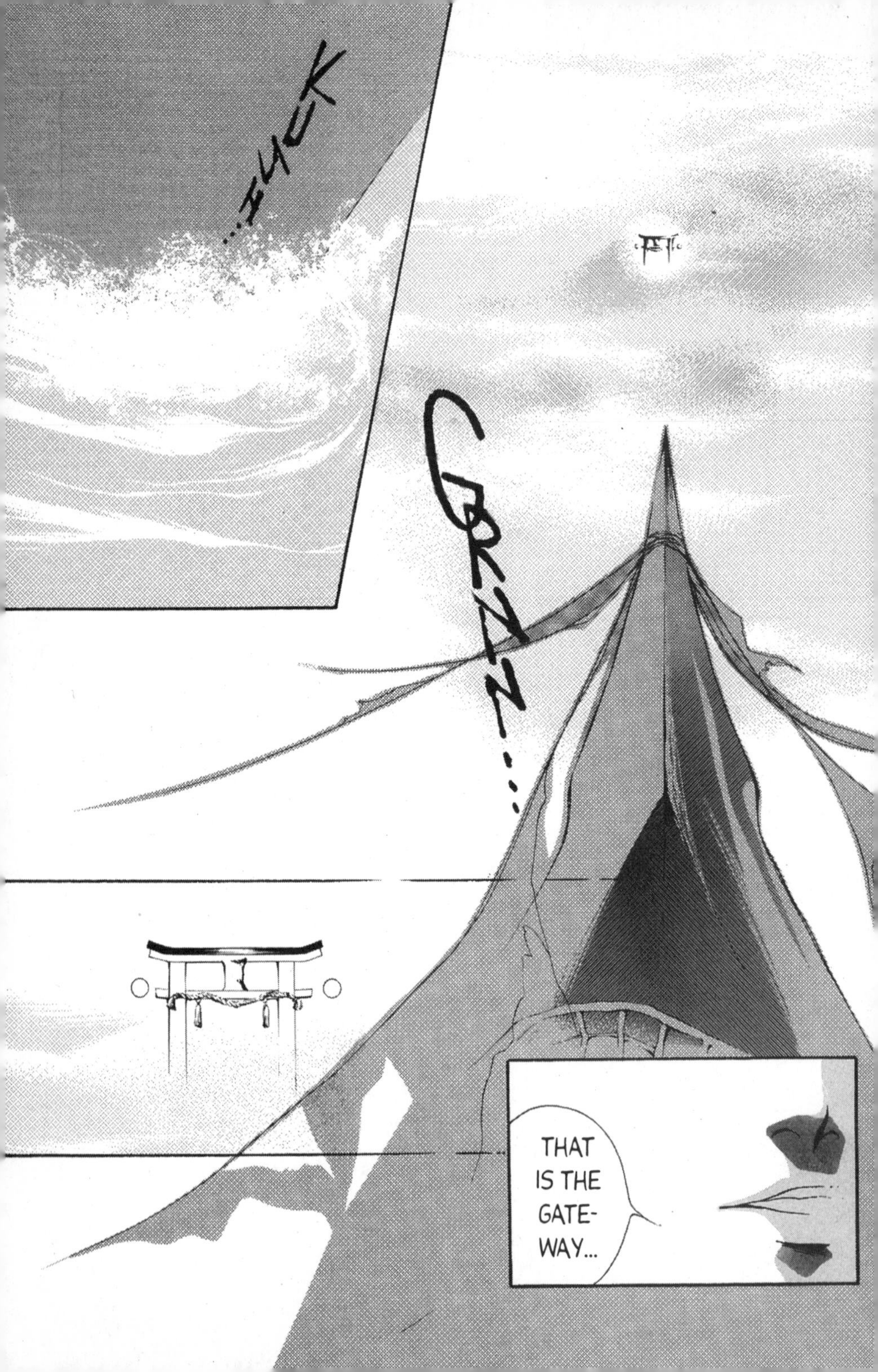
...IYUK
GRZZZ...
THAT IS THE GATE-WAY...

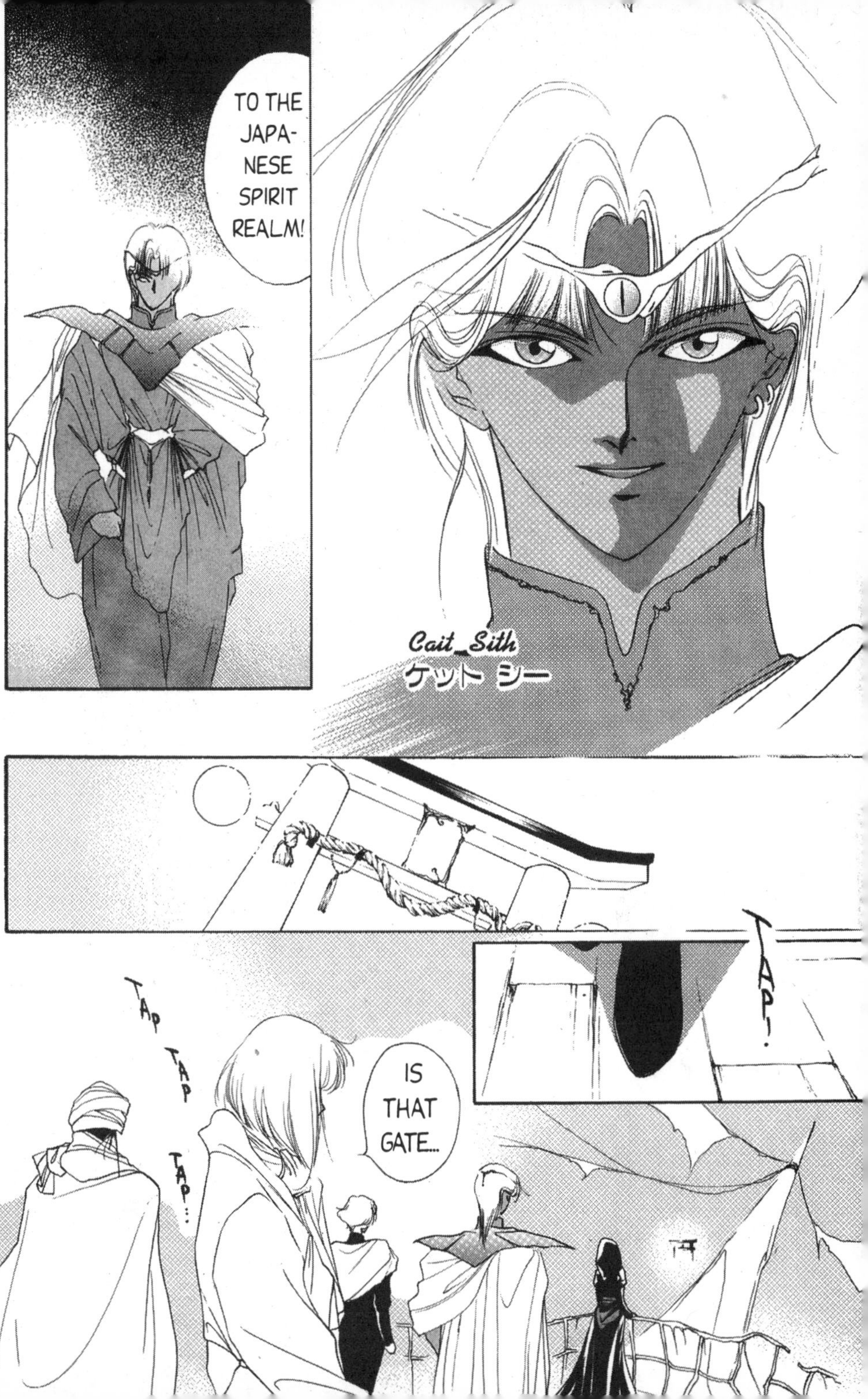
TO THE JAPA-NESE SPIRIT REALM!
Cait Sith
ケット シー
TAP!
IS THAT GATE...
TAP TAP TAP...

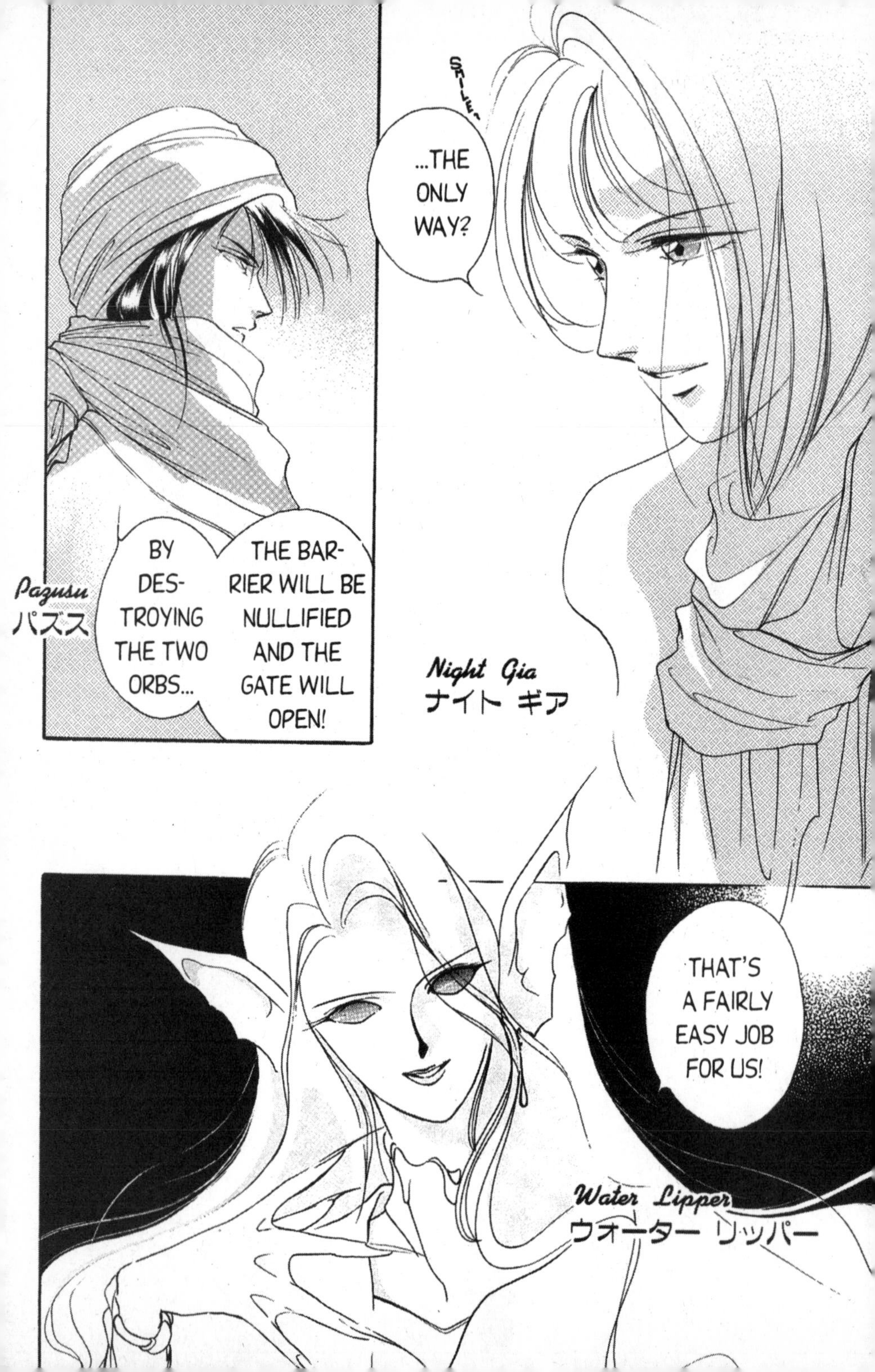

BY DES-TROYING THE TWO ORBS...
THE BAR-RIER WILL BE NULLIFIED AND THE GATE WILL OPEN!
Pazusu
パズス
SMILE~
...THE ONLY WAY?
Night Gia
ナイト ギア
THAT'S A FAIRLY EASY JOB FOR US!
Water Lipper
ウォーター リッパー

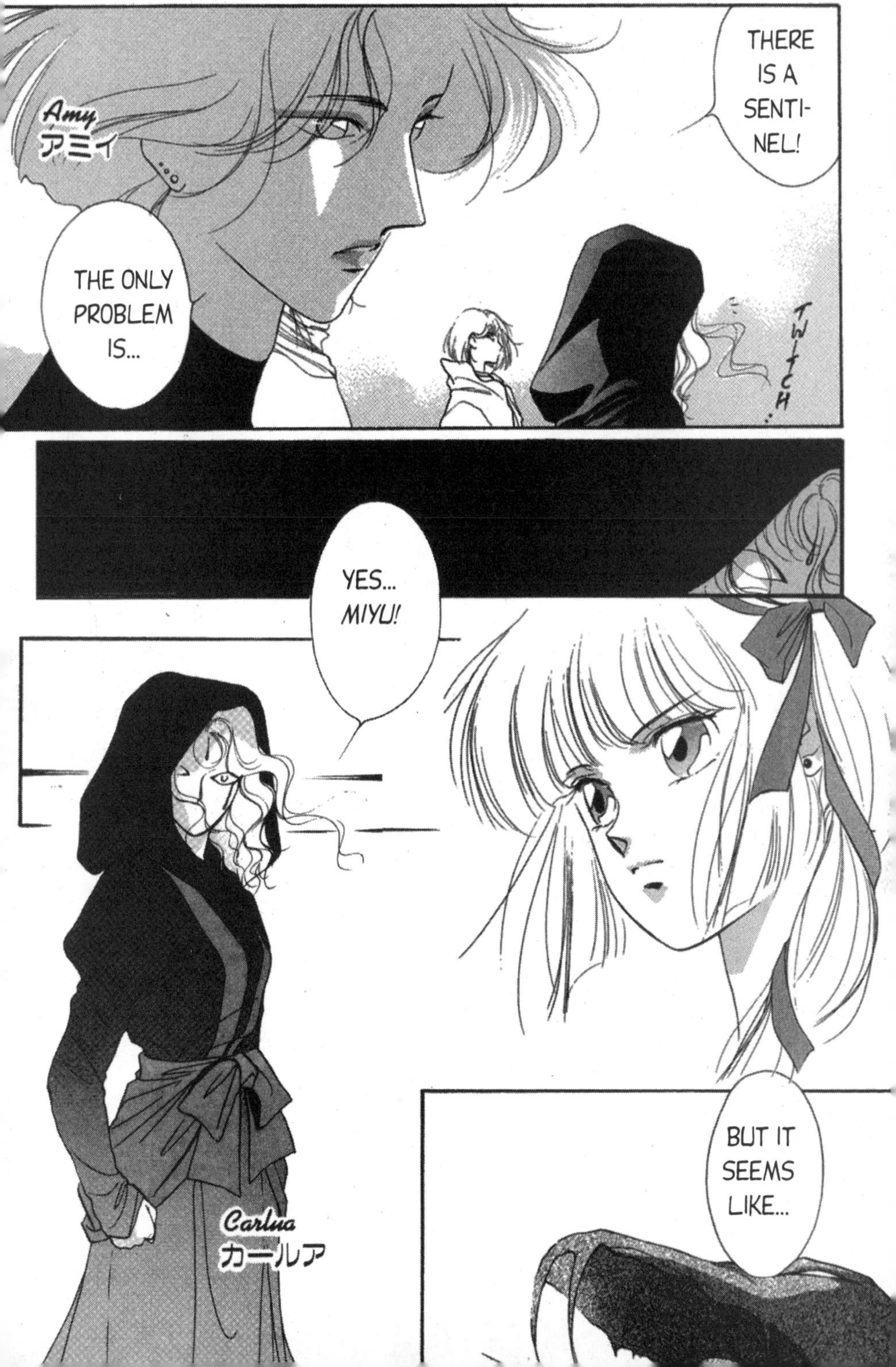
THERE IS A SENTI-NEL!
Amy
アミィ
THE ONLY PROBLEM IS...
TWITCH...
YES... MIYU!
Carlua
カールア
BUT IT SEEMS LIKE...

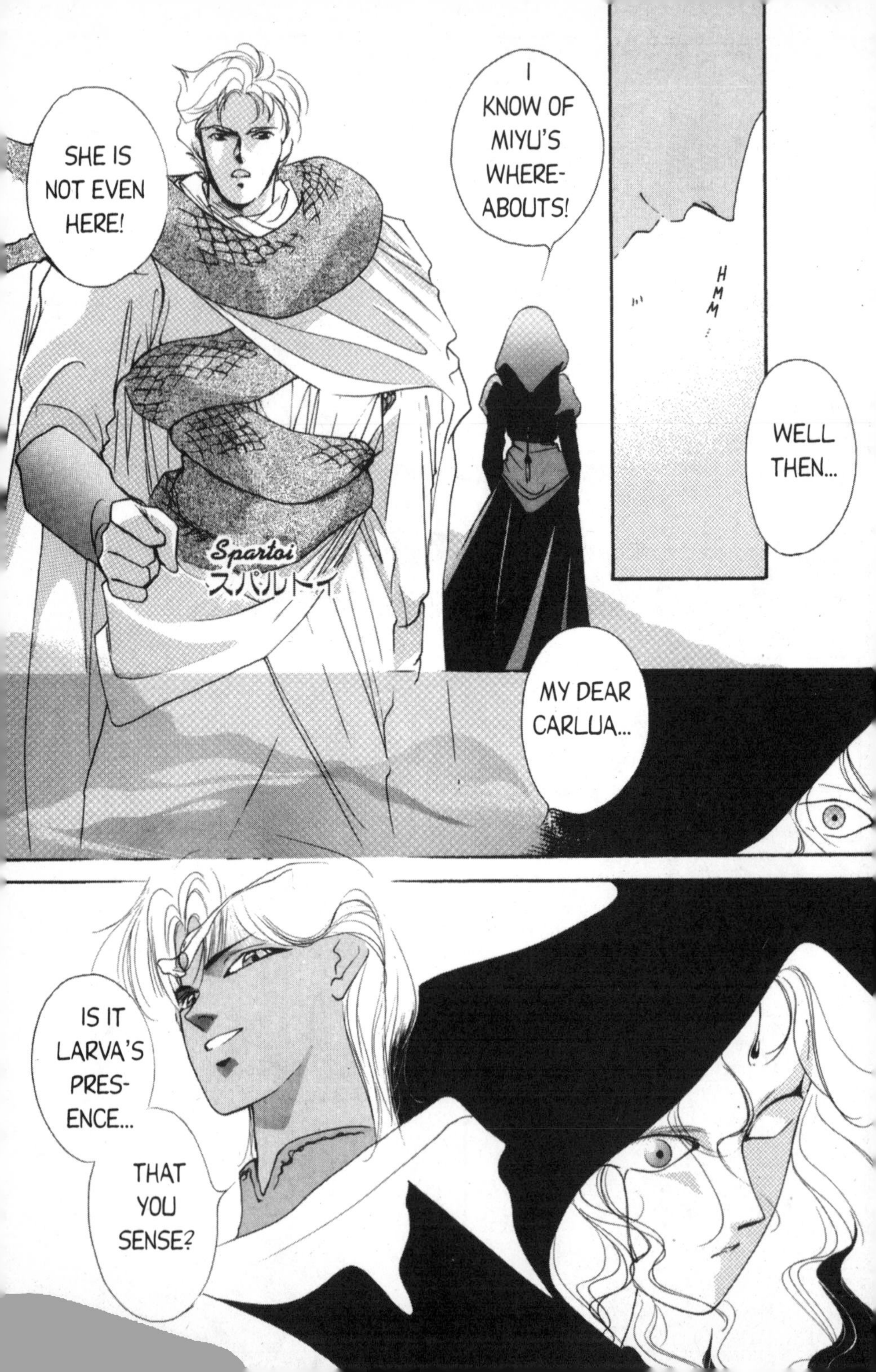
I KNOW OF MIYU'S WHERE-ABOUTS!
SHE IS NOT EVEN HERE!
HMM...
WELL THEN...
Spartoi
スパルトイ
MY DEAR CARLUA...
IS IT LARVA'S PRES-ENCE...
THAT YOU SENSE?

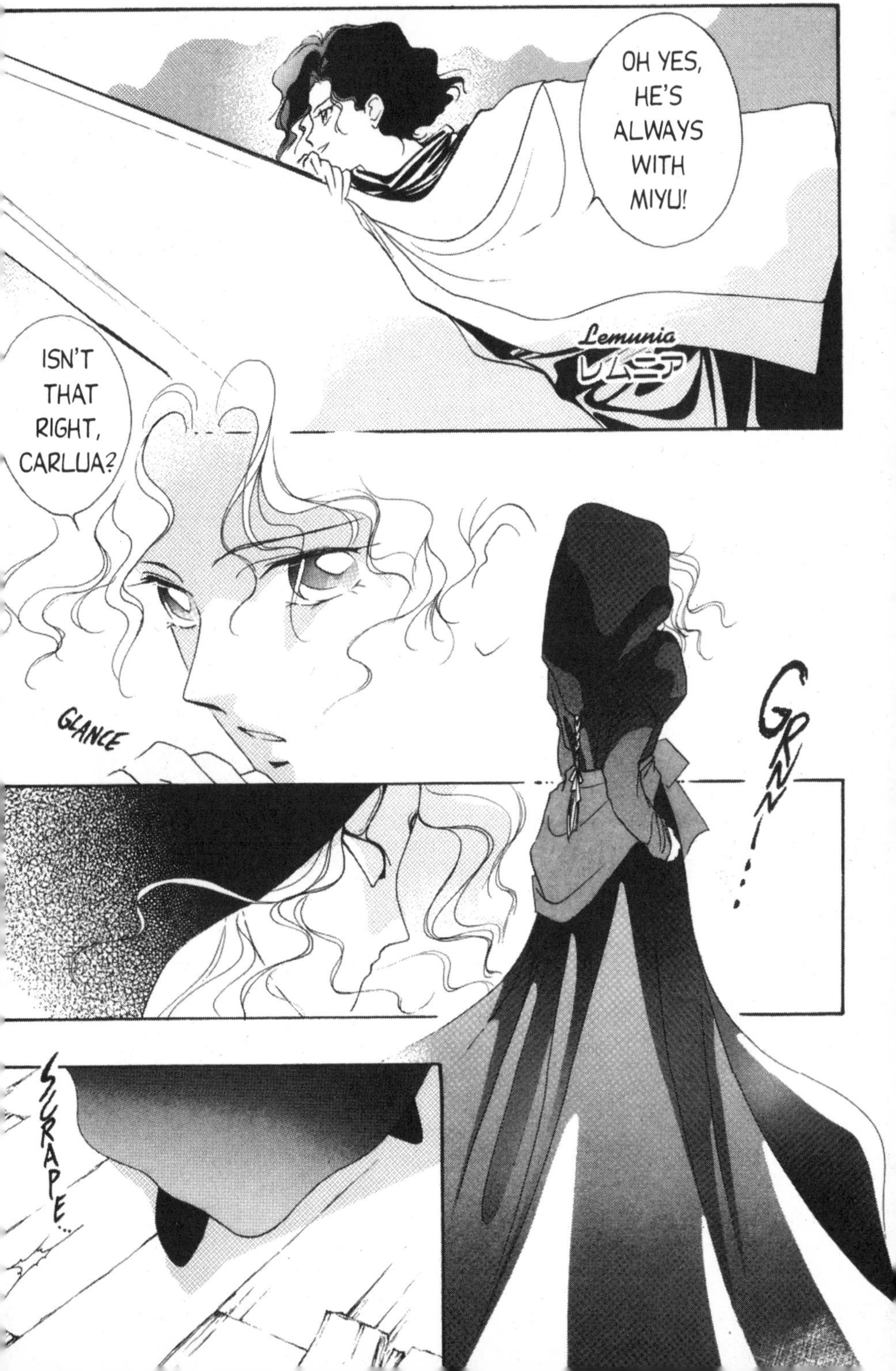

OH YES, HE'S ALWAYS WITH MIYU!
Lemunia
レムニア
ISN'T THAT RIGHT, CARLUA?
GLANCE
GRNN...
SCRAPE...

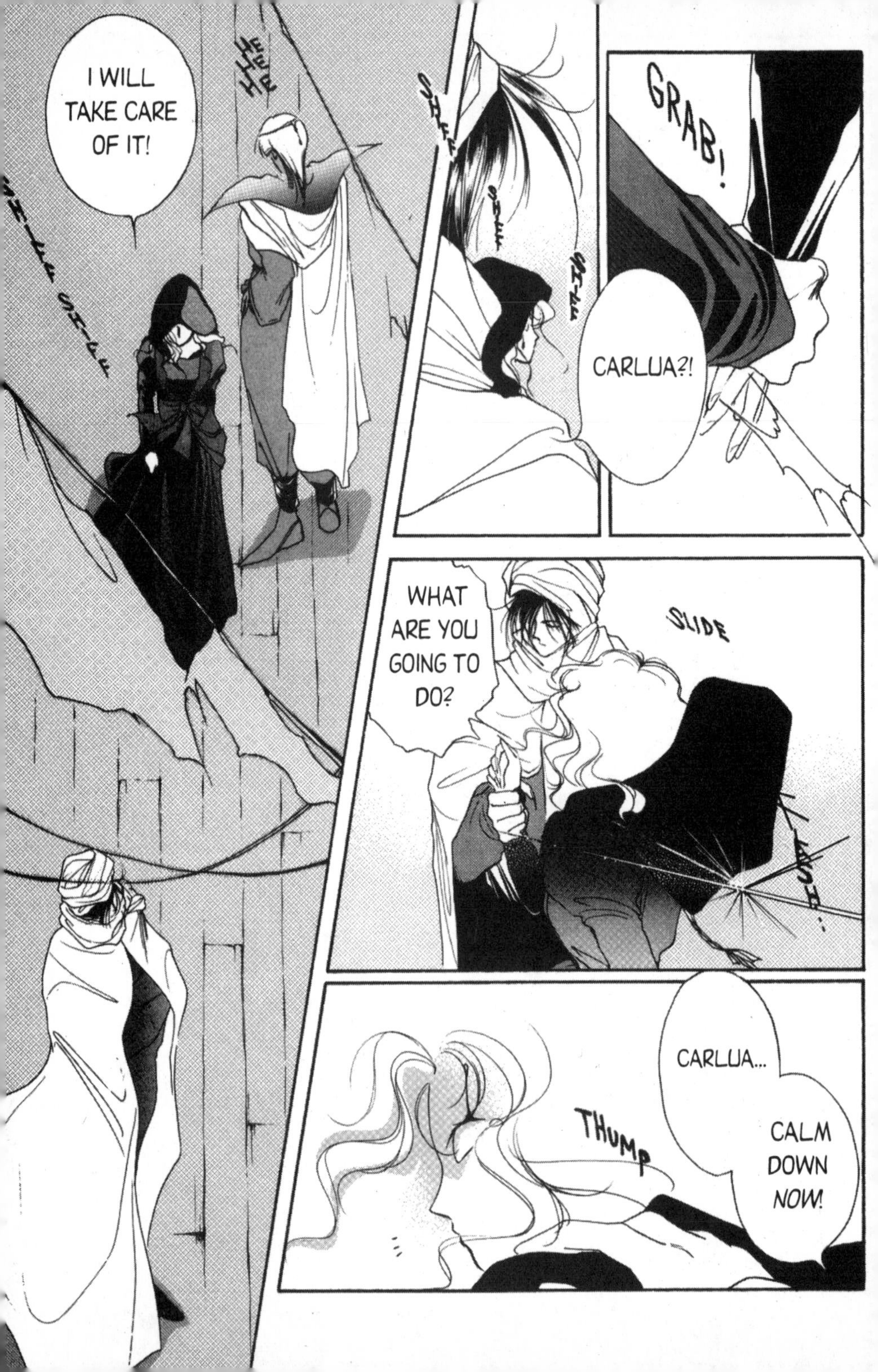
I WILL TAKE CARE OF IT!
HE HE HE
GRAB!
CARLUA?!
WHAT ARE YOU GOING TO DO?
SLIDE
CARLUA...
CALM DOWN NOW!
THUMP

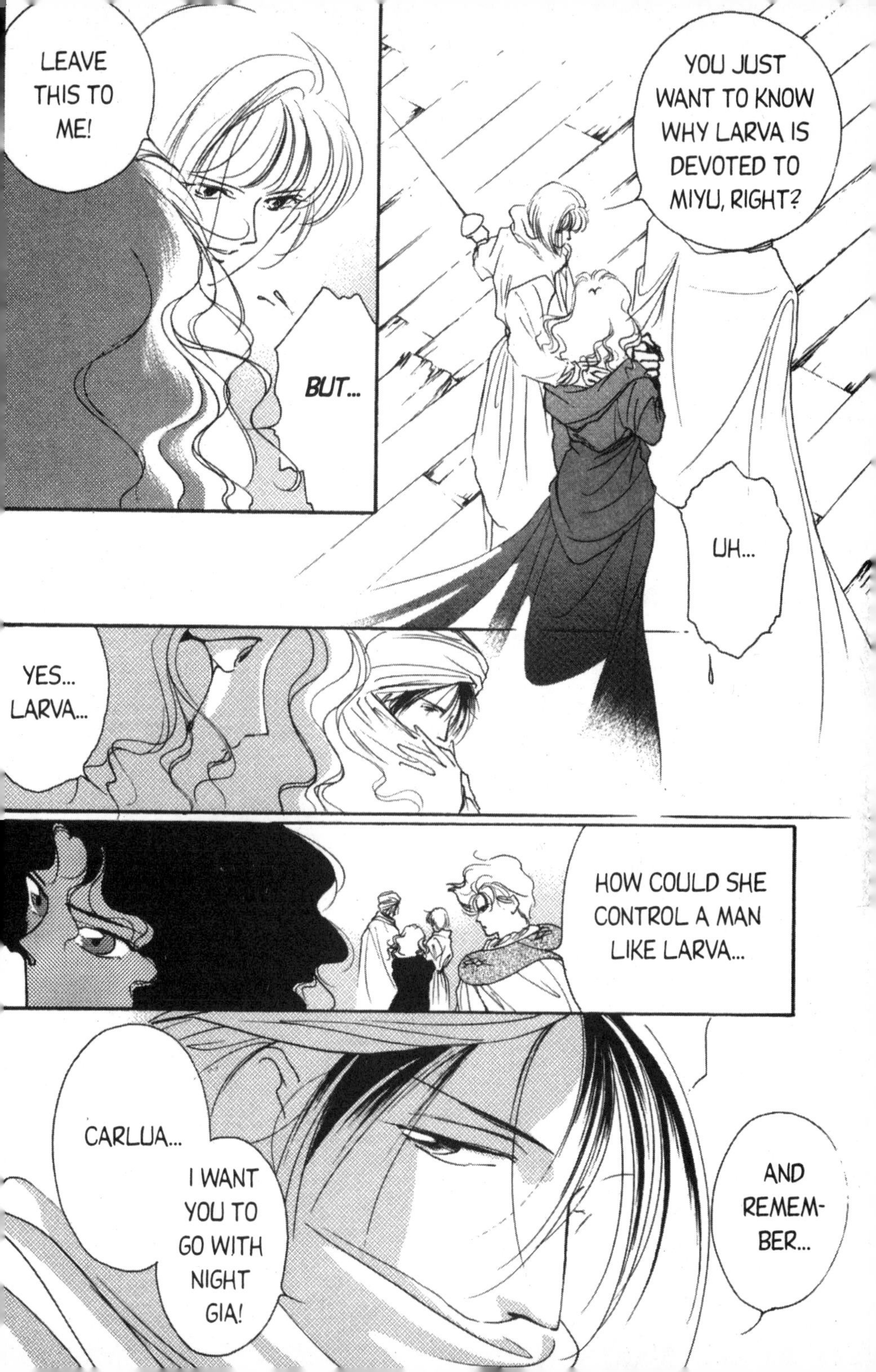
YOU JUST WANT TO KNOW WHY LARVA IS DEVOTED TO MIYU, RIGHT?
LEAVE THIS TO ME!
BUT...
UH...
YES... LARVA...
HOW COULD SHE CONTROL A MAN LIKE LARVA...
AND REMEM-BER...
CARLUA...
I WANT YOU TO GO WITH NIGHT GIA!

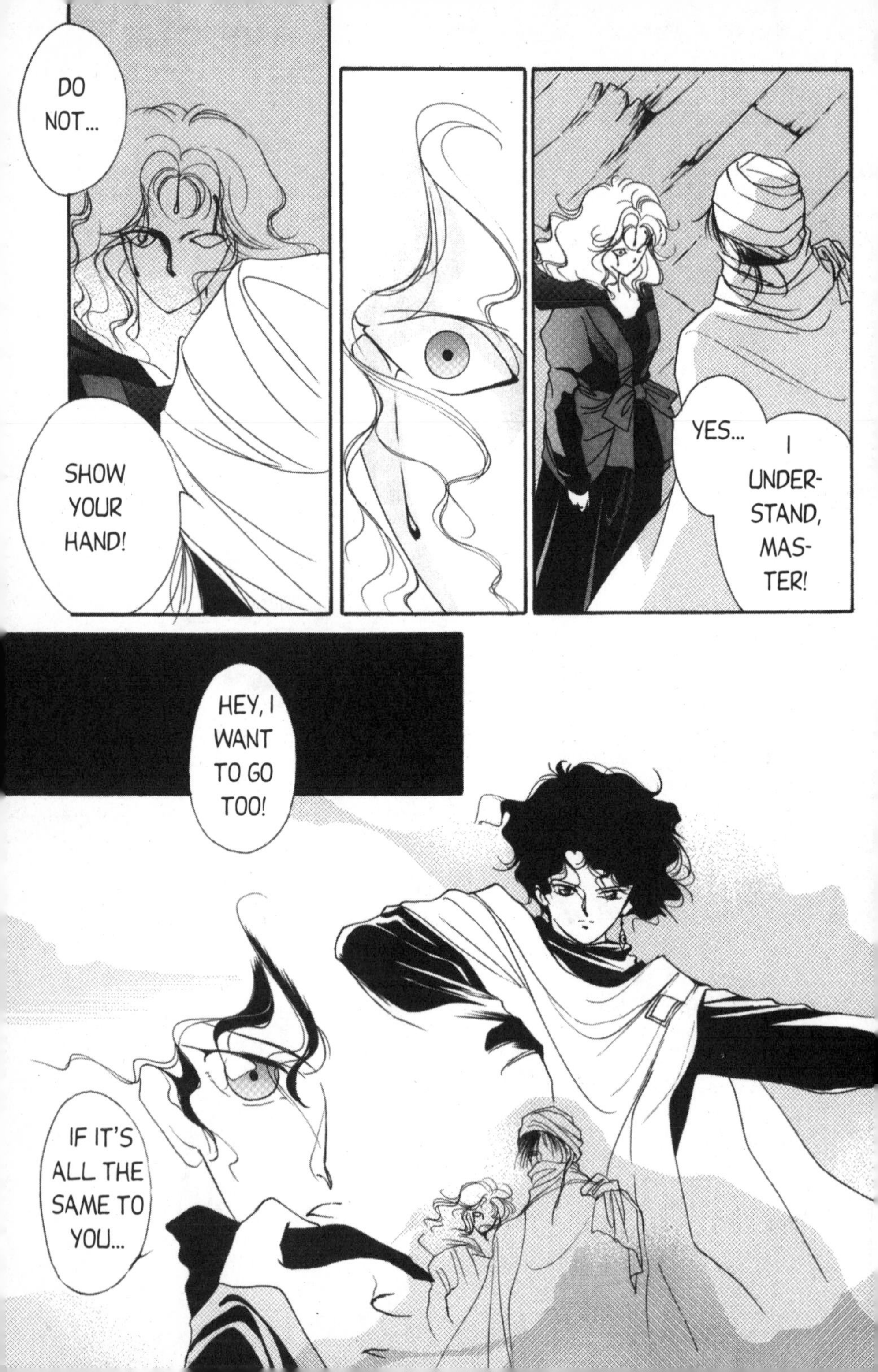
DO NOT...
SHOW YOUR HAND!
YES...
I UNDERSTAND, MASTER!
HEY, I WANT TO GO TOO!
IF IT'S ALL THE SAME TO YOU...

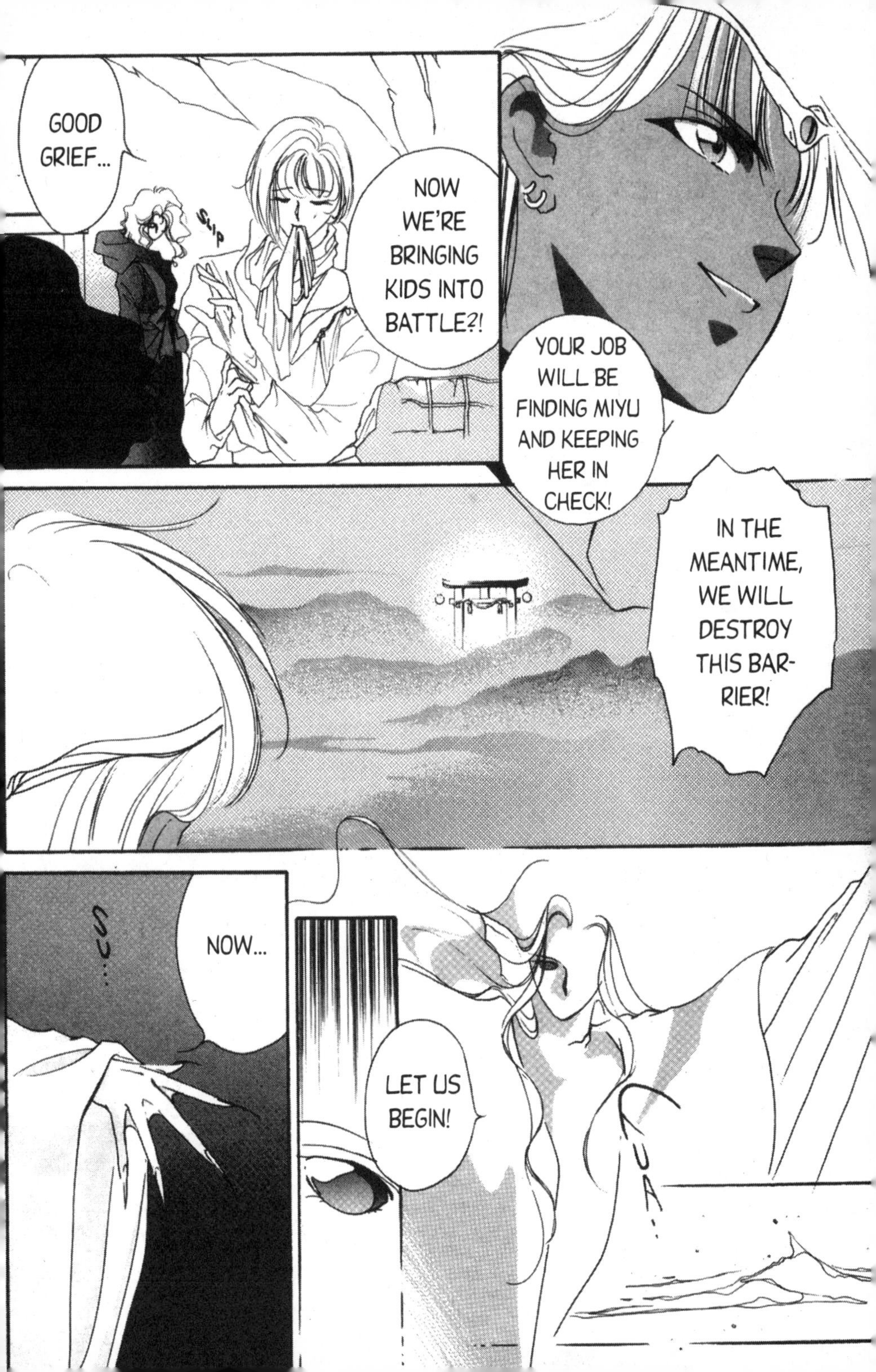
GOOD GRIEF...
SLIP
NOW WE'RE BRINGING KIDS INTO BATTLE?!
YOUR JOB WILL BE FINDING MIYU AND KEEPING HER IN CHECK!
IN THE MEANTIME, WE WILL DESTROY THIS BAR-RIER!
SU...
NOW...
LET US BEGIN!
FUA...

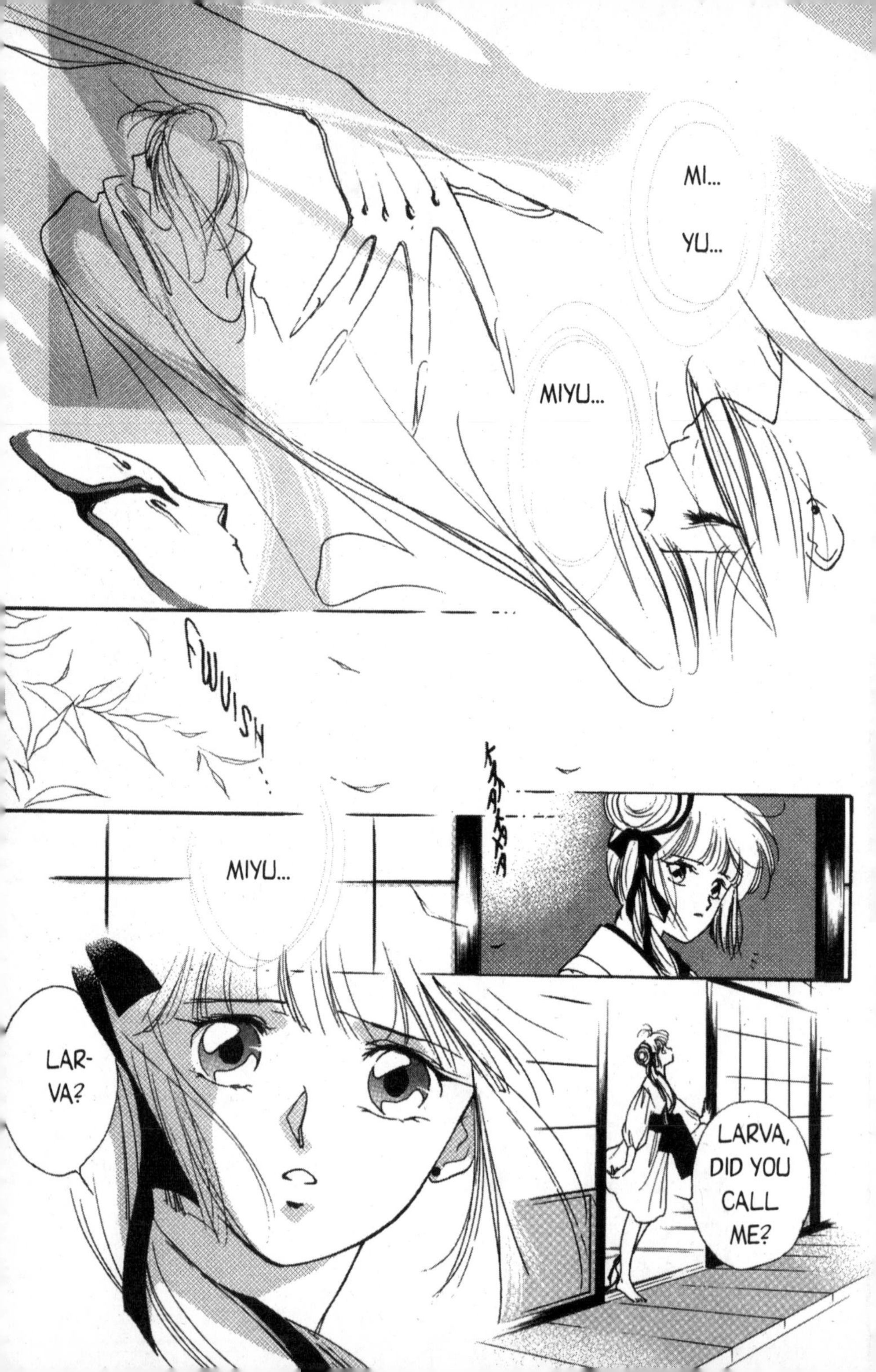
MI...
YU...
MIYU...
FWUISH
KATAKATA
MIYU...
LARVA, DID YOU CALL ME?
LAR-VA?

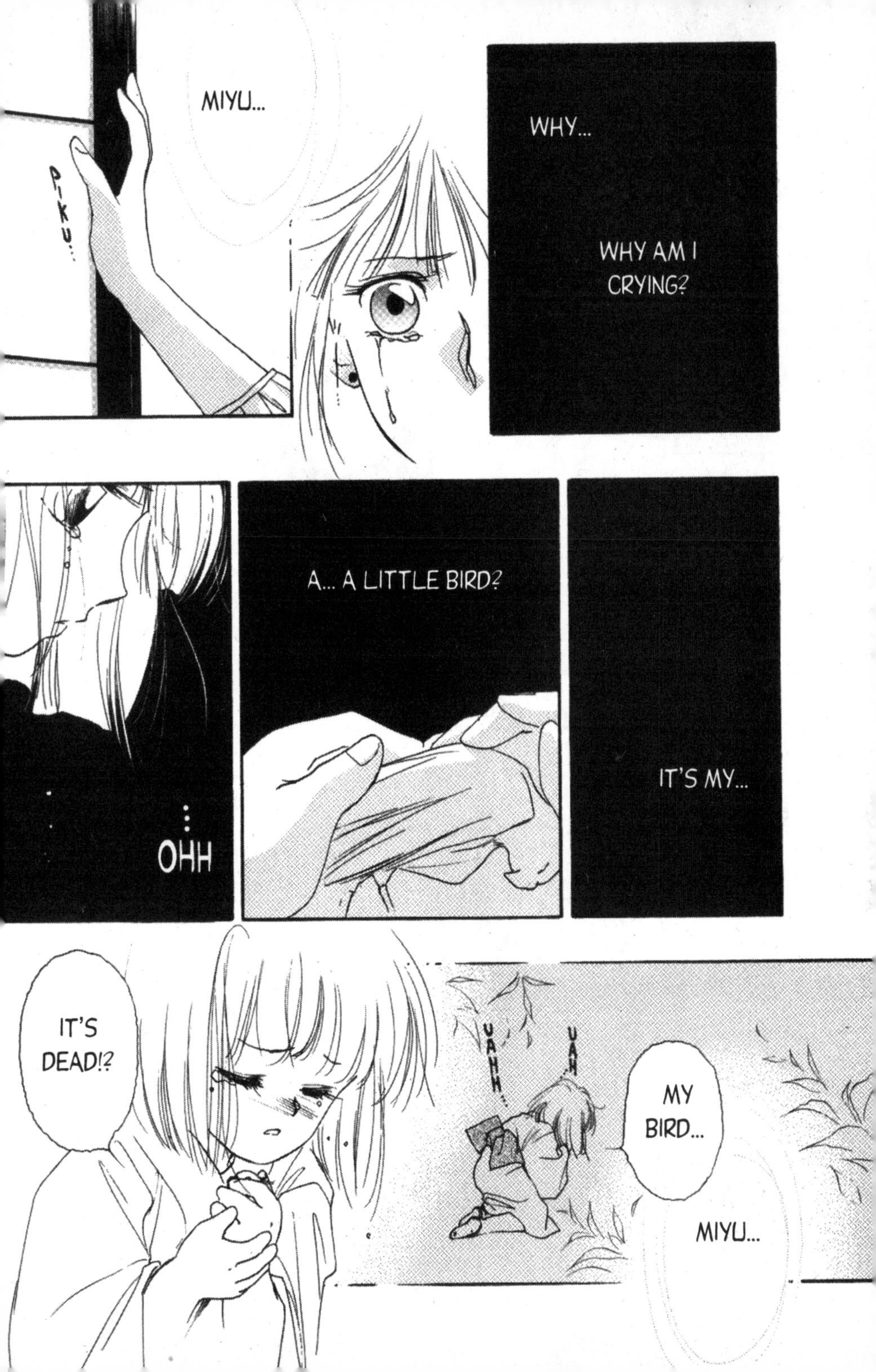
MIYU...
PIKU...
WHY...
WHY AM I CRYING?
IT'S MY...
A... A LITTLE BIRD?
...OHH
MY BIRD...
UAHH...
UAH
MIYU...
IT'S DEAD!?

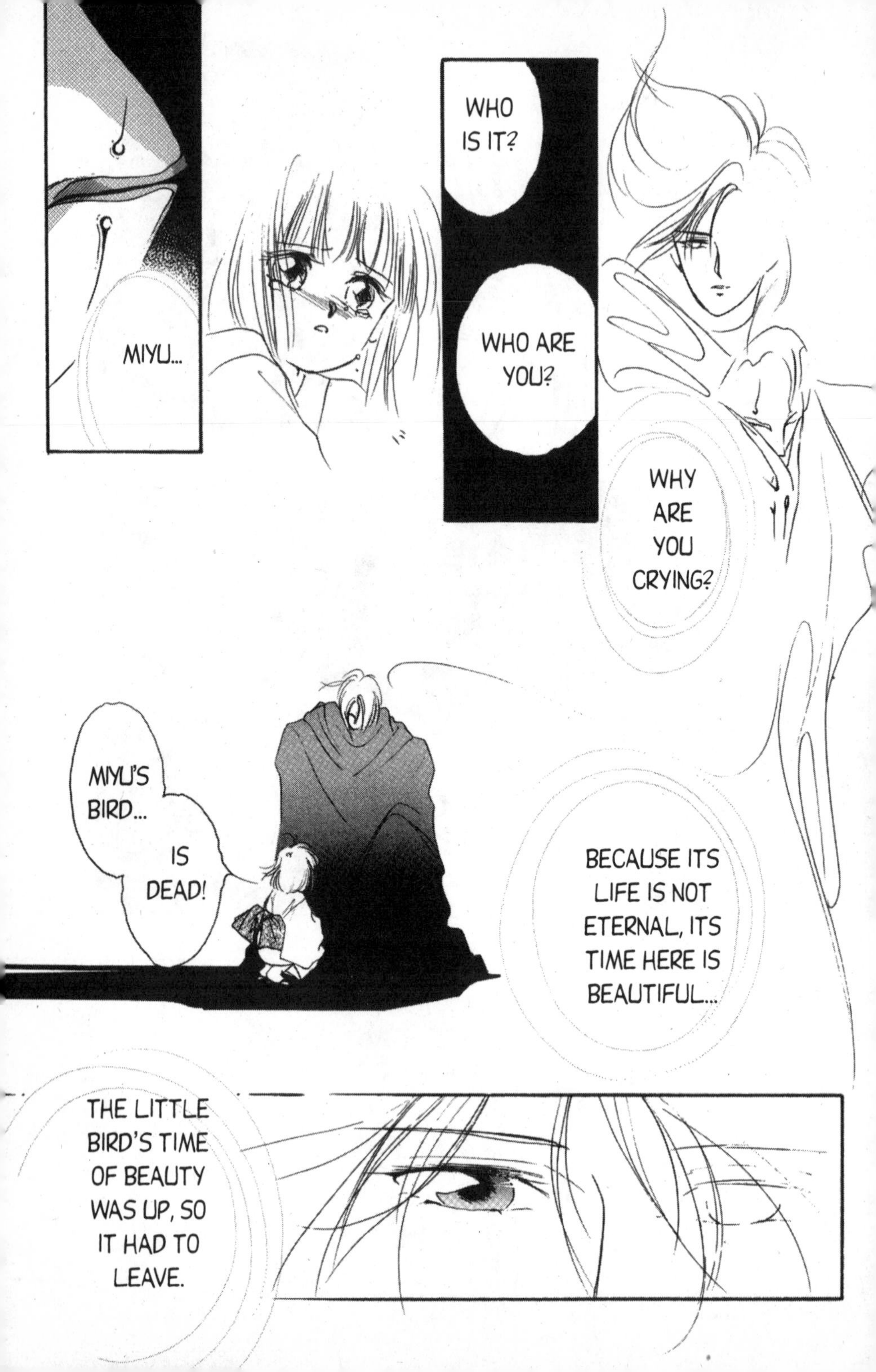
MIYU...
WHO IS IT?
WHO ARE YOU?
WHY ARE YOU CRYING?
MIYU'S BIRD...
IS DEAD!
BECAUSE ITS LIFE IS NOT ETERNAL, ITS TIME HERE IS BEAUTIFUL...
THE LITTLE BIRD'S TIME OF BEAUTY WAS UP, SO IT HAD TO LEAVE.

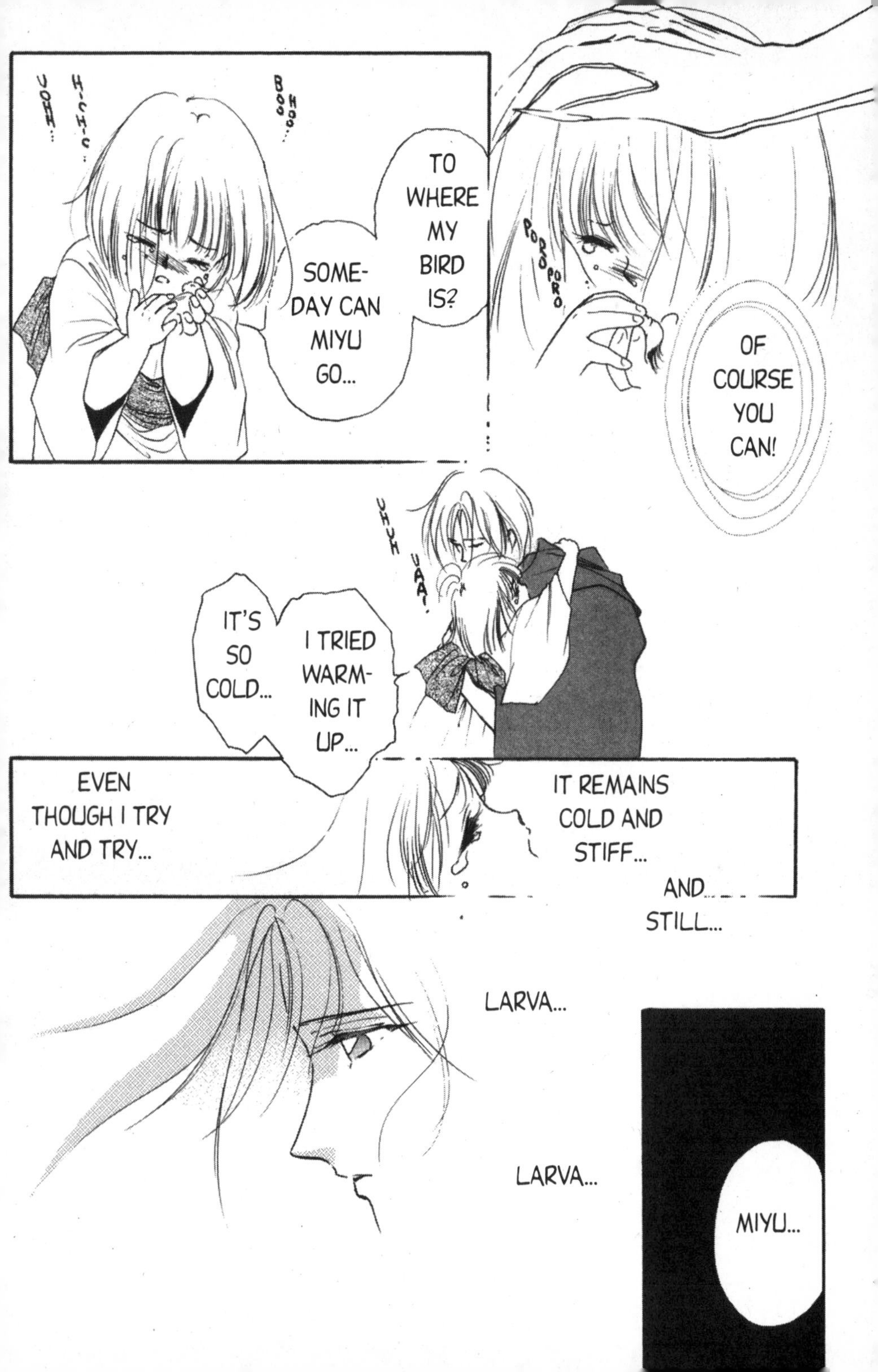

OF COURSE YOU CAN!
PORO PORO
TO WHERE MY BIRD IS?
SOME-DAY CAN MIYU GO...
BOO HOO...
HIC HIC...
UOHH...
UHUH
UAA!
I TRIED WARM-ING IT UP...
IT'S SO COLD...
IT REMAINS COLD AND STIFF...
AND... STILL...
EVEN THOUGH I TRY AND TRY...
MIYU...
LARVA...
LARVA...

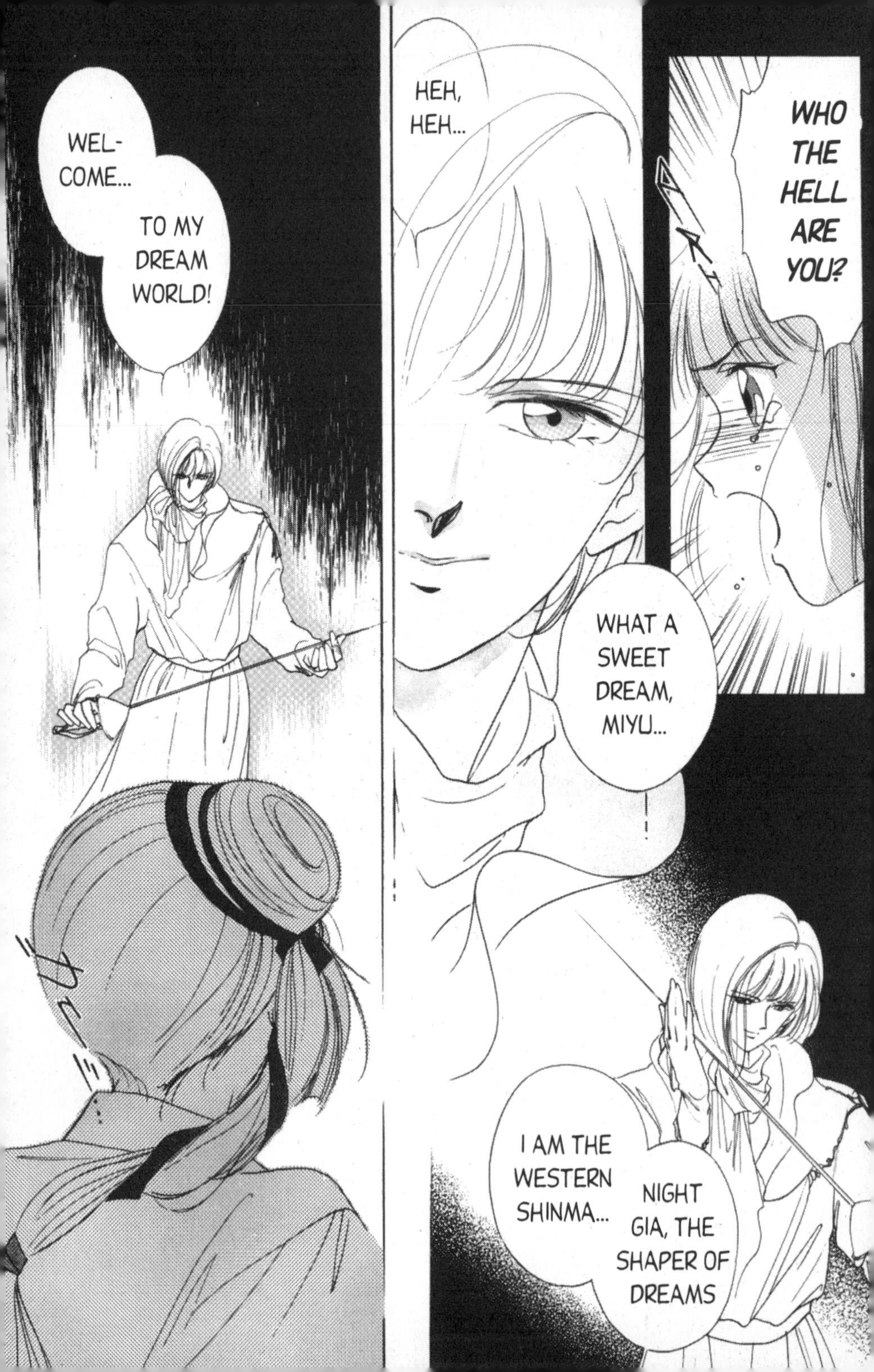
WHO THE HELL ARE YOU?
HEH, HEH...
WHAT A SWEET DREAM, MIYU...
I AM THE WESTERN SHINMA...
NIGHT GIA, THE SHAPER OF DREAMS
WEL-COME...
TO MY DREAM WORLD!

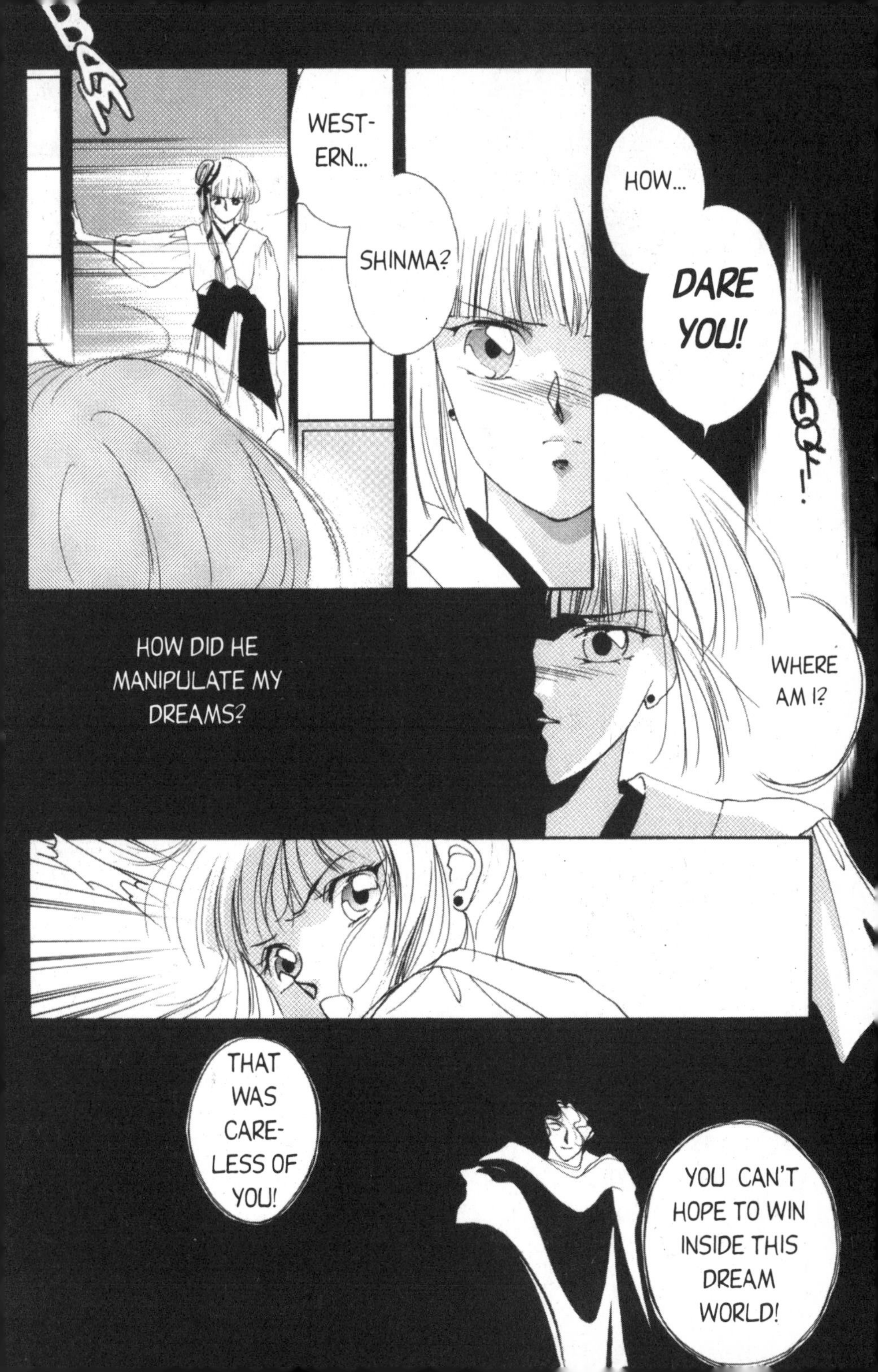
HOW... DARE YOU!
WEST-ERN... SHINMA?
BAM
WHERE AM I?
HOW DID HE MANIPULATE MY DREAMS?
YOU CAN'T HOPE TO WIN INSIDE THIS DREAM WORLD!
THAT WAS CARE-LESS OF YOU!

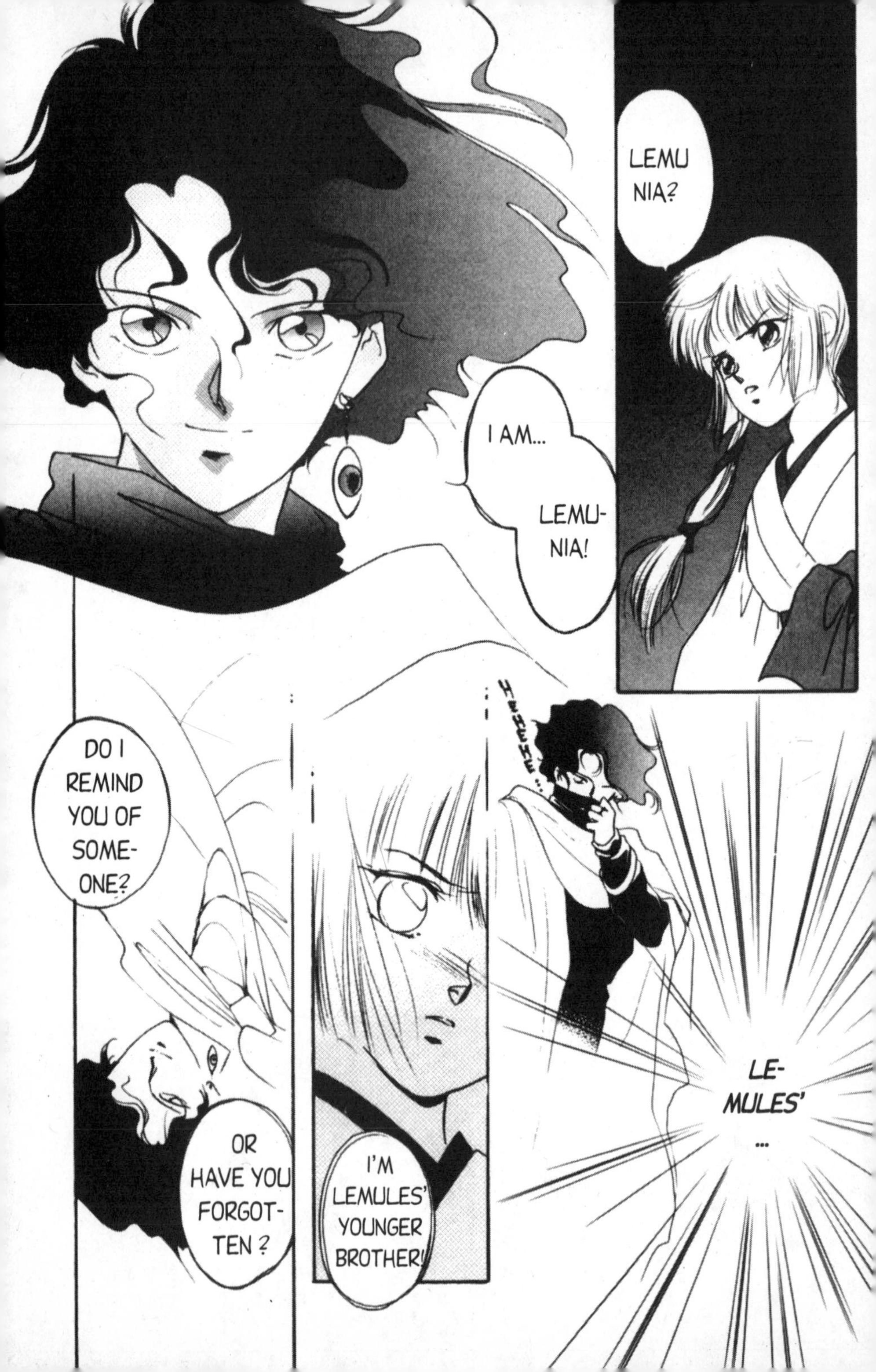
LEMU NIA?
I AM...
LEMU-NIA!
HEHEHE...
LE-MULES' ...
I'M LEMULES' YOUNGER BROTHER!
DO I REMIND YOU OF SOME-ONE?
OR HAVE YOU FORGOT-TEN?

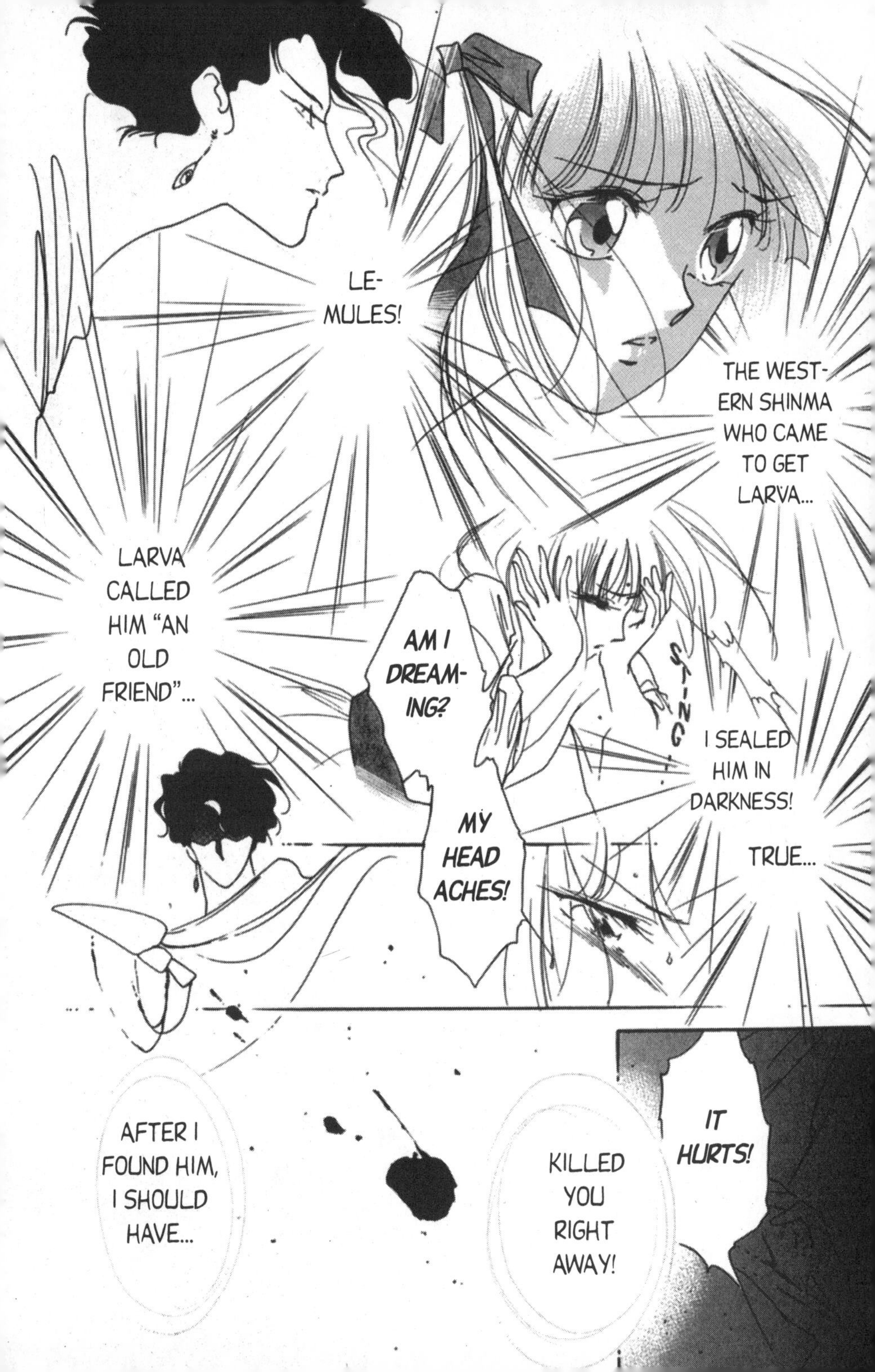
LE-MULES!
THE WEST-ERN SHINMA WHO CAME TO GET LARVA...
LARVA CALLED HIM "AN OLD FRIEND"...
I SEALED HIM IN DARKNESS!
TRUE...
AM I DREAMING?
STING
MY HEAD ACHES!
IT HURTS!
AFTER I FOUND HIM, I SHOULD HAVE...
KILLED YOU RIGHT AWAY!

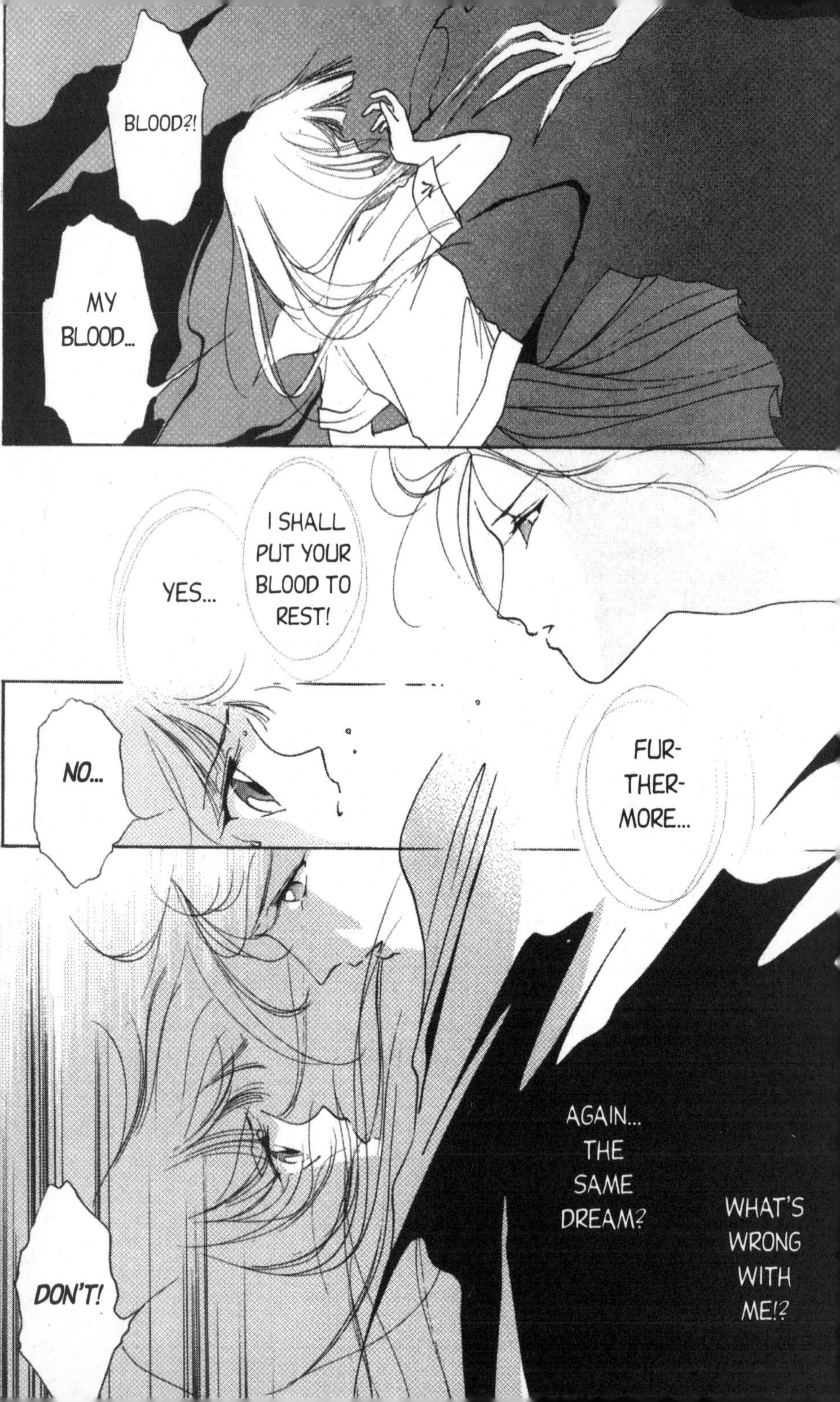
BLOOD?!
MY BLOOD...
I SHALL PUT YOUR BLOOD TO REST!
YES...
FURTHERMORE...
NO...
WHAT'S WRONG WITH ME!?
AGAIN... THE SAME DREAM?
DON'T!

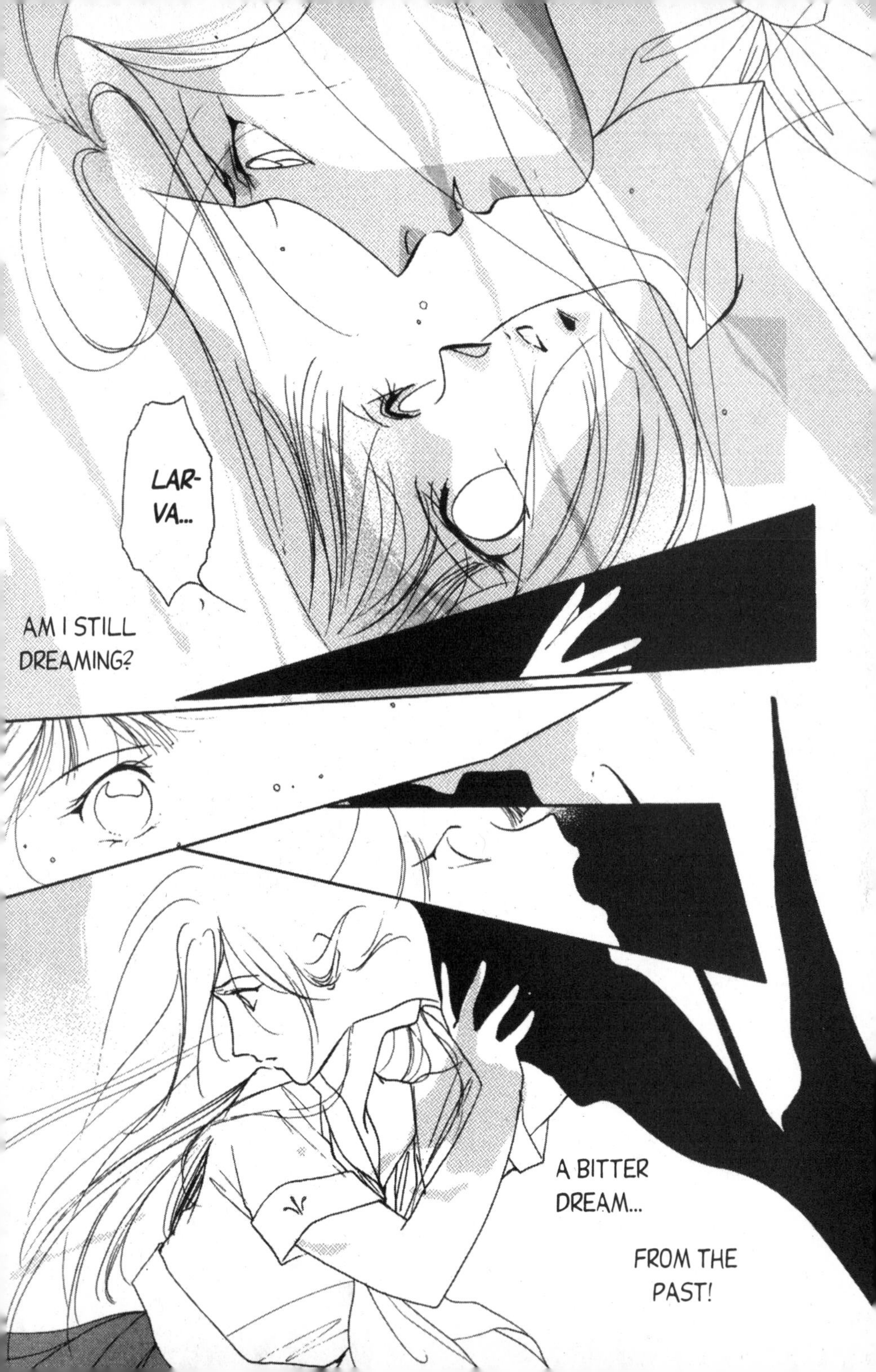
LAR-
VA...
AM I STILL
DREAMING?
A BITTER
DREAM...
FROM THE
PAST!

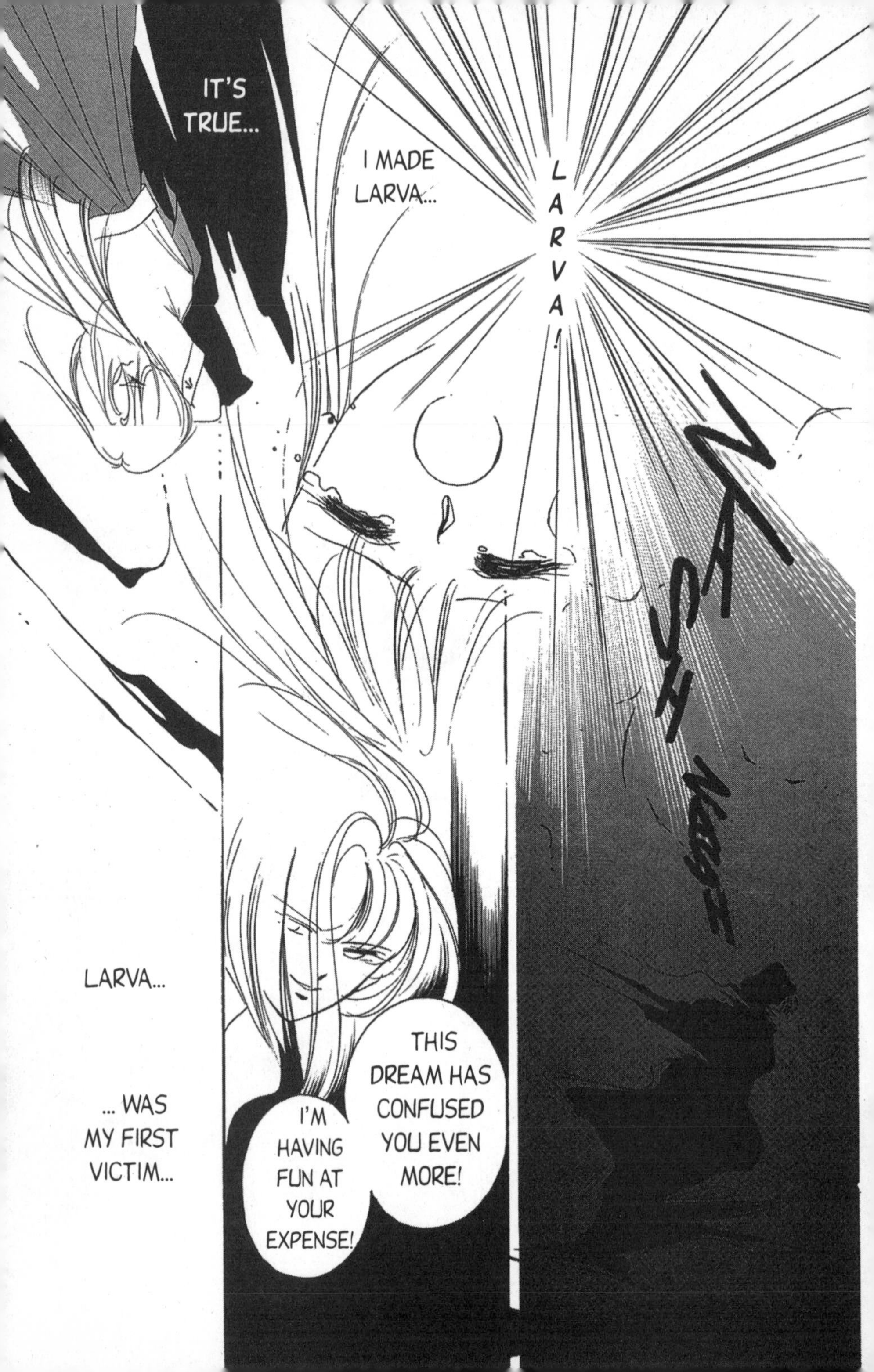
LARVA!
I MADE LARVA...
IT'S TRUE...
ZASH
THIS DREAM HAS CONFUSED YOU EVEN MORE!
I'M HAVING FUN AT YOUR EXPENSE!
LARVA...
... WAS MY FIRST VICTIM...

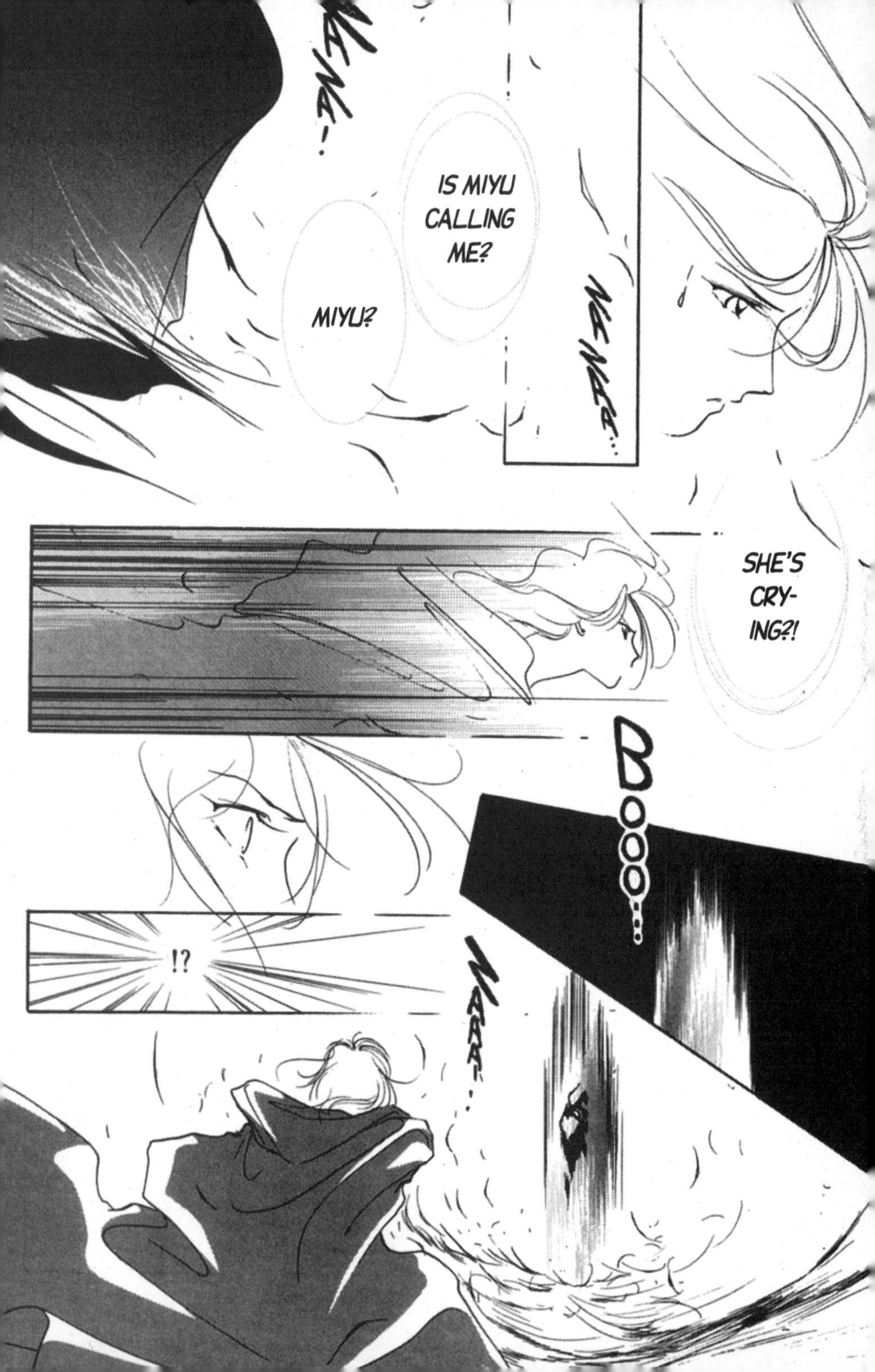

IS MIYU CALLING ME?
MIYU?
SHE'S CRY-ING?!
BOOOO...
!?

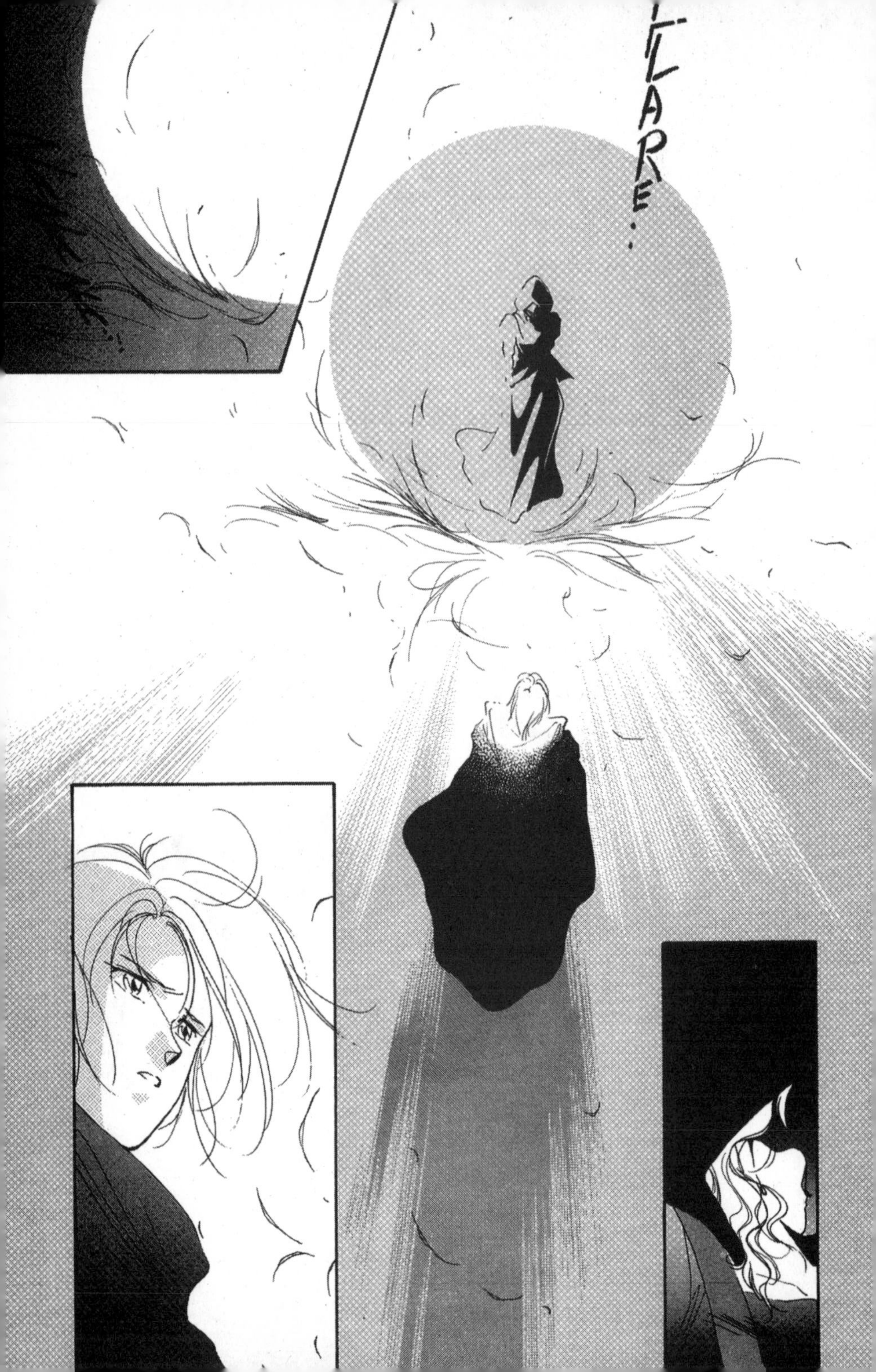
FLARE...

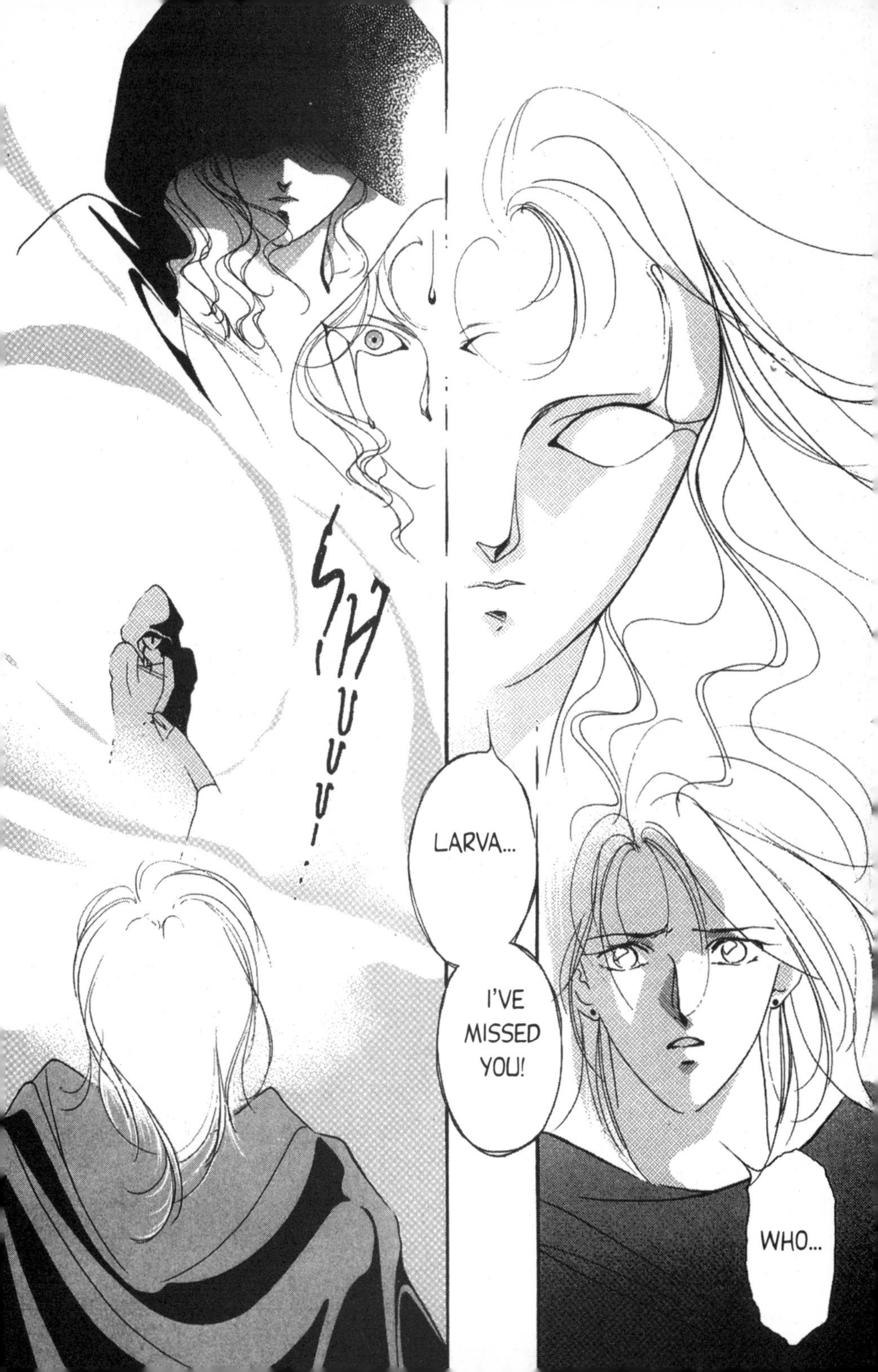
SHUUUU...
LARVA...
I'VE MISSED YOU!
WHO...

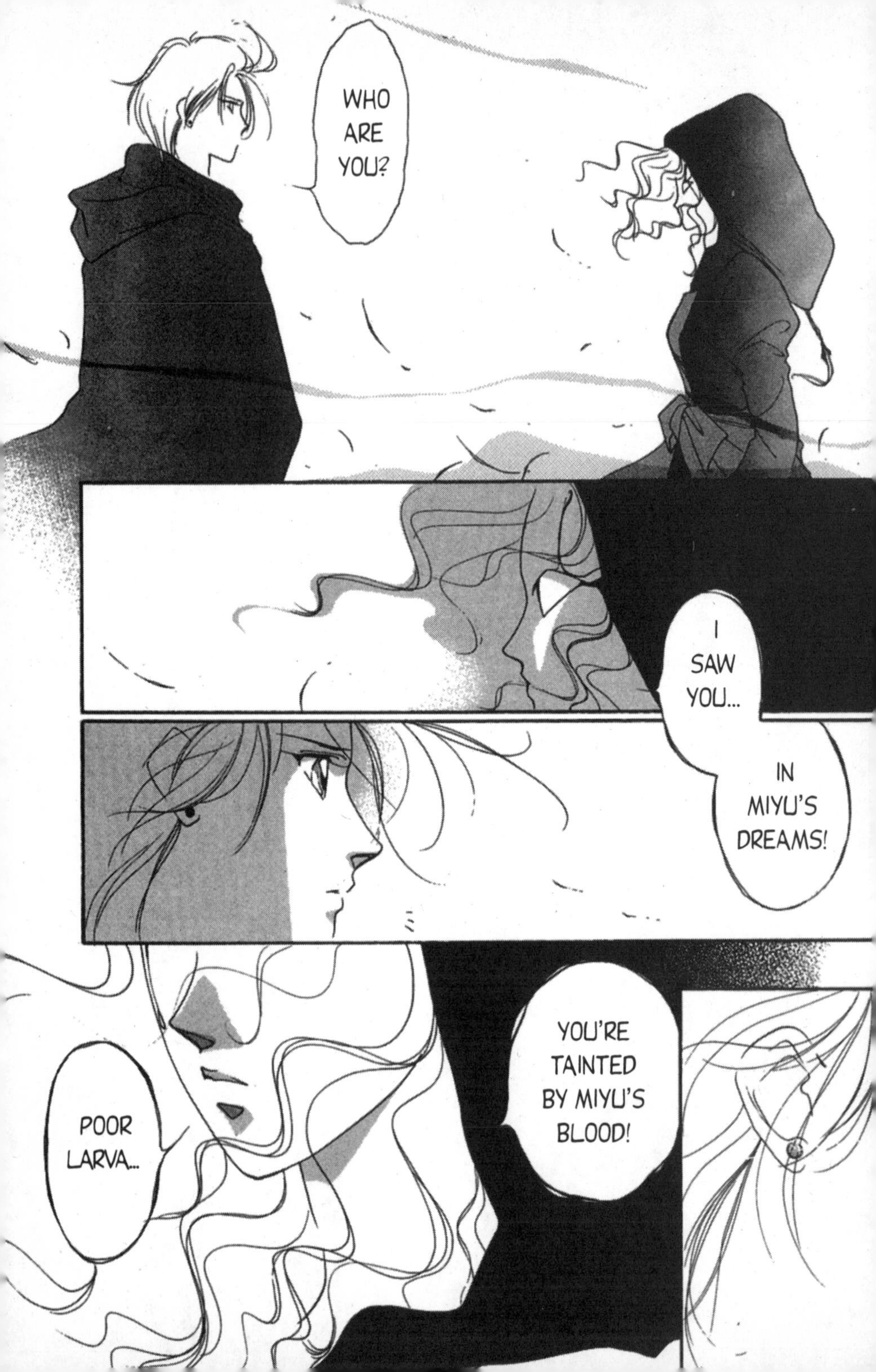
WHO ARE YOU?
I SAW YOU...
IN MIYU'S DREAMS!
YOU'RE TAINTED BY MIYU'S BLOOD!
POOR LARVA...

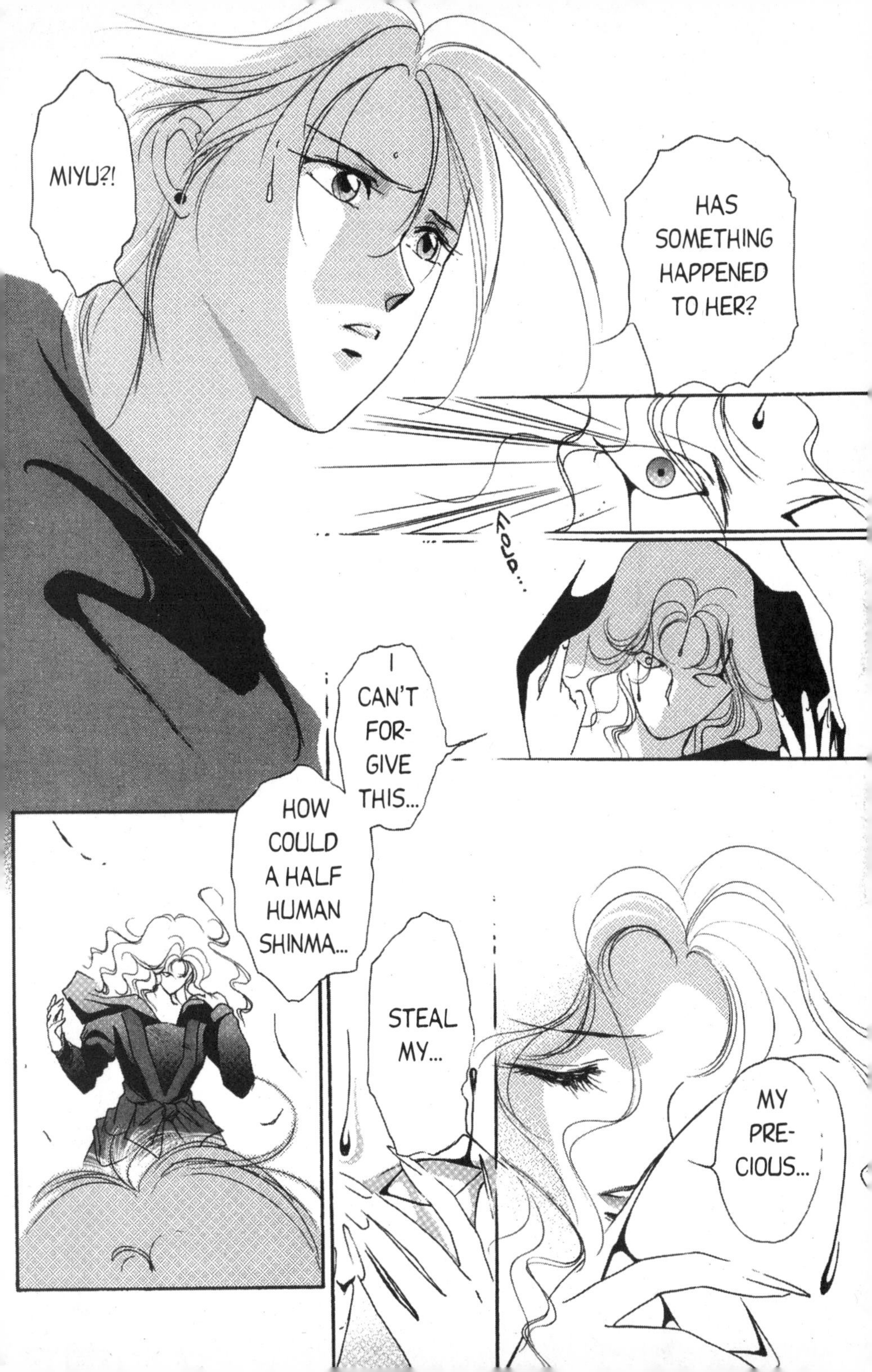
MIYU?!
HAS SOMETHING HAPPENED TO HER?
I CAN'T FOR-GIVE THIS...
HOW COULD A HALF HUMAN SHINMA...
STEAL MY...
MY PRE-CIOUS...

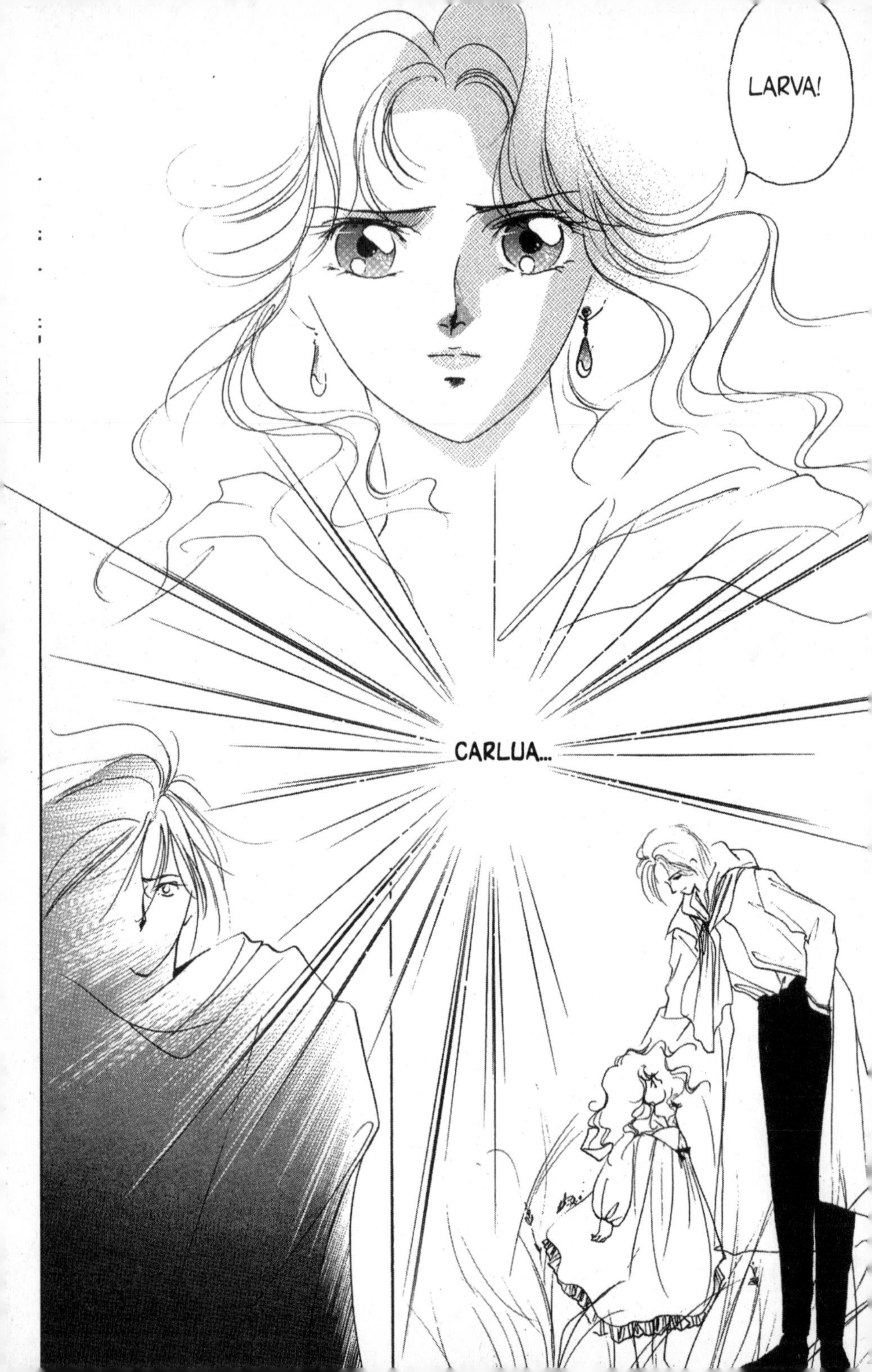

LARVA!
CARLUA...

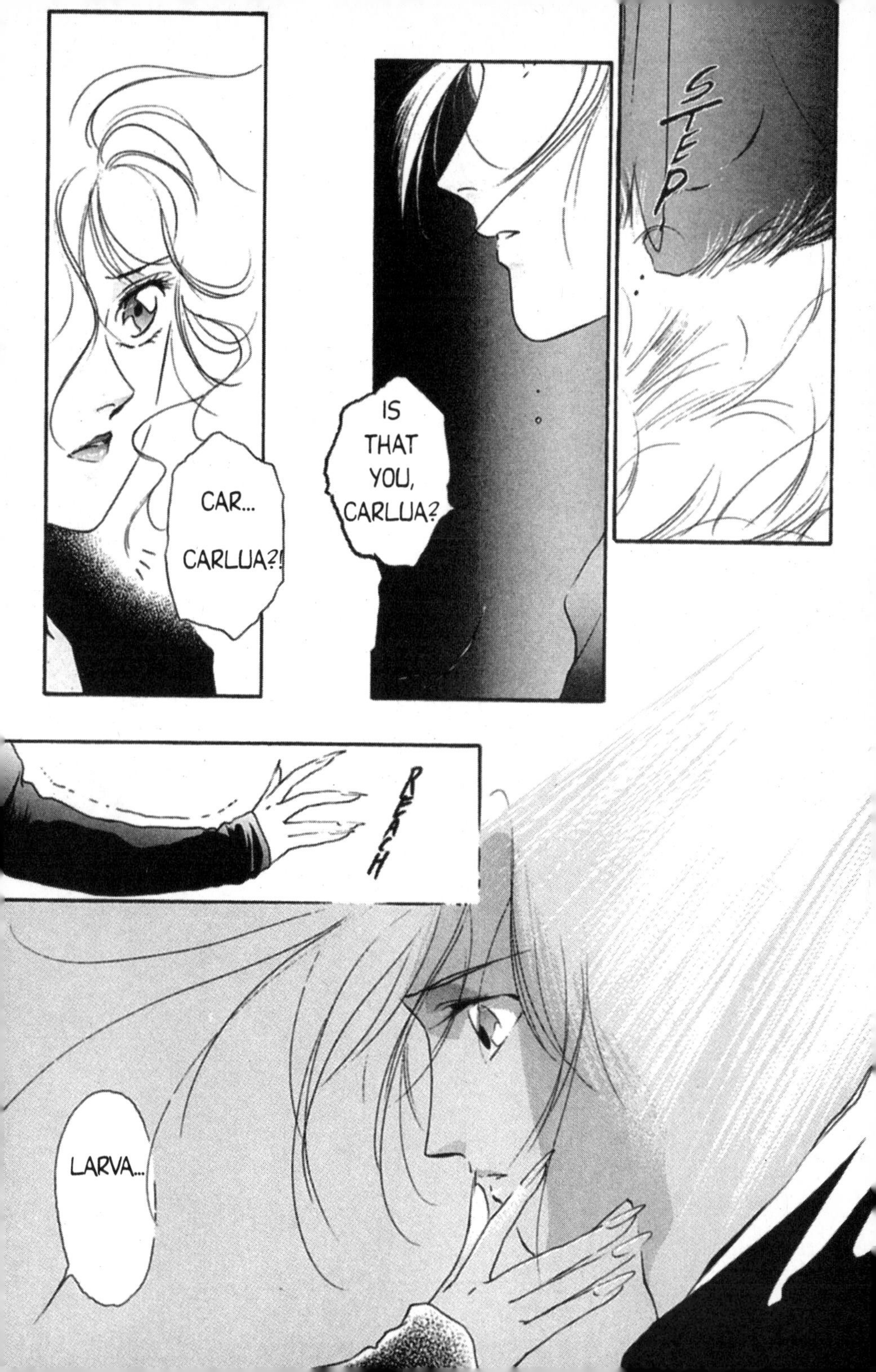
STEP
IS THAT YOU, CARLUA?
CAR... CARLUA?!
REACH
LARVA...

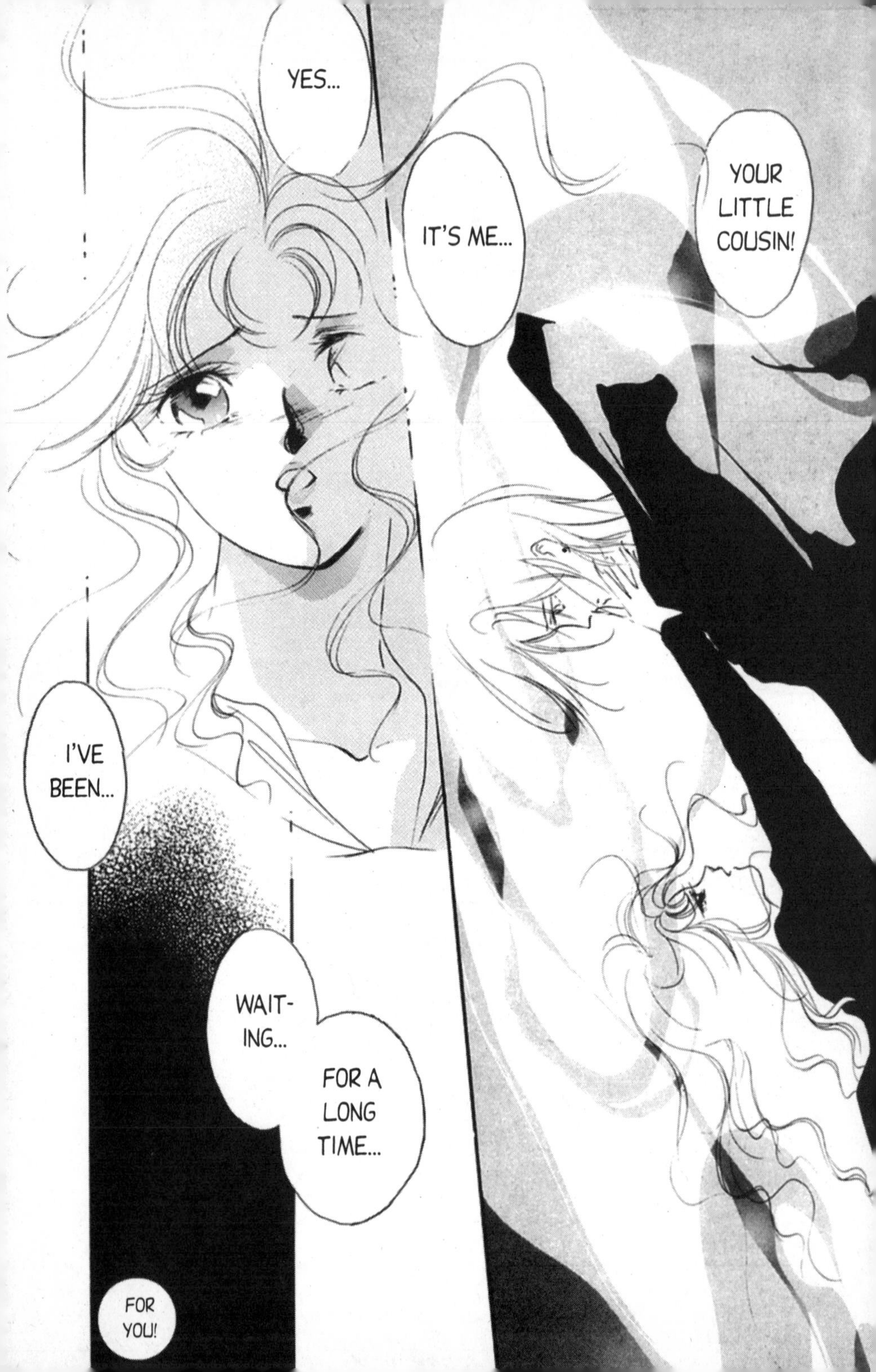
YES...
IT'S ME...
YOUR LITTLE COUSIN!
I'VE BEEN...
WAITING...
FOR A LONG TIME...
FOR YOU!

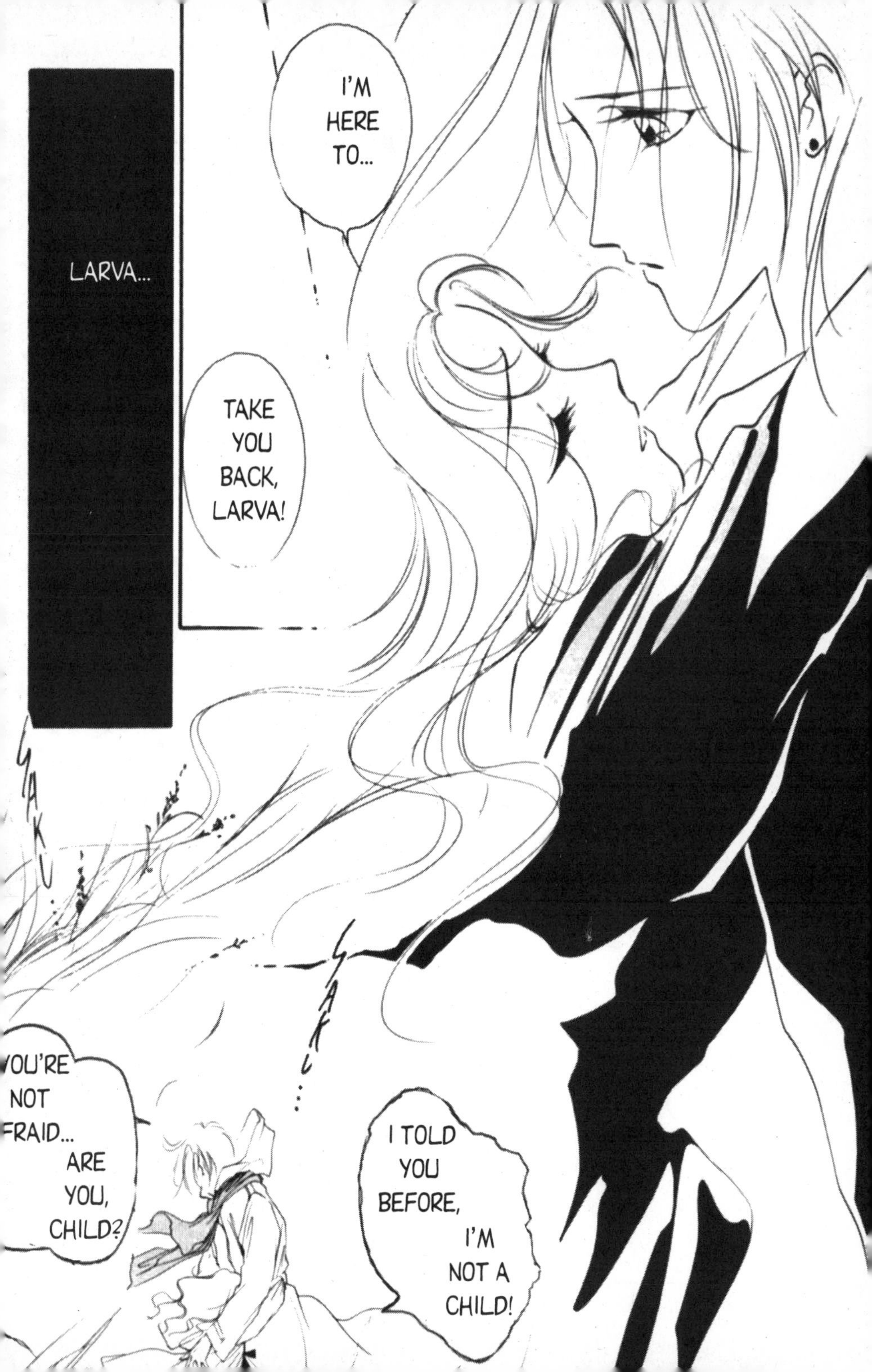
I'M HERE TO...
LARVA...
TAKE YOU BACK, LARVA!
SAKU
SAKU...
I TOLD YOU BEFORE, I'M NOT A CHILD!
OU'RE NOT FRAID... ARE YOU, CHILD?

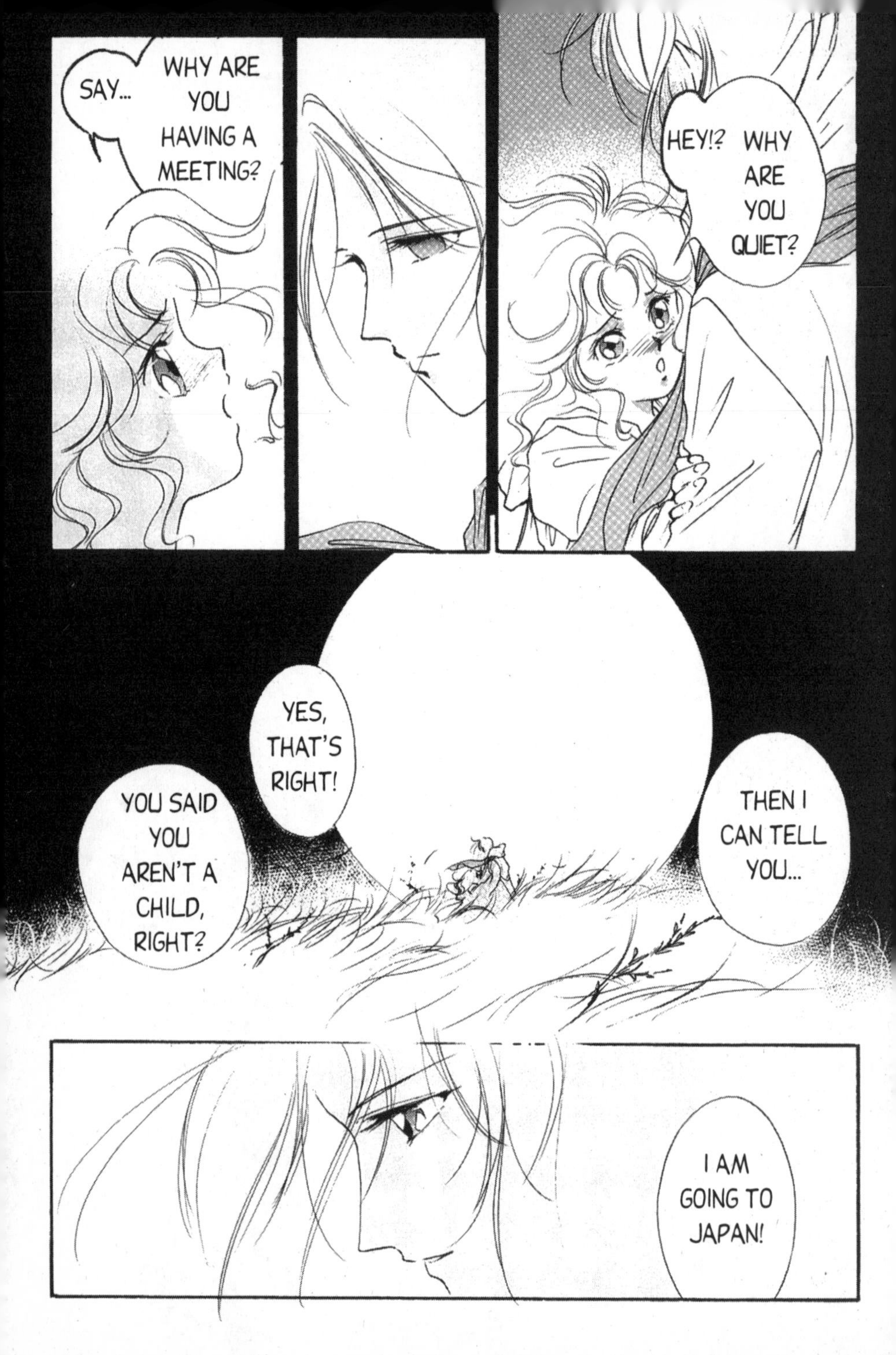

SAY...
WHY ARE YOU HAVING A MEETING?
HEY!? WHY ARE YOU QUIET?
YES, THAT'S RIGHT!
YOU SAID YOU AREN'T A CHILD, RIGHT?
THEN I CAN TELL YOU...
I AM GOING TO JAPAN!

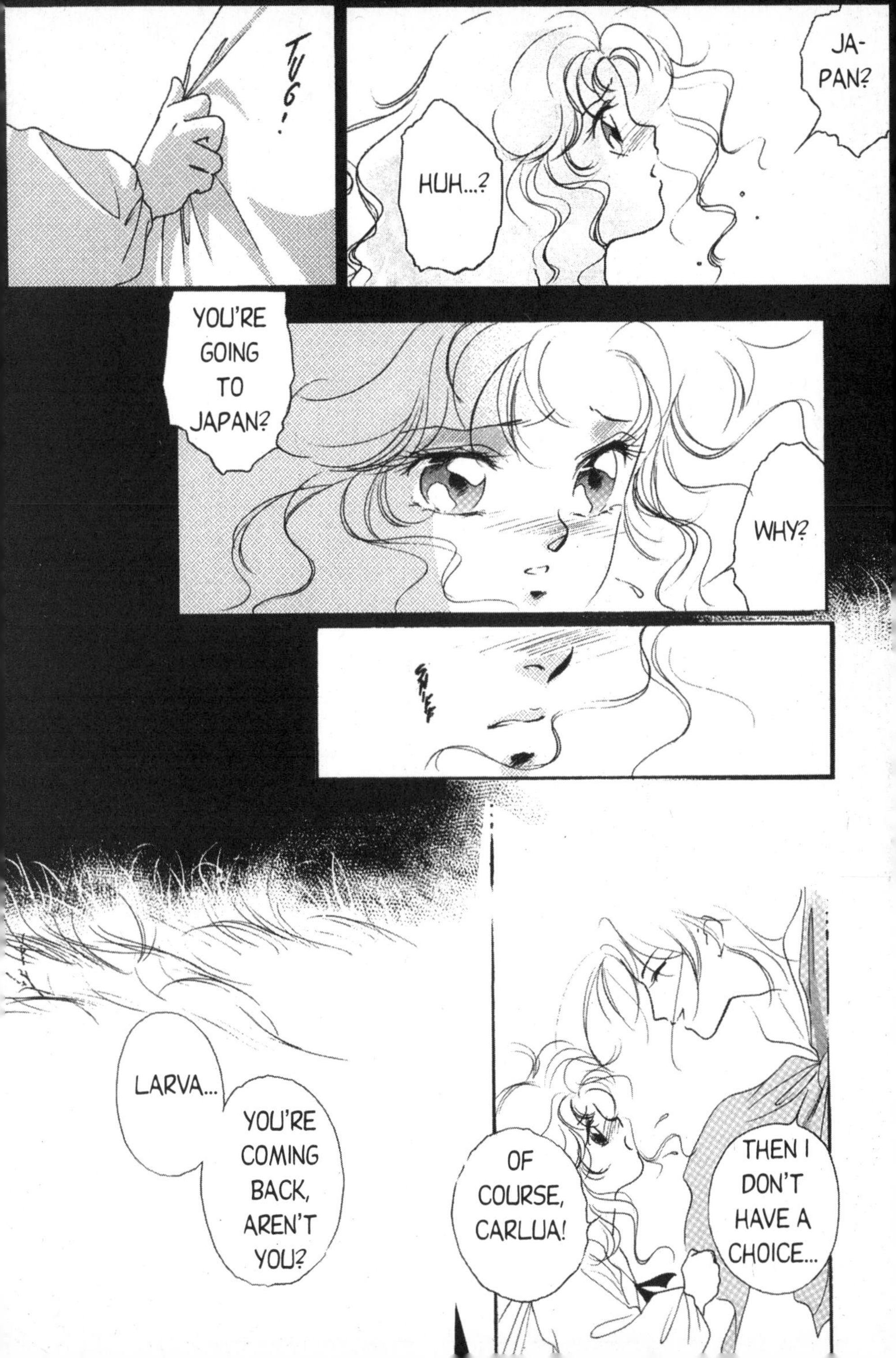
TUG!
HUH...?
JA-PAN?
YOU'RE GOING TO JAPAN?
WHY?
LARVA...
YOU'RE COMING BACK, AREN'T YOU?
OF COURSE, CARLUA!
THEN I DON'T HAVE A CHOICE...

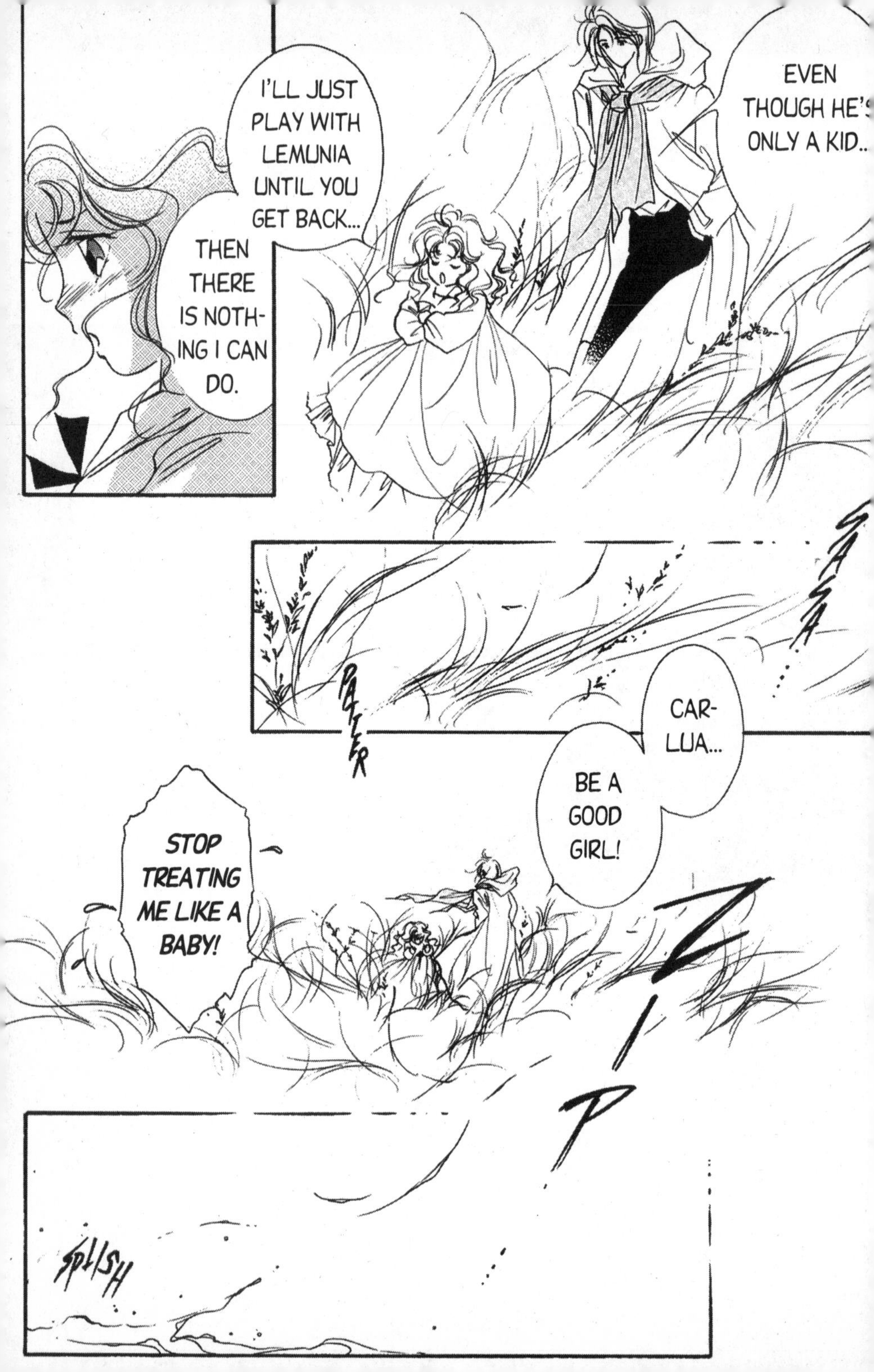
EVEN THOUGH HE' ONLY A KID...
I'LL JUST PLAY WITH LEMUNIA UNTIL YOU GET BACK...
THEN THERE IS NOTH-ING I CAN DO.
SASA...
PATTER
CAR-LUA...
BE A GOOD GIRL!
STOP TREATING ME LIKE A BABY!
ZIP
SPLISH

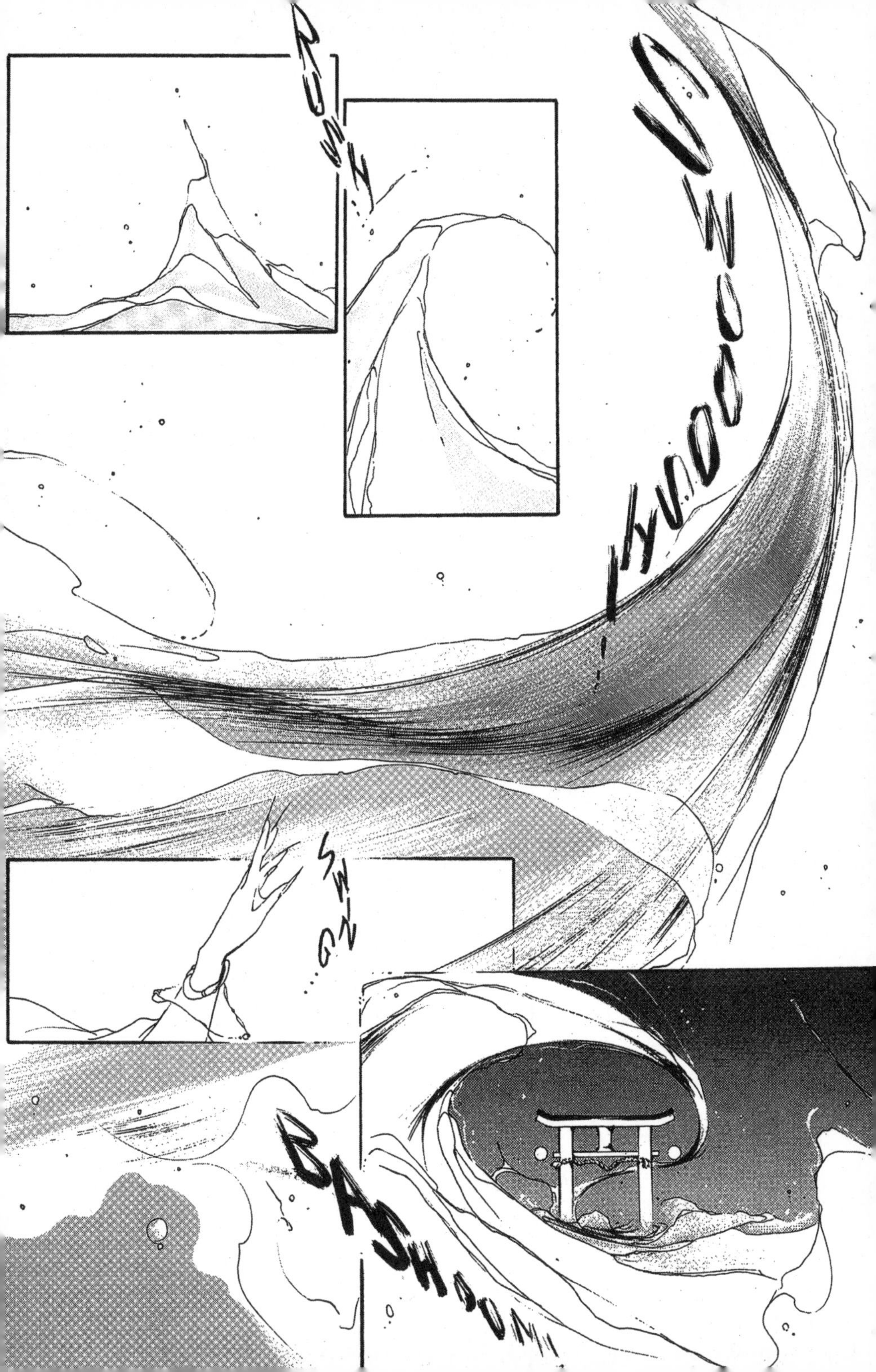
RUSH
HYOOOOOOO
SWING...
BASHOOM!!

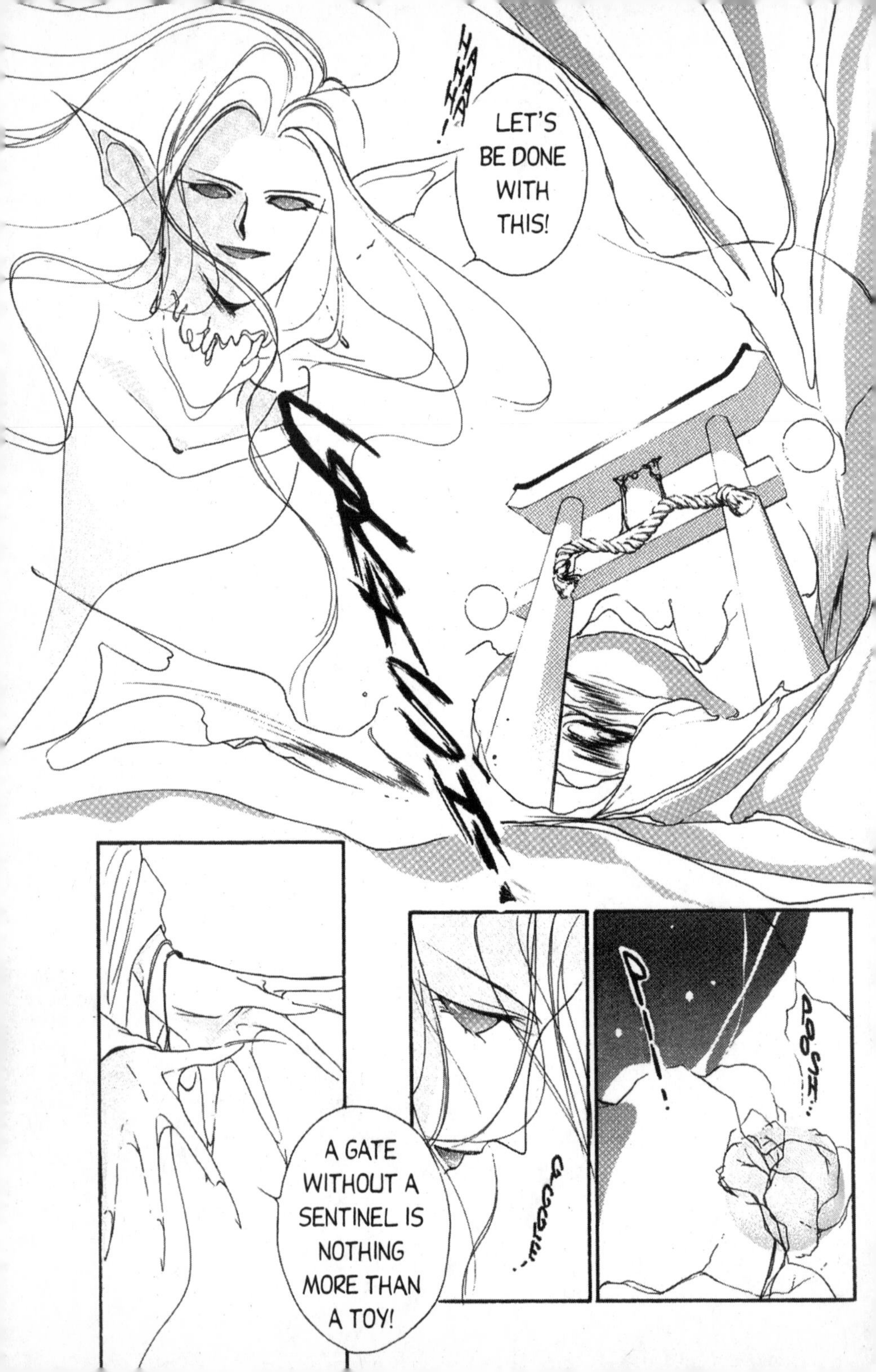
HAHAHA!
LET'S BE DONE WITH THIS!
A GATE WITHOUT A SENTINEL IS NOTHING MORE THAN A TOY!
POOF...

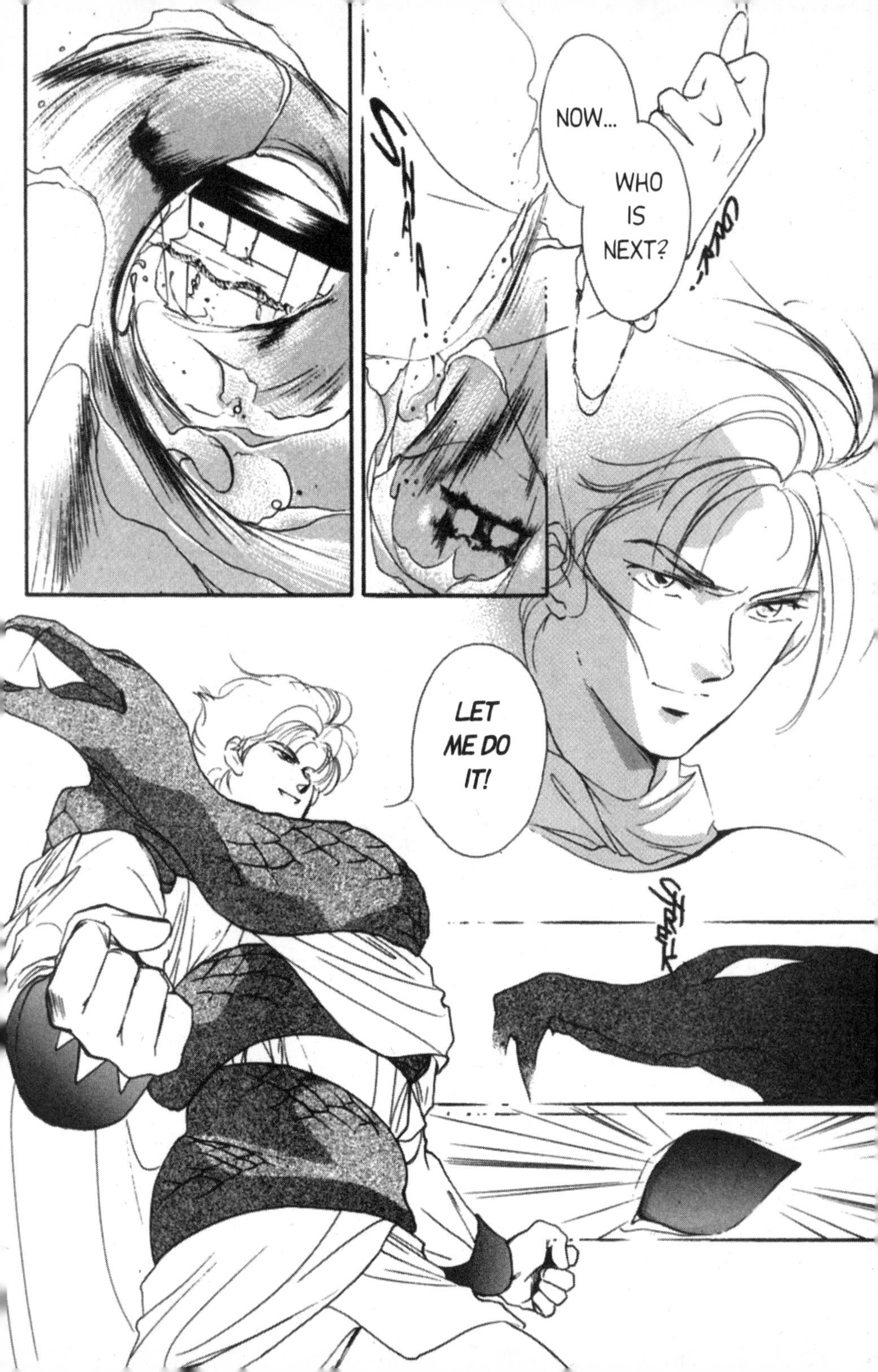
NOW...
WHO IS NEXT?
LET ME DO IT!

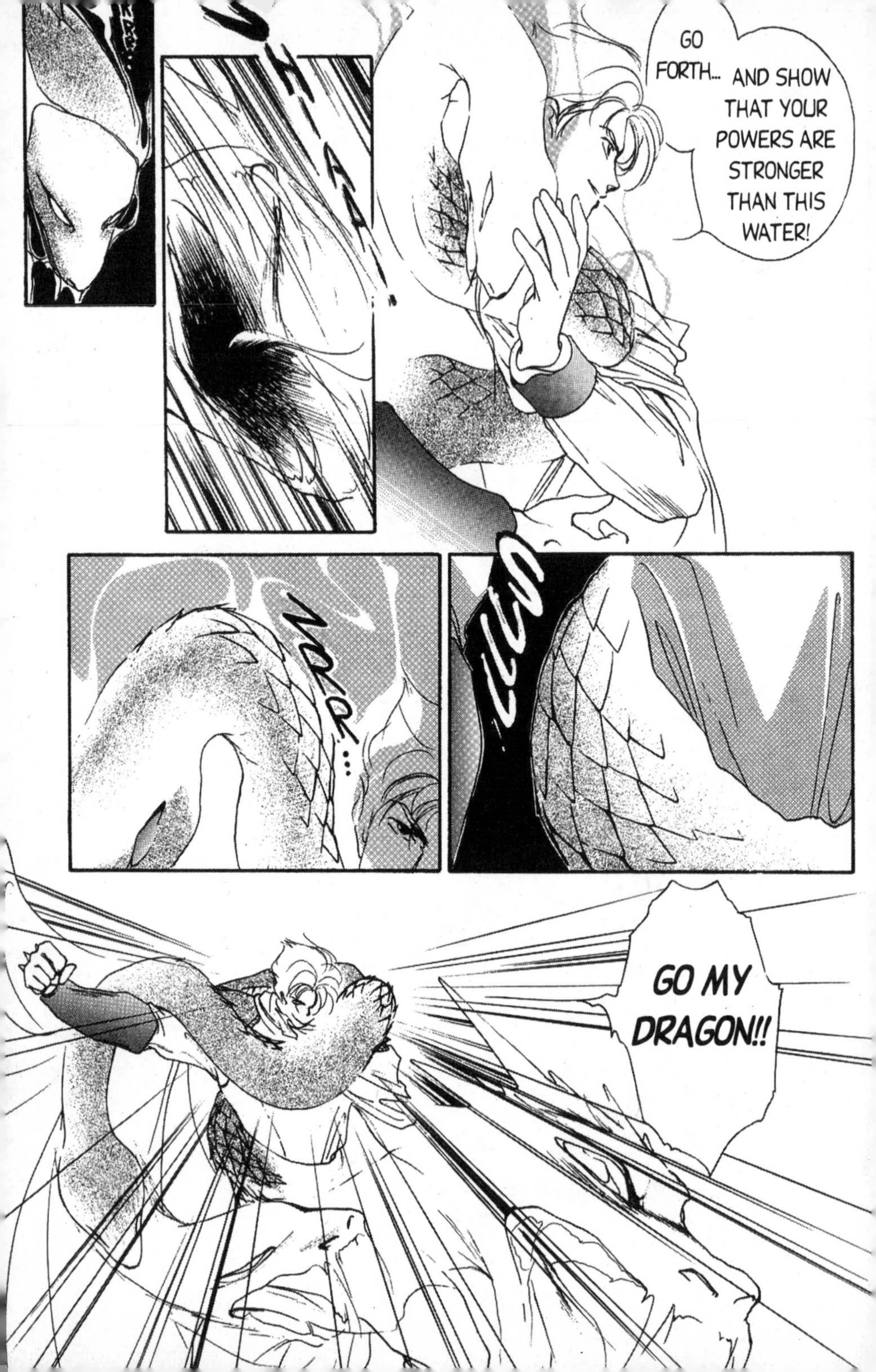
KRR...
GO FORTH... AND SHOW THAT YOUR POWERS ARE STRONGER THAN THIS WATER!
GO MY DRAGON!!

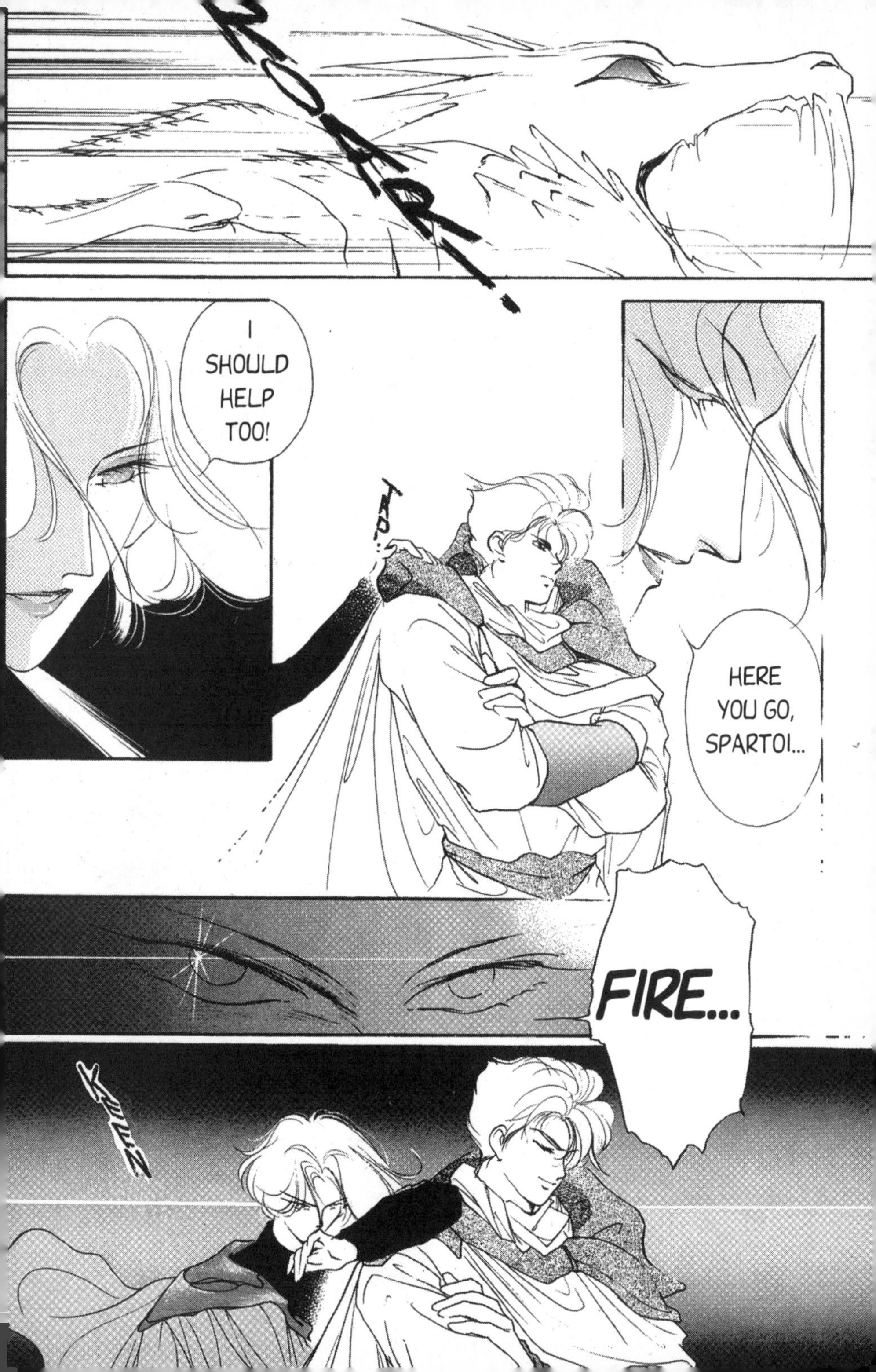
ROAR...
I SHOULD HELP TOO!
TAP...
HERE YOU GO, SPARTOI...
FIRE...

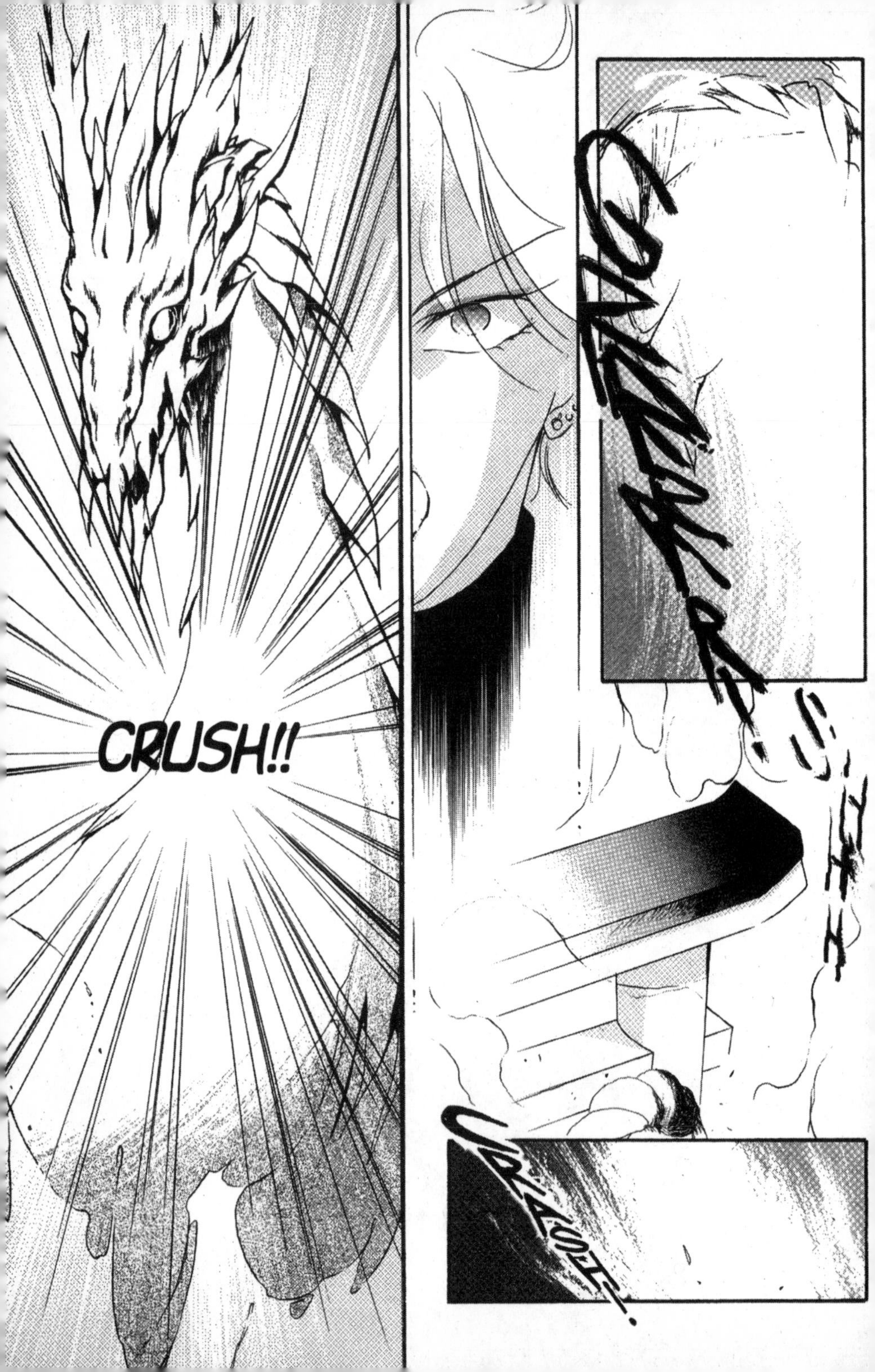
CRUMBLE!
CRACK!
CRUSH!!

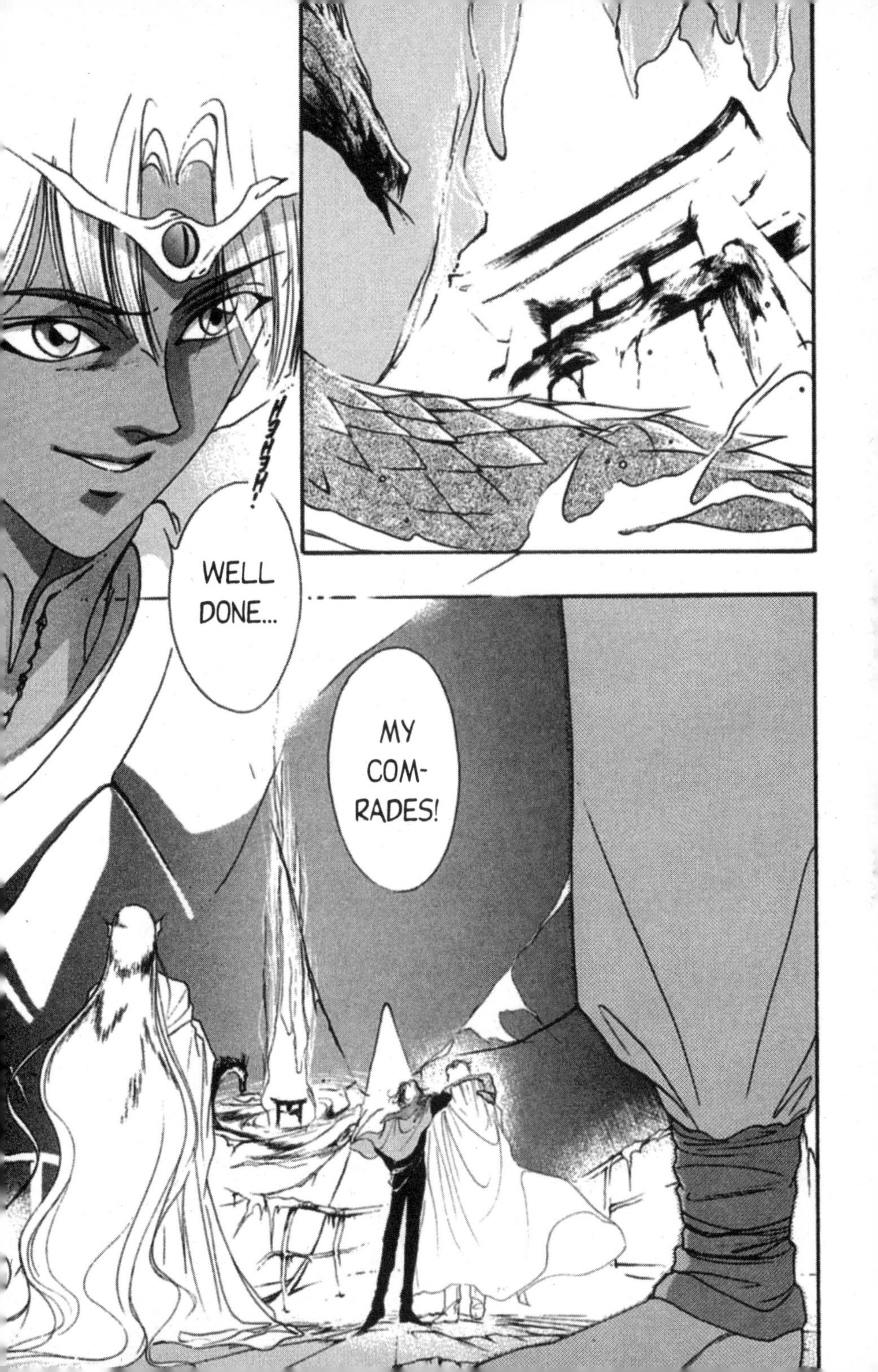
WELL DONE...
MY COM-RADES!

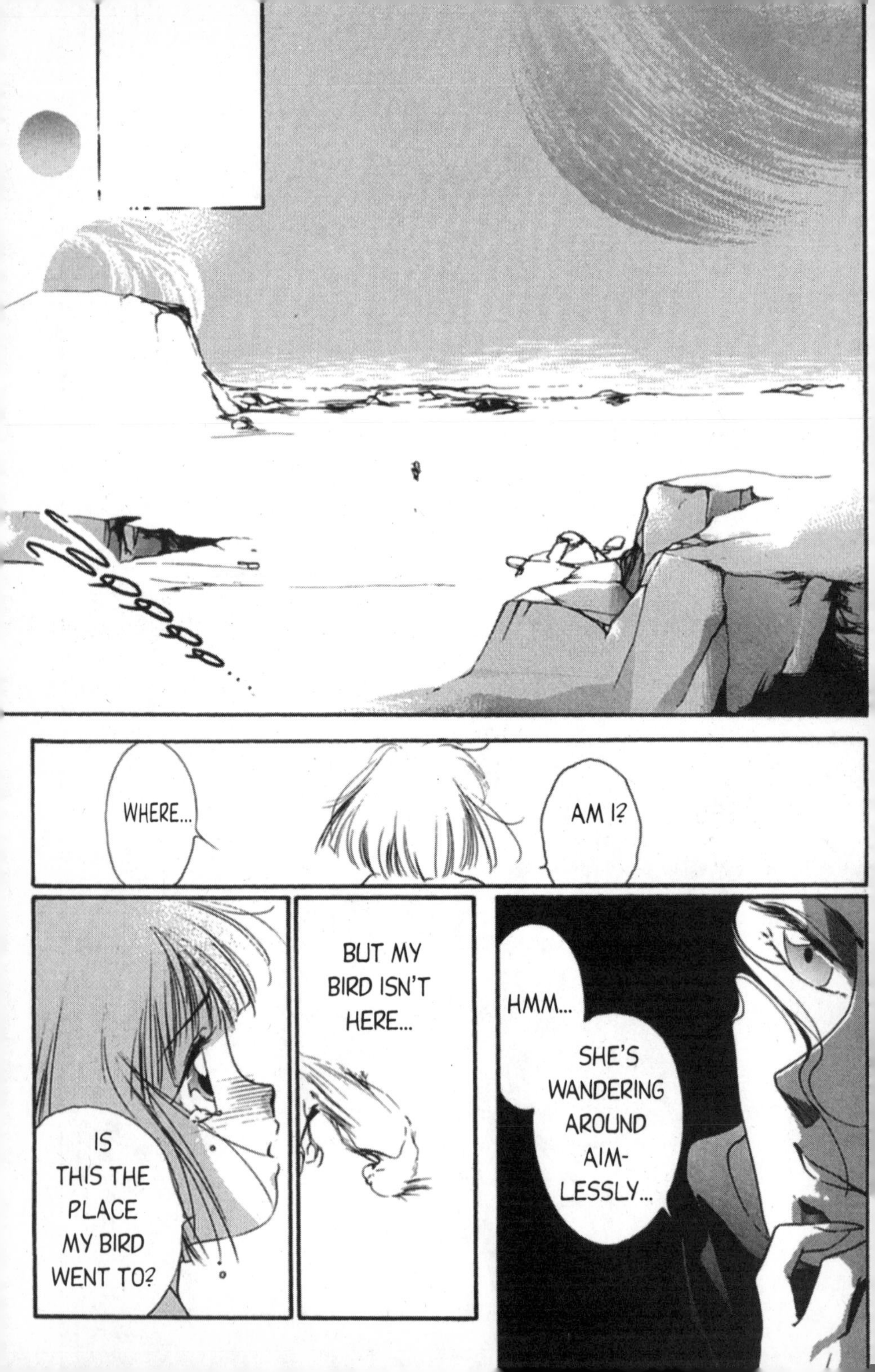
WHERE...
AM I?
IS THIS THE PLACE MY BIRD WENT TO?
BUT MY BIRD ISN'T HERE...
HMM...
SHE'S WANDERING AROUND AIM-LESSLY...

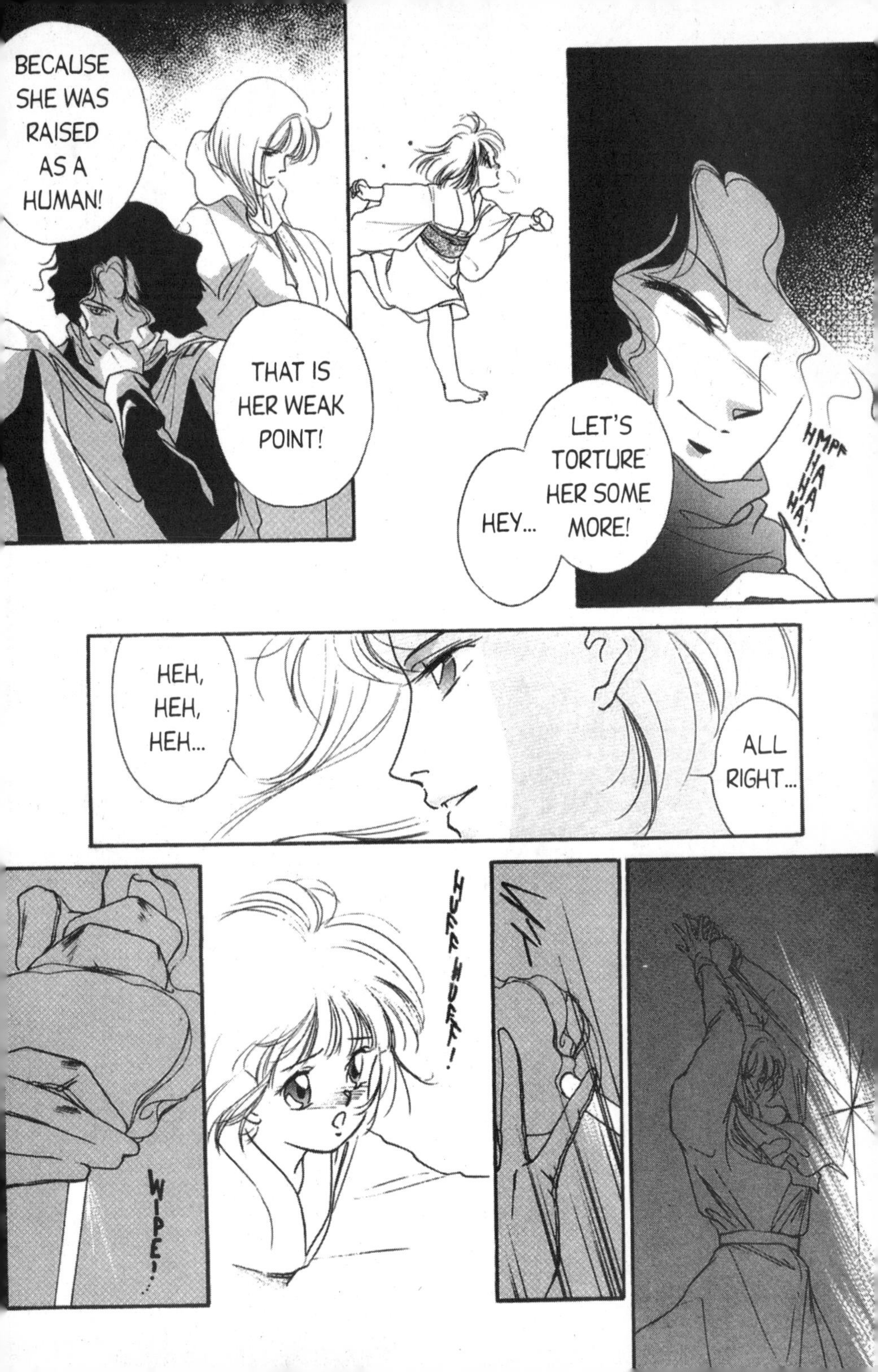
BECAUSE SHE WAS RAISED AS A HUMAN!
THAT IS HER WEAK POINT!
HEY...
LET'S TORTURE HER SOME MORE!
HMPF HA HA HA!
HEH, HEH, HEH...
ALL RIGHT...
WIPE!...
HUFF HUFF!

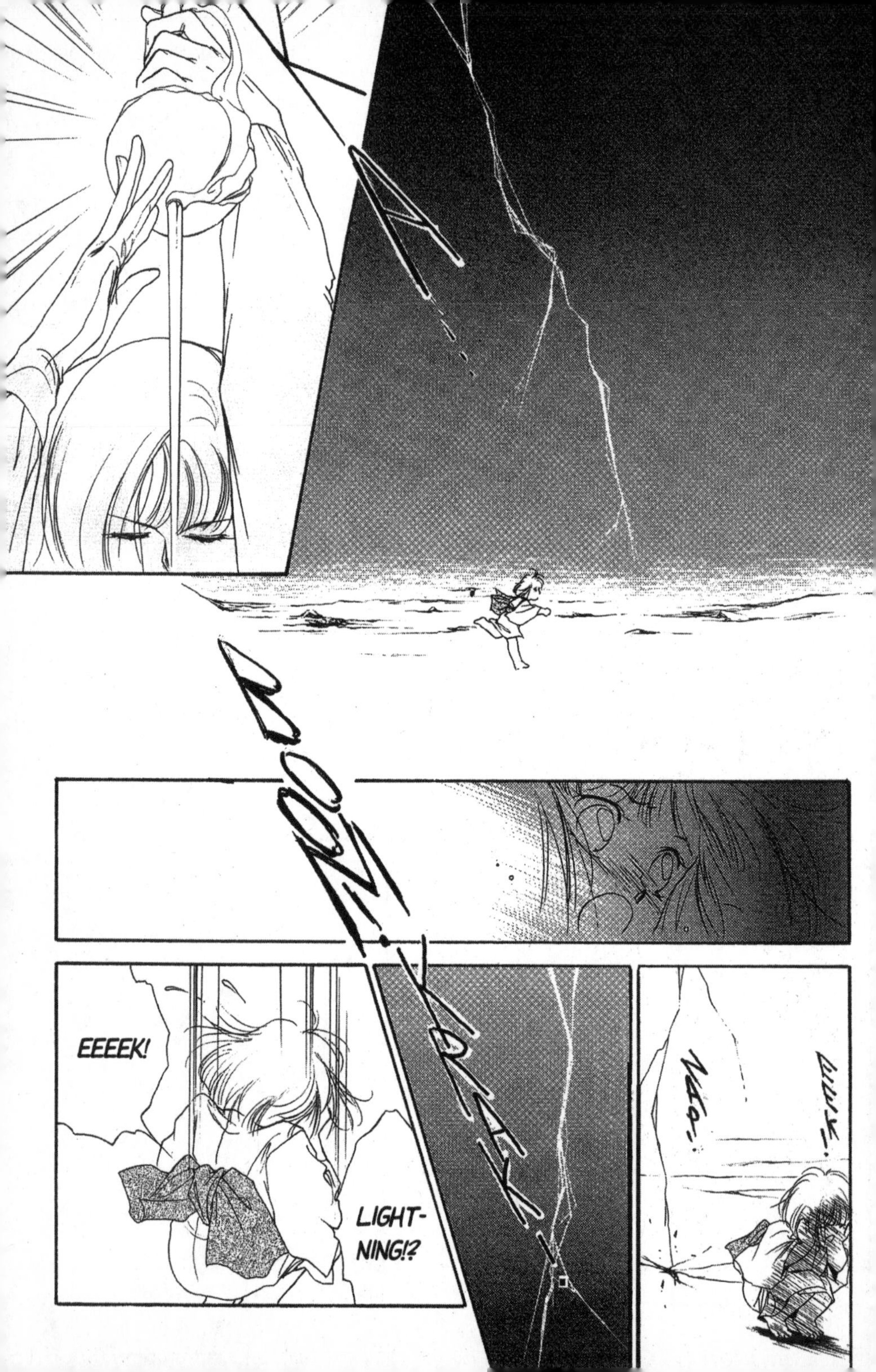
BOOM
KRASH
EEEEK!
LIGHT-
NING!?

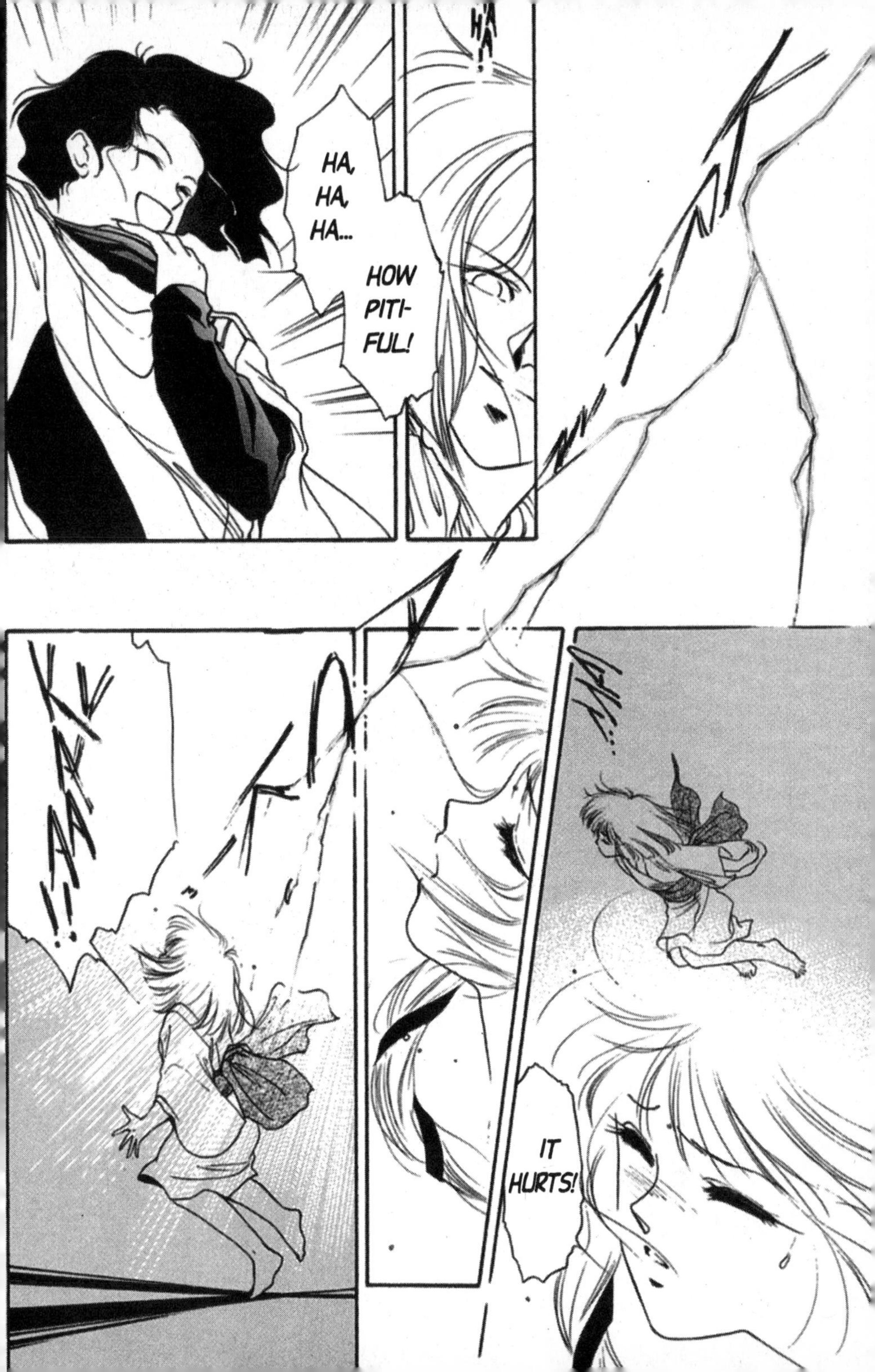

HA, HA, HA...
HOW PITI-FUL!
HA HA!
KYAAA!!
AHH...
IT HURTS!

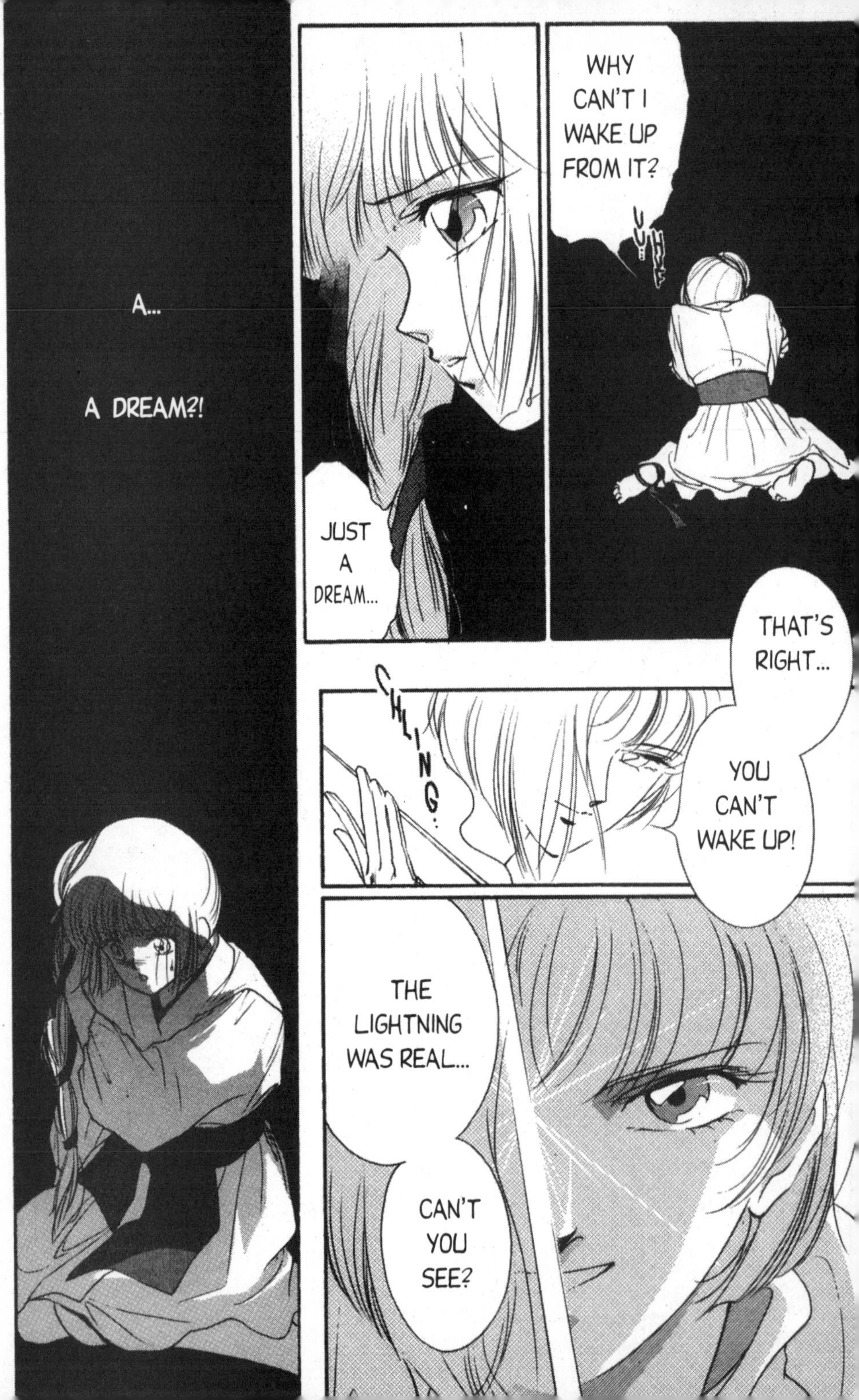
A...
A DREAM?!
JUST A DREAM...
WHY CAN'T I WAKE UP FROM IT?
THAT'S RIGHT...
CHLING..
YOU CAN'T WAKE UP!
THE LIGHTNING WAS REAL...
CAN'T YOU SEE?

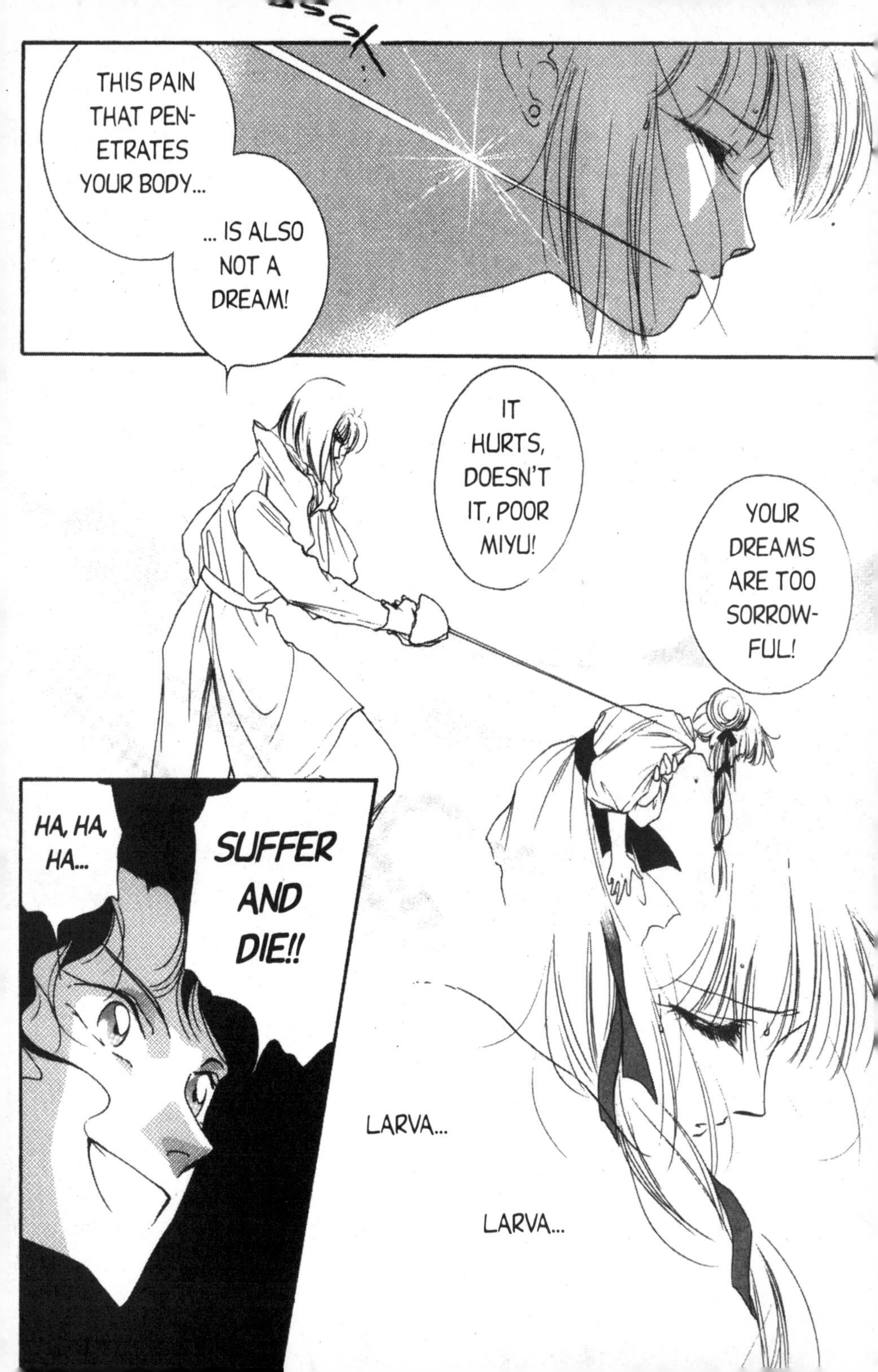
THIS PAIN THAT PEN-ETRATES YOUR BODY...
... IS ALSO NOT A DREAM!
IT HURTS, DOESN'T IT, POOR MIYU!
YOUR DREAMS ARE TOO SORROW-FUL!
SUFFER AND DIE!!
HA, HA, HA...
LARVA...
LARVA...

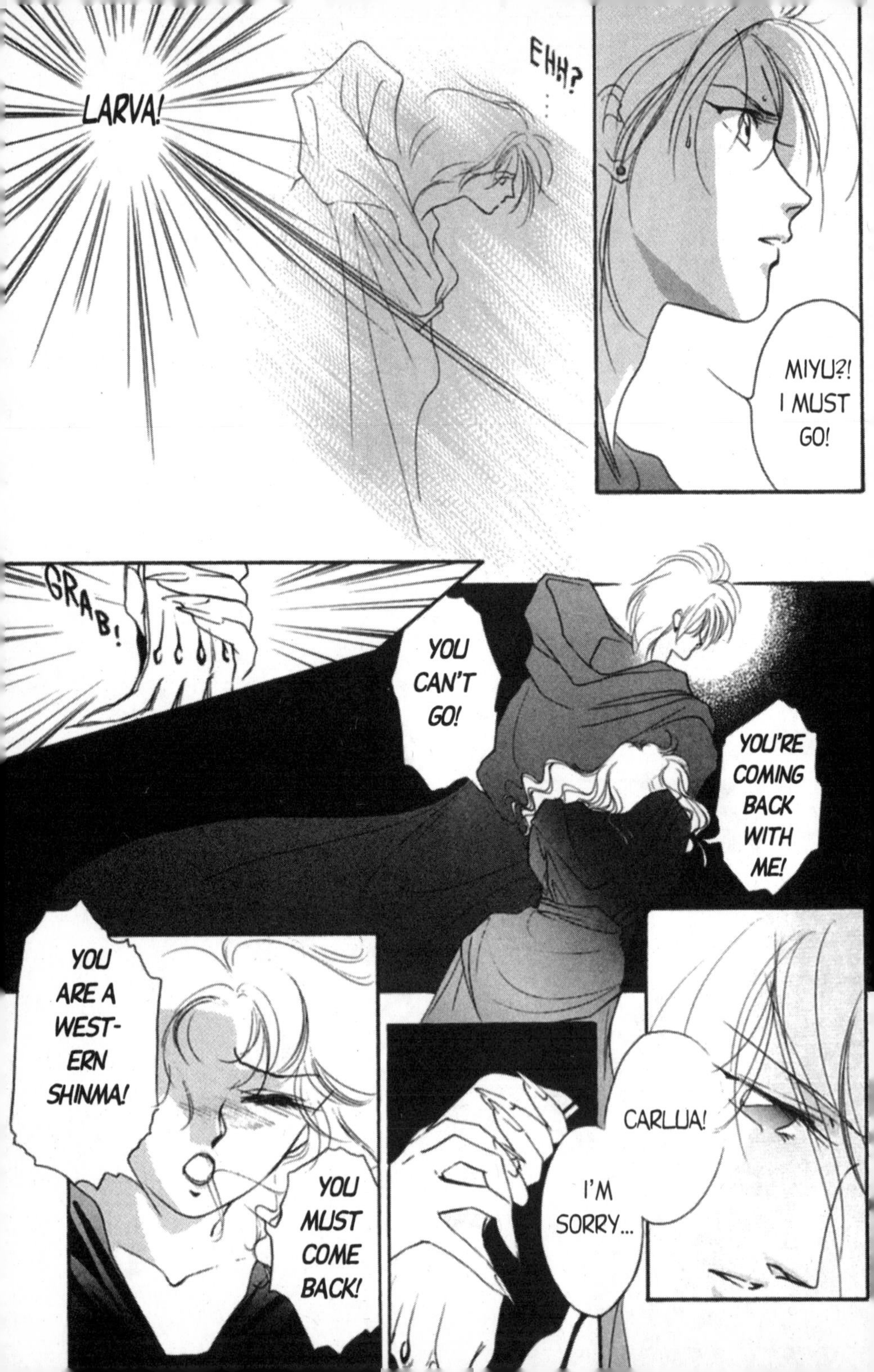
LARVA!
EHH?
MIYU?! I MUST GO!
GRAB!
YOU CAN'T GO!
YOU'RE COMING BACK WITH ME!
YOU ARE A WEST-ERN SHINMA!
YOU MUST COME BACK!
CARLUA!
I'M SORRY...

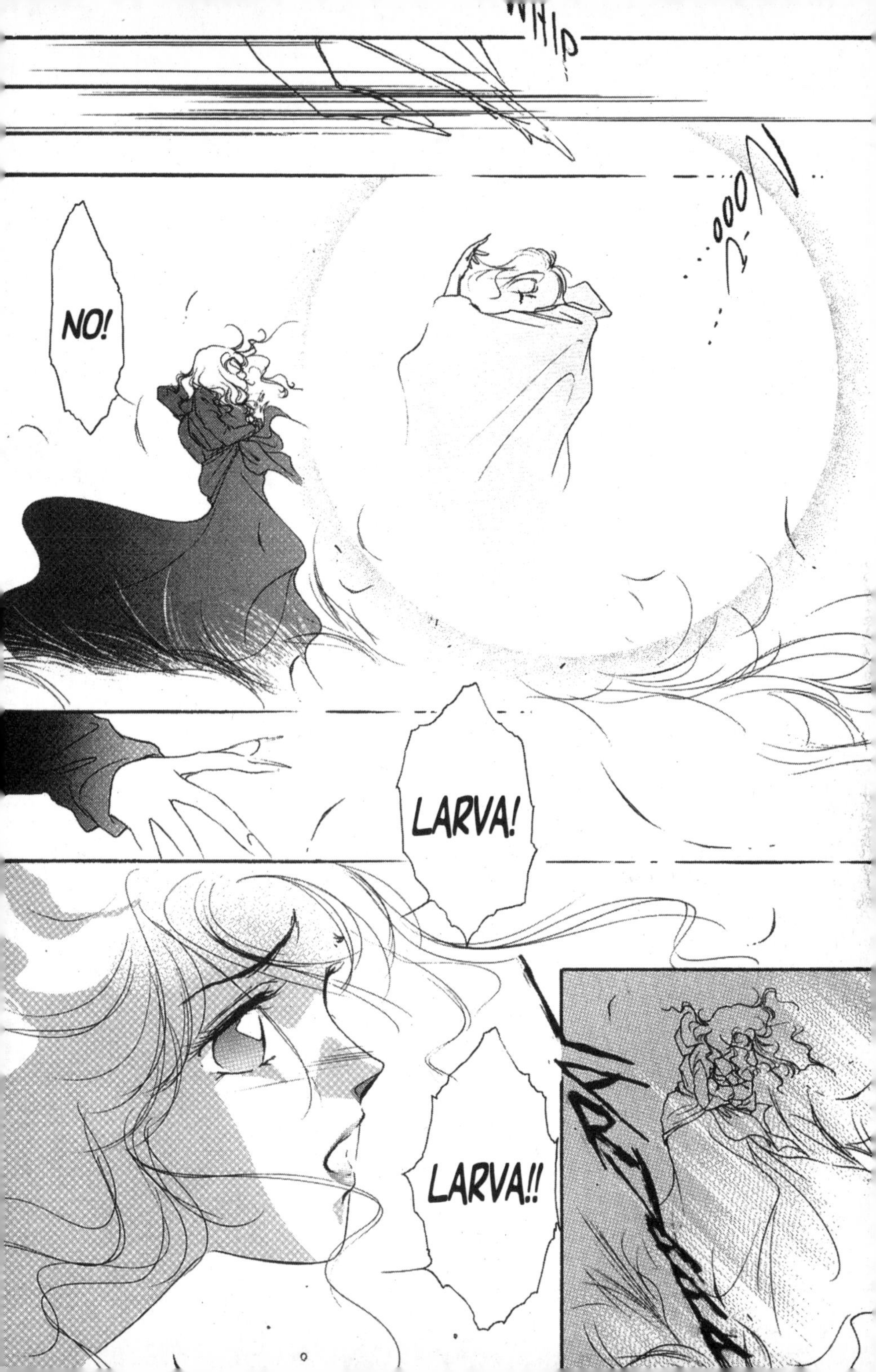
NO!
LARVA!
LARVA!!

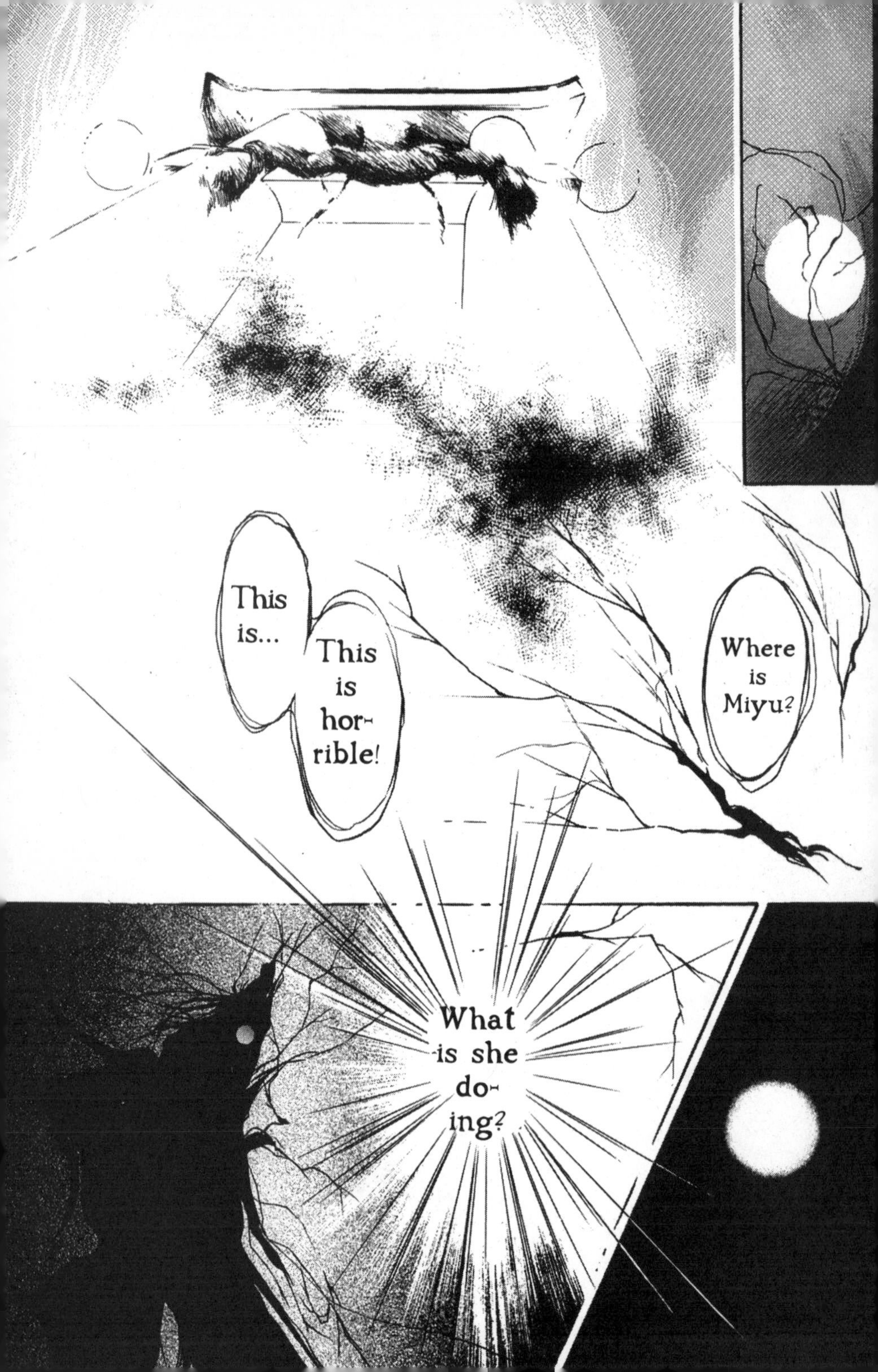
This is...
This is hor-rible!
Where is Miyu?
What is she do-ing?

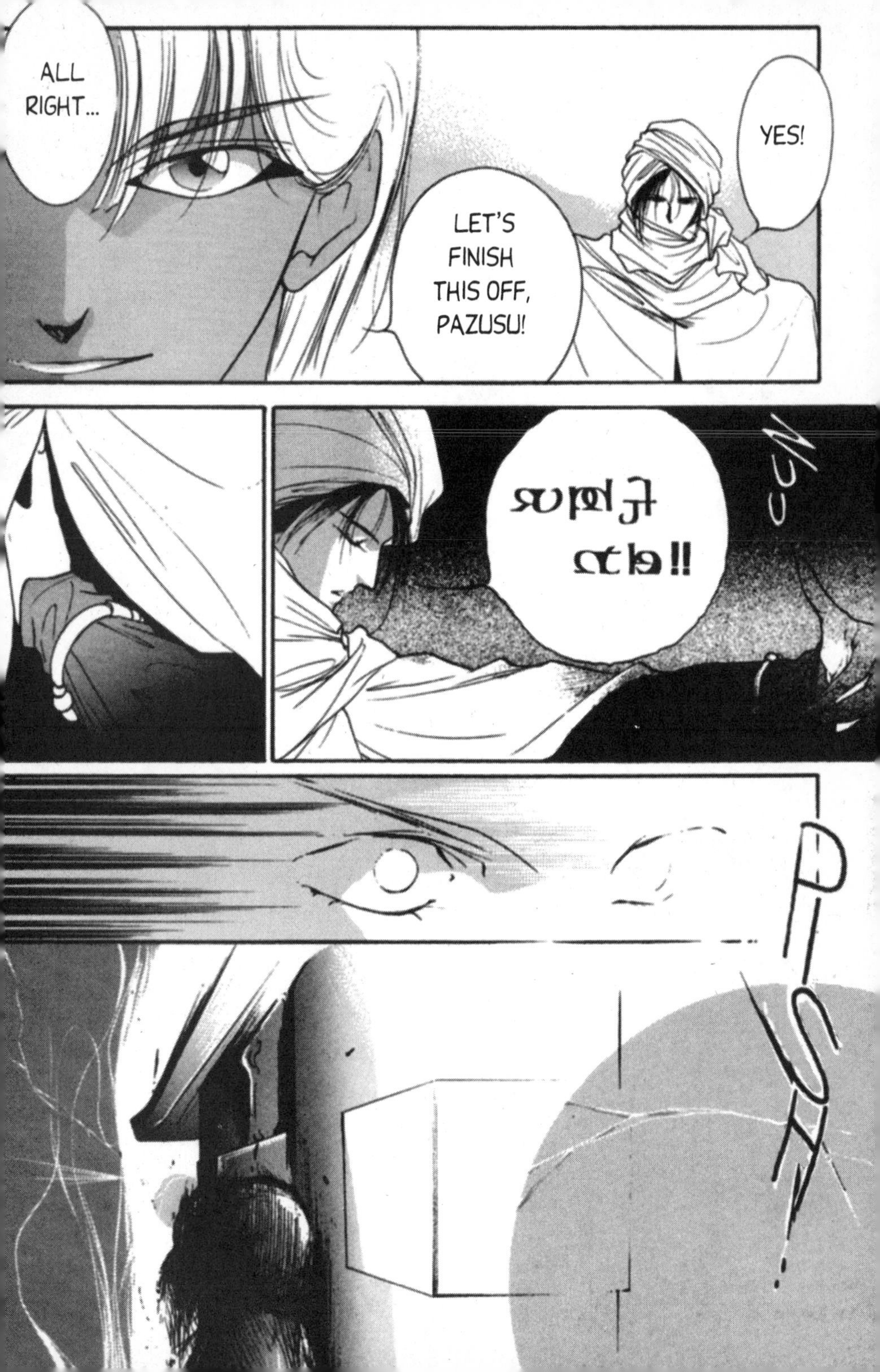
ALL RIGHT...
LET'S FINISH THIS OFF, PAZUSU!
YES!

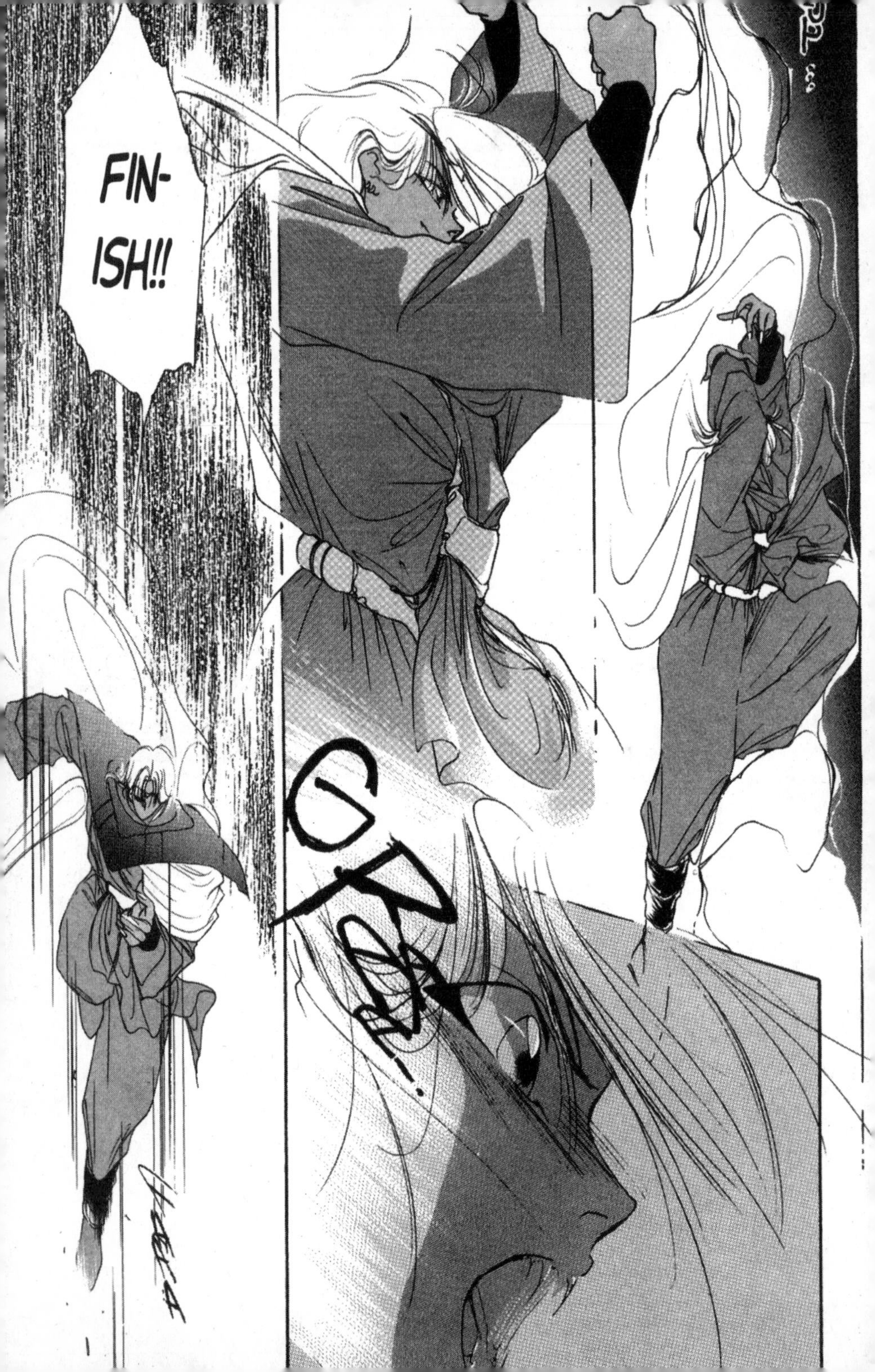
FIN-
ISH!!

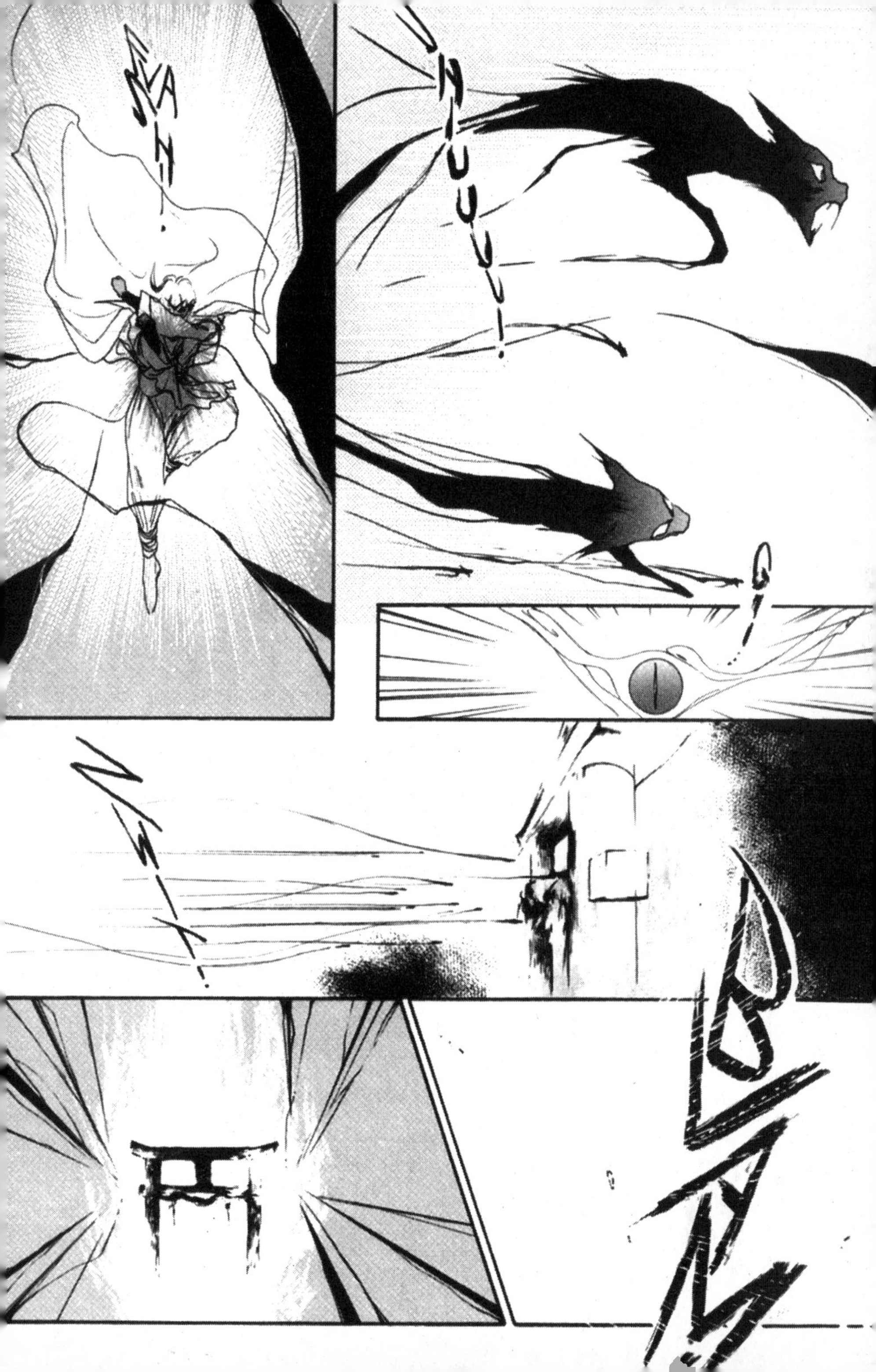
SHUUUUU—!
ZVASH!
NSST!!
BZZZ—

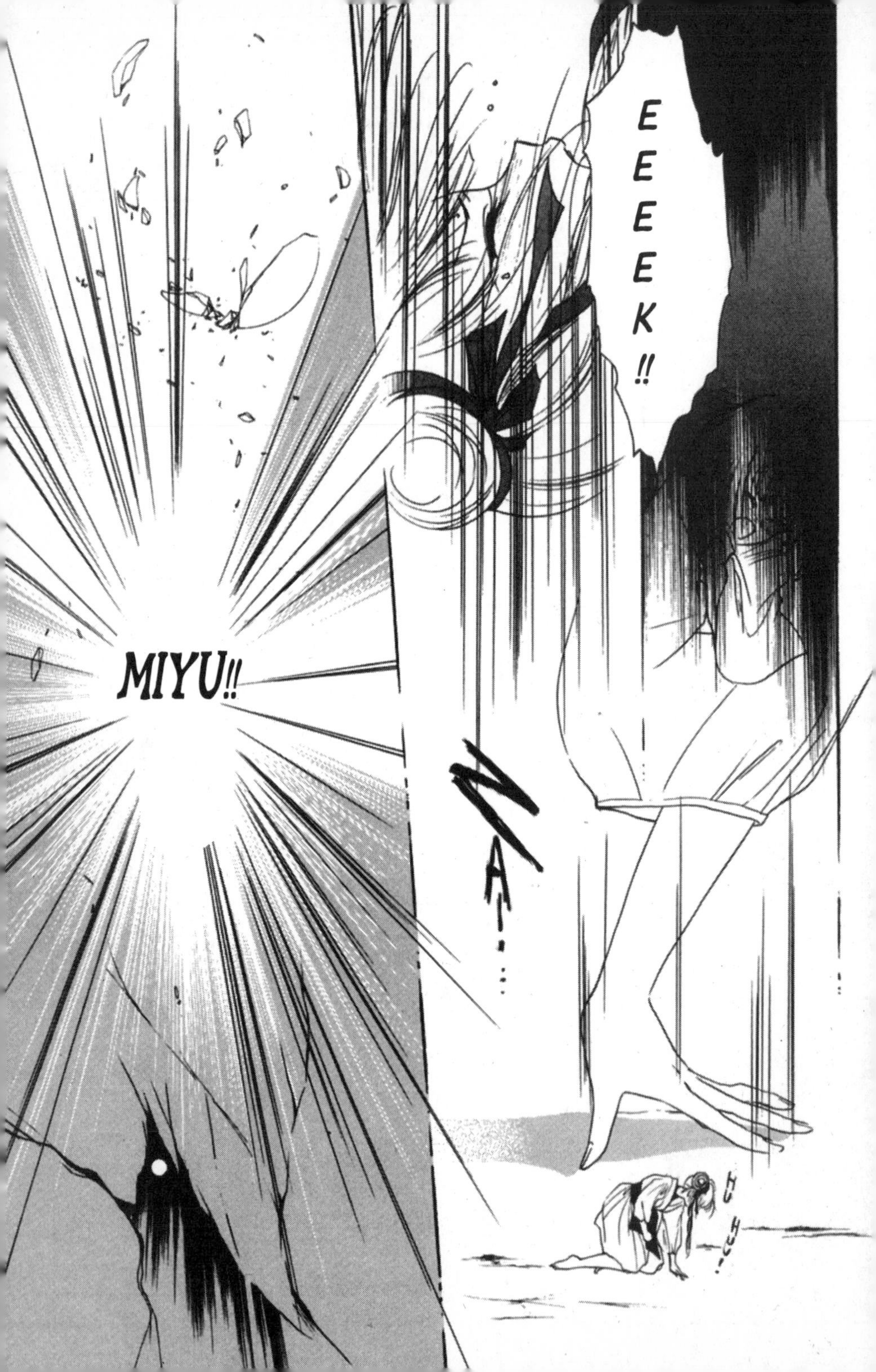
EEEEEK!!
NA....
HU HU..
MIYU!!

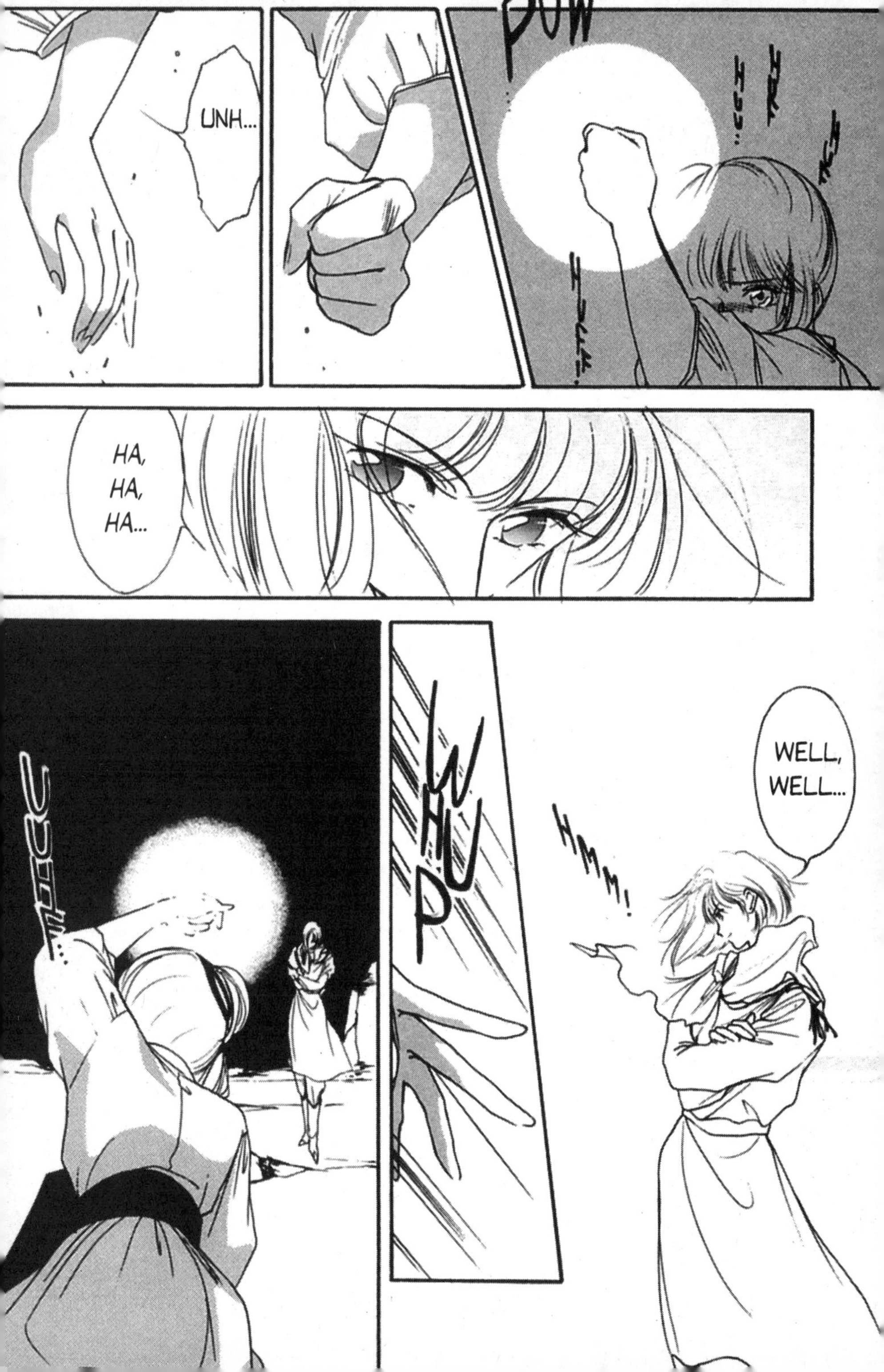
UNH...
PUW
HA,
HA,
HA...
WELL,
WELL...
HMM!
WHUP

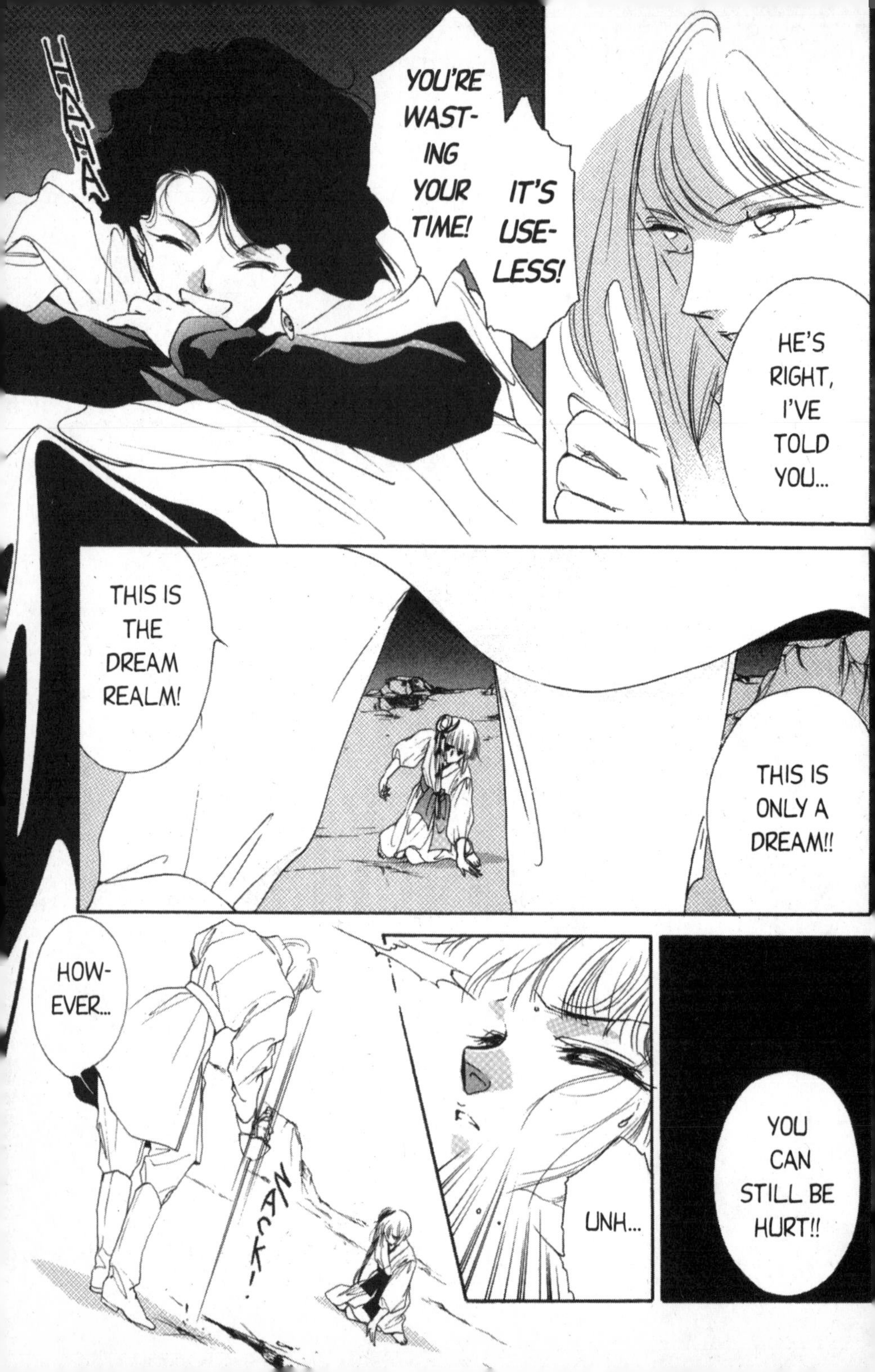

HAHAHA
YOU'RE WASTING YOUR TIME!
IT'S USELESS!
HE'S RIGHT, I'VE TOLD YOU...
THIS IS THE DREAM REALM!
THIS IS ONLY A DREAM!!
HOW-EVER...
ZACK!
UNH...
YOU CAN STILL BE HURT!!

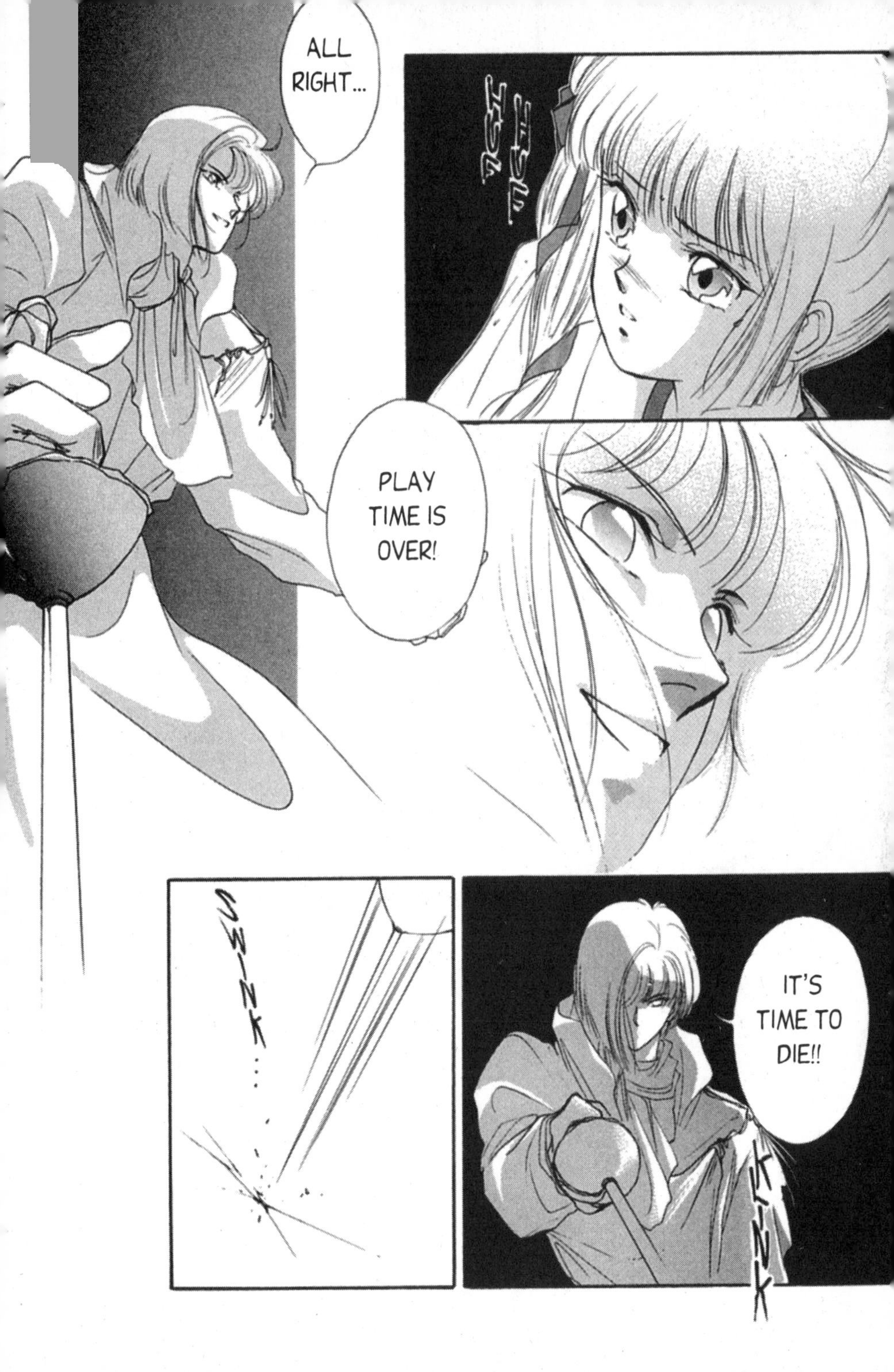
ALL RIGHT...
PLAY TIME IS OVER!
SWINK...
IT'S TIME TO DIE!!
KLINK

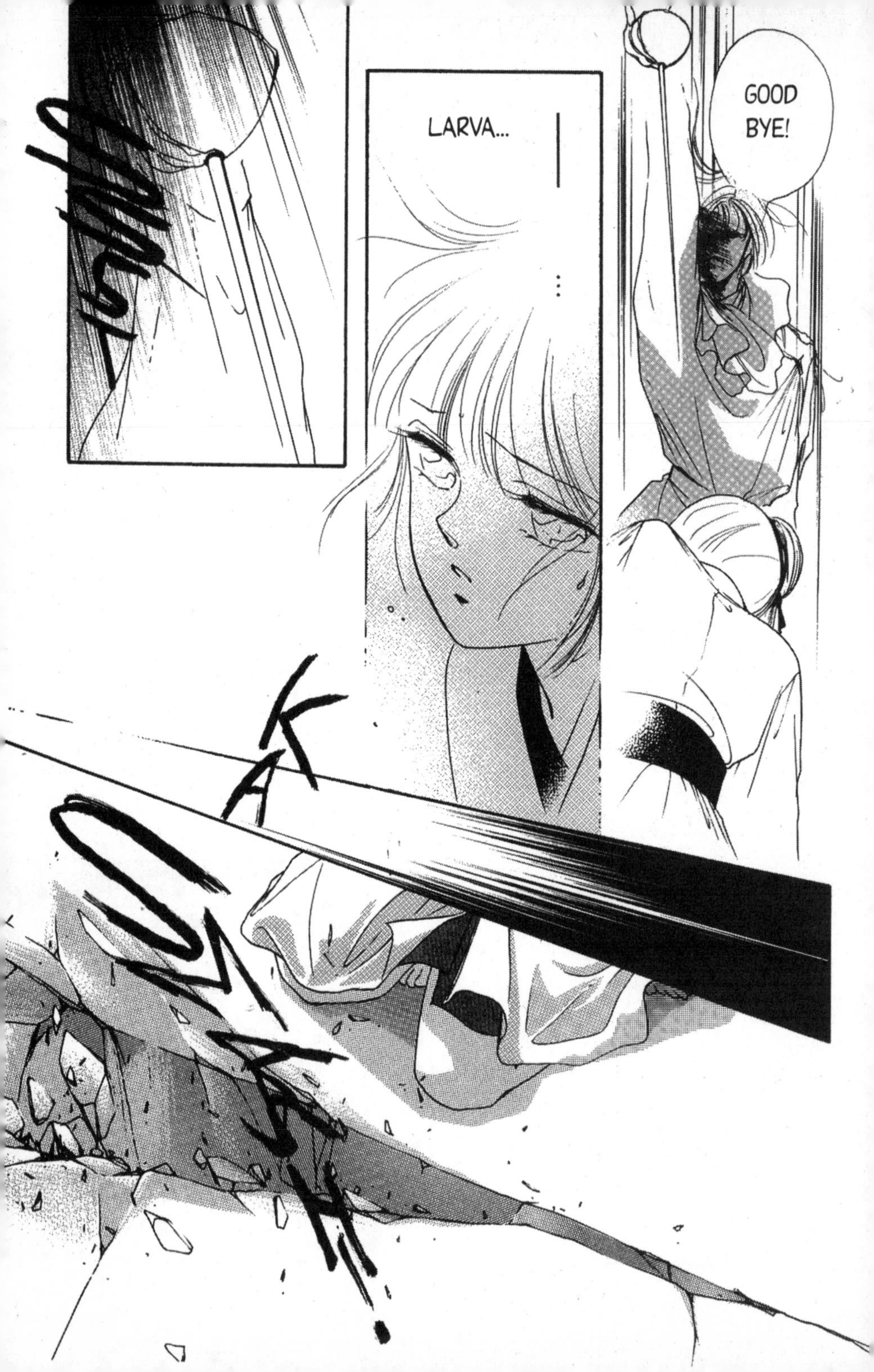
GOOD BYE!
LARVA...
KA
SMASH

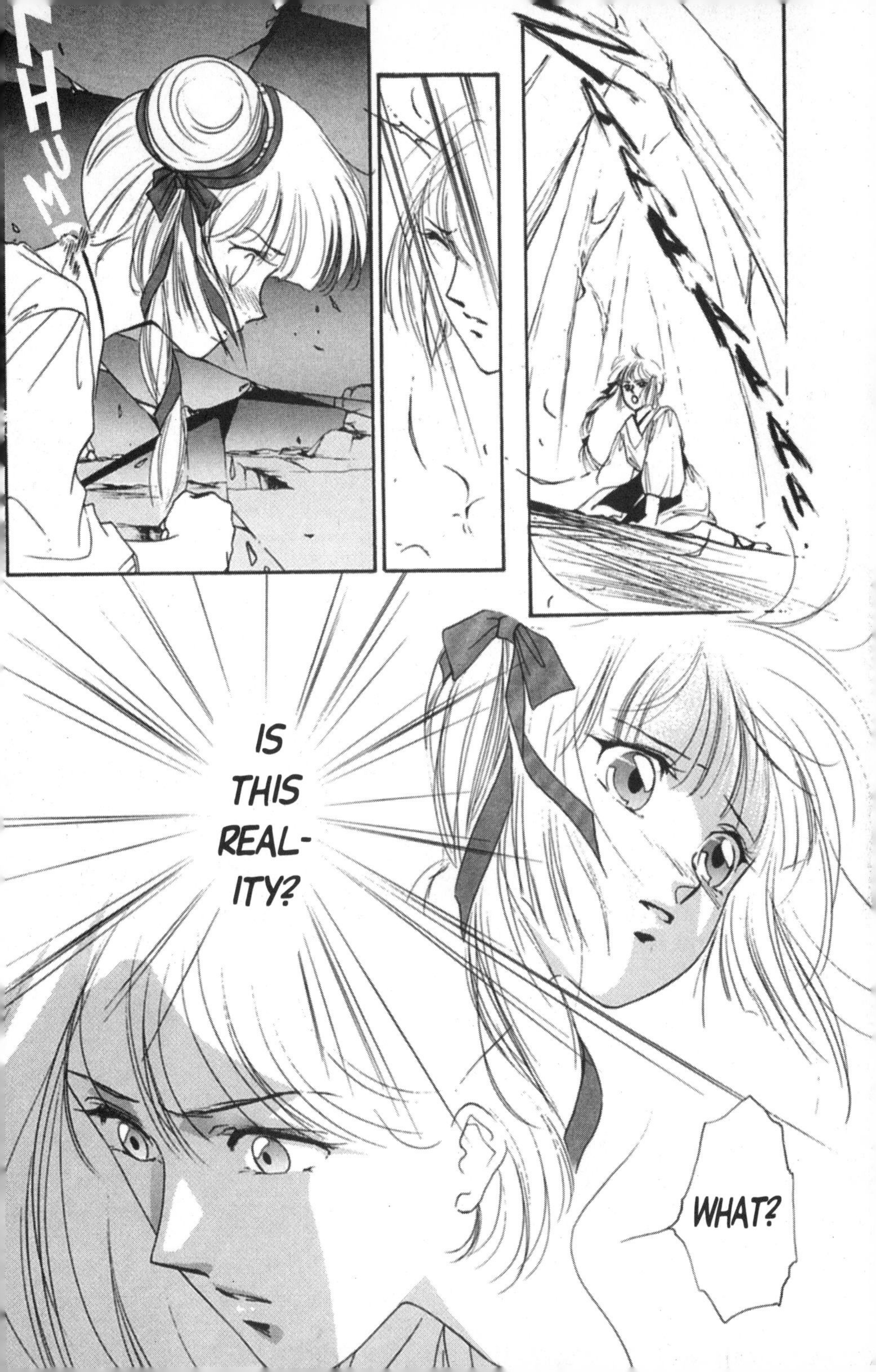
IS THIS REAL-
ITY?
WHAT?

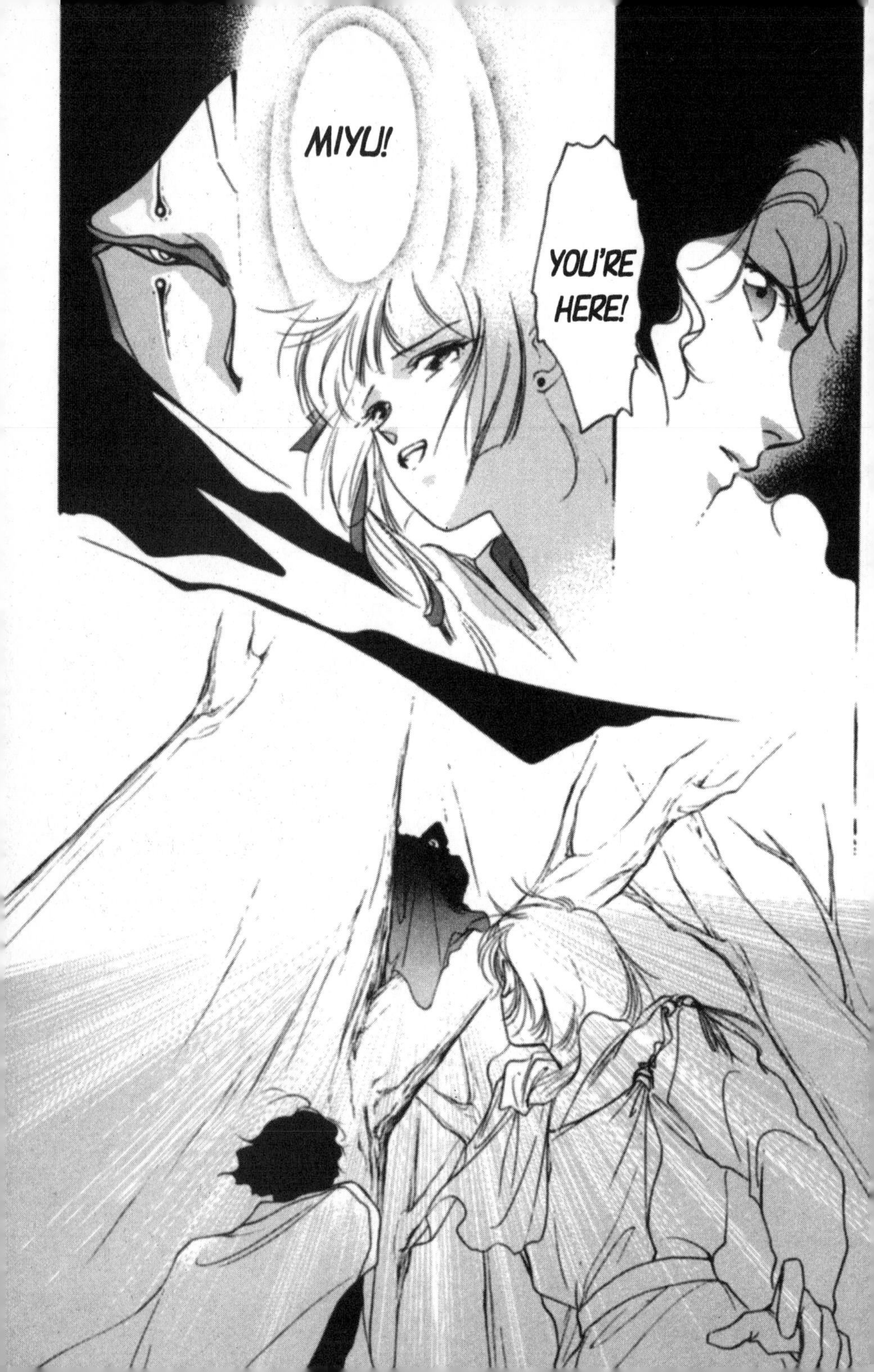
YOU'RE HERE!
MIYU!

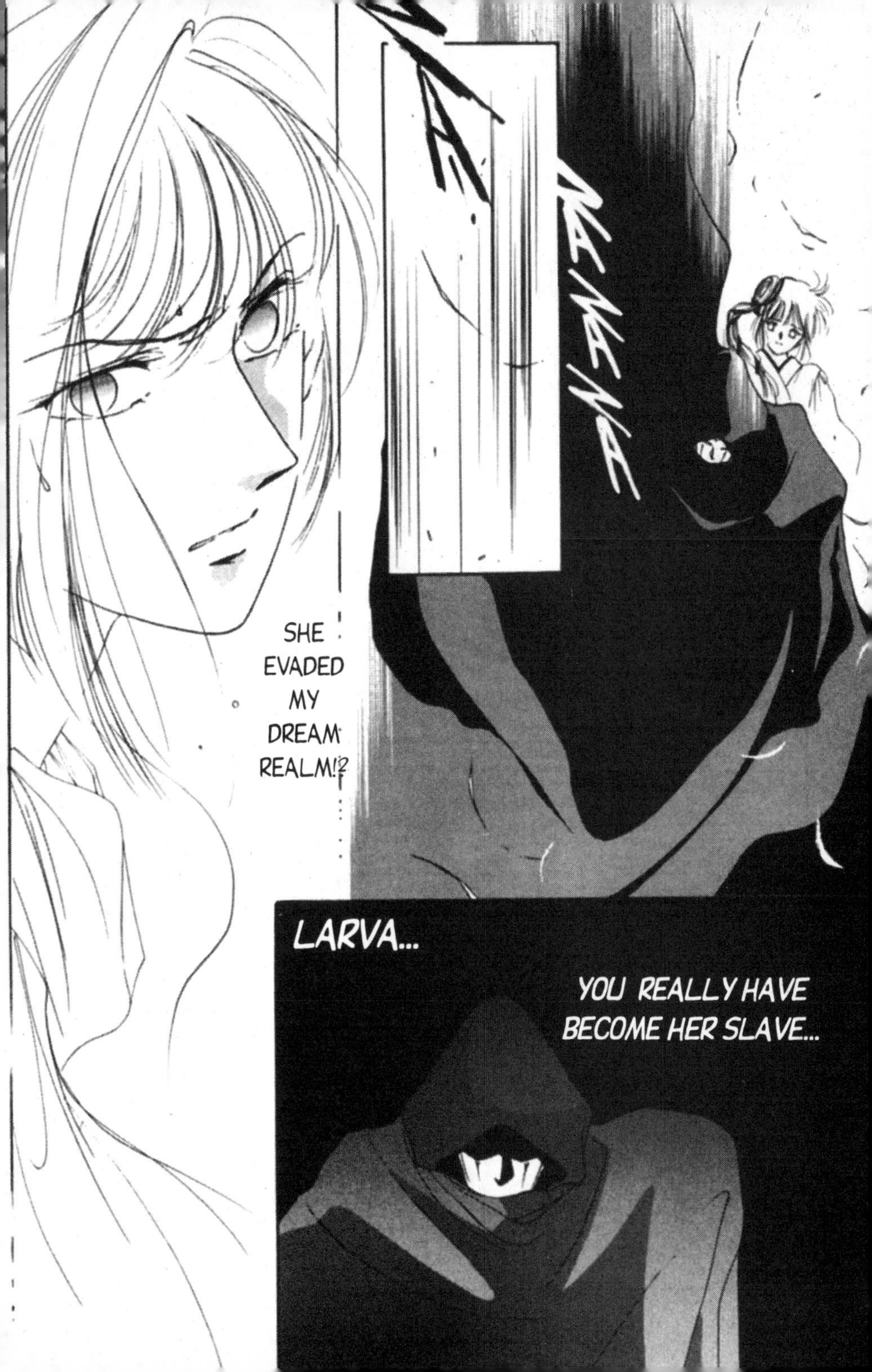

SHE EVADED MY DREAM REALM!?
LARVA...
YOU REALLY HAVE BECOME HER SLAVE...

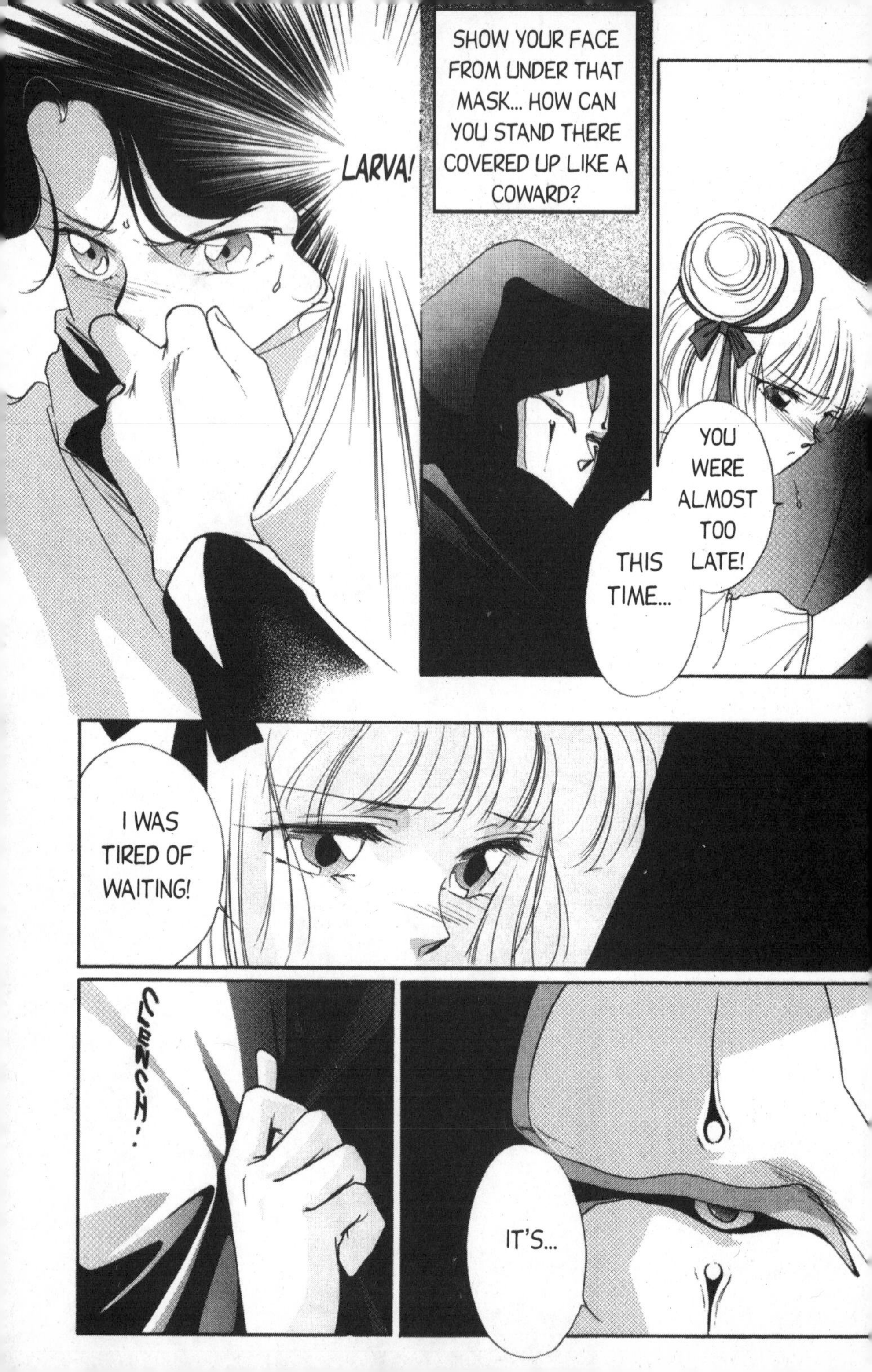
YOU WERE ALMOST TOO LATE!
THIS TIME...
SHOW YOUR FACE FROM UNDER THAT MASK... HOW CAN YOU STAND THERE COVERED UP LIKE A COWARD?
LARVA!
I WAS TIRED OF WAITING!
IT'S...
CLENCH!

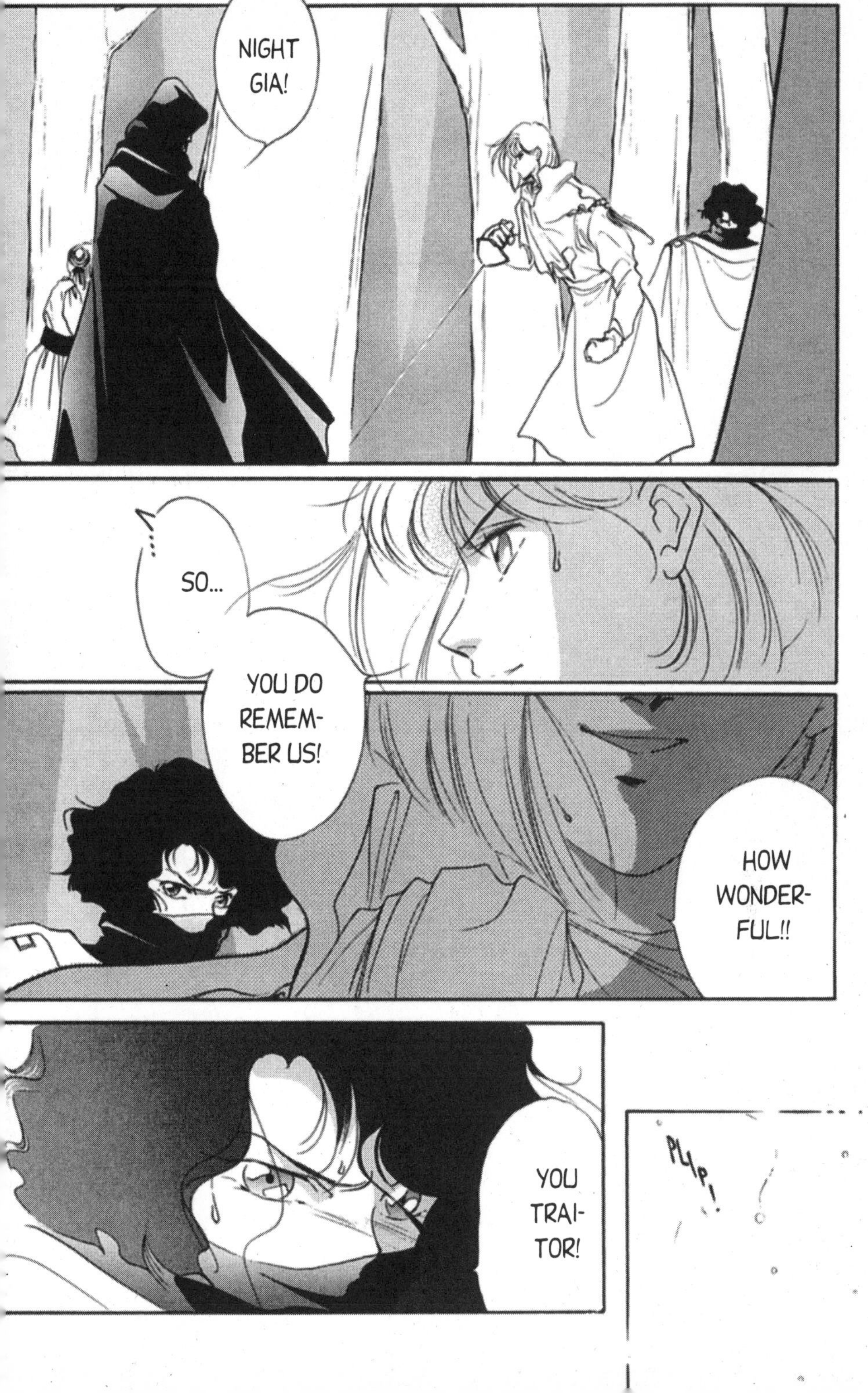
NIGHT GIA!
...
SO...
YOU DO REMEMBER US!
HOW WONDERFUL!!
YOU TRAITOR!
PLIP!

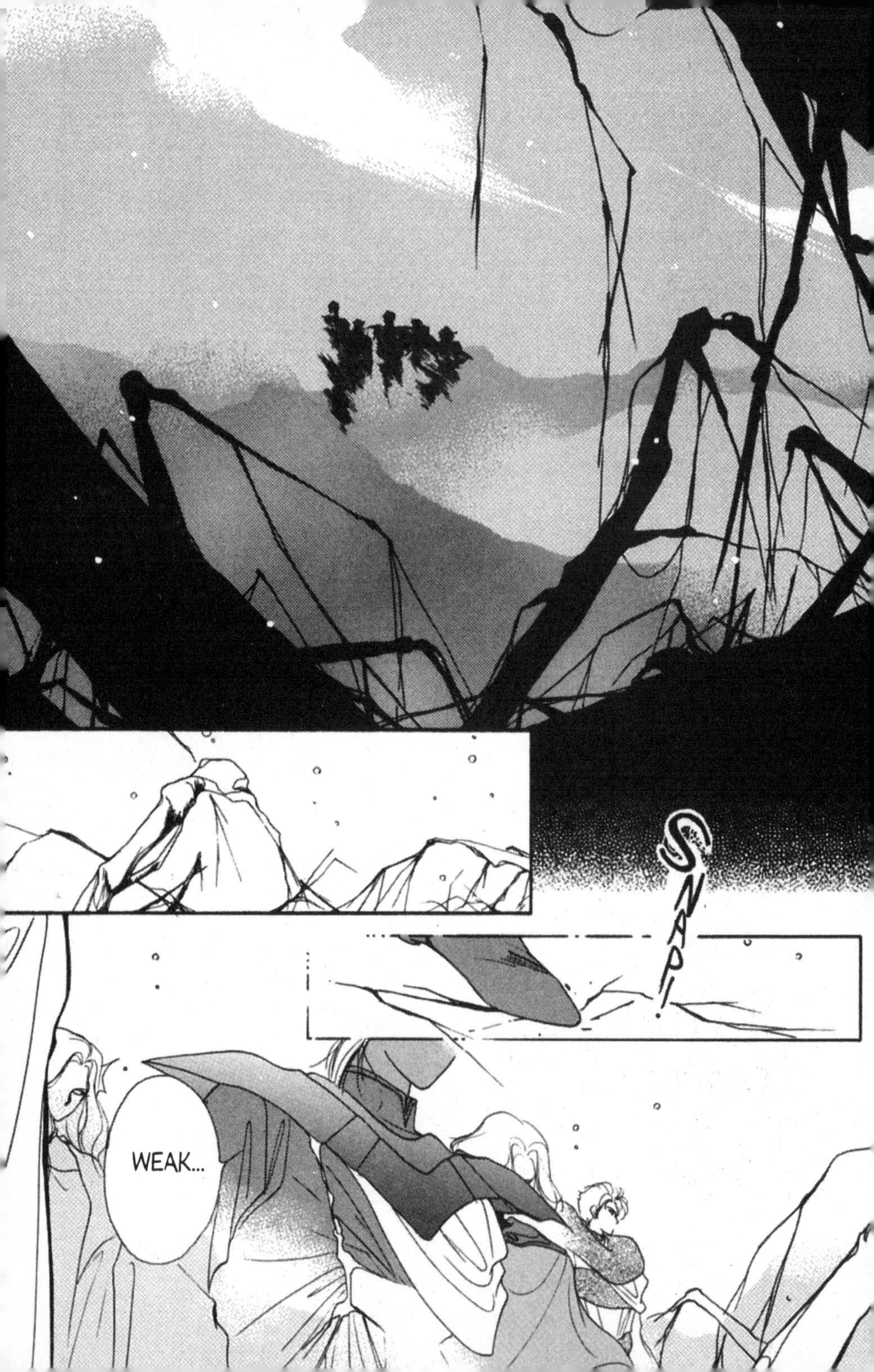
SNAP!
WEAK...

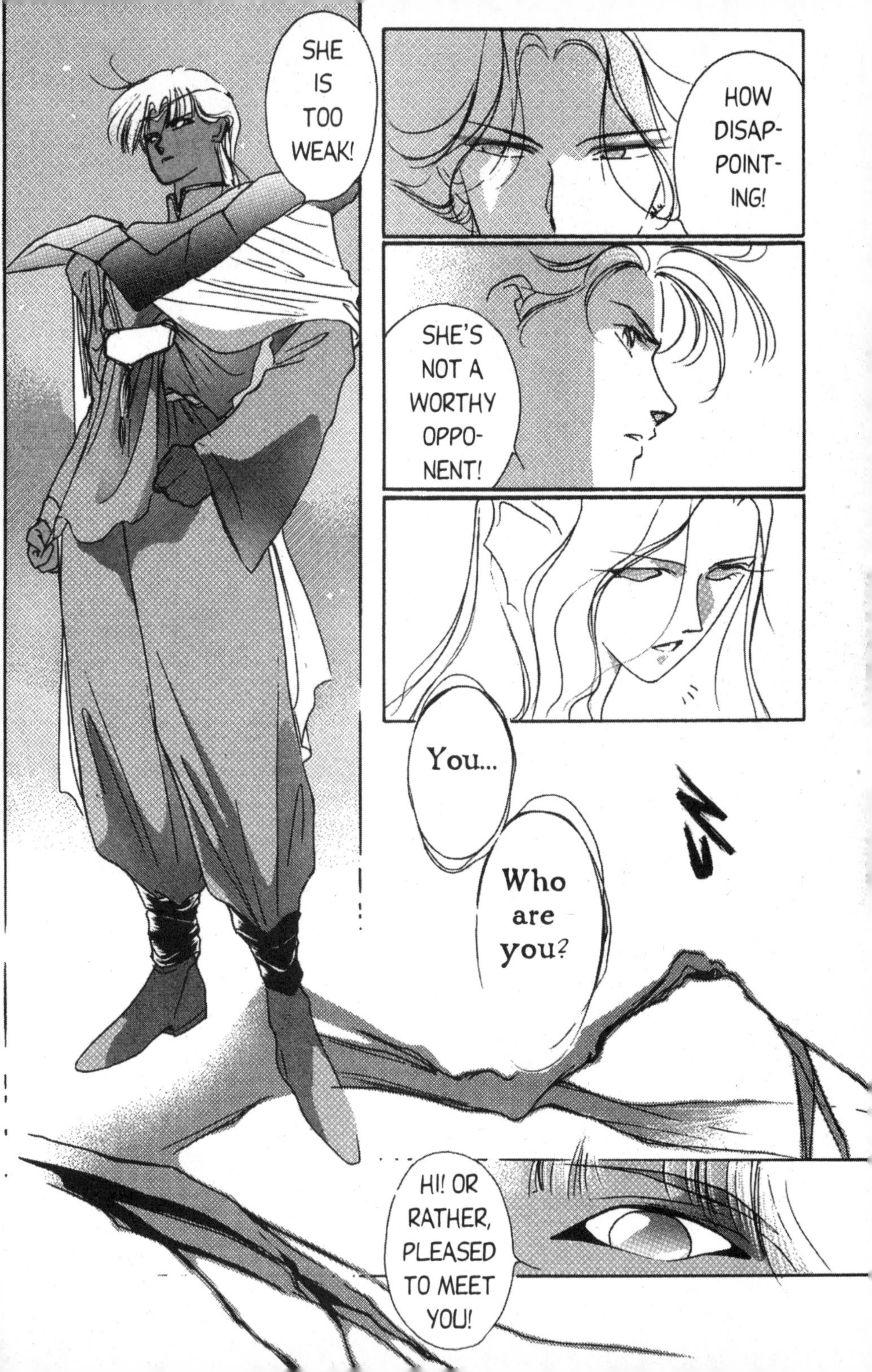
SHE IS TOO WEAK!
HOW DISAP-POINT-ING!
SHE'S NOT A WORTHY OPPO-NENT!
You...
Who are you?
HI! OR RATHER, PLEASED TO MEET YOU!

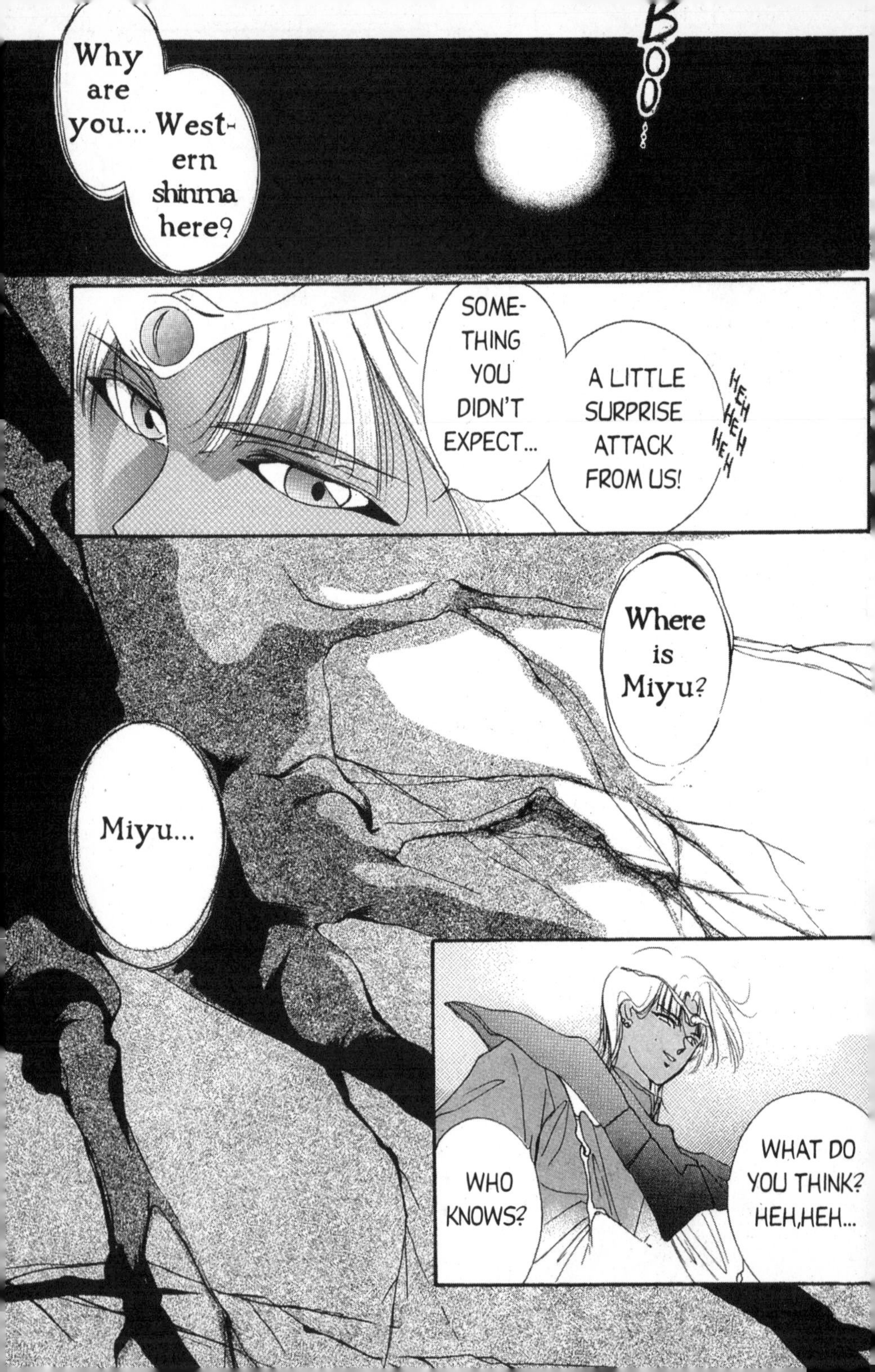
BOOO...
Why are you... Western shinma here?
SOMETHING YOU DIDN'T EXPECT...
A LITTLE SURPRISE ATTACK FROM US!
HEH HEH HEH
Where is Miyu?
Miyu...
WHAT DO YOU THINK? HEH,HEH...
WHO KNOWS?

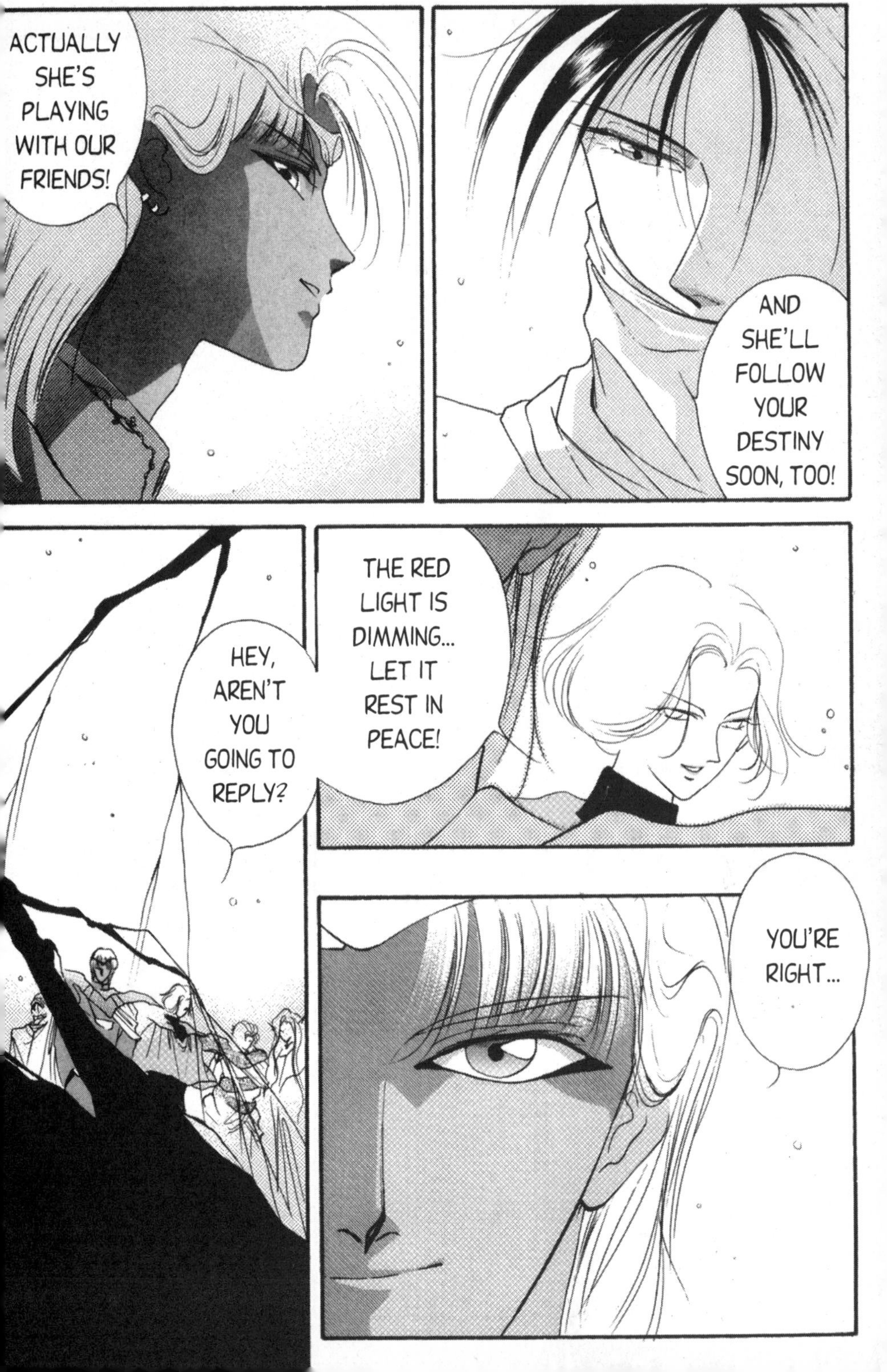

ACTUALLY SHE'S PLAYING WITH OUR FRIENDS!
AND SHE'LL FOLLOW YOUR DESTINY SOON, TOO!
THE RED LIGHT IS DIMMING... LET IT REST IN PEACE!
HEY, AREN'T YOU GOING TO REPLY?
YOU'RE RIGHT...

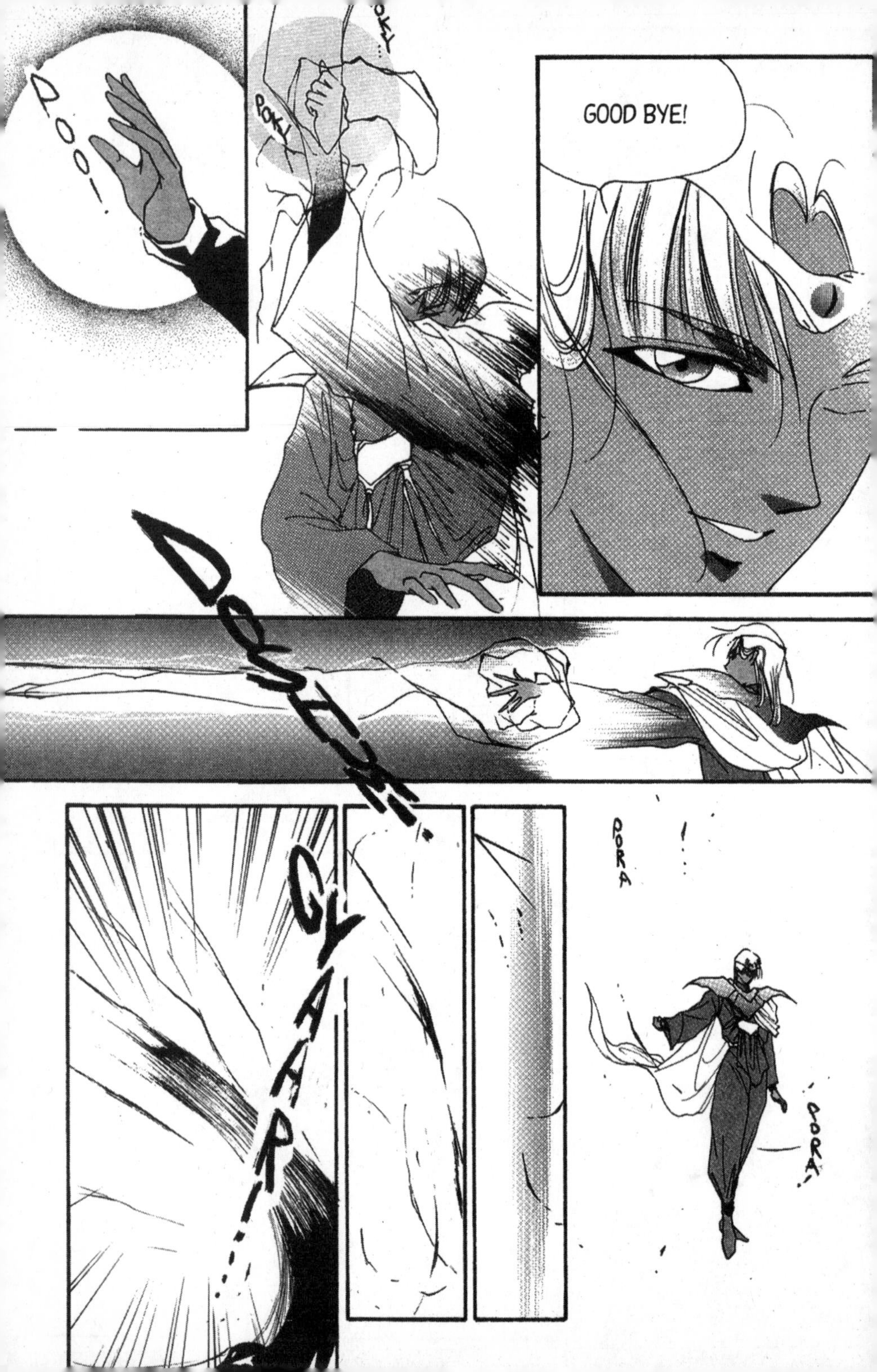
GOOD BYE!
POKY ... POKY
POOI...
DOSHUM!!
GYAAAR!...
PORA PORA

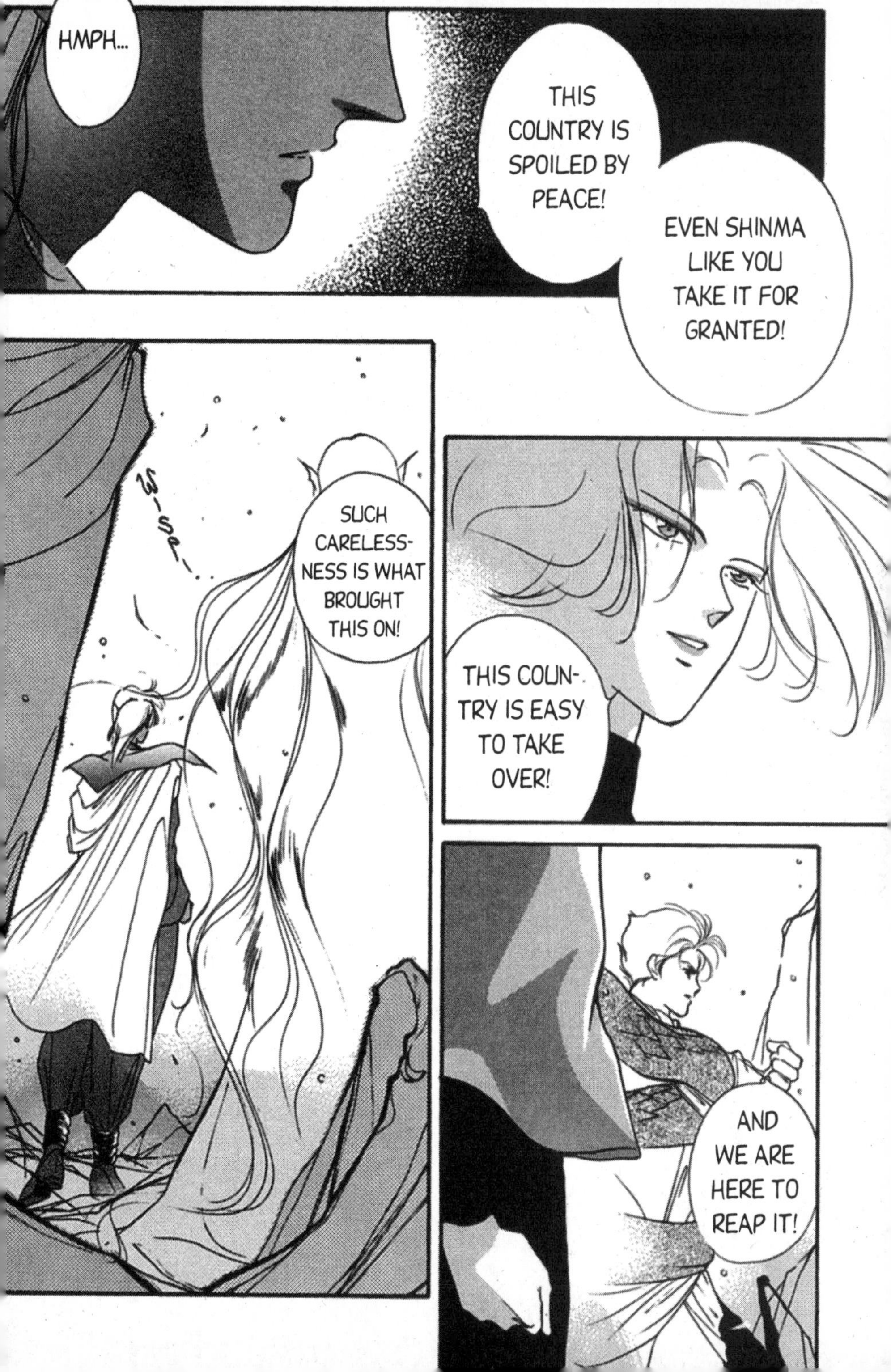
HMPH...
THIS COUNTRY IS SPOILED BY PEACE!
EVEN SHINMA LIKE YOU TAKE IT FOR GRANTED!
SUCH CARELESS-NESS IS WHAT BROUGHT THIS ON!
THIS COUN-TRY IS EASY TO TAKE OVER!
AND WE ARE HERE TO REAP IT!

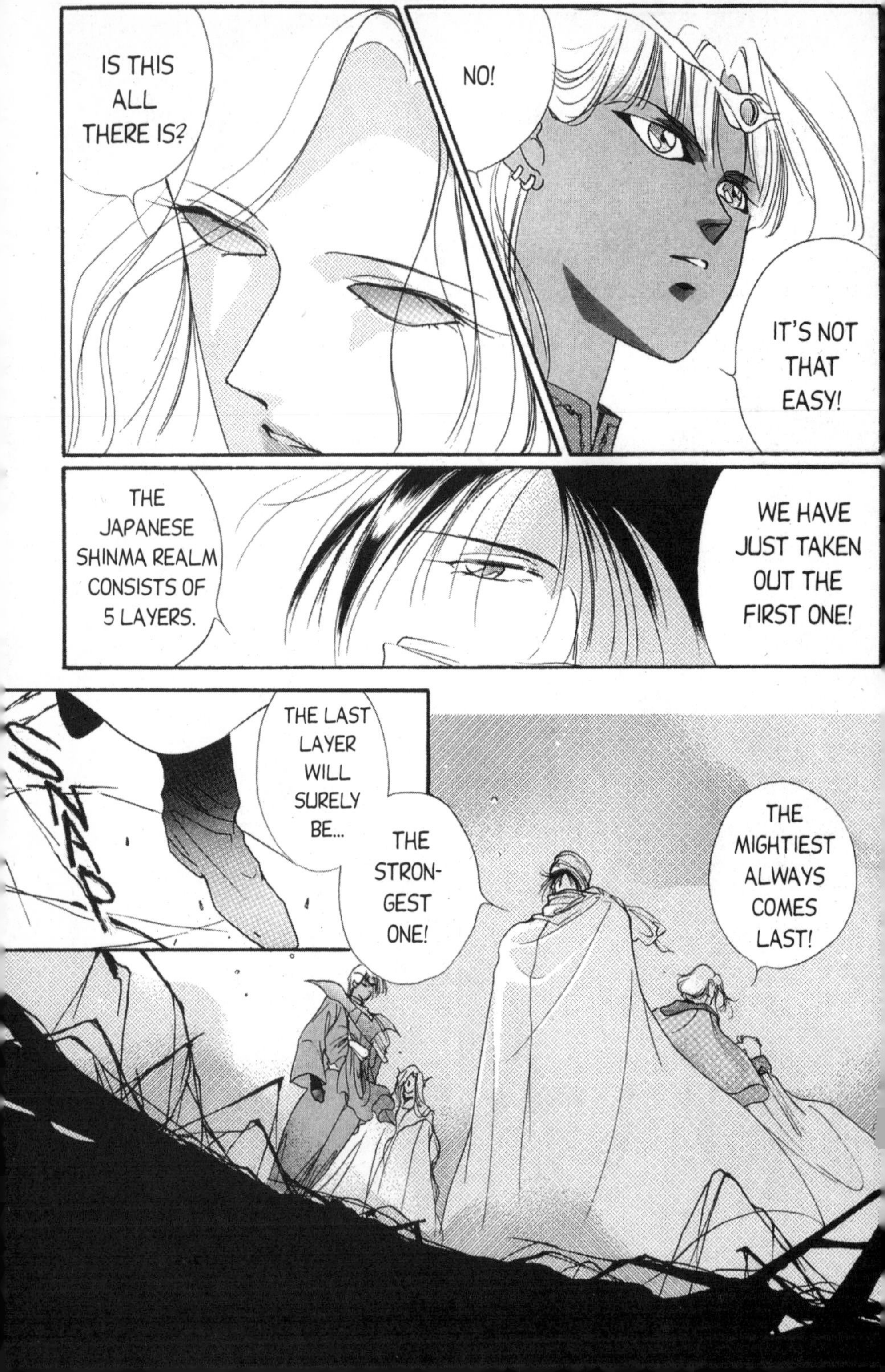
IS THIS ALL THERE IS?
NO!
IT'S NOT THAT EASY!
THE JAPANESE SHINMA REALM CONSISTS OF 5 LAYERS.
WE HAVE JUST TAKEN OUT THE FIRST ONE!
THE LAST LAYER WILL SURELY BE...
THE STRON-GEST ONE!
THE MIGHTIEST ALWAYS COMES LAST!

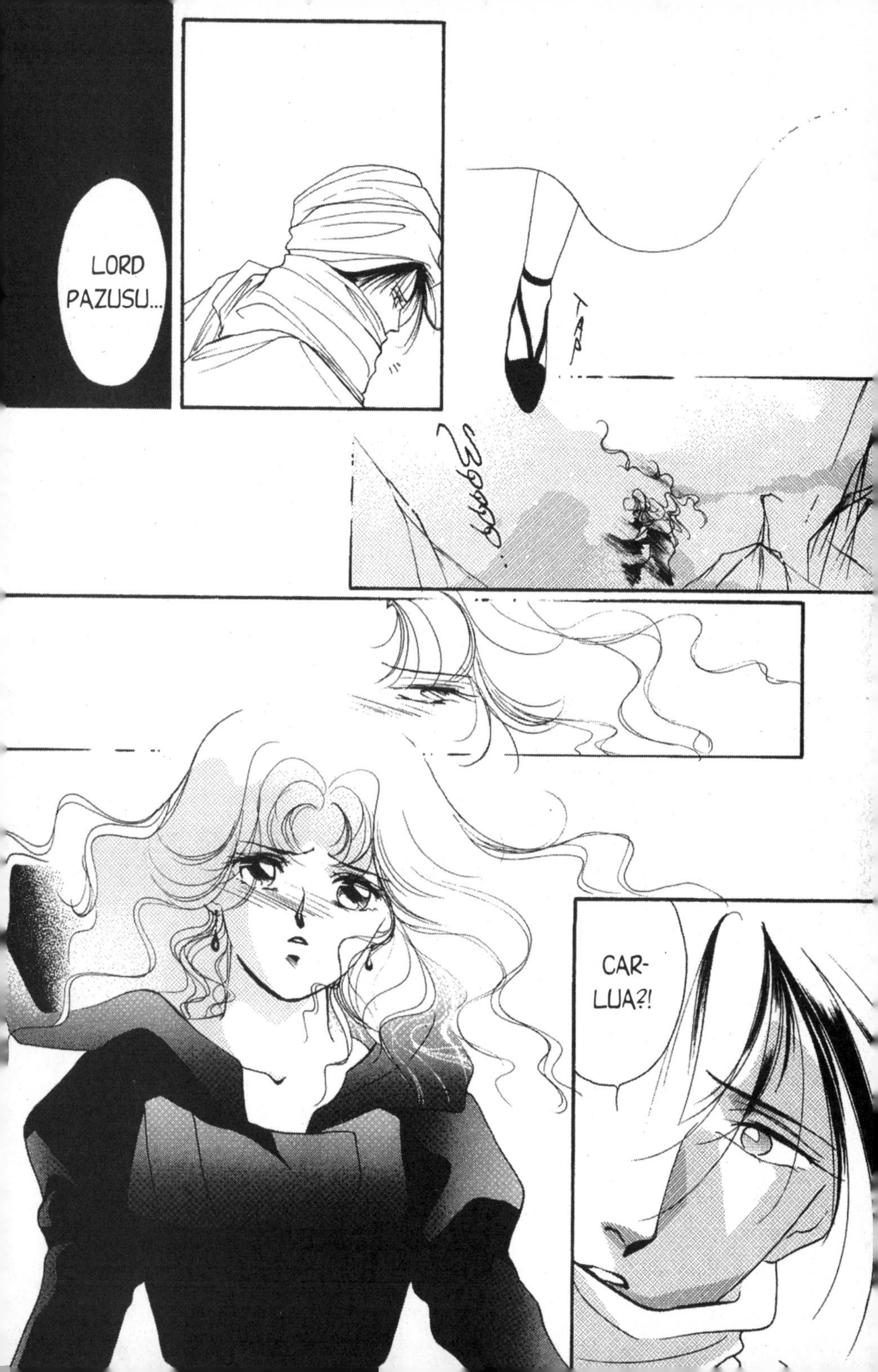
LORD PAZUSU...
TAP
Swooosh
CAR-
LUA?!

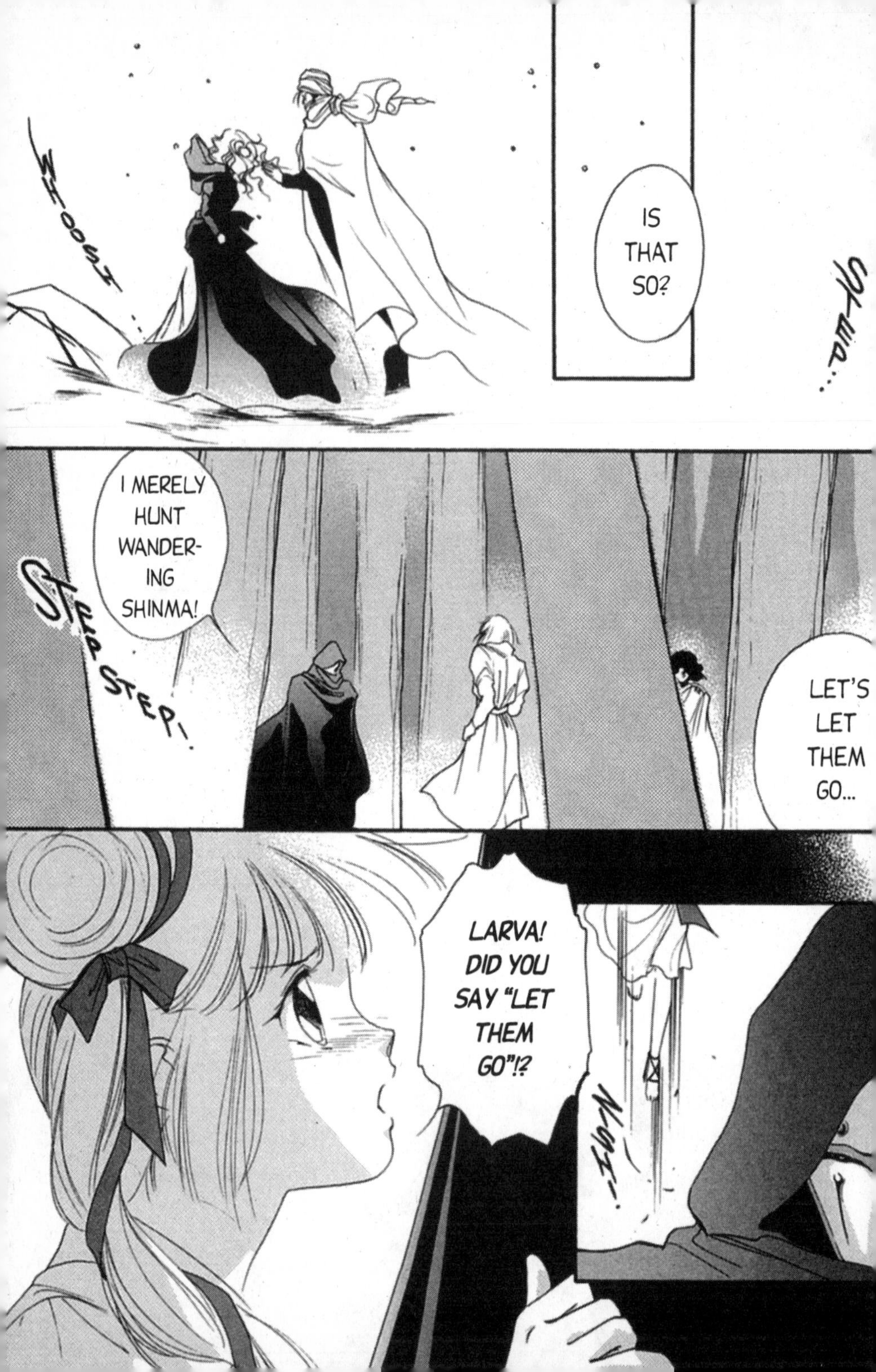
SKRID...
IS THAT SO?
WHOOSH...
LET'S LET THEM GO...
I MERELY HUNT WANDER-ING SHINMA!
STEP STEP!
LARVA! DID YOU SAY "LET THEM GO"!?
NOD...

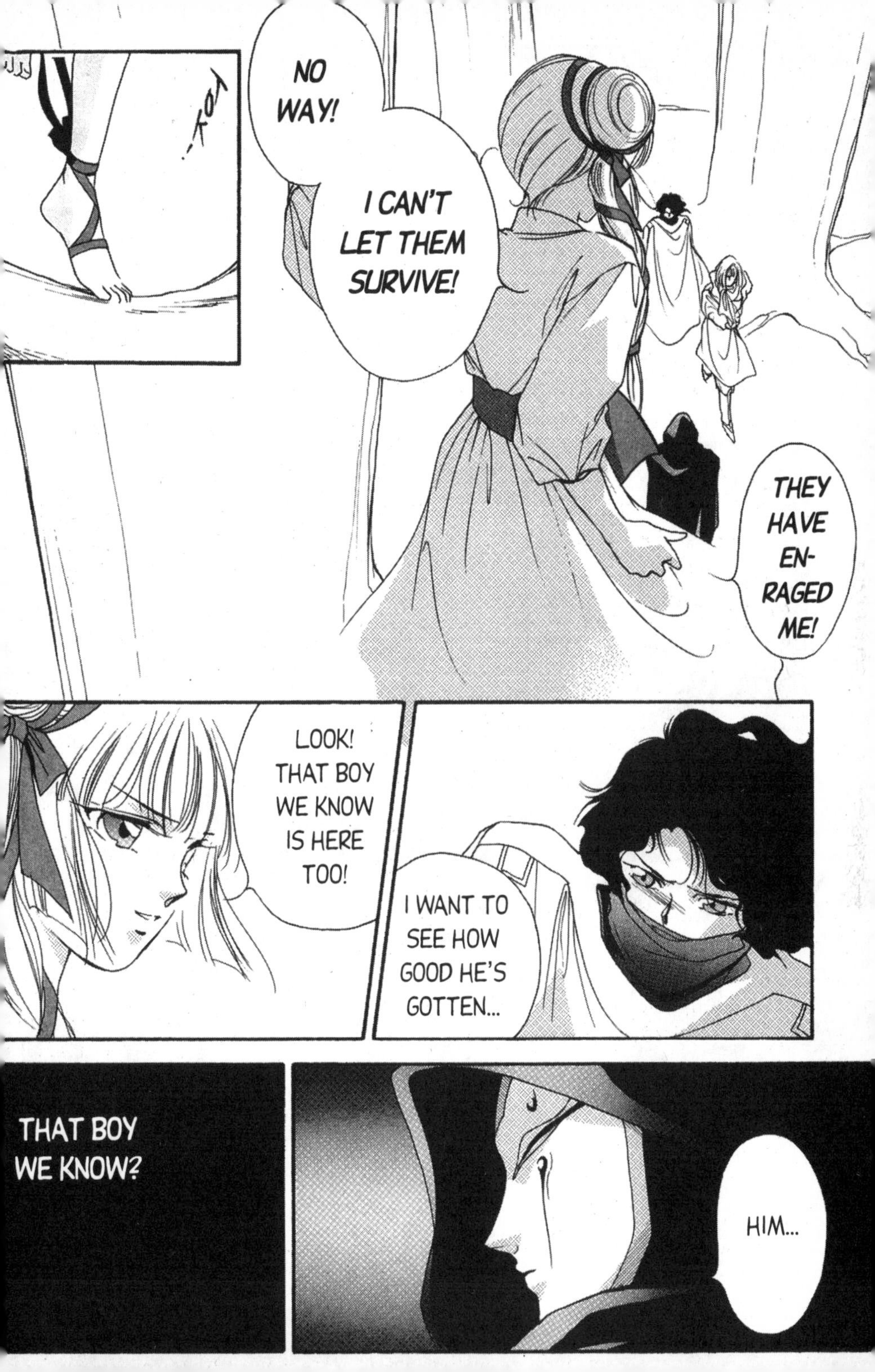
NO WAY!
I CAN'T LET THEM SURVIVE!
THEY HAVE EN-RAGED ME!
LOOK! THAT BOY WE KNOW IS HERE TOO!
I WANT TO SEE HOW GOOD HE'S GOTTEN...
THAT BOY WE KNOW?
HIM...

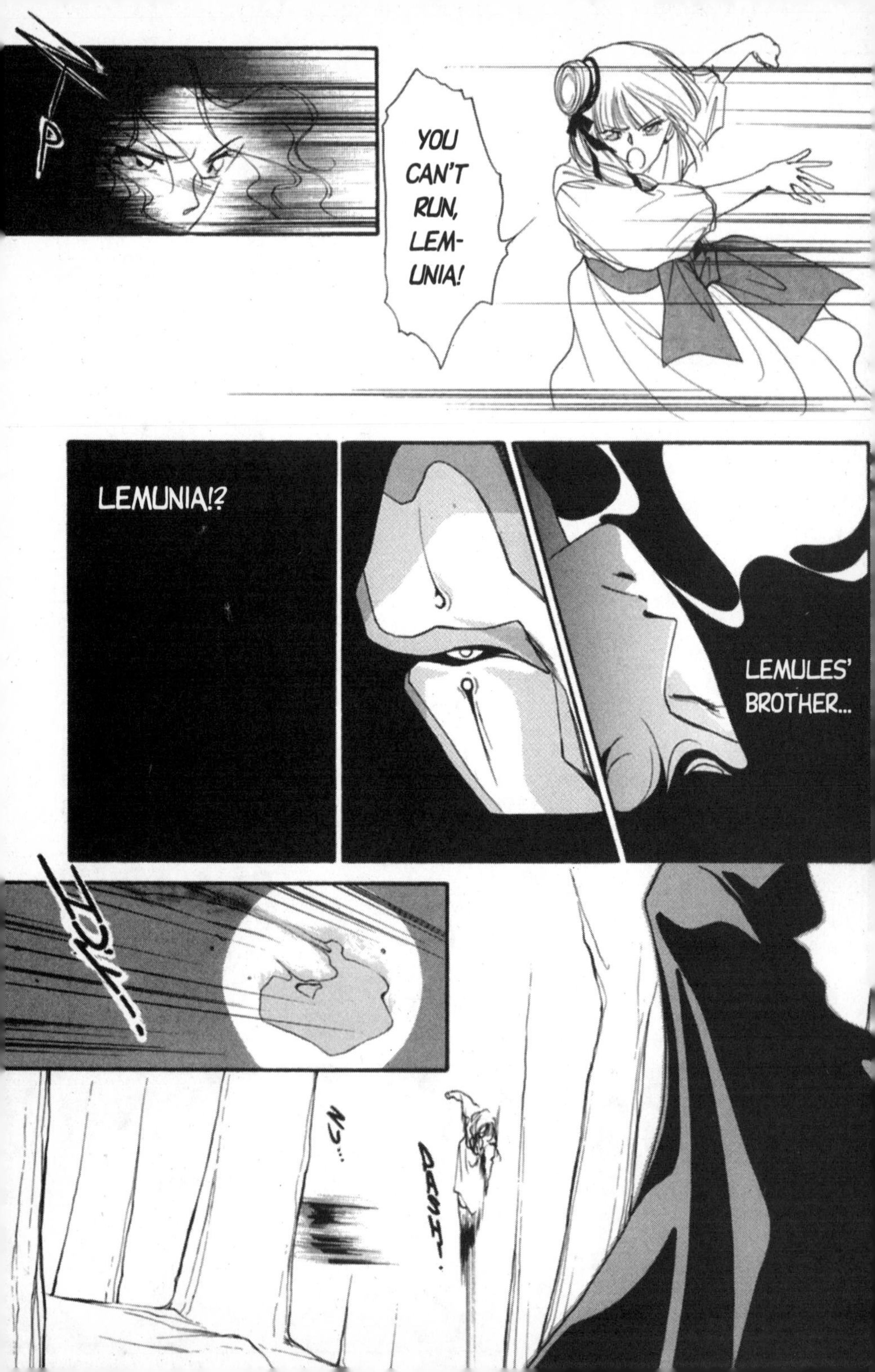
YOU CAN'T RUN, LEMUNIA!
LEMULES' BROTHER...
LEMUNIA!?

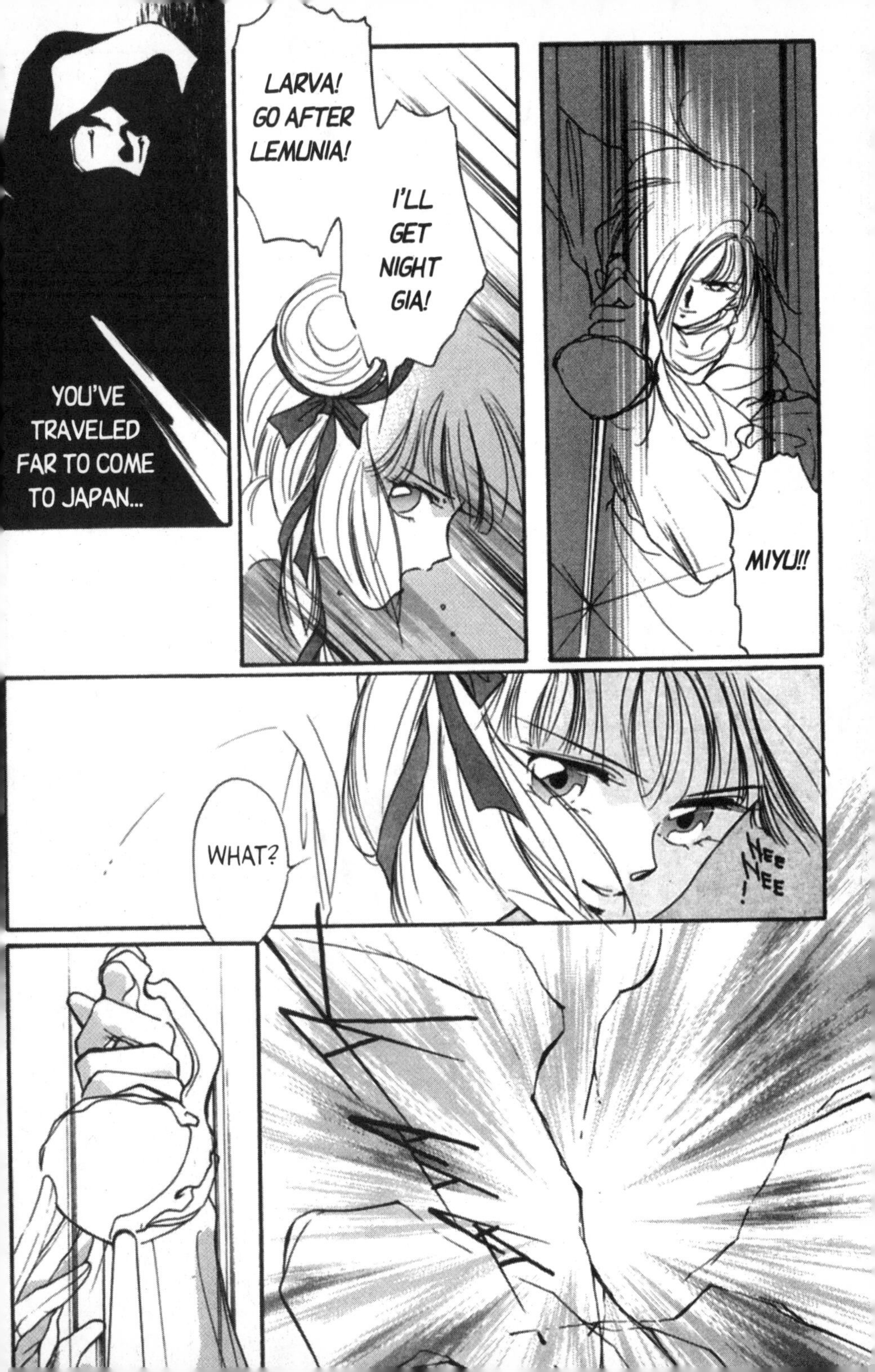
YOU'VE TRAVELED FAR TO COME TO JAPAN...
LARVA! GO AFTER LEMUNIA!
I'LL GET NIGHT GIA!
MIYU!!
WHAT?
HEE HEE!

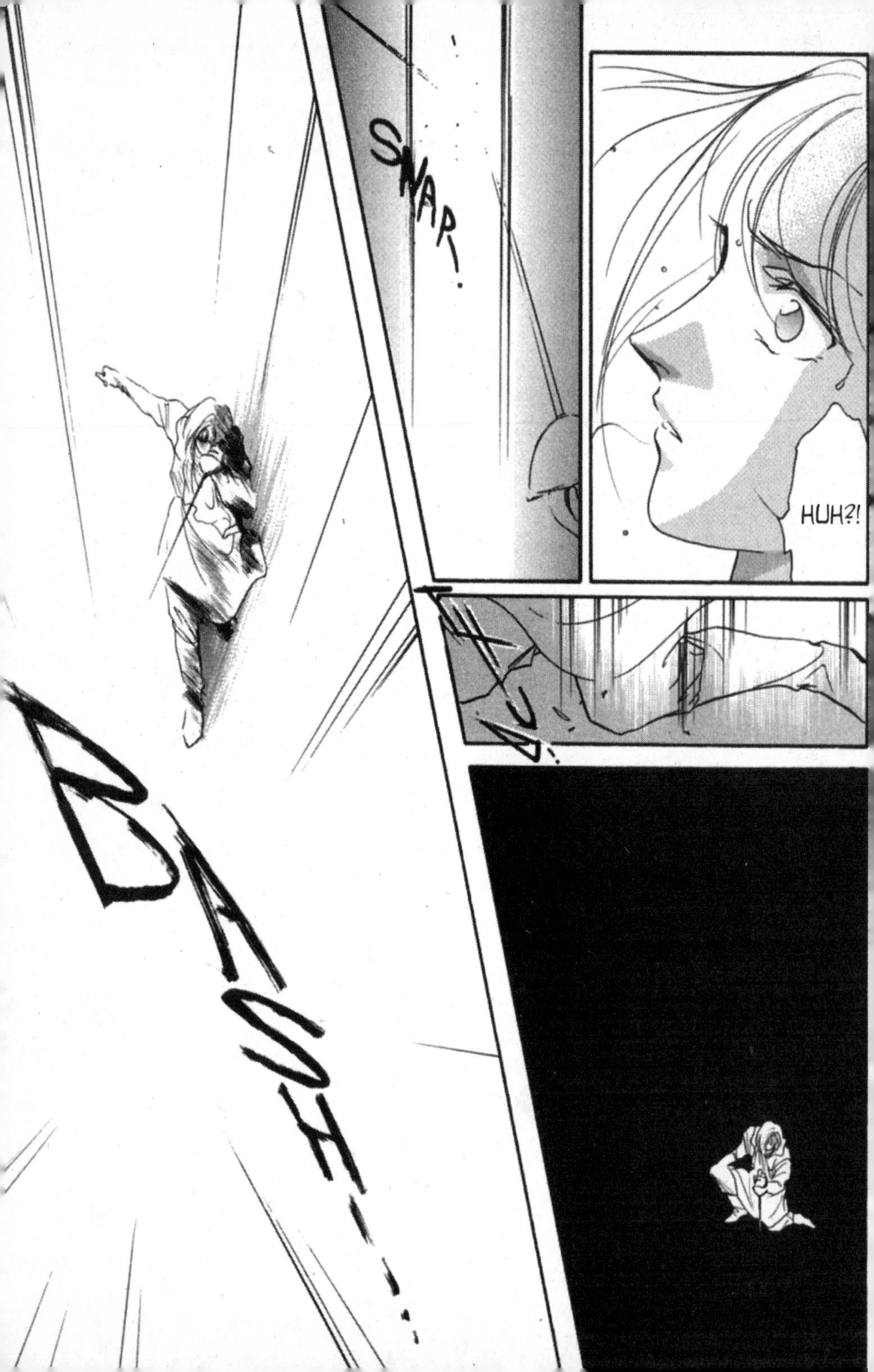
HUH?!
SNAP!
THUD!
BDASH...

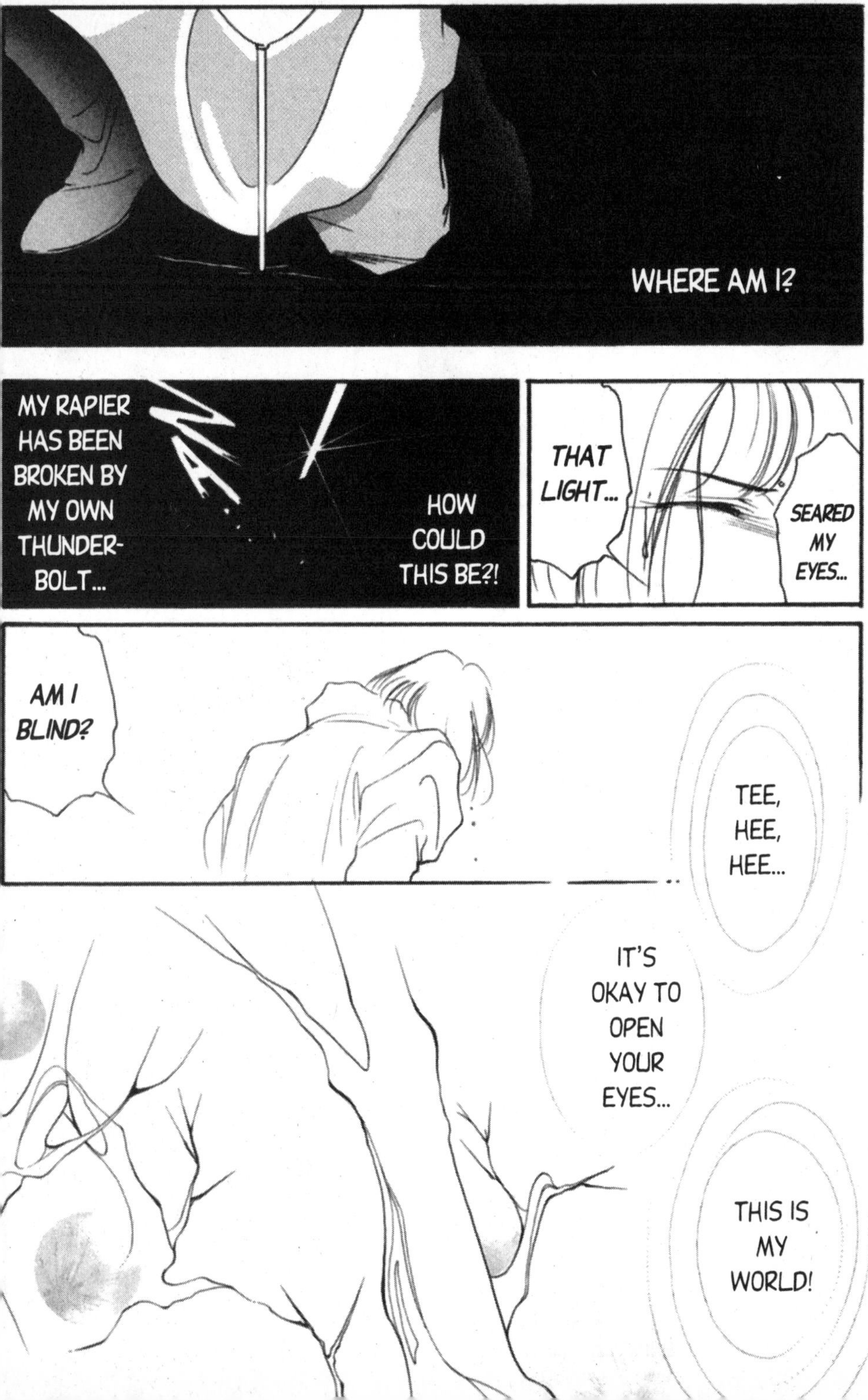
WHERE AM I?
MY RAPIER HAS BEEN BROKEN BY MY OWN THUNDERBOLT...
HOW COULD THIS BE?!
THAT LIGHT...
SEARED MY EYES...
AM I BLIND?
TEE, HEE, HEE...
IT'S OKAY TO OPEN YOUR EYES...
THIS IS MY WORLD!

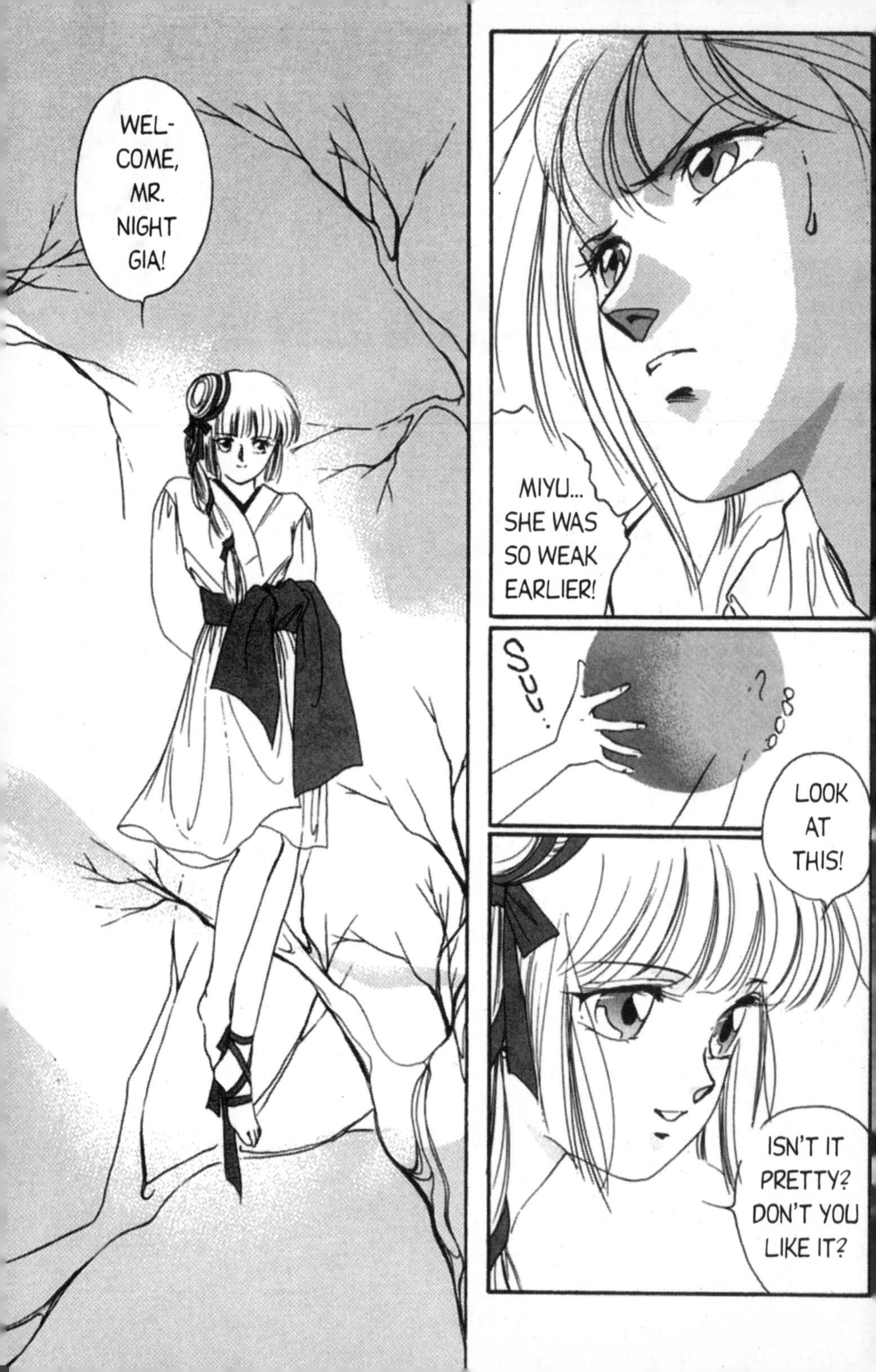
WEL-COME, MR. NIGHT GIA!
MIYU... SHE WAS SO WEAK EARLIER!
SUUU...
LOOK AT THIS!
ISN'T IT PRETTY? DON'T YOU LIKE IT?

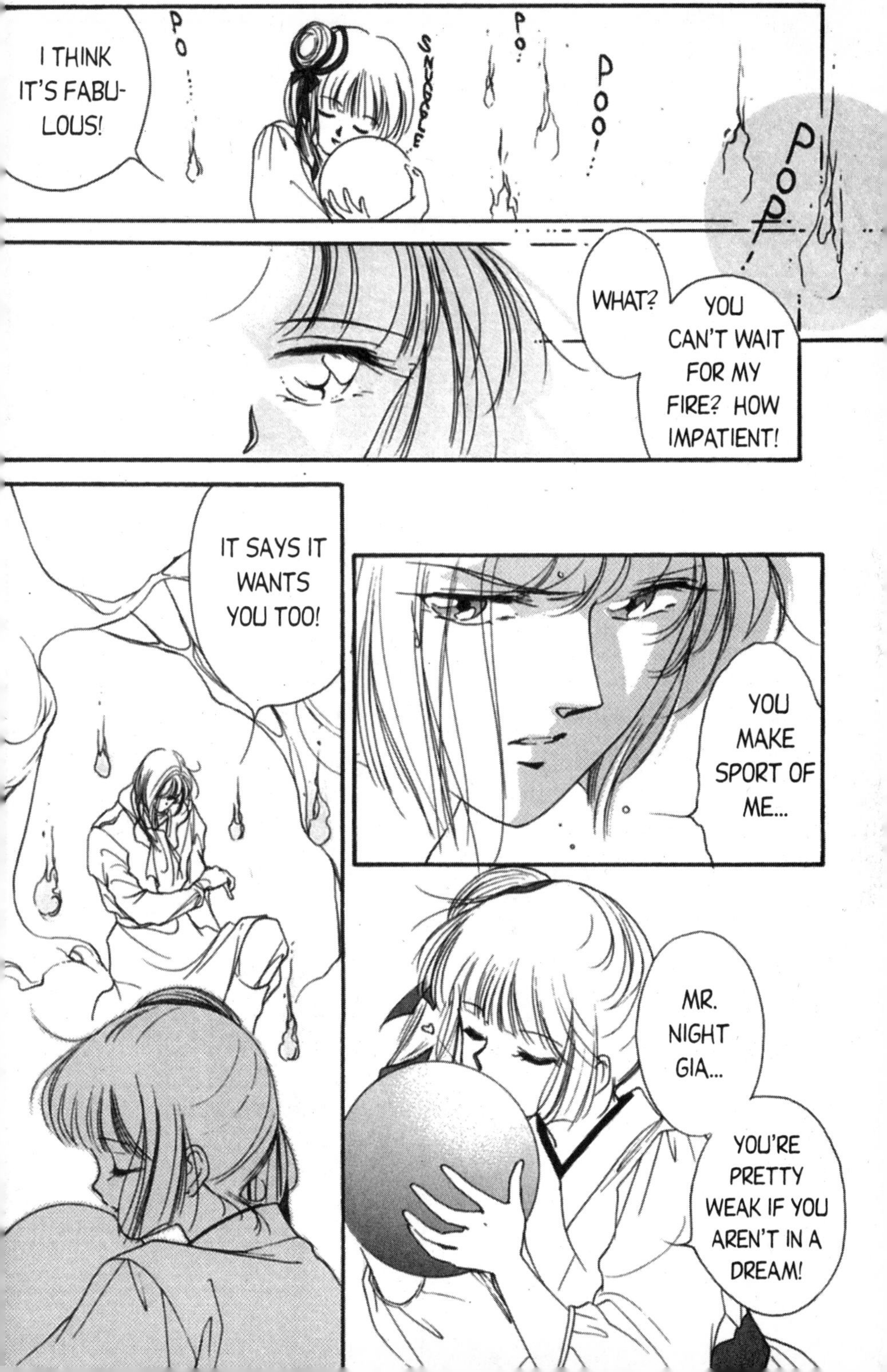
I THINK IT'S FABULOUS!
PO...
PO...
POO...
POP!
WHAT?
YOU CAN'T WAIT FOR MY FIRE? HOW IMPATIENT!
IT SAYS IT WANTS YOU TOO!
YOU MAKE SPORT OF ME...
MR. NIGHT GIA...
YOU'RE PRETTY WEAK IF YOU AREN'T IN A DREAM!

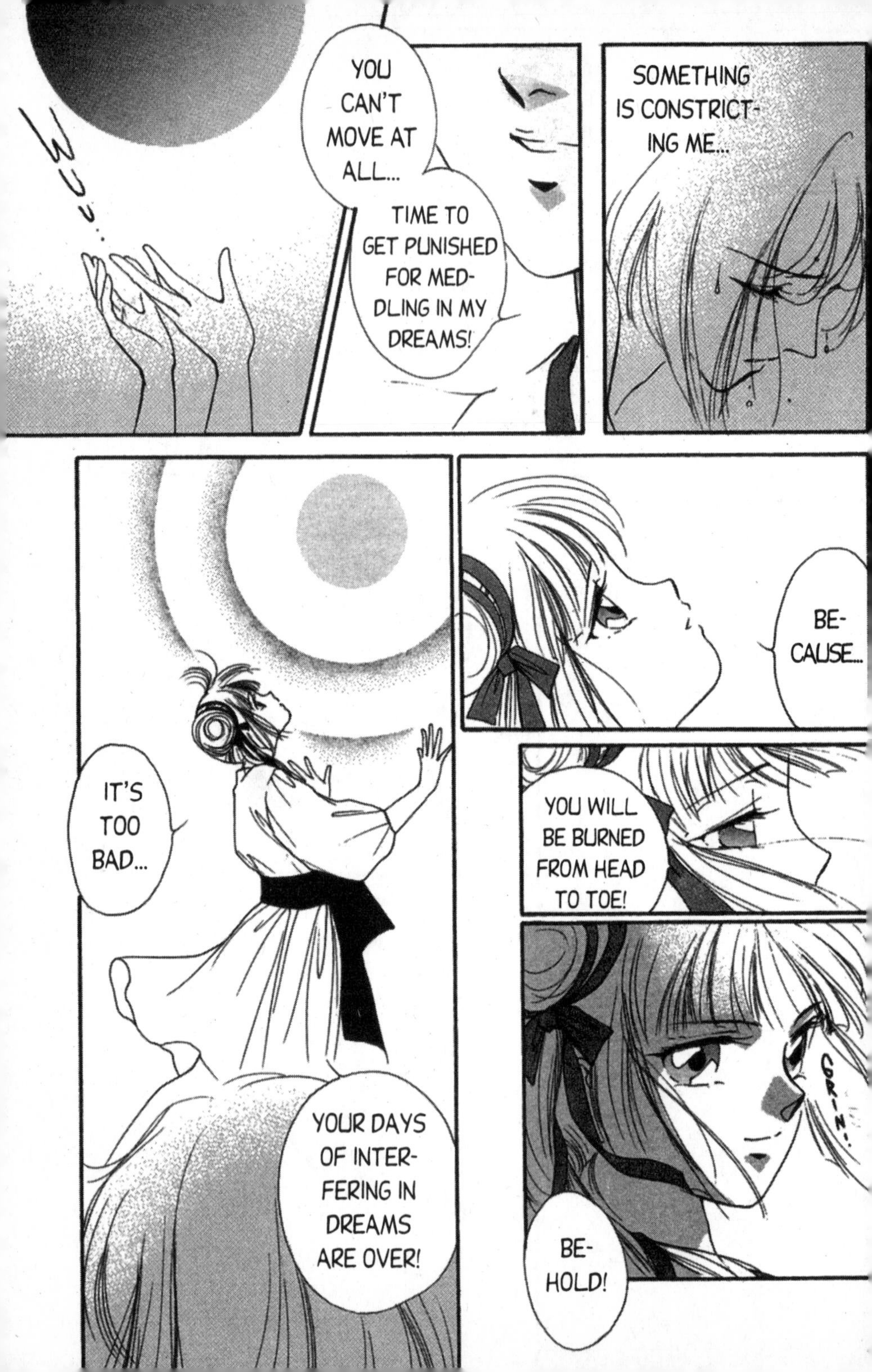
WUU...
YOU CAN'T MOVE AT ALL...
TIME TO GET PUNISHED FOR MED-DLING IN MY DREAMS!
SOMETHING IS CONSTRICT-ING ME...
IT'S TOO BAD...
BE-CAUSE...
YOU WILL BE BURNED FROM HEAD TO TOE!
GRIN..
BE-HOLD!
YOUR DAYS OF INTER-FERING IN DREAMS ARE OVER!

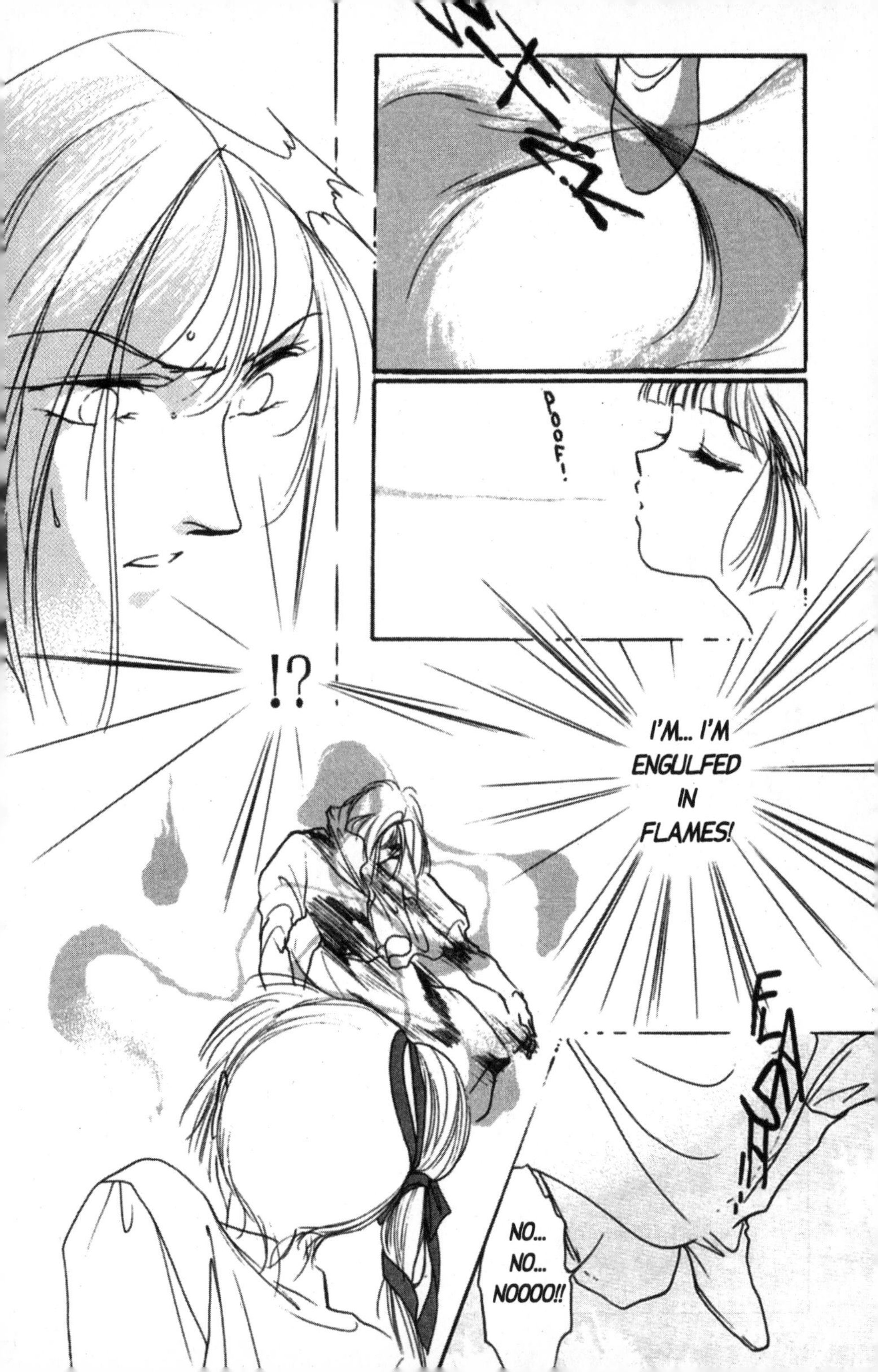
POOF!
!?
I'M... I'M ENGULFED IN FLAMES!
FLASH!!
NO... NO... NOOOO!!

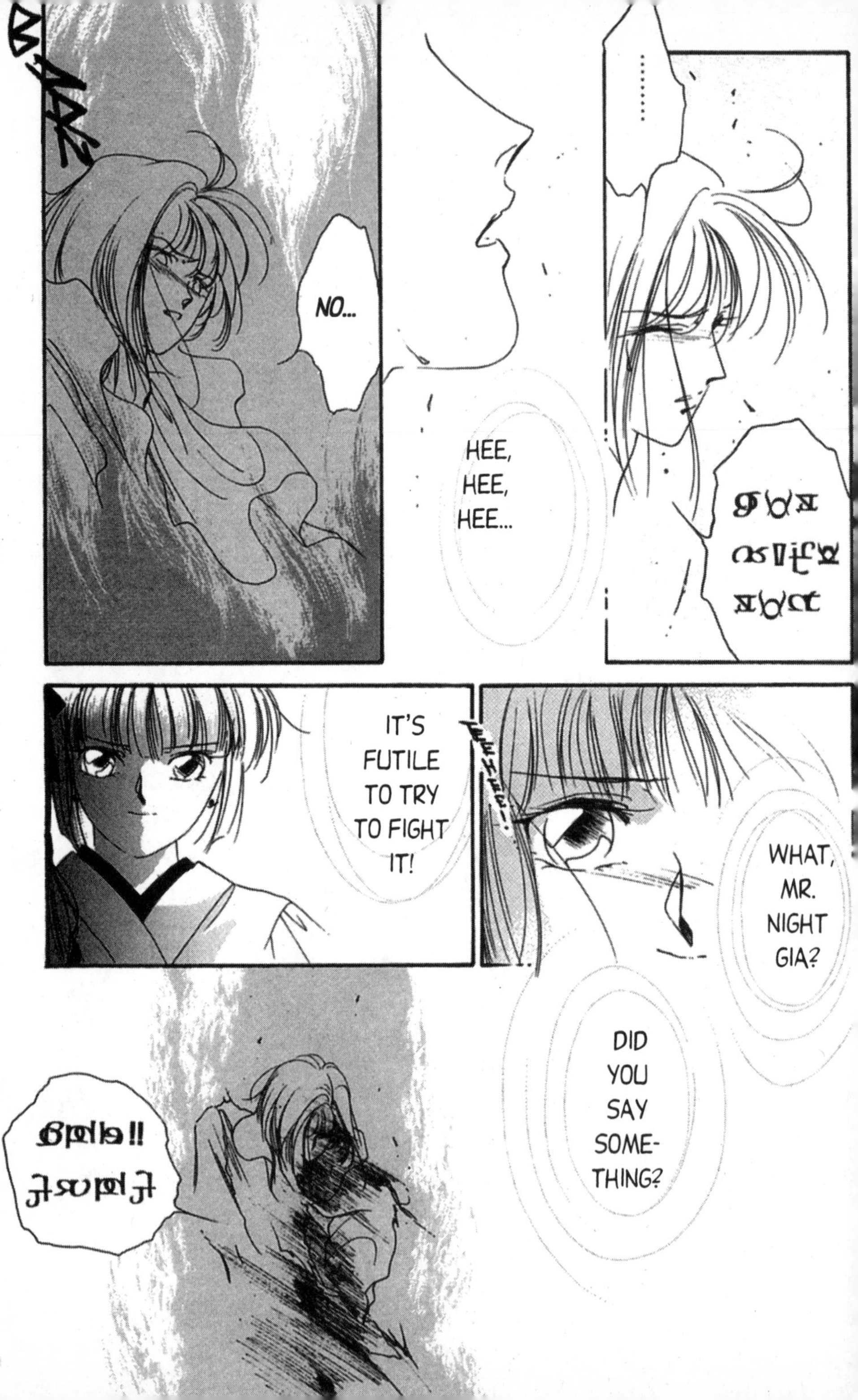
......
HEE, HEE, HEE...
NO...
WHAT, MR. NIGHT GIA?
IT'S FUTILE TO TRY TO FIGHT IT!
DID YOU SAY SOME-THING?

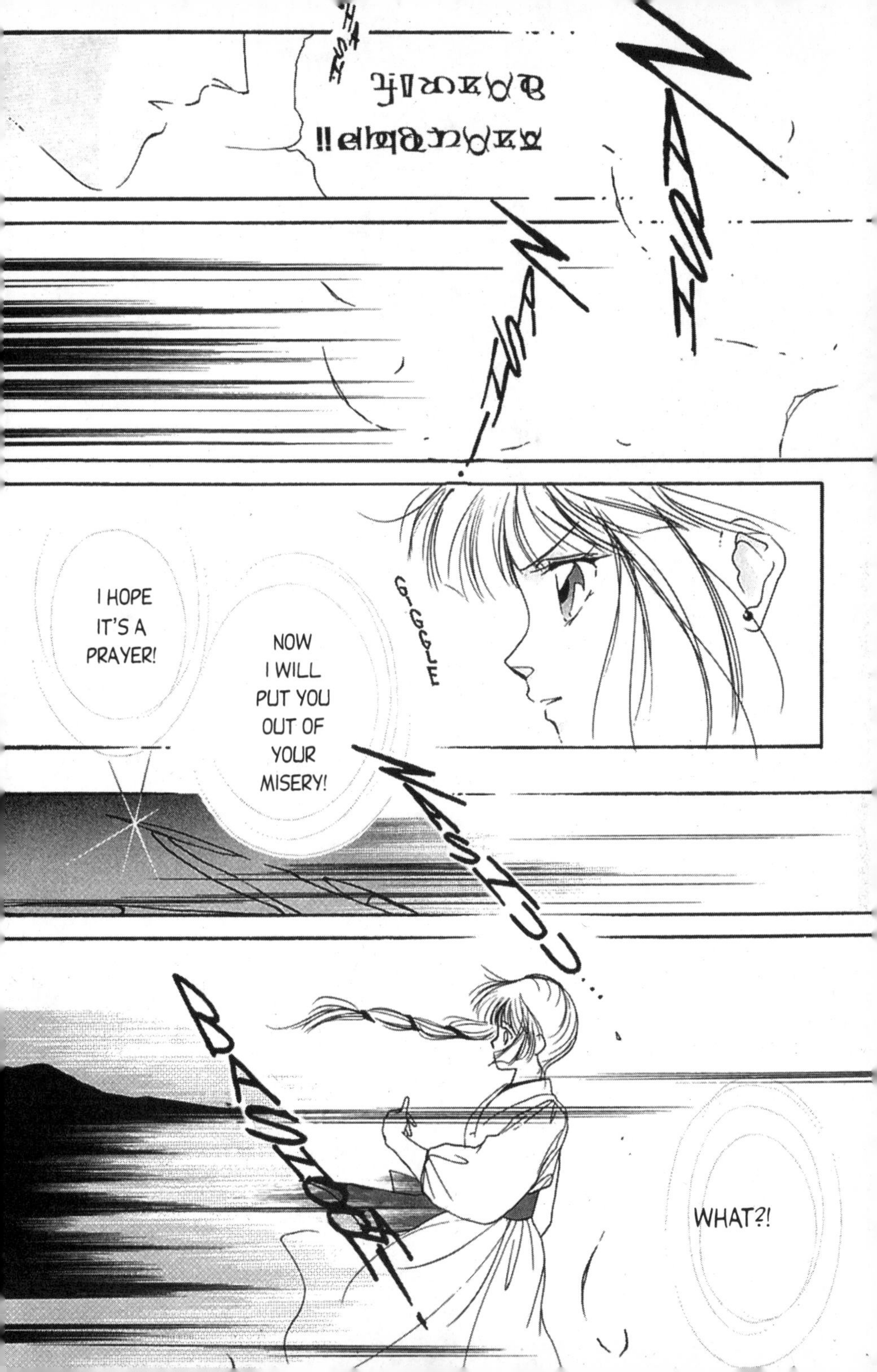
NOW I WILL PUT YOU OUT OF YOUR MISERY!
I HOPE IT'S A PRAYER!
WHAT?!

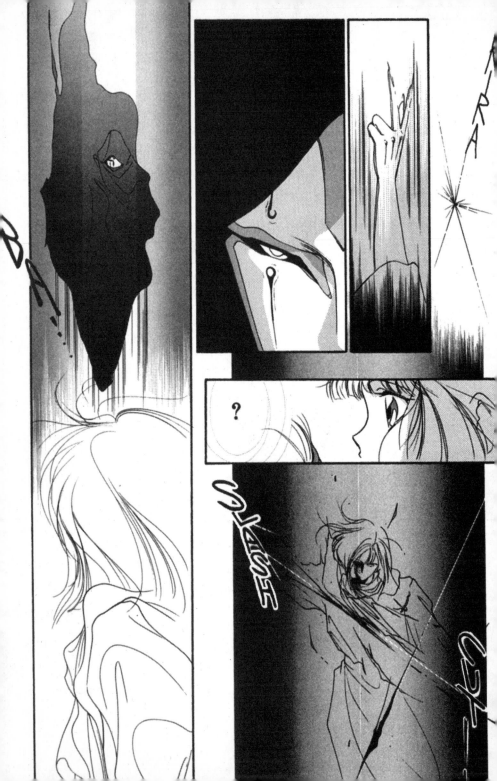

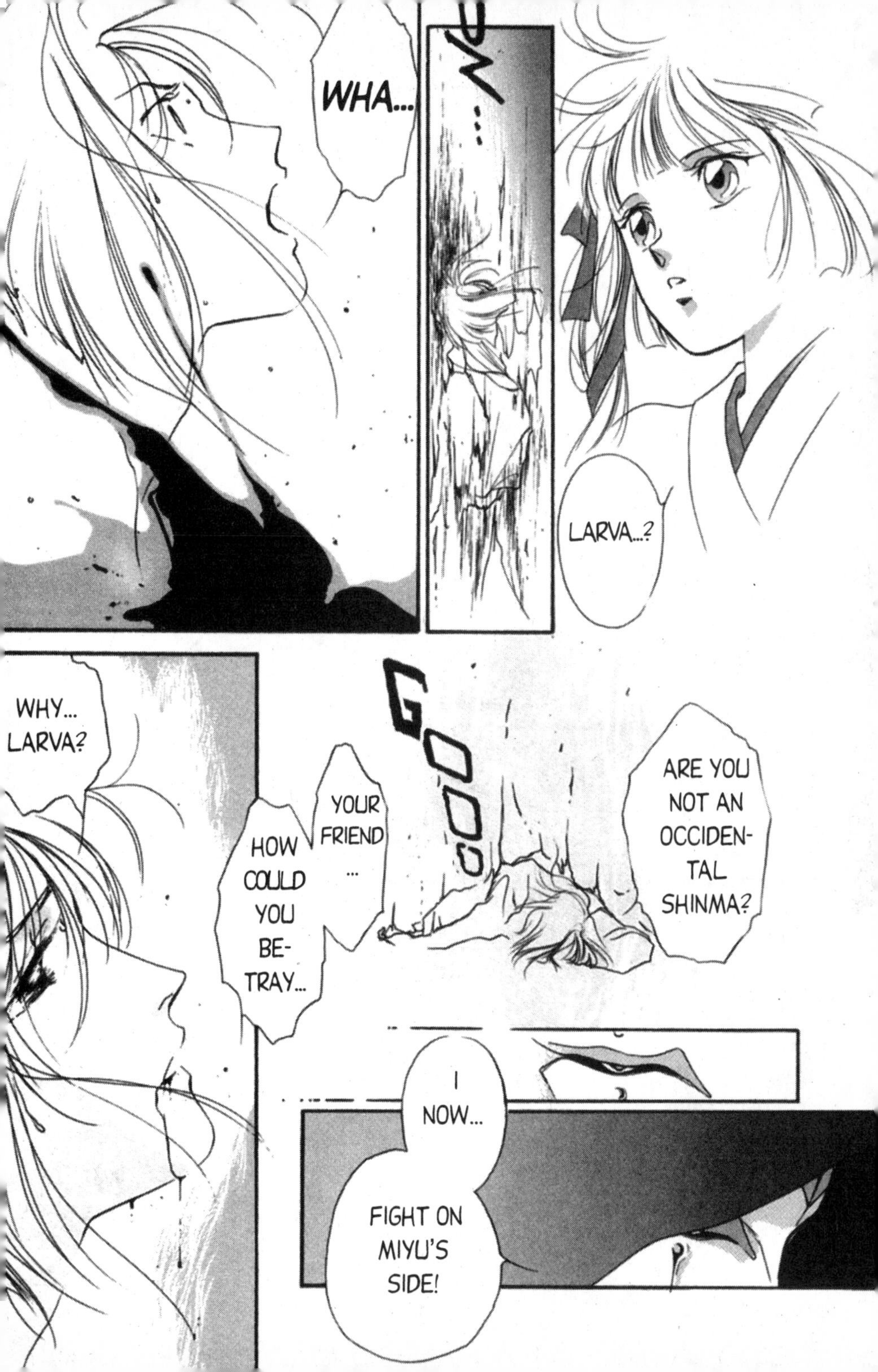
WHA...
LARVA...?
WHY... LARVA?
HOW COULD YOU BE-TRAY...
YOUR FRIEND ...
GOOO
ARE YOU NOT AN OCCIDEN-TAL SHINMA?
I NOW...
FIGHT ON MIYU'S SIDE!

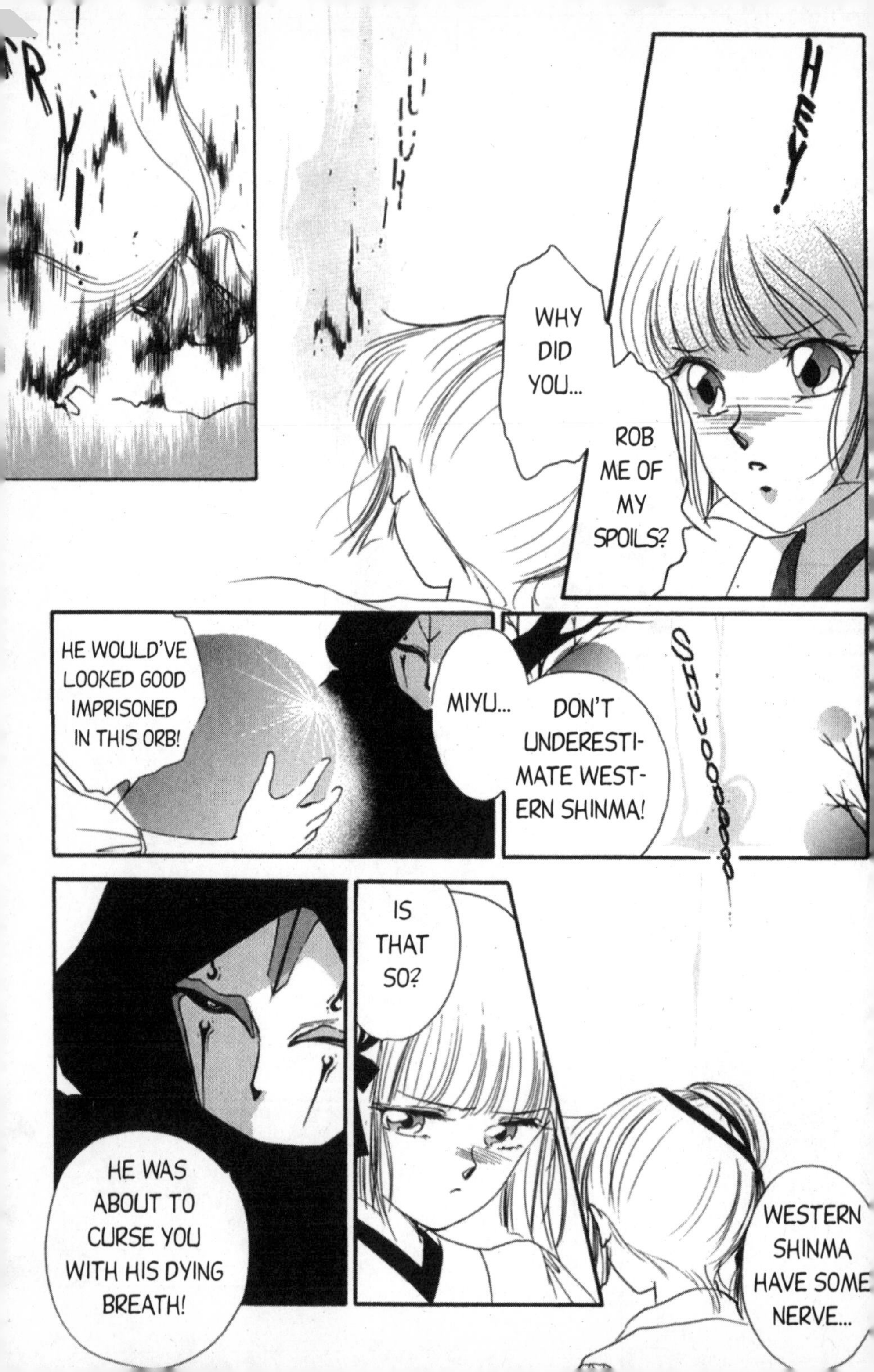
HEY!
WHY DID YOU...
ROB ME OF MY SPOILS?
MIYU...
DON'T UNDERESTI-MATE WEST-ERN SHINMA!
HE WOULD'VE LOOKED GOOD IMPRISONED IN THIS ORB!
IS THAT SO?
WESTERN SHINMA HAVE SOME NERVE...
HE WAS ABOUT TO CURSE YOU WITH HIS DYING BREATH!

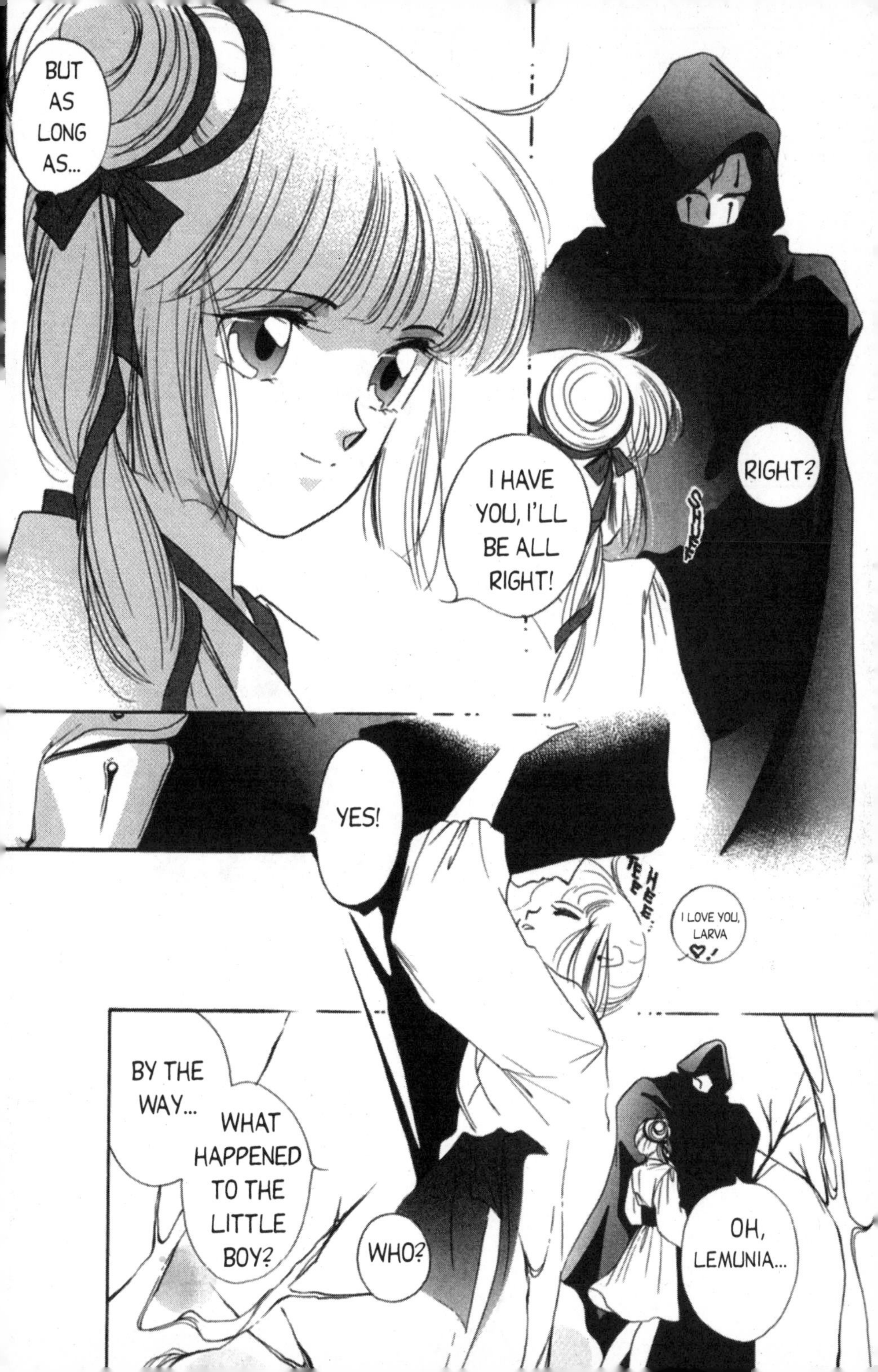
BUT AS LONG AS...
I HAVE YOU, I'LL BE ALL RIGHT!
RIGHT?
SHUFF
YES!
TEE HEE...
I LOVE YOU, LARVA ♡!
BY THE WAY...
WHAT HAPPENED TO THE LITTLE BOY?
WHO?
OH, LEMUNIA...

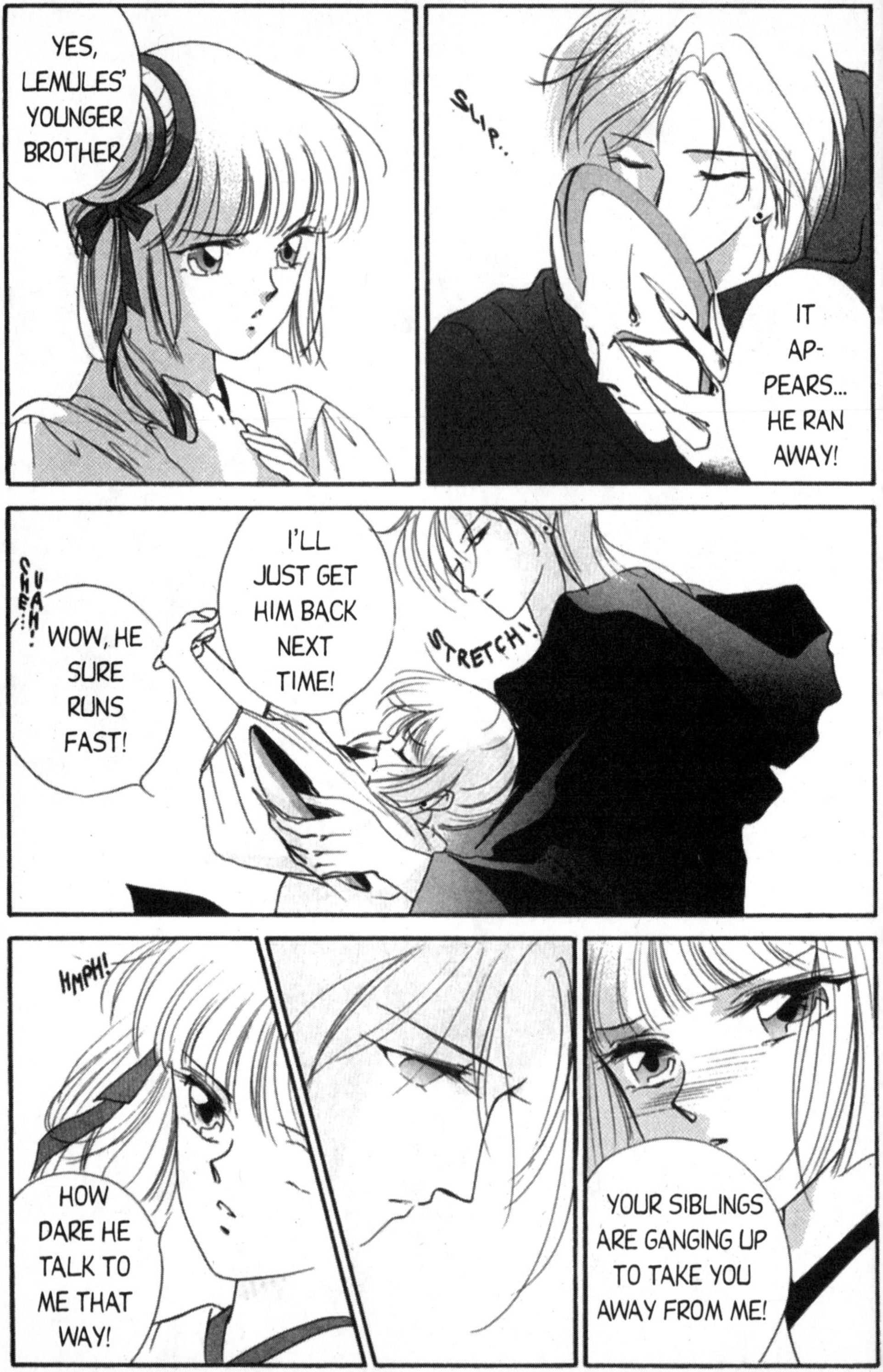
YES, LEMULES' YOUNGER BROTHER.
SLIP...
IT APPEARS... HE RAN AWAY!
SHE...UAH!
WOW, HE SURE RUNS FAST!
I'LL JUST GET HIM BACK NEXT TIME!
STRETCH!
HMPH!
HOW DARE HE TALK TO ME THAT WAY!
YOUR SIBLINGS ARE GANGING UP TO TAKE YOU AWAY FROM ME!

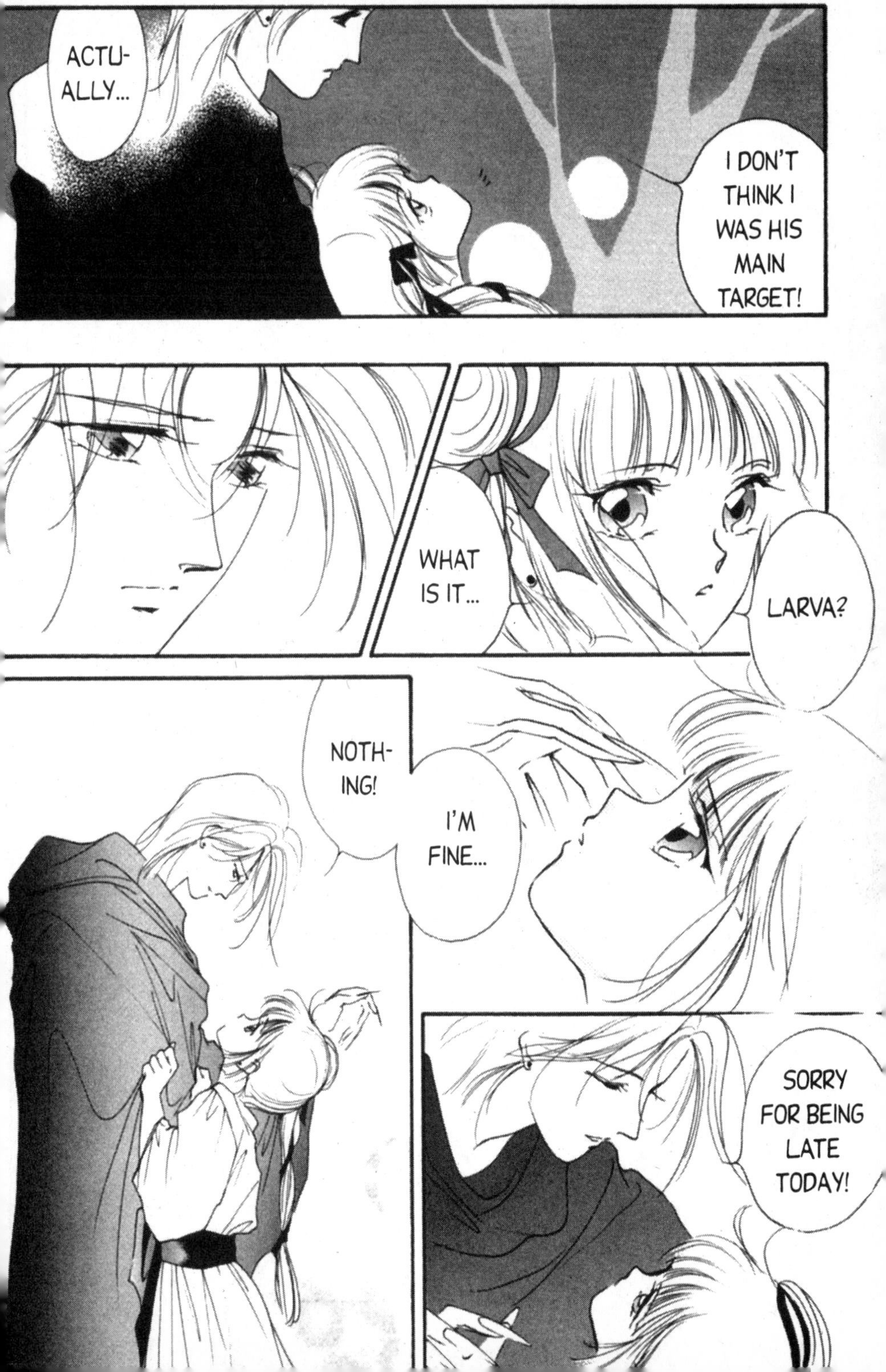
ACTU-ALLY...
I DON'T THINK I WAS HIS MAIN TARGET!
WHAT IS IT...
LARVA?
NOTH-ING!
I'M FINE...
SORRY FOR BEING LATE TODAY!

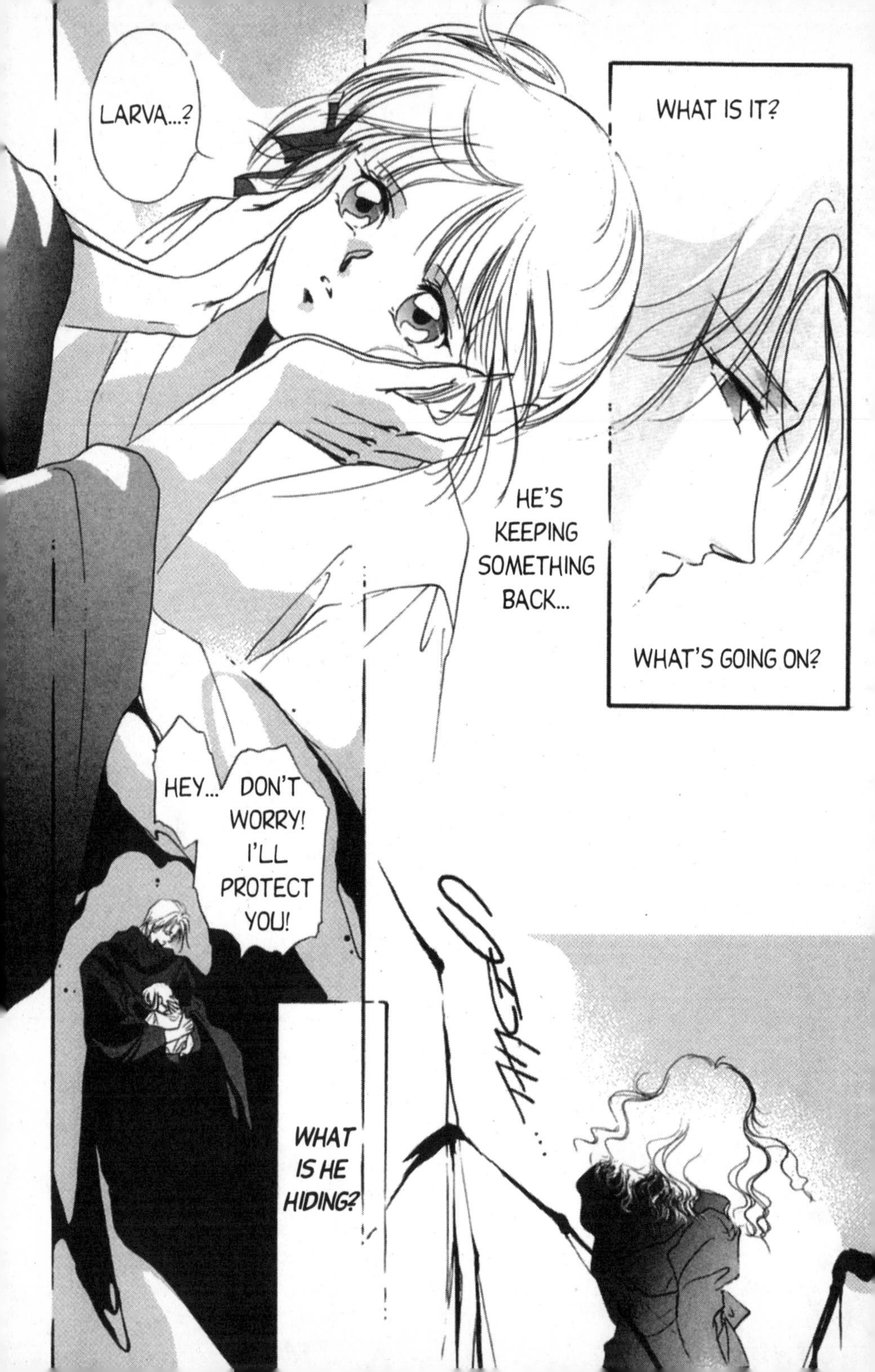
WHAT IS IT?
HE'S KEEPING SOMETHING BACK...
WHAT'S GOING ON?
LARVA...?
HEY... DON'T WORRY! I'LL PROTECT YOU!
WHAT IS HE HIDING?

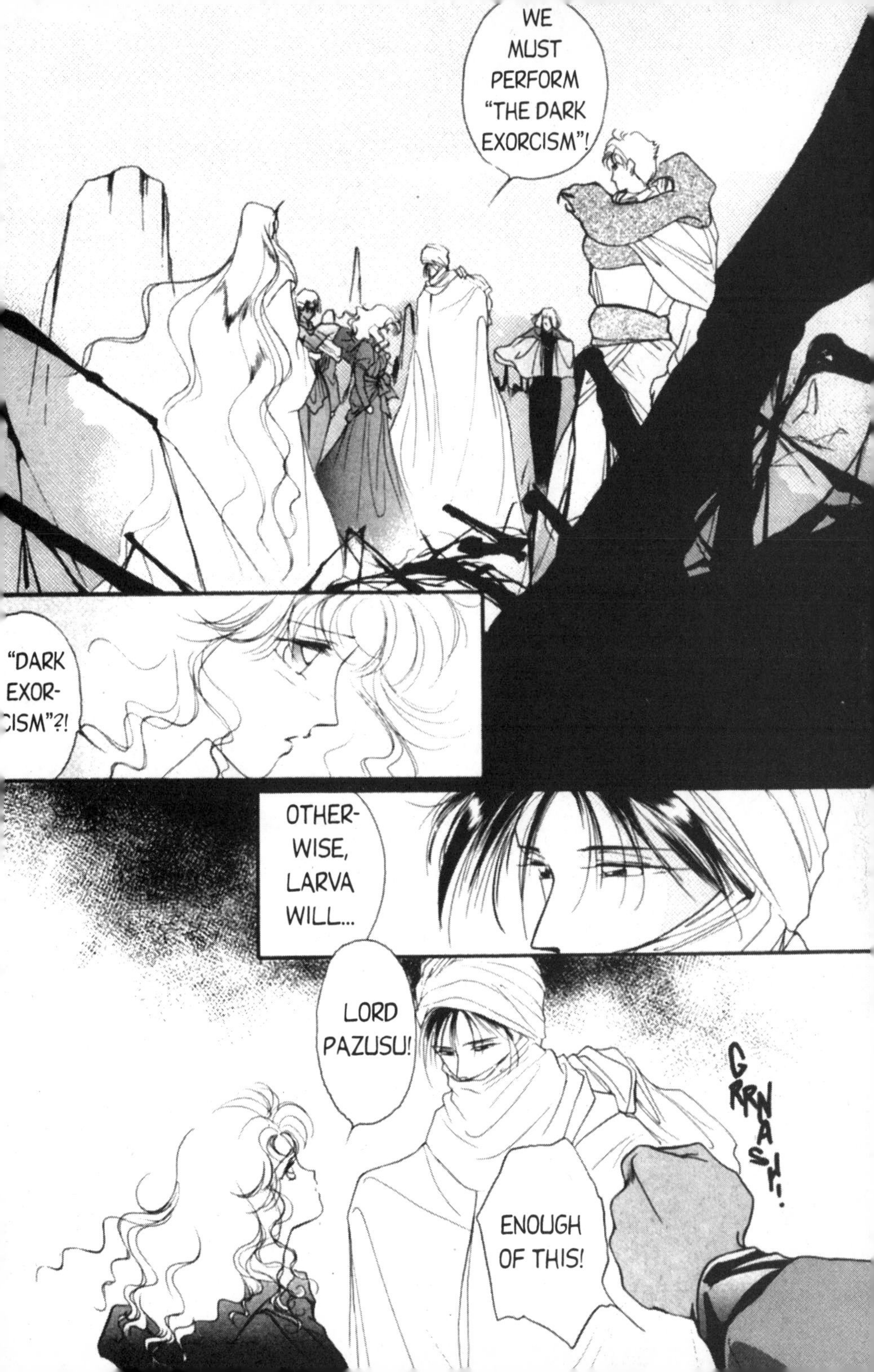
WE MUST PERFORM "THE DARK EXORCISM"!
"DARK EXOR-CISM"?!
OTHER-WISE, LARVA WILL...
LORD PAZUSU!
GRRNASH!
ENOUGH OF THIS!

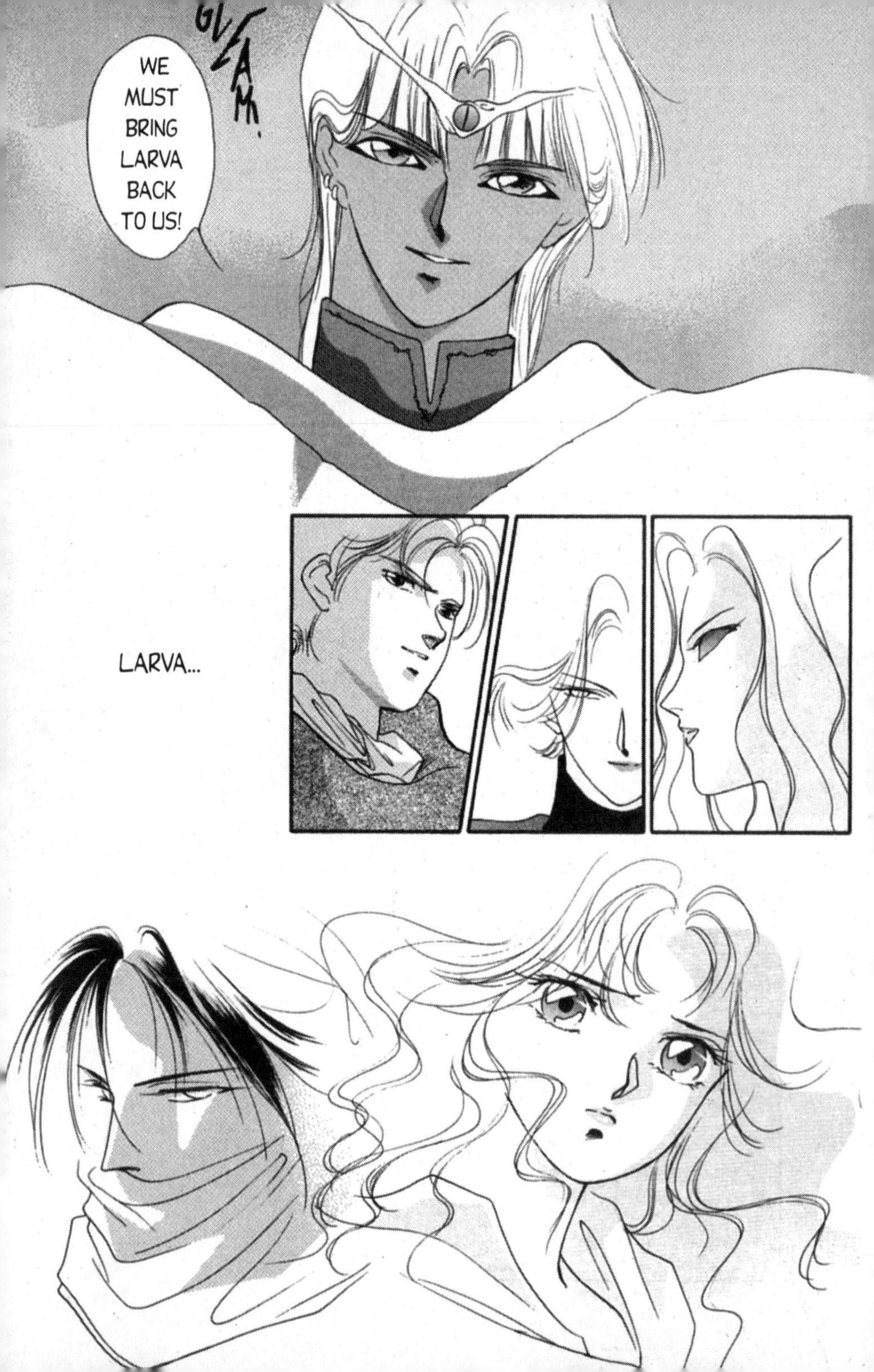
WE MUST BRING LARVA BACK TO US!
GLEAM!
LARVA...

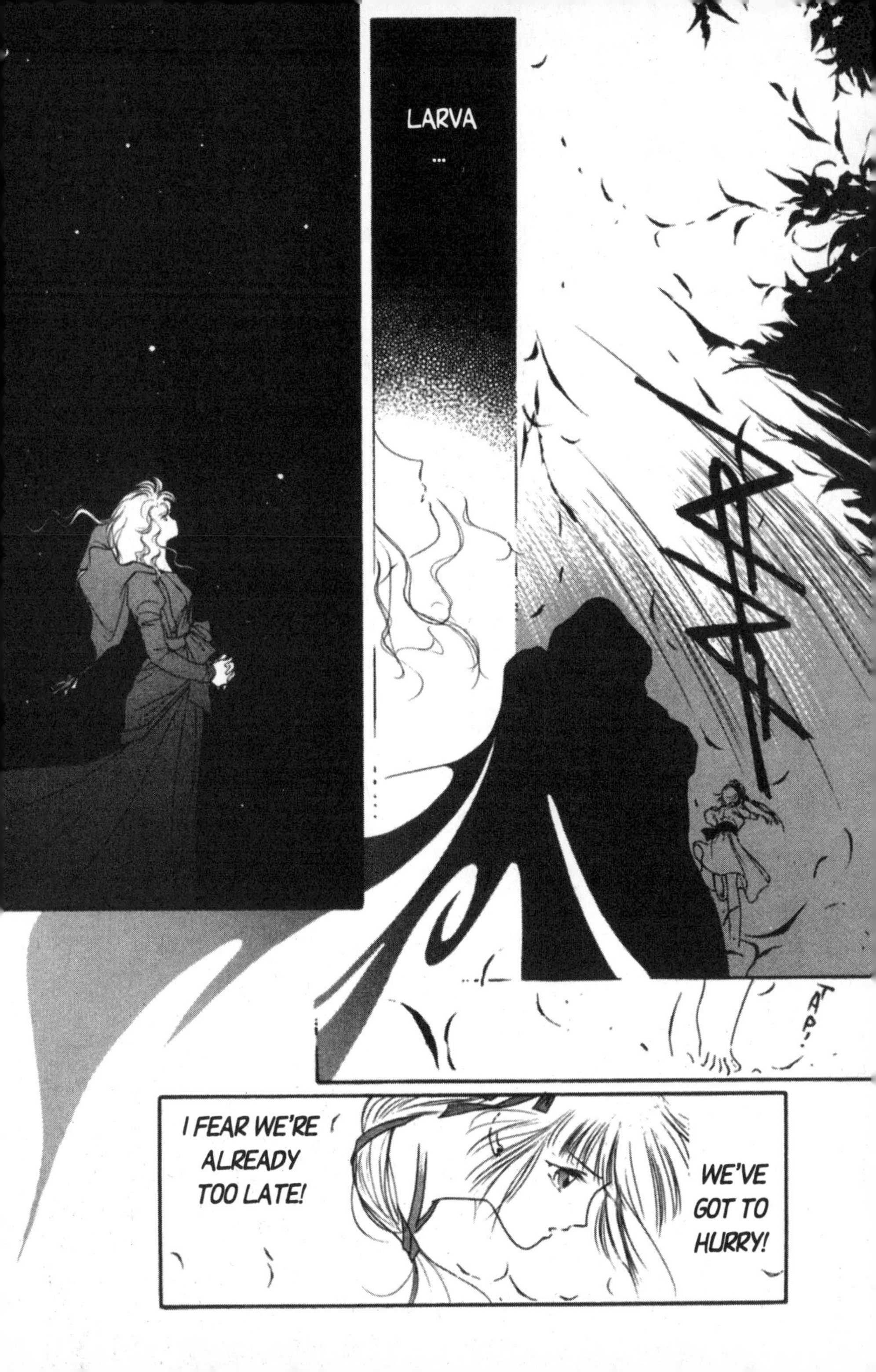
LARVA
...
TAP...
I FEAR WE'RE ALREADY TOO LATE!
WE'VE GOT TO HURRY!

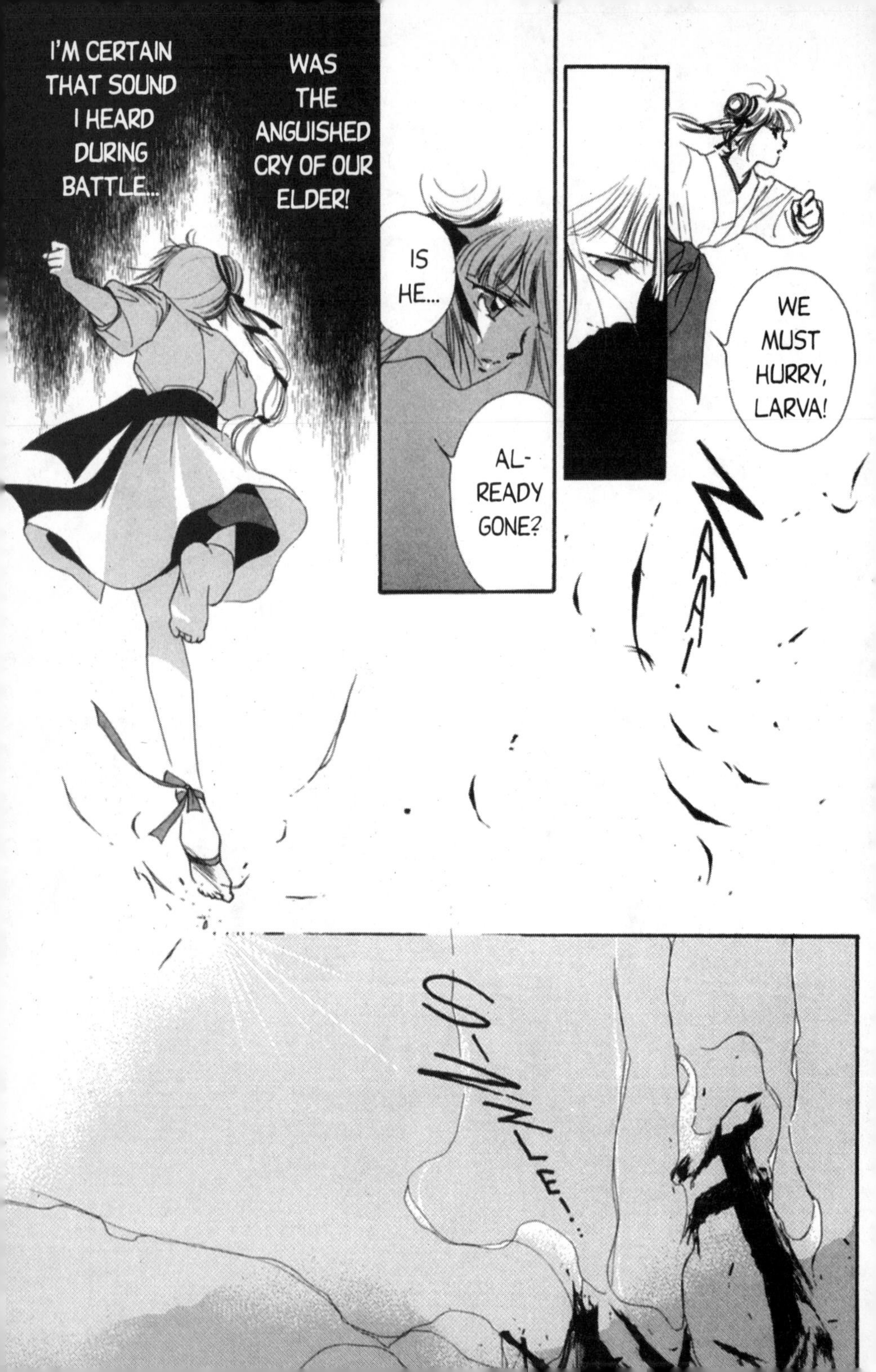
I'M CERTAIN THAT SOUND I HEARD DURING BATTLE...
WAS THE ANGUISHED CRY OF OUR ELDER!
IS HE...
AL-READY GONE?
WE MUST HURRY, LARVA!

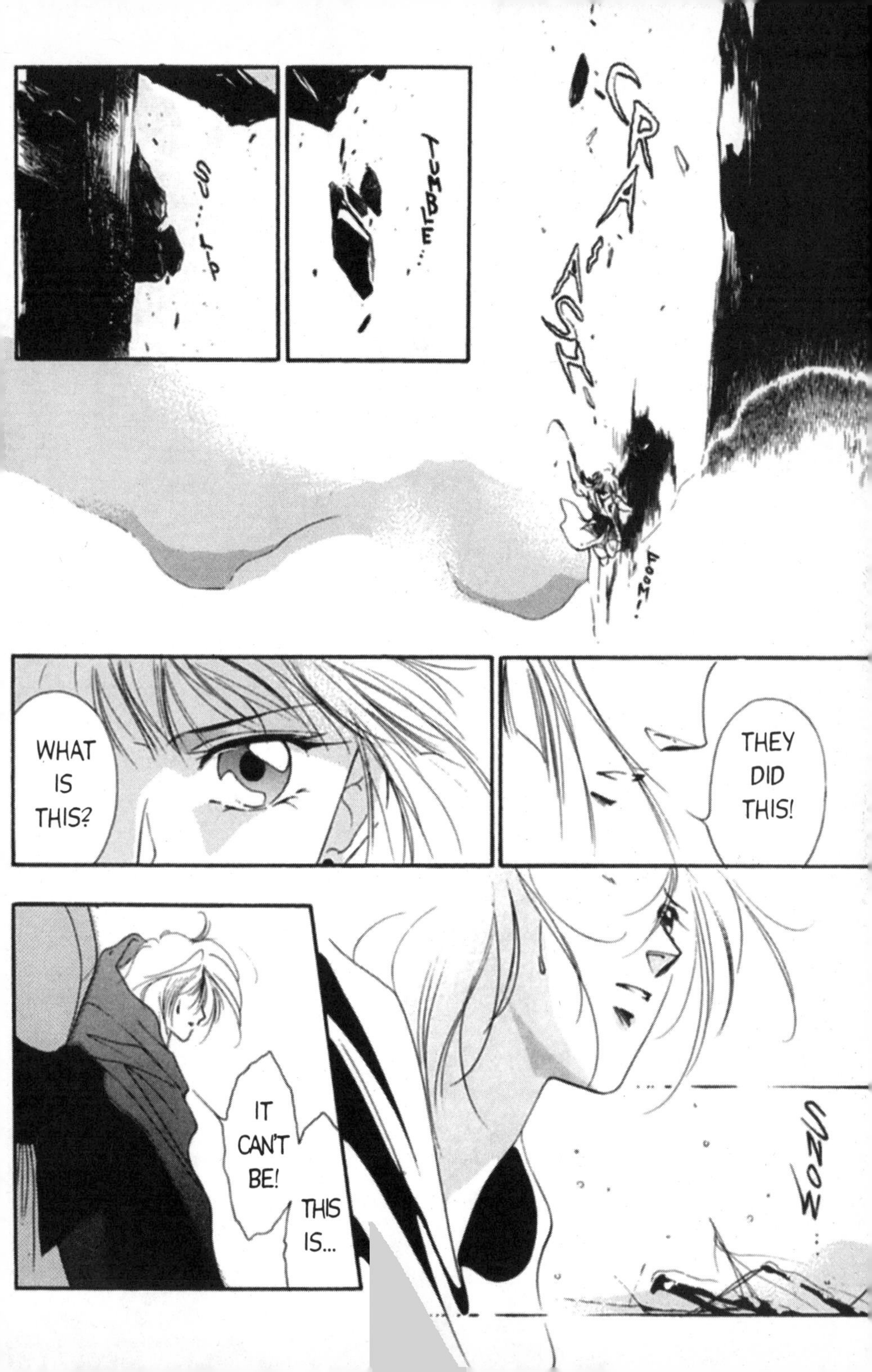
CRA-ASH
TUMBLE...
BOOM...
THEY DID THIS!
WHAT IS THIS?
SNOW...
IT CAN'T BE!
THIS IS...

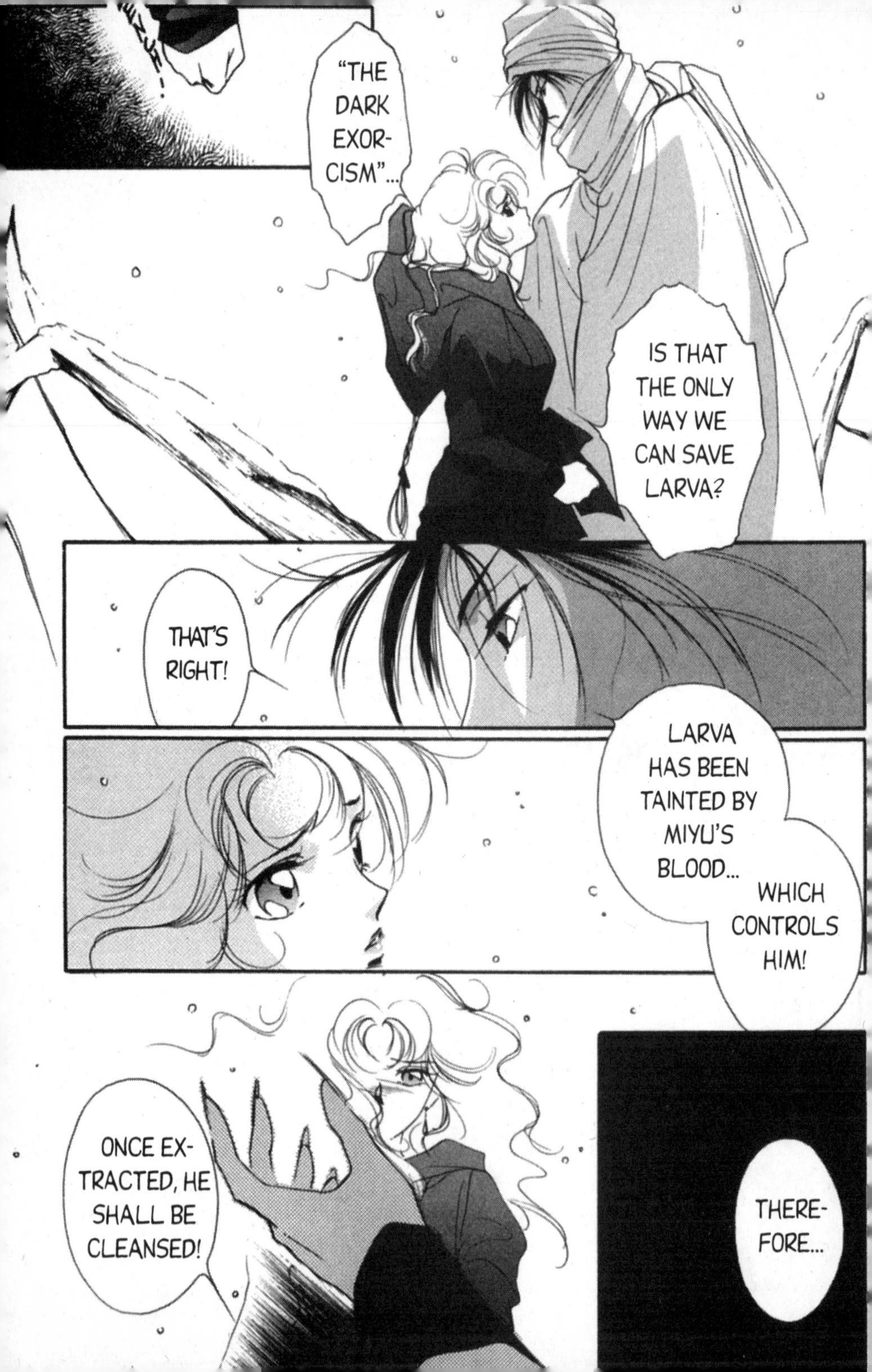
"THE DARK EXORCISM"...
IS THAT THE ONLY WAY WE CAN SAVE LARVA?
THAT'S RIGHT!
LARVA HAS BEEN TAINTED BY MIYU'S BLOOD...
WHICH CONTROLS HIM!
THEREFORE...
ONCE EXTRACTED, HE SHALL BE CLEANSED!

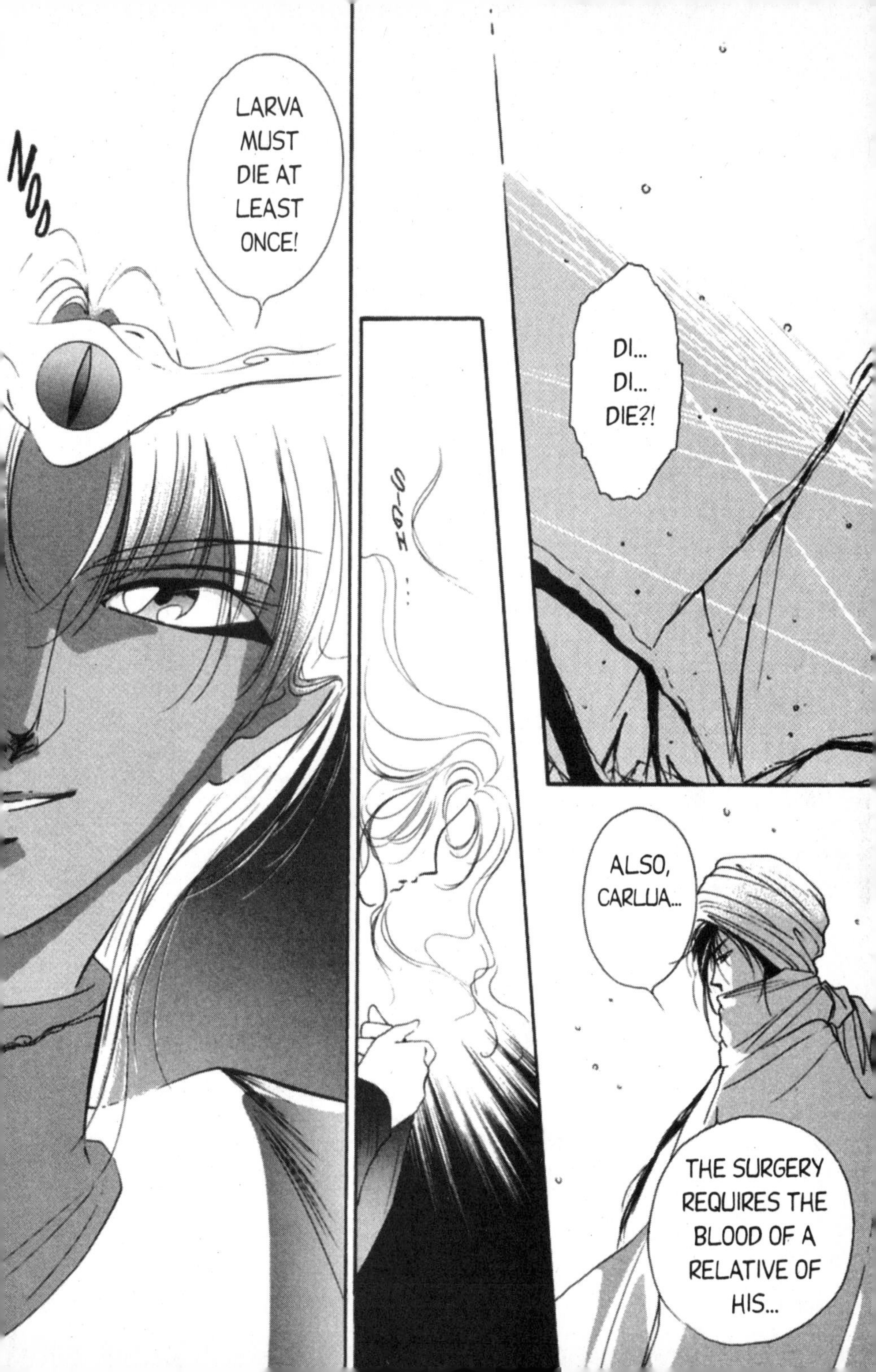
DI... DI... DIE?!
ALSO, CARLUA...
THE SURGERY REQUIRES THE BLOOD OF A RELATIVE OF HIS...
S-SIGH...
LARVA MUST DIE AT LEAST ONCE!
NOD

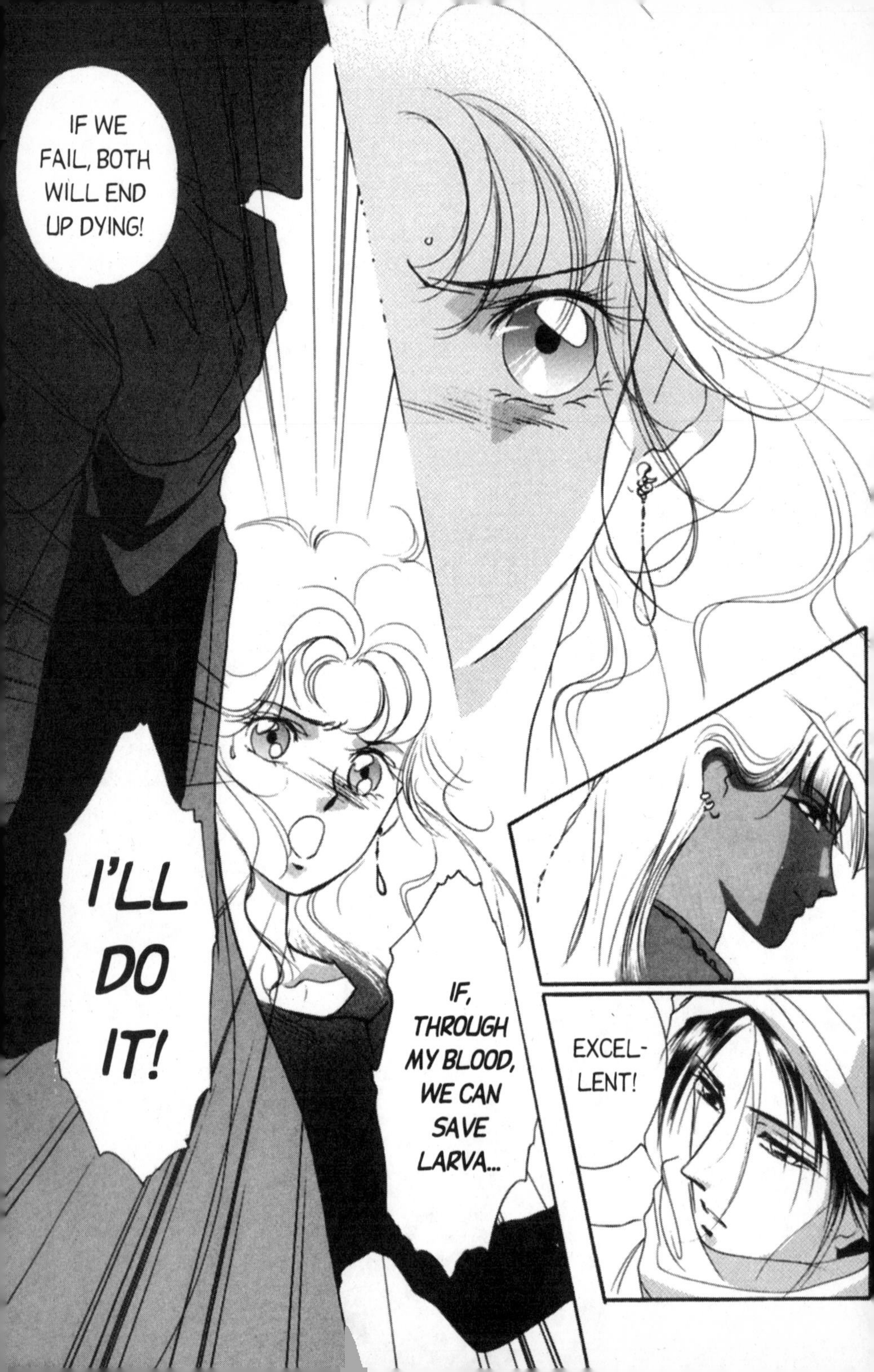
IF WE FAIL, BOTH WILL END UP DYING!
I'LL DO IT!
IF, THROUGH MY BLOOD, WE CAN SAVE LARVA...
EXCEL-LENT!

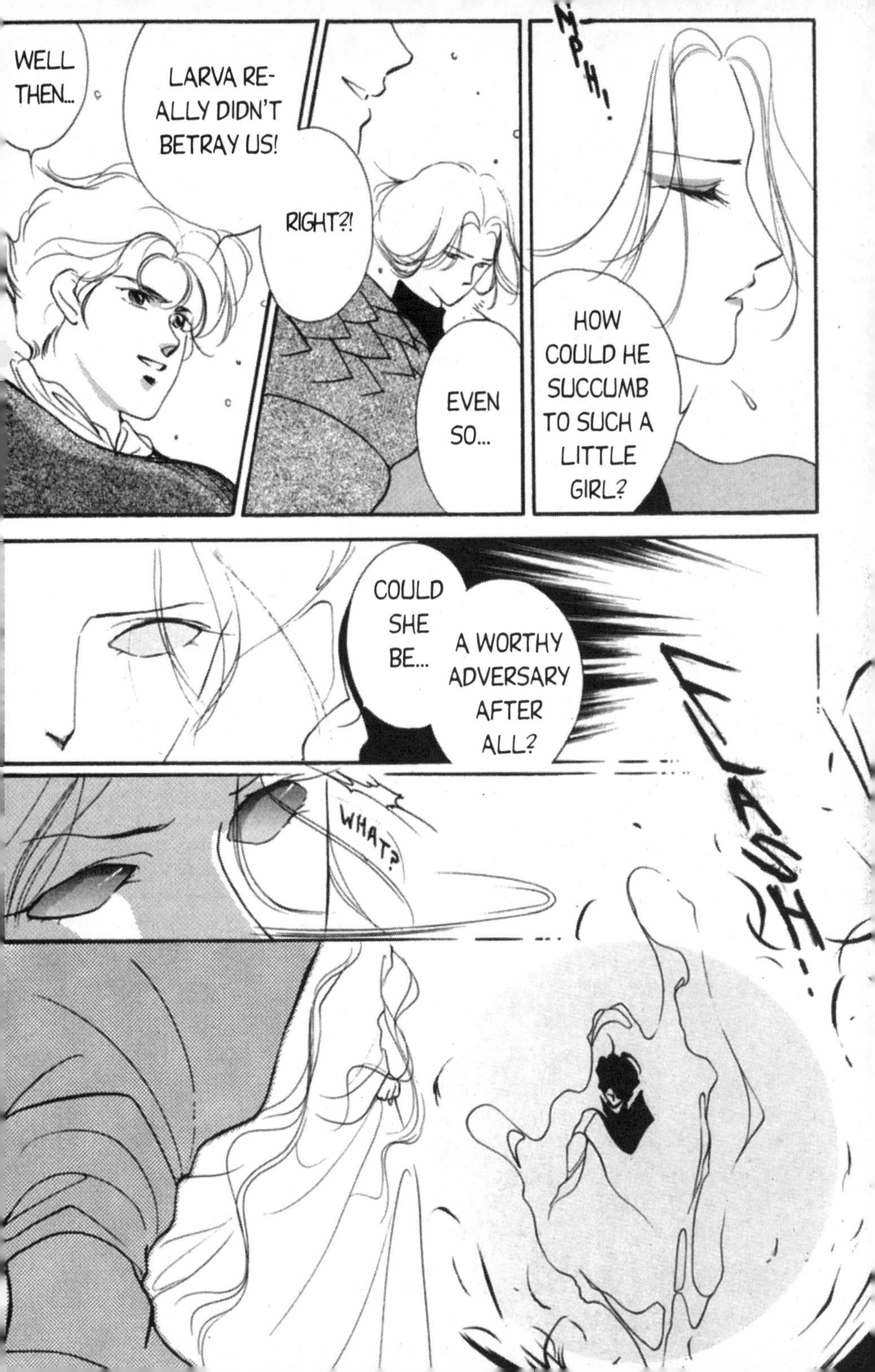
WELL THEN...
LARVA REALLY DIDN'T BETRAY US!
RIGHT?!
EVEN SO...
NPH!
HOW COULD HE SUCCUMB TO SUCH A LITTLE GIRL?
COULD SHE BE...
A WORTHY ADVERSARY AFTER ALL?
WHAT?
FLASH...

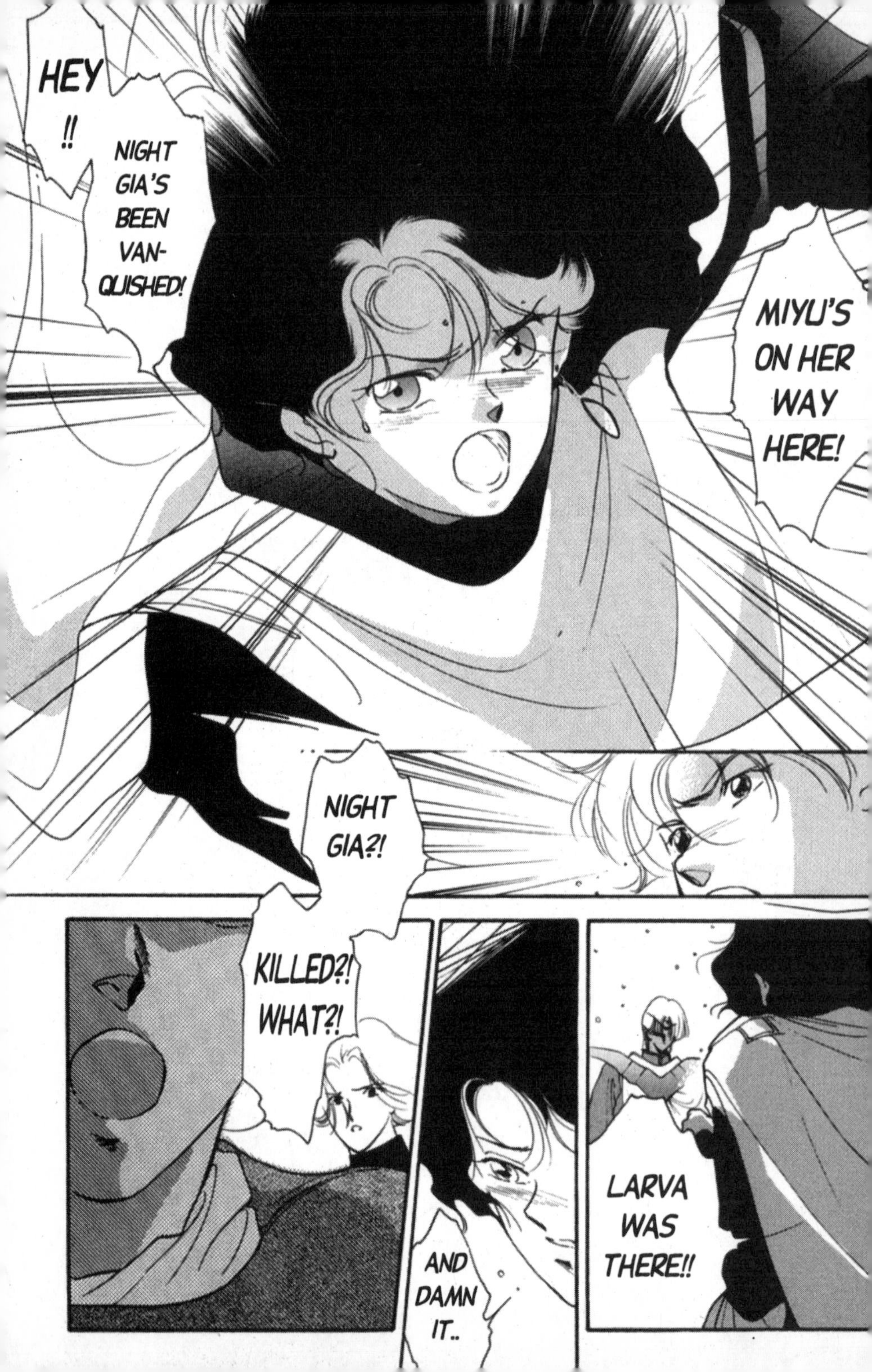
HEY !!
NIGHT GIA'S BEEN VAN-QUISHED!
MIYU'S ON HER WAY HERE!
NIGHT GIA?!
KILLED?! WHAT?!
AND DAMN IT..
LARVA WAS THERE!!

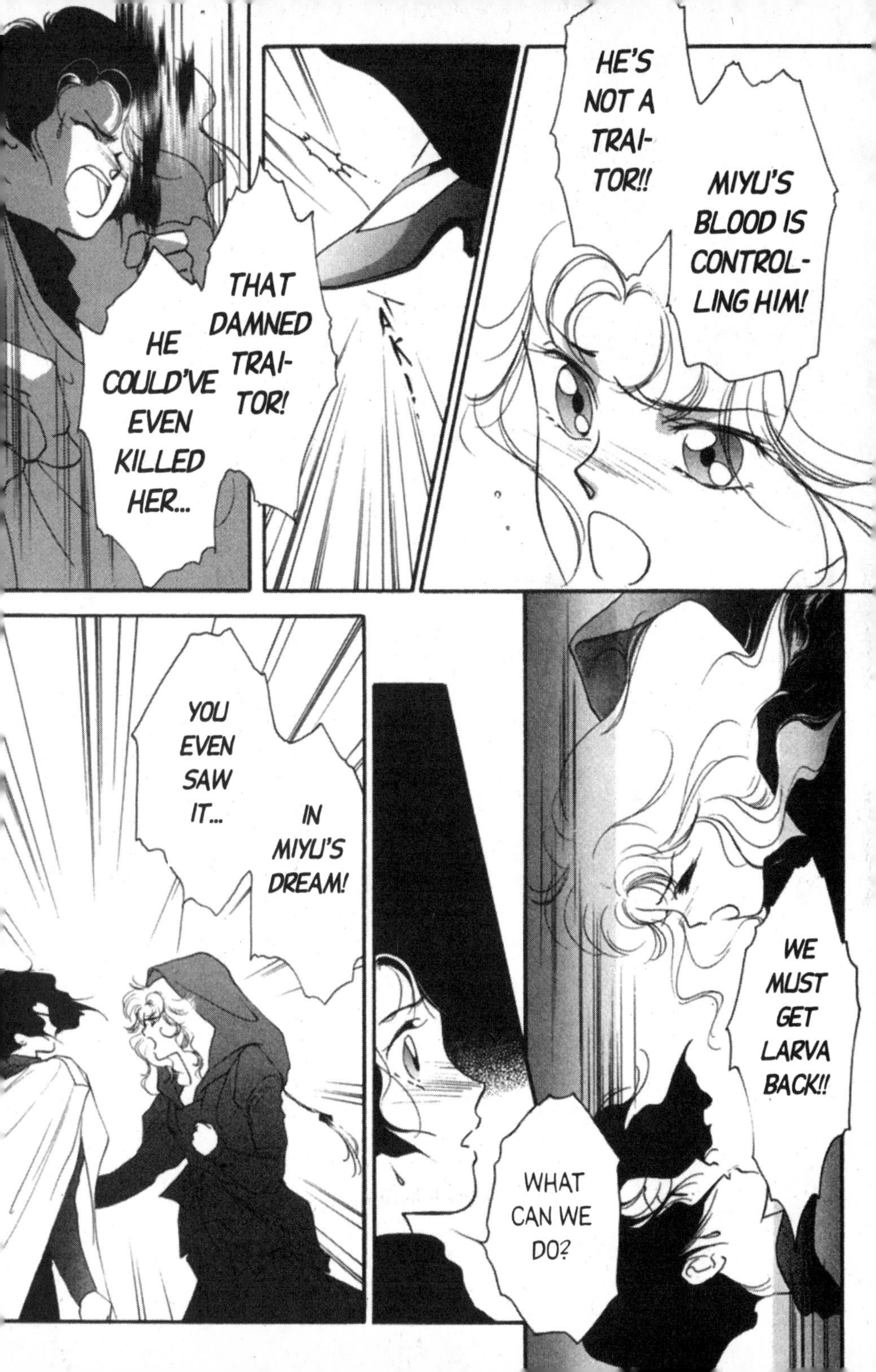
THAT DAMNED TRAITOR!
HE COULD'VE EVEN KILLED HER...
HE'S NOT A TRAITOR!!
MIYU'S BLOOD IS CONTROLLING HIM!
YOU EVEN SAW IT...
IN MIYU'S DREAM!
WHAT CAN WE DO?
WE MUST GET LARVA BACK!!

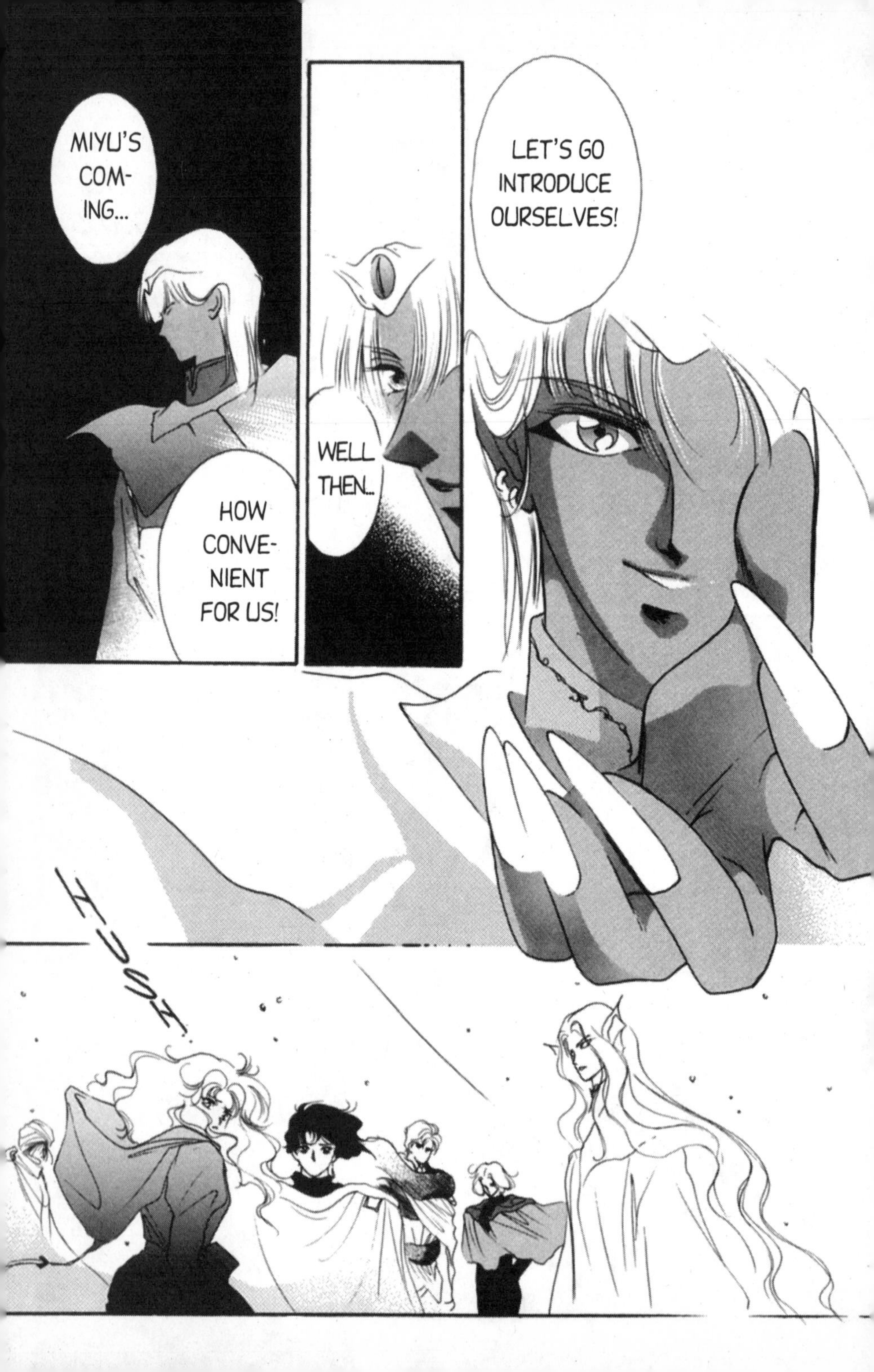
LET'S GO INTRODUCE OURSELVES!
WELL THEN...
MIYU'S COM-ING...
HOW CONVE-NIENT FOR US!
HUSH!

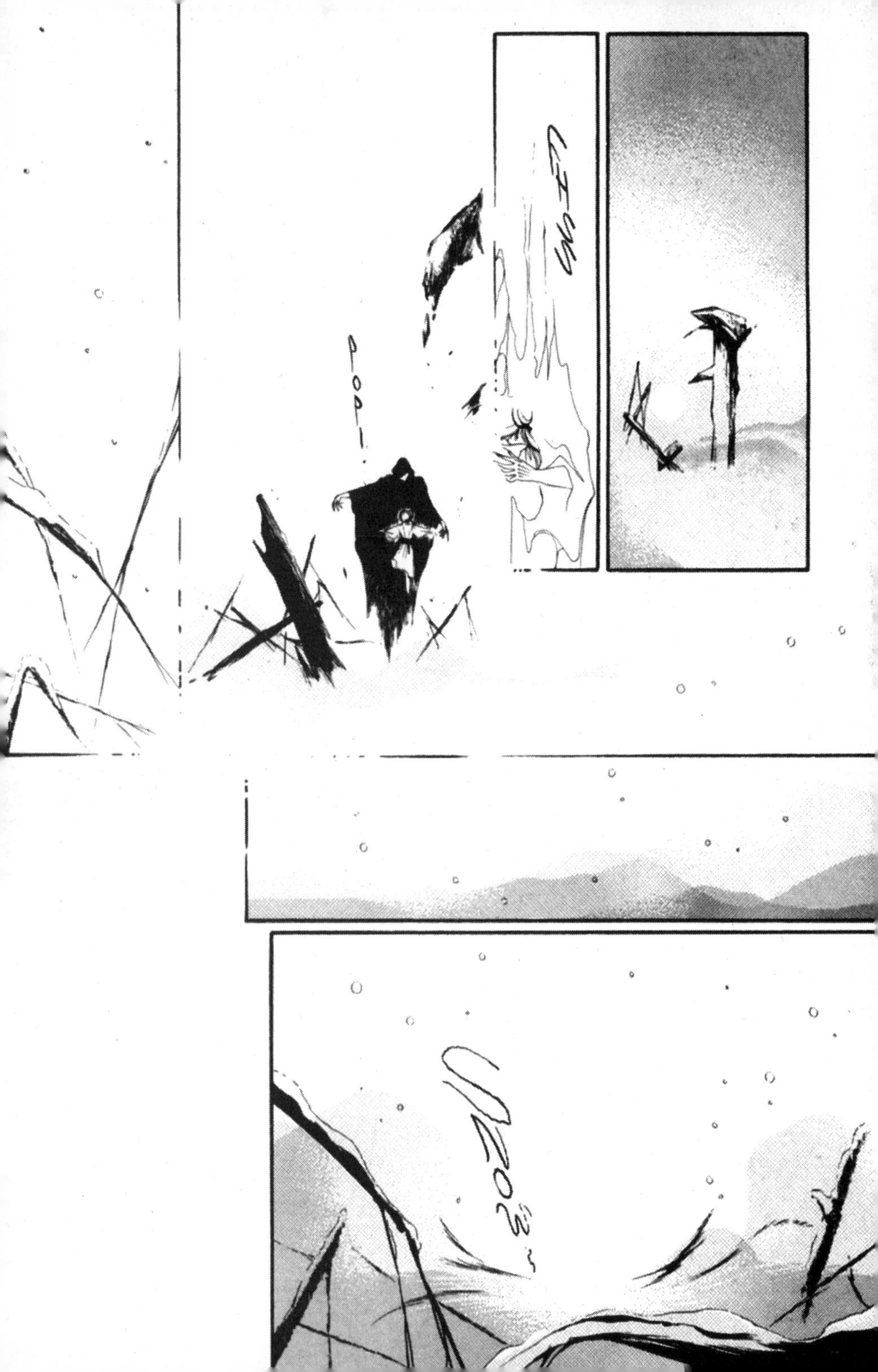
POP!

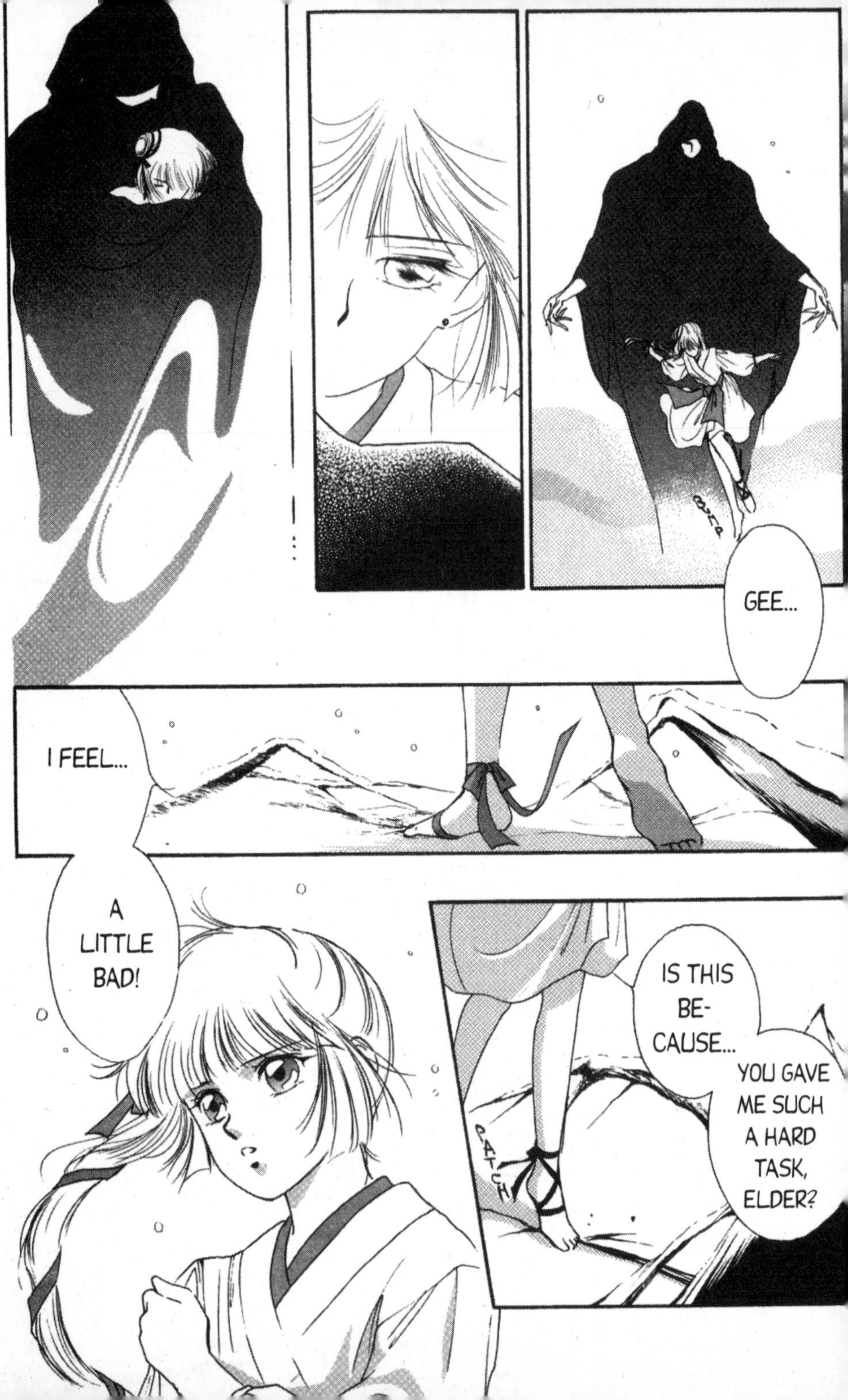
...
GEE...
I FEEL...
A LITTLE BAD!
IS THIS BE-CAUSE...
YOU GAVE ME SUCH A HARD TASK, ELDER?
CATCH

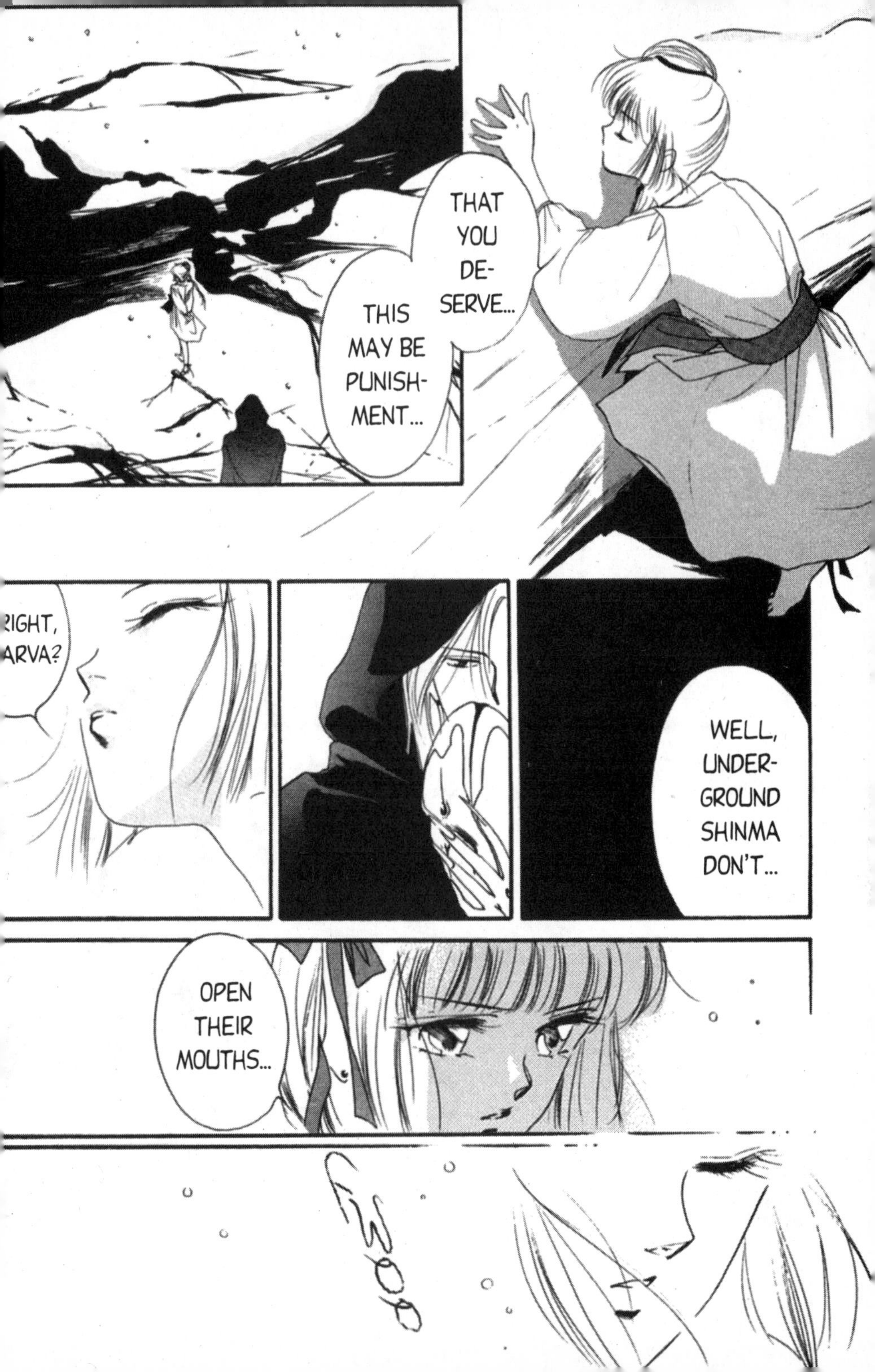

THIS MAY BE PUNISHMENT...
THAT YOU DE-SERVE...
RIGHT, ARVA?
WELL, UNDER-GROUND SHINMA DON'T...
OPEN THEIR MOUTHS...

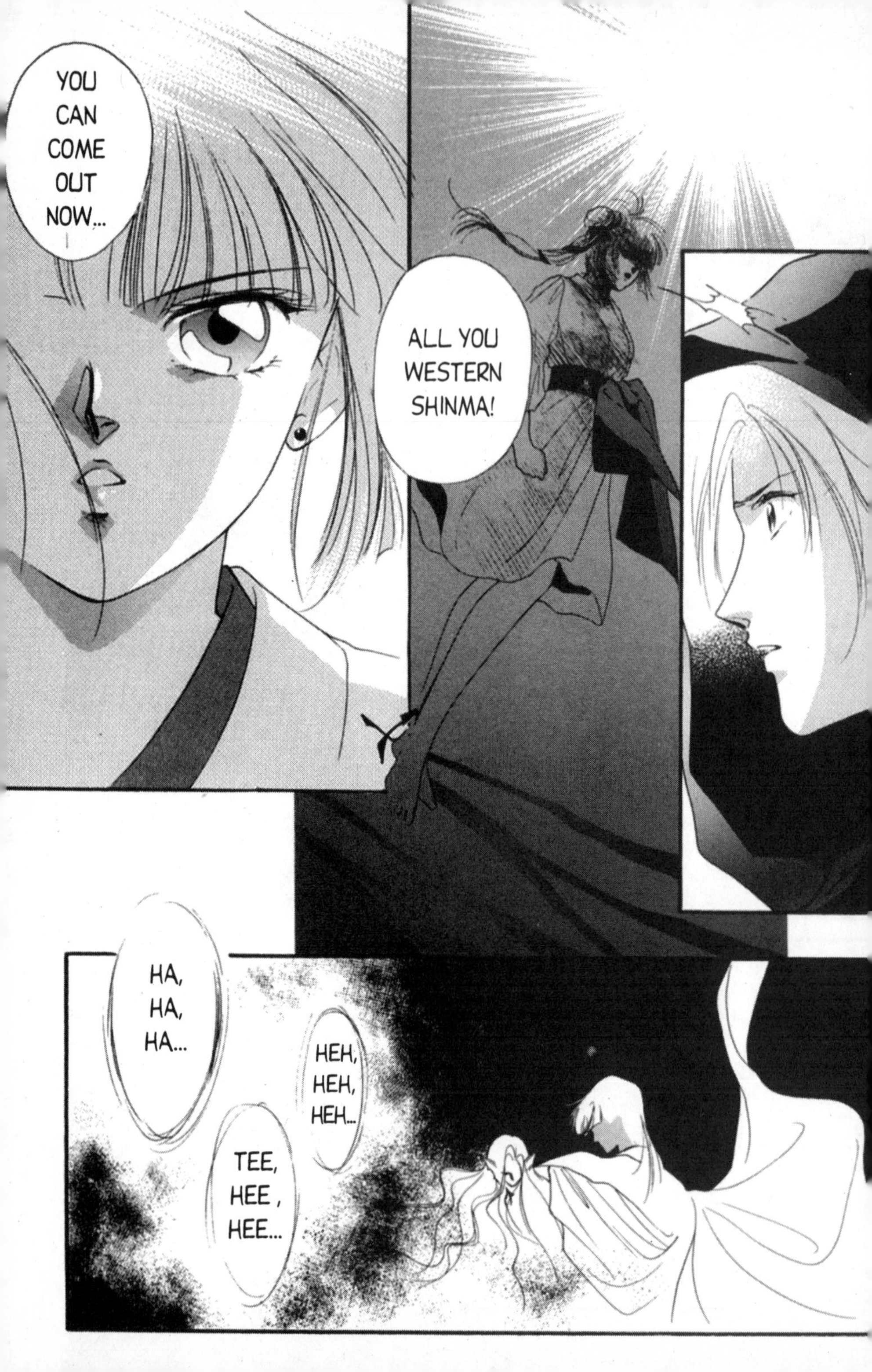
YOU CAN COME OUT NOW...
ALL YOU WESTERN SHINMA!
HA, HA, HA...
HEH, HEH, HEH...
TEE, HEE , HEE...

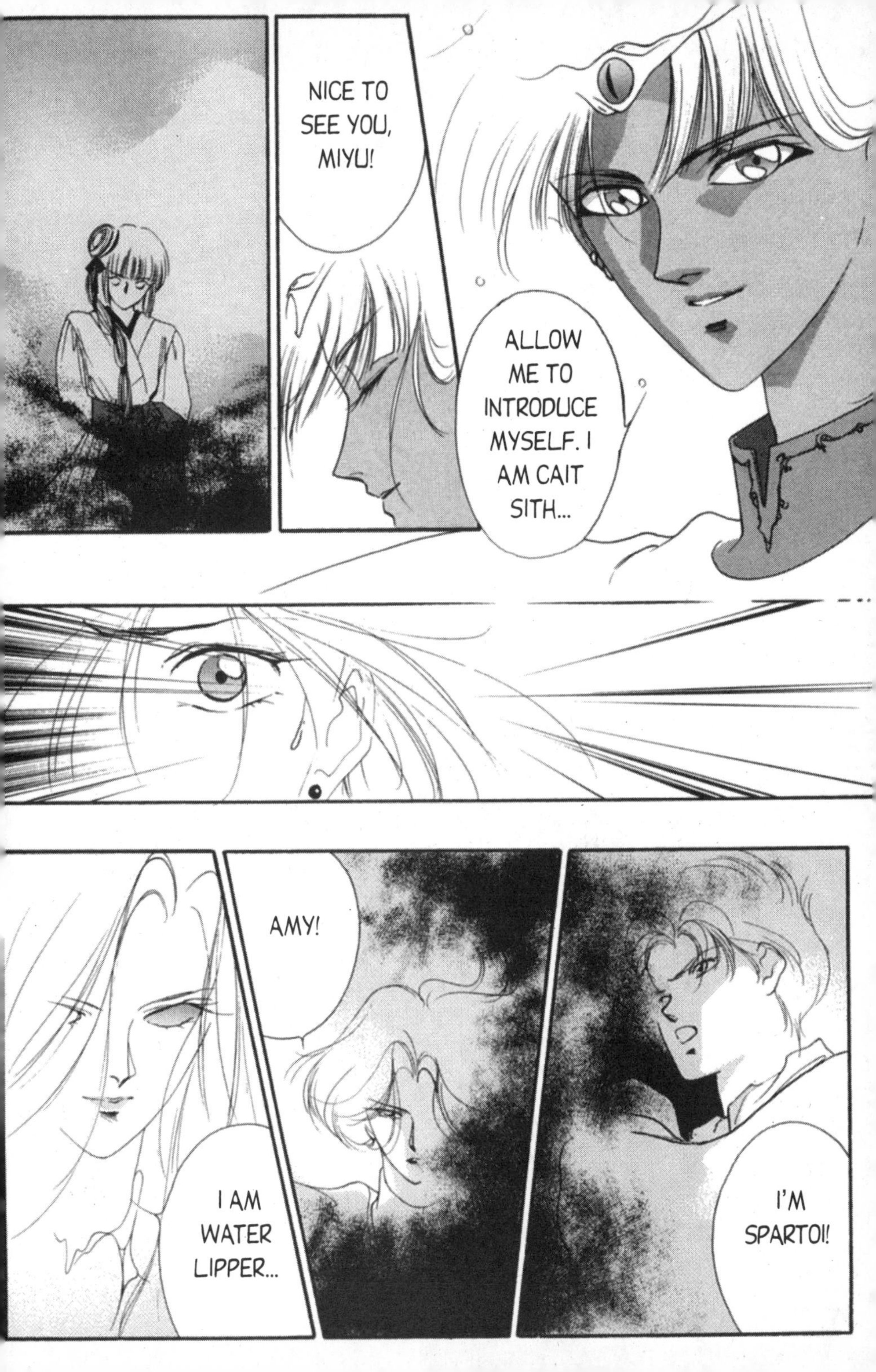
NICE TO SEE YOU, MIYU!
ALLOW ME TO INTRODUCE MYSELF. I AM CAIT SITH...
AMY!
I AM WATER LIPPER...
I'M SPARTOI!

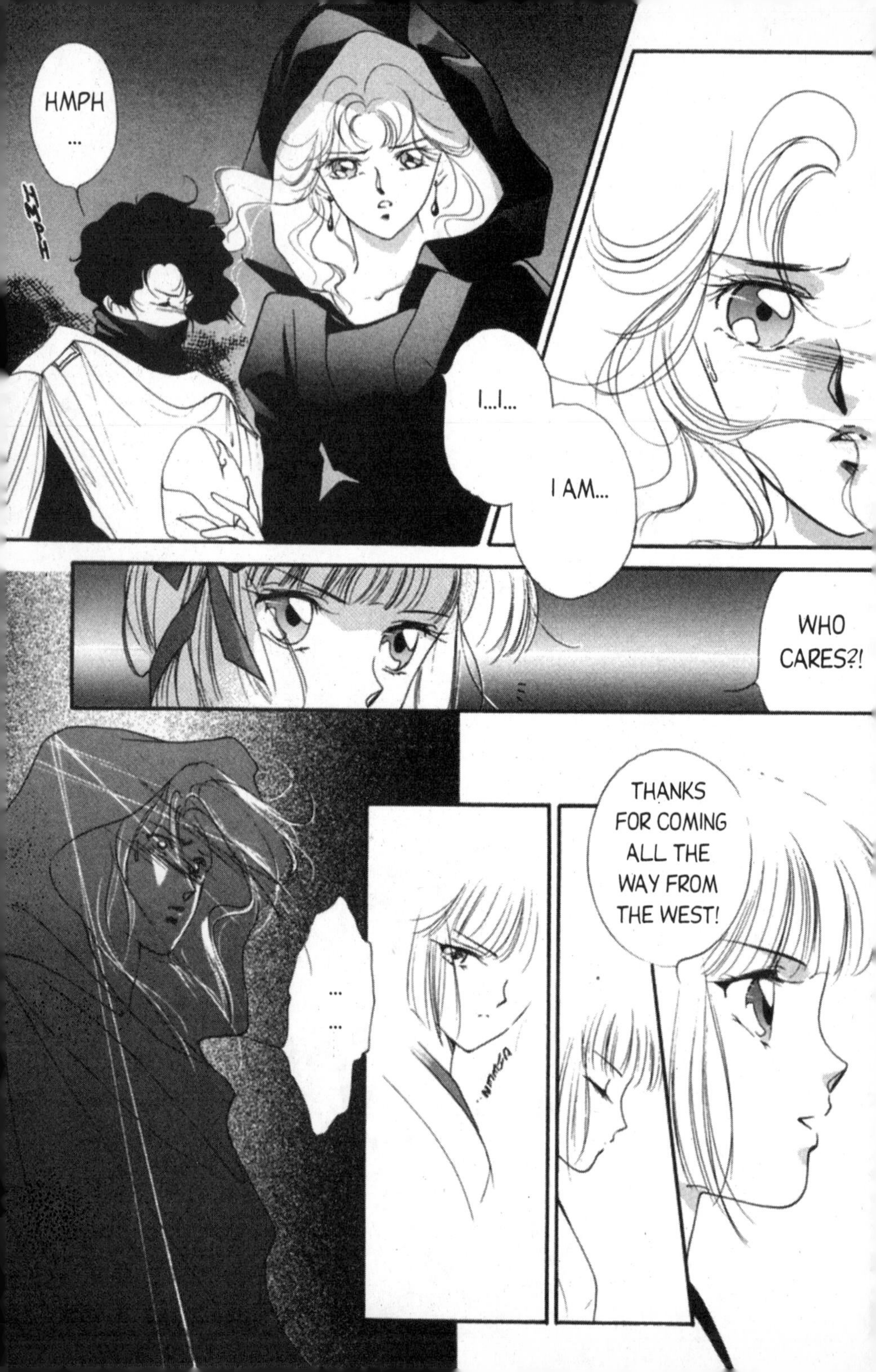
I...I...
I AM...
HMPH
...
HMPH
WHO CARES?!
THANKS FOR COMING ALL THE WAY FROM THE WEST!
...
...

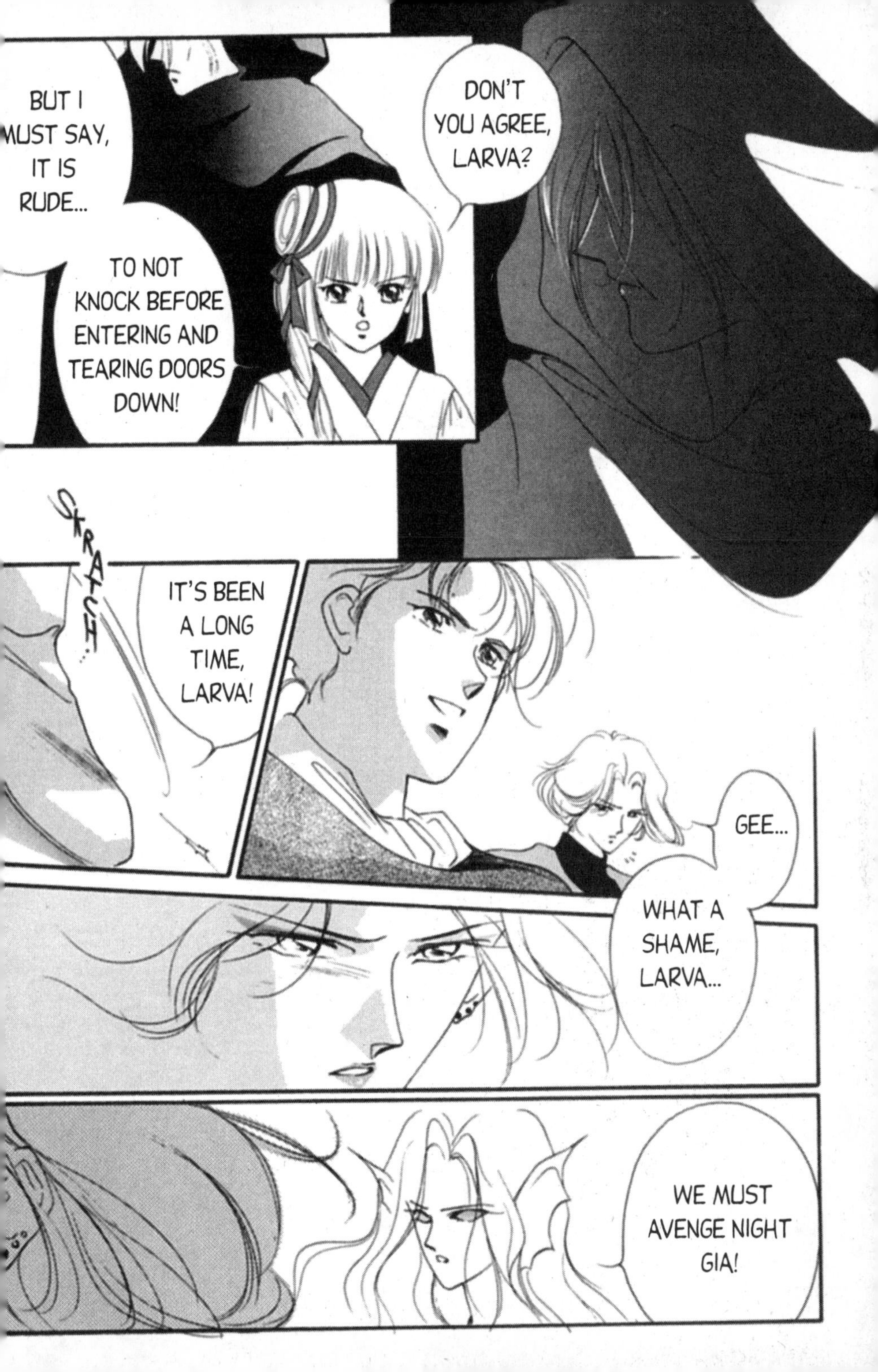
BUT I MUST SAY, IT IS RUDE...
TO NOT KNOCK BEFORE ENTERING AND TEARING DOORS DOWN!
DON'T YOU AGREE, LARVA?
SKRATCH...
IT'S BEEN A LONG TIME, LARVA!
GEE...
WHAT A SHAME, LARVA...
WE MUST AVENGE NIGHT GIA!

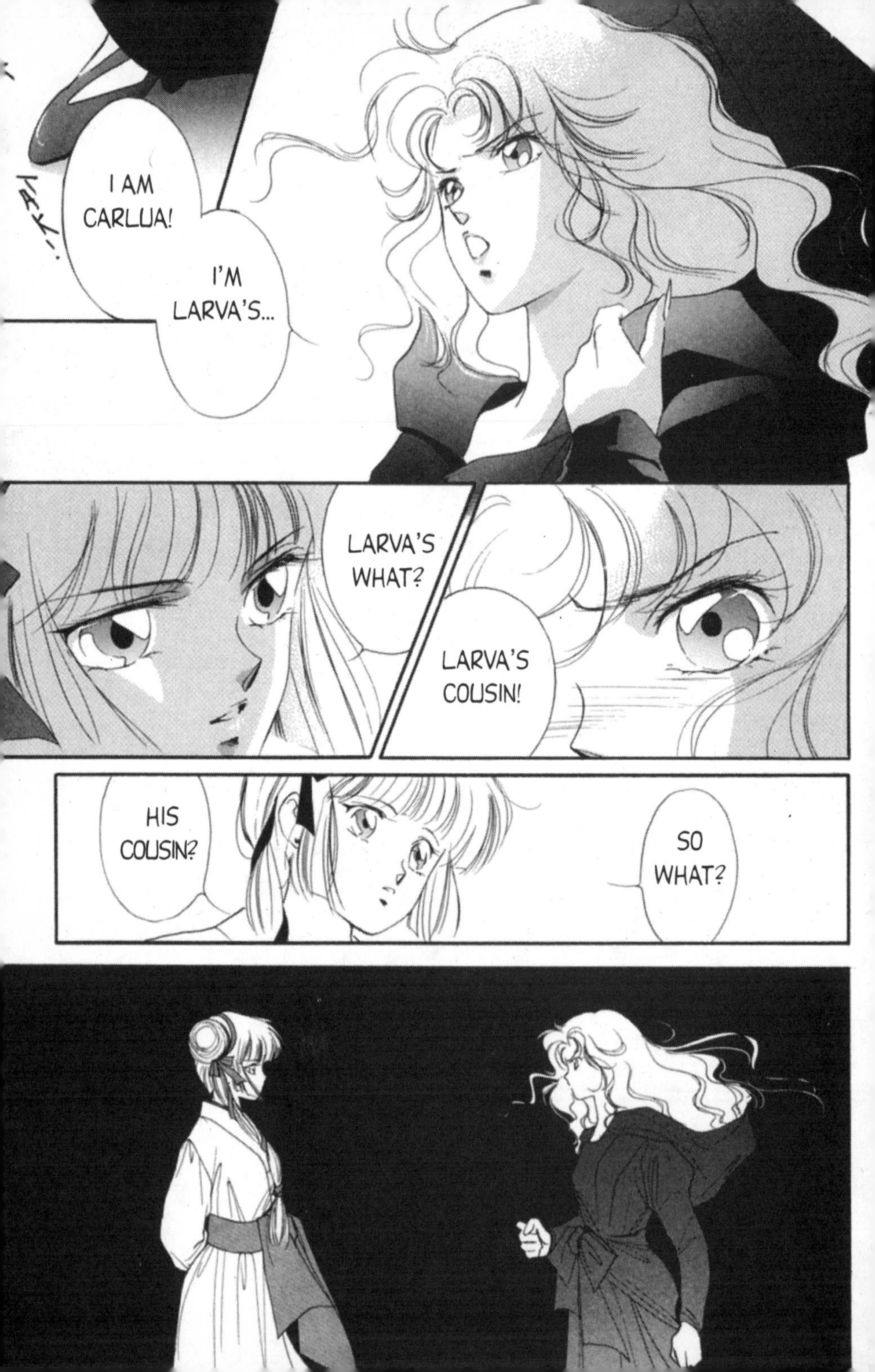
TAK!
I AM CARLUA!
I'M LARVA'S...
LARVA'S WHAT?
LARVA'S COUSIN!
HIS COUSIN?
SO WHAT?

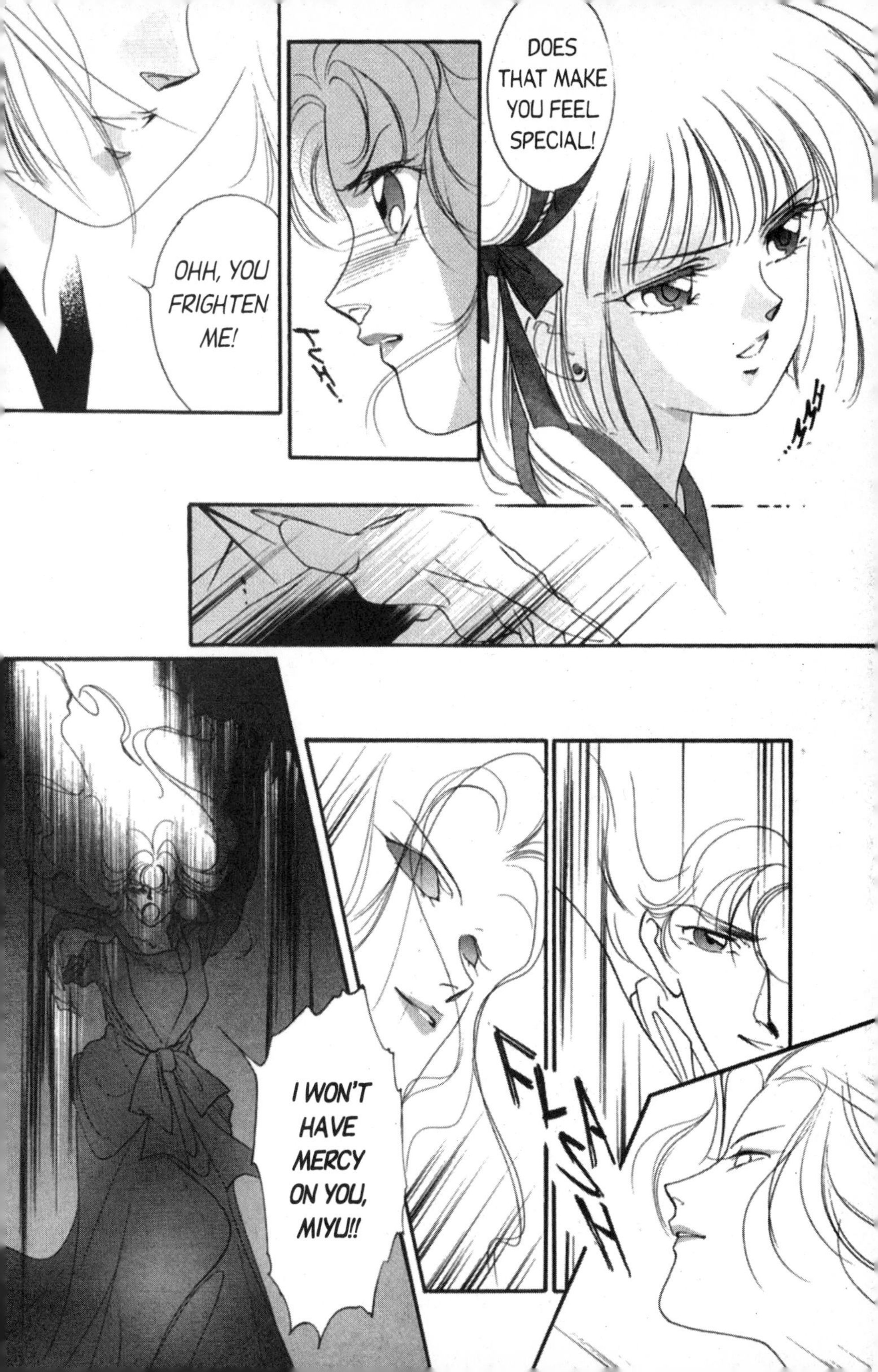
DOES THAT MAKE YOU FEEL SPECIAL!
OHH, YOU FRIGHTEN ME!
I WON'T HAVE MERCY ON YOU, MIYU!!
FLASH

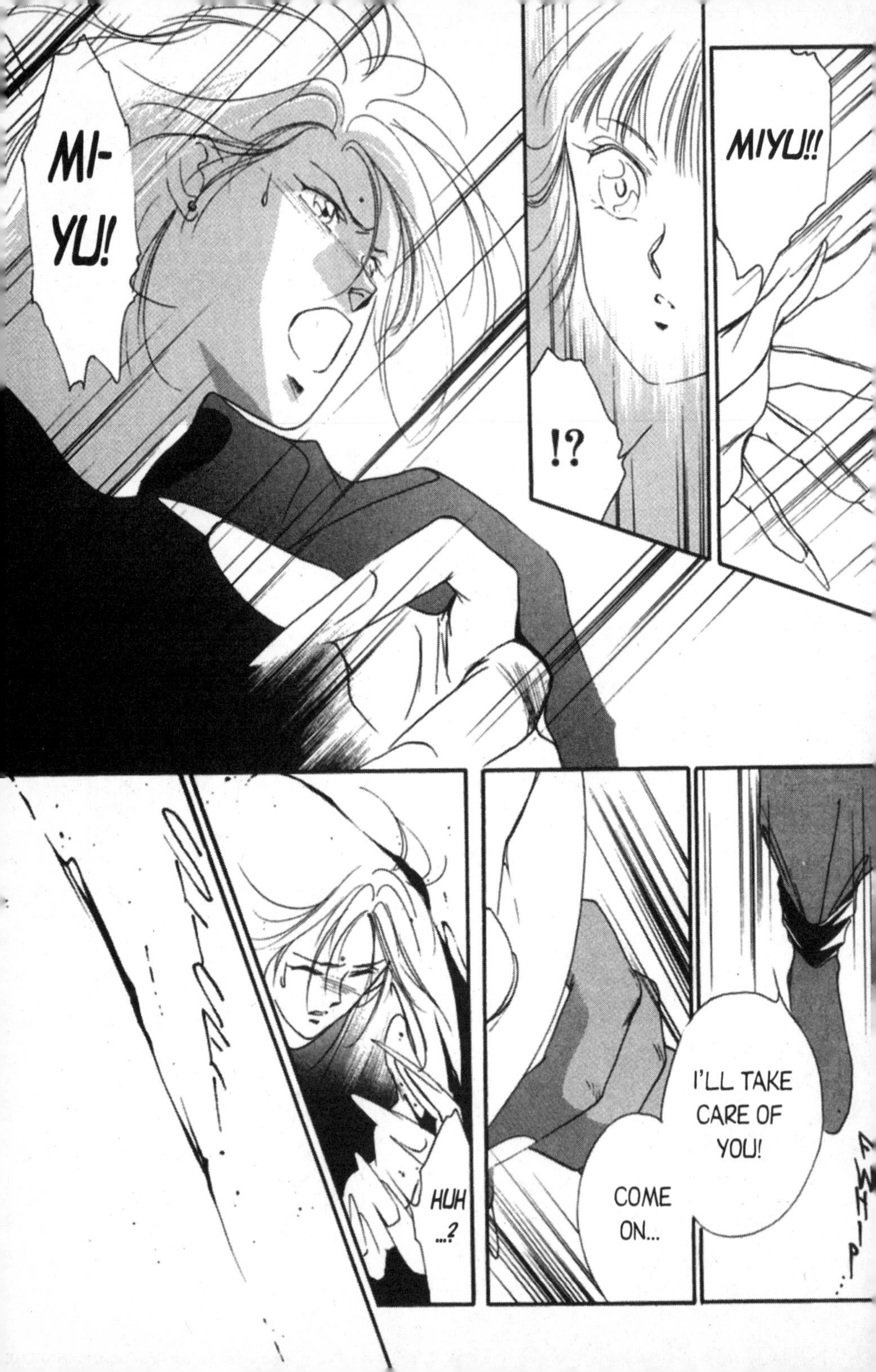
MIYU!!
!?
MI-YU!
I'LL TAKE CARE OF YOU!
COME ON...
HUH ...?

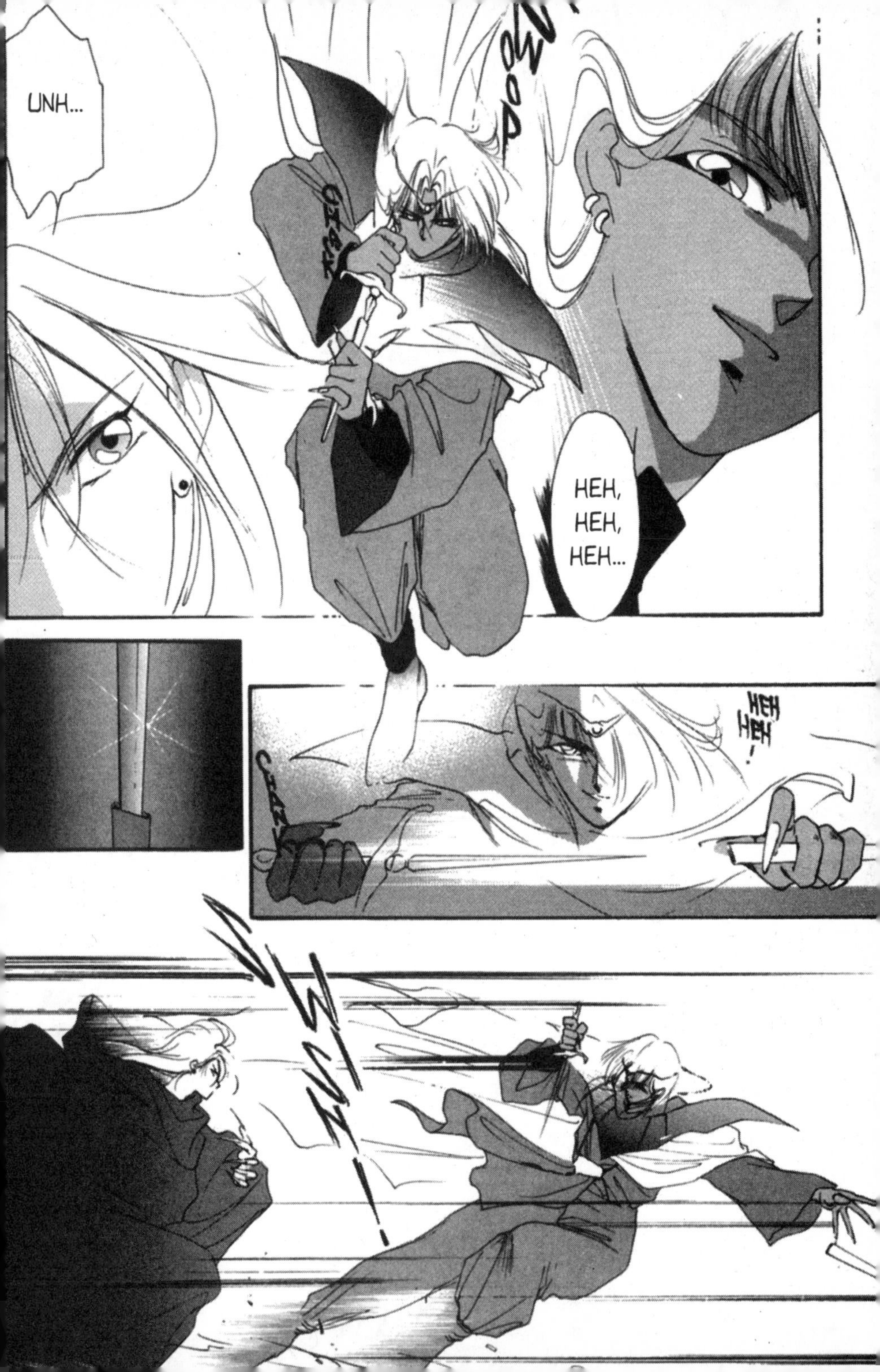
HEH, HEH, HEH...
UNH...
HEH HEH!

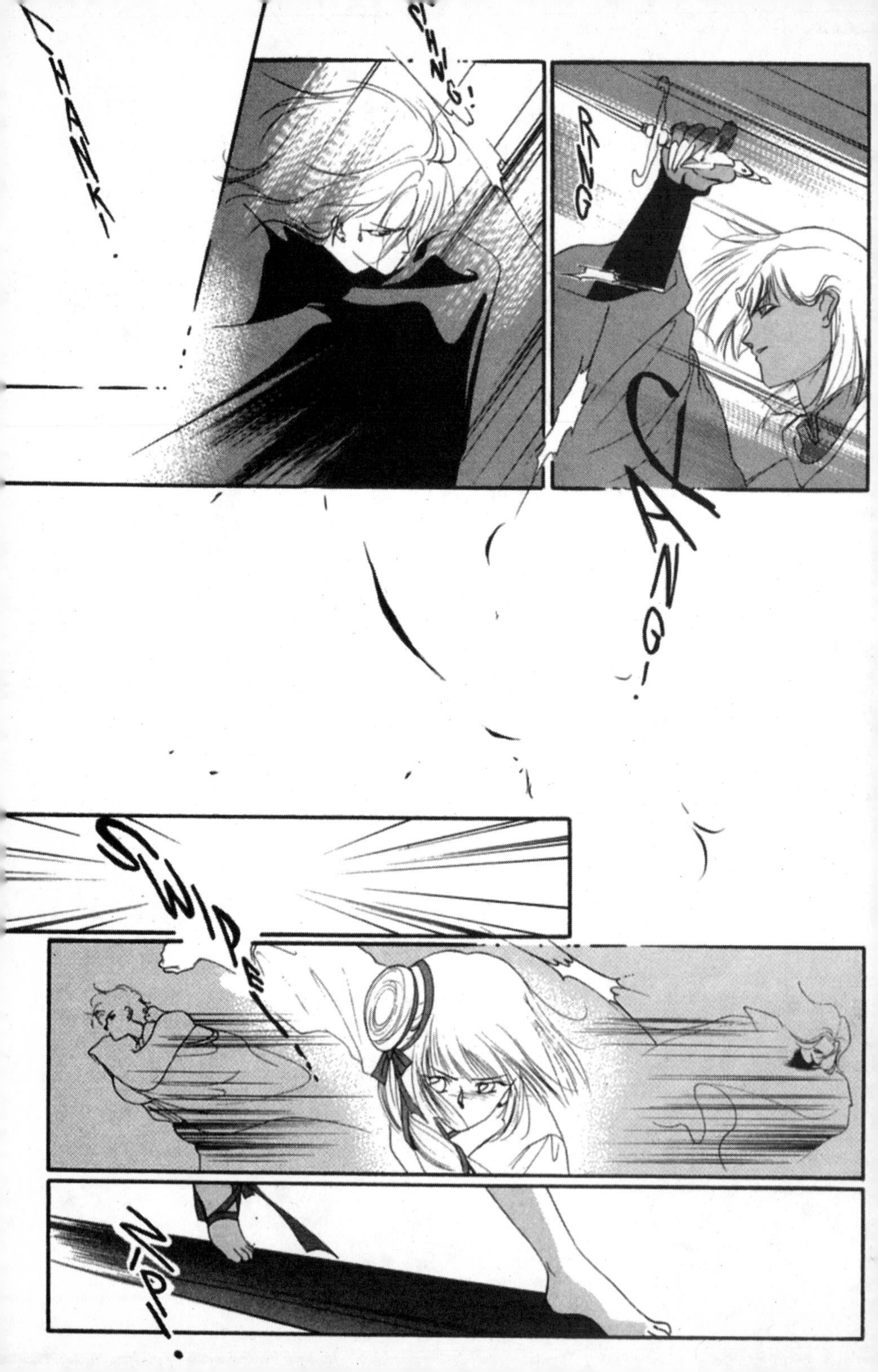
RING
SHING!
CHANK!
CLANG!
SWIPE!
ZIP!

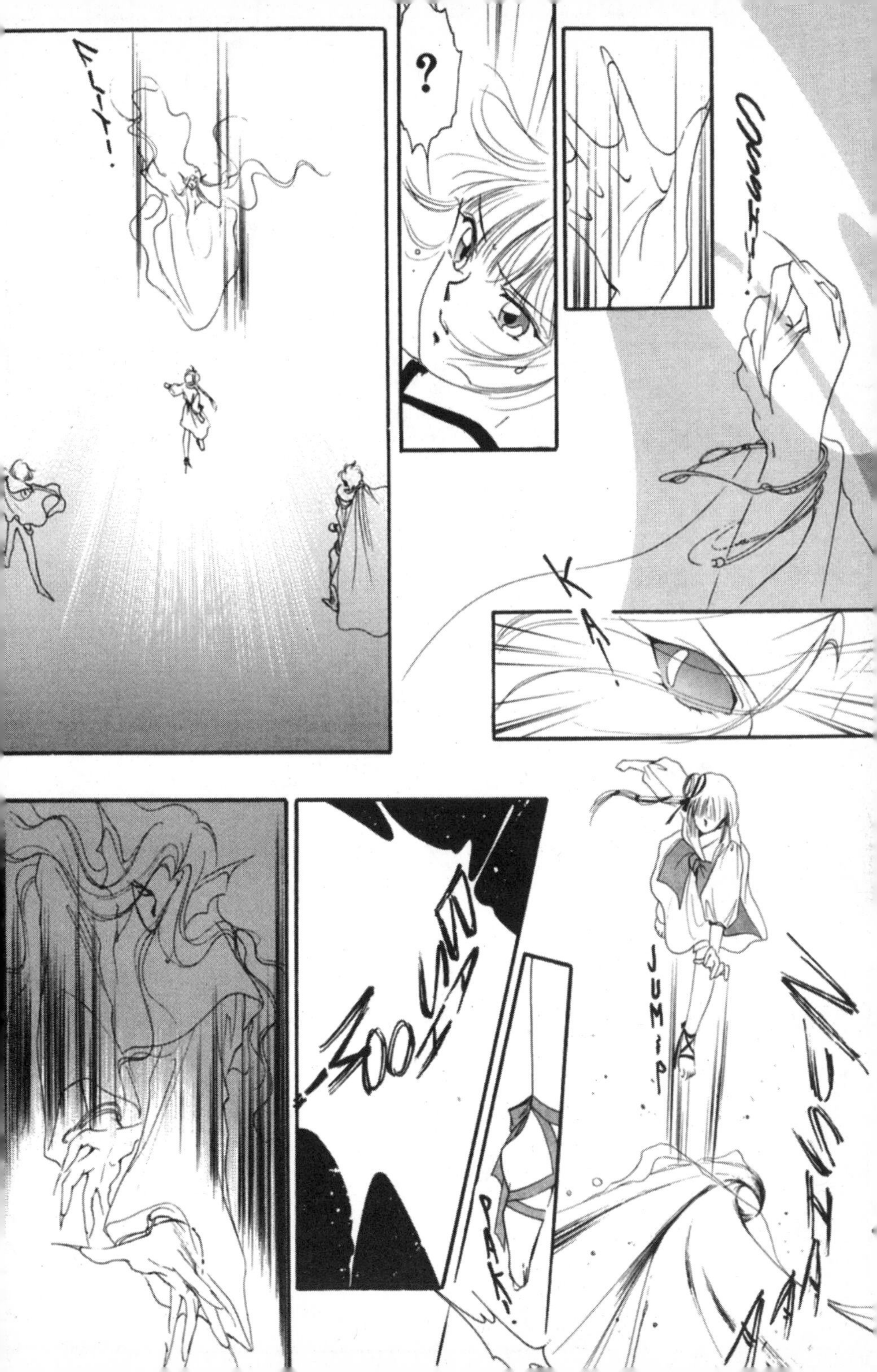
?
KA!
JUMP

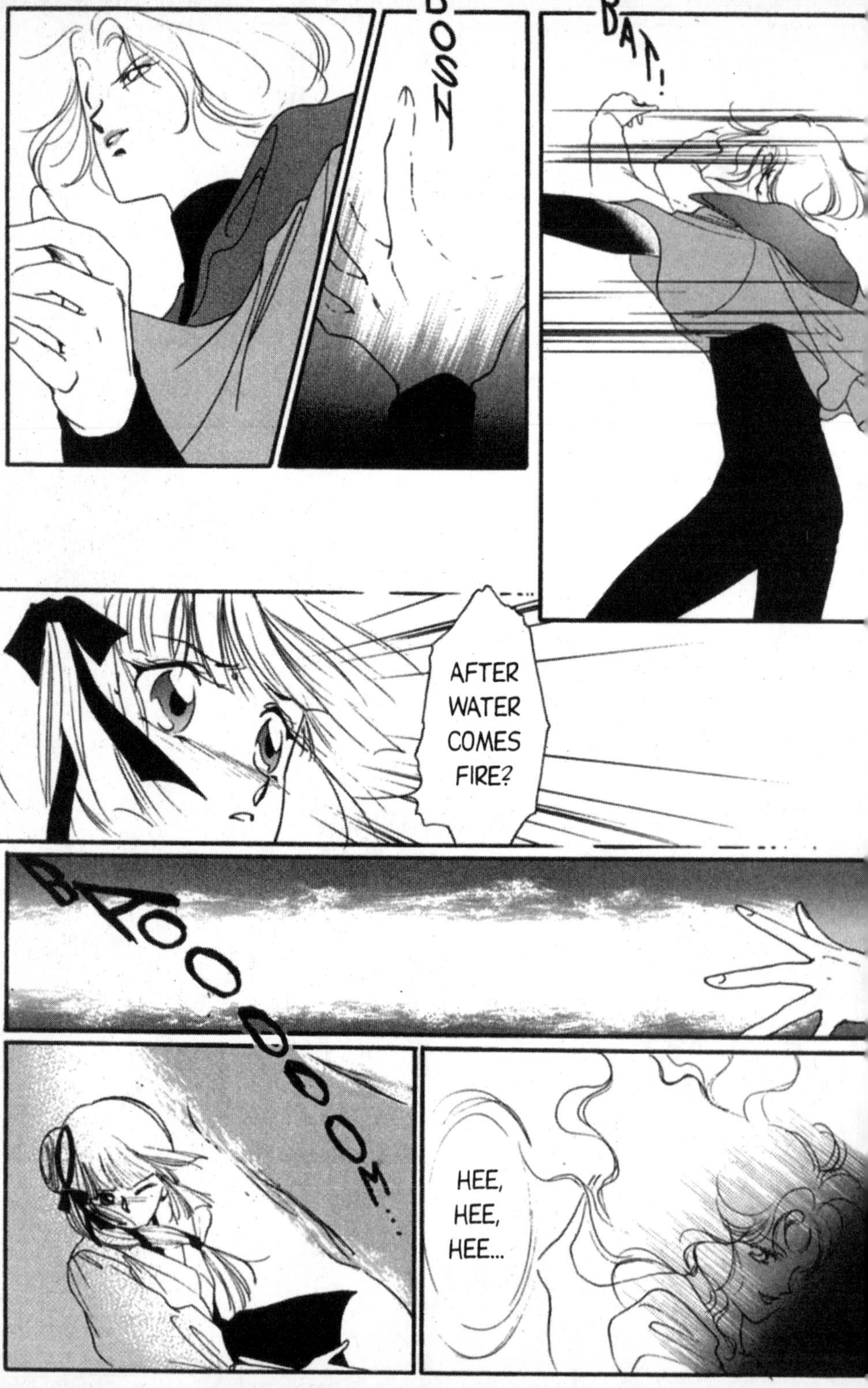
BAT!
BOSH
AFTER WATER COMES FIRE?
BAOOOOOOM...
HEE, HEE, HEE...

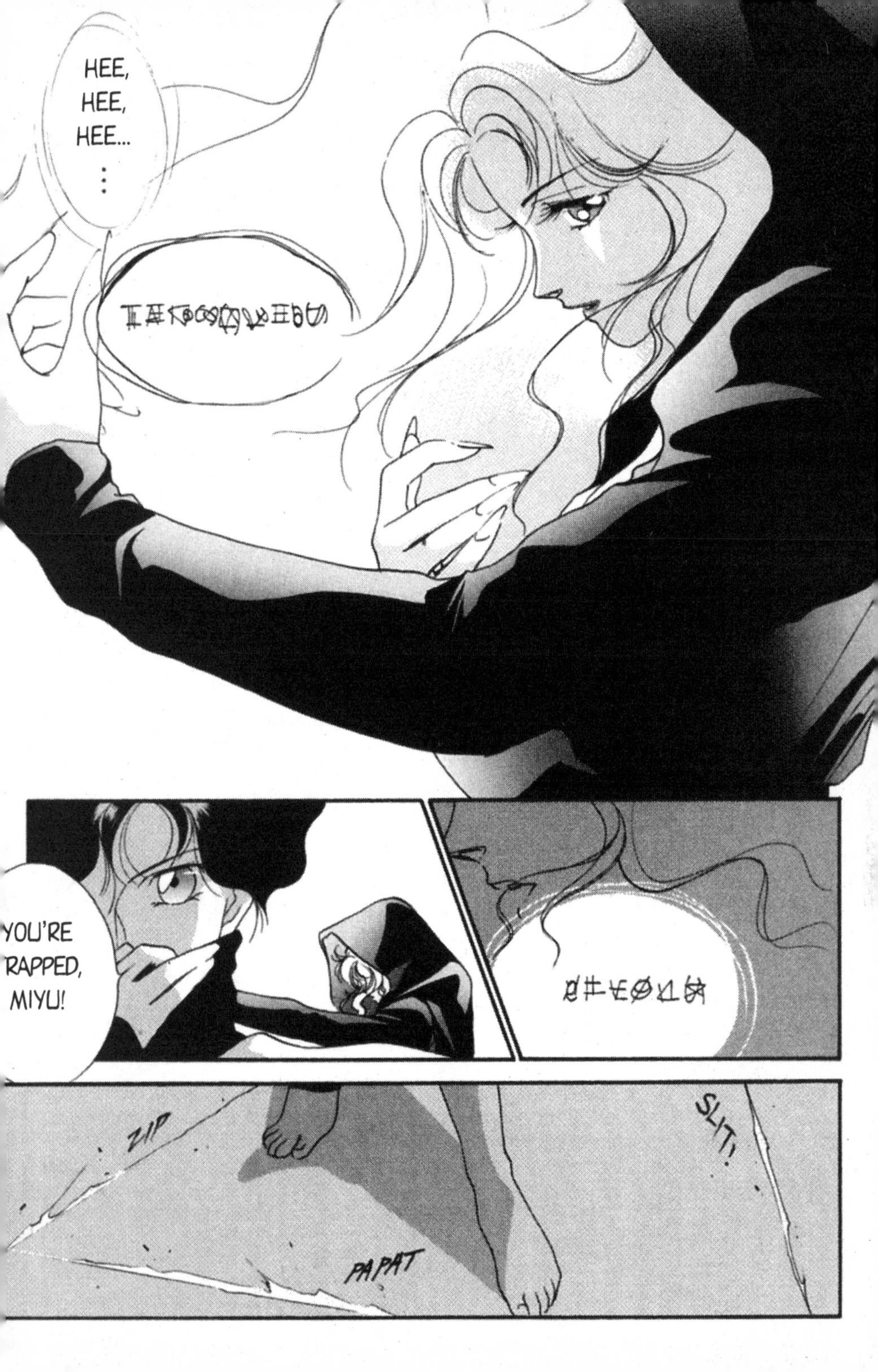
HEE, HEE, HEE...
...
YOU'RE RAPPED, MIYU!
SLIT!
ZIP
PAPAT

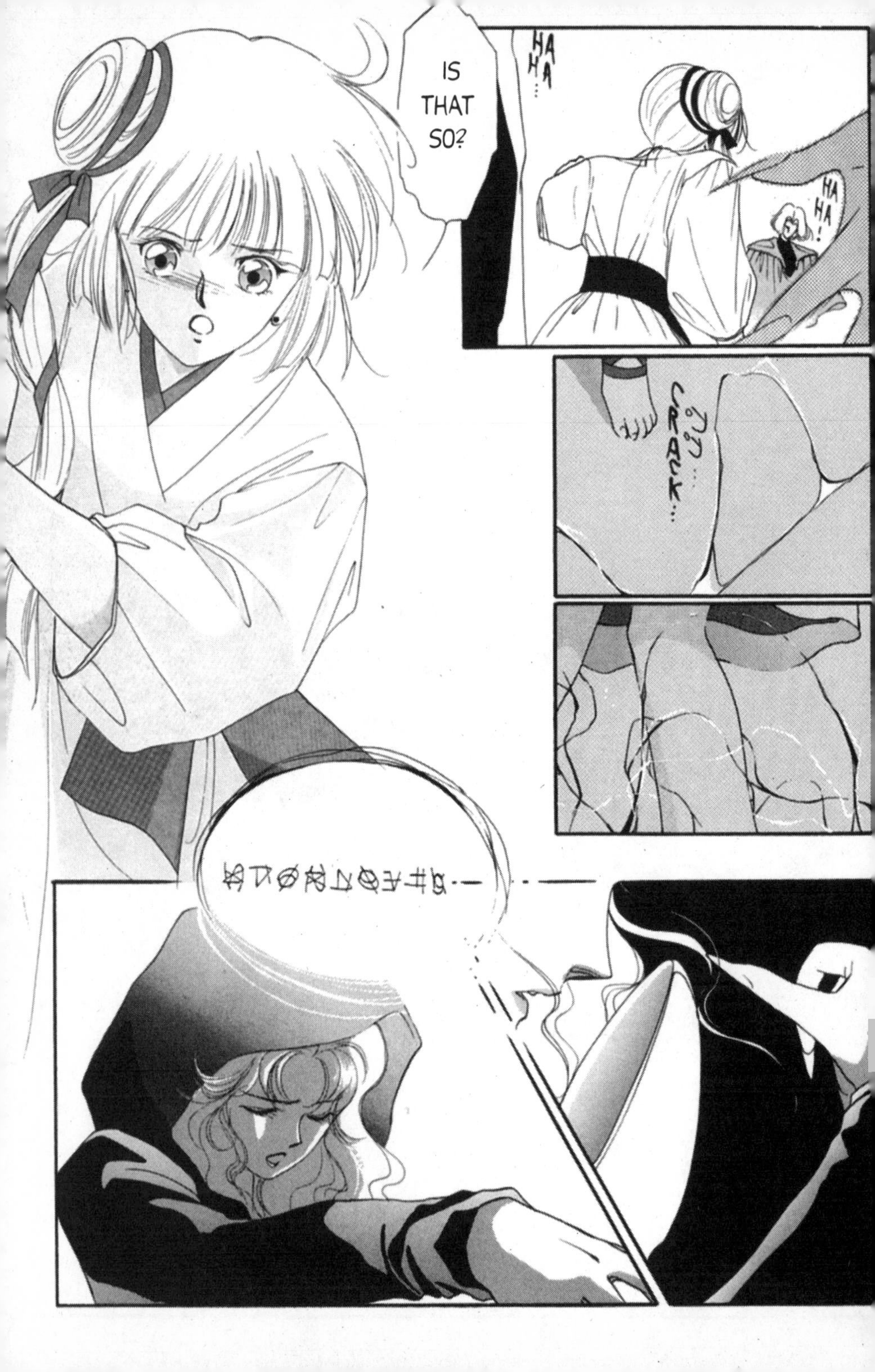

HA HA...
HA HA!
IS THAT SO?
CRACK...

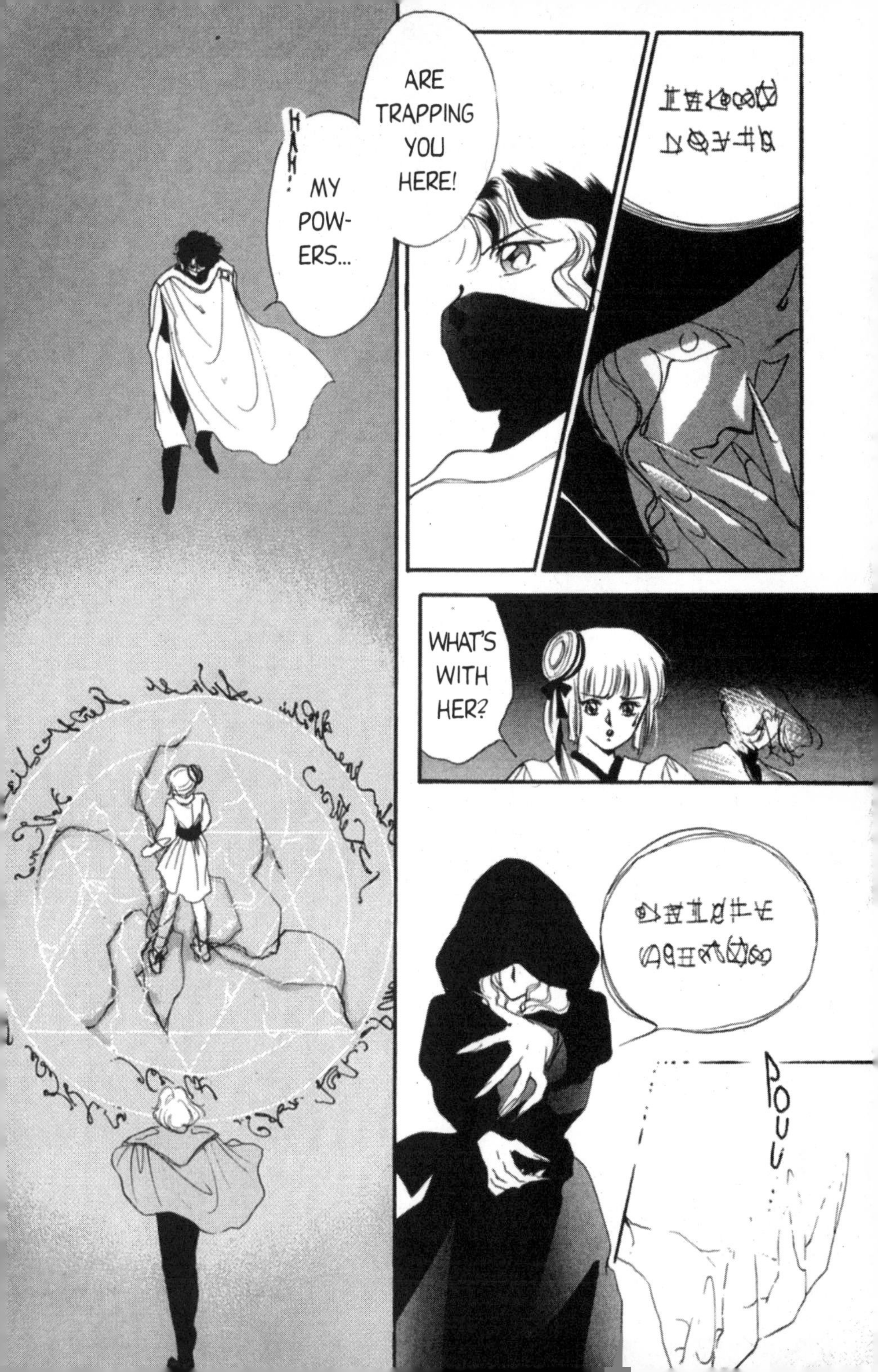
HAH!
MY POW-ERS...
ARE TRAPPING YOU HERE!
WHAT'S WITH HER?
POUU...

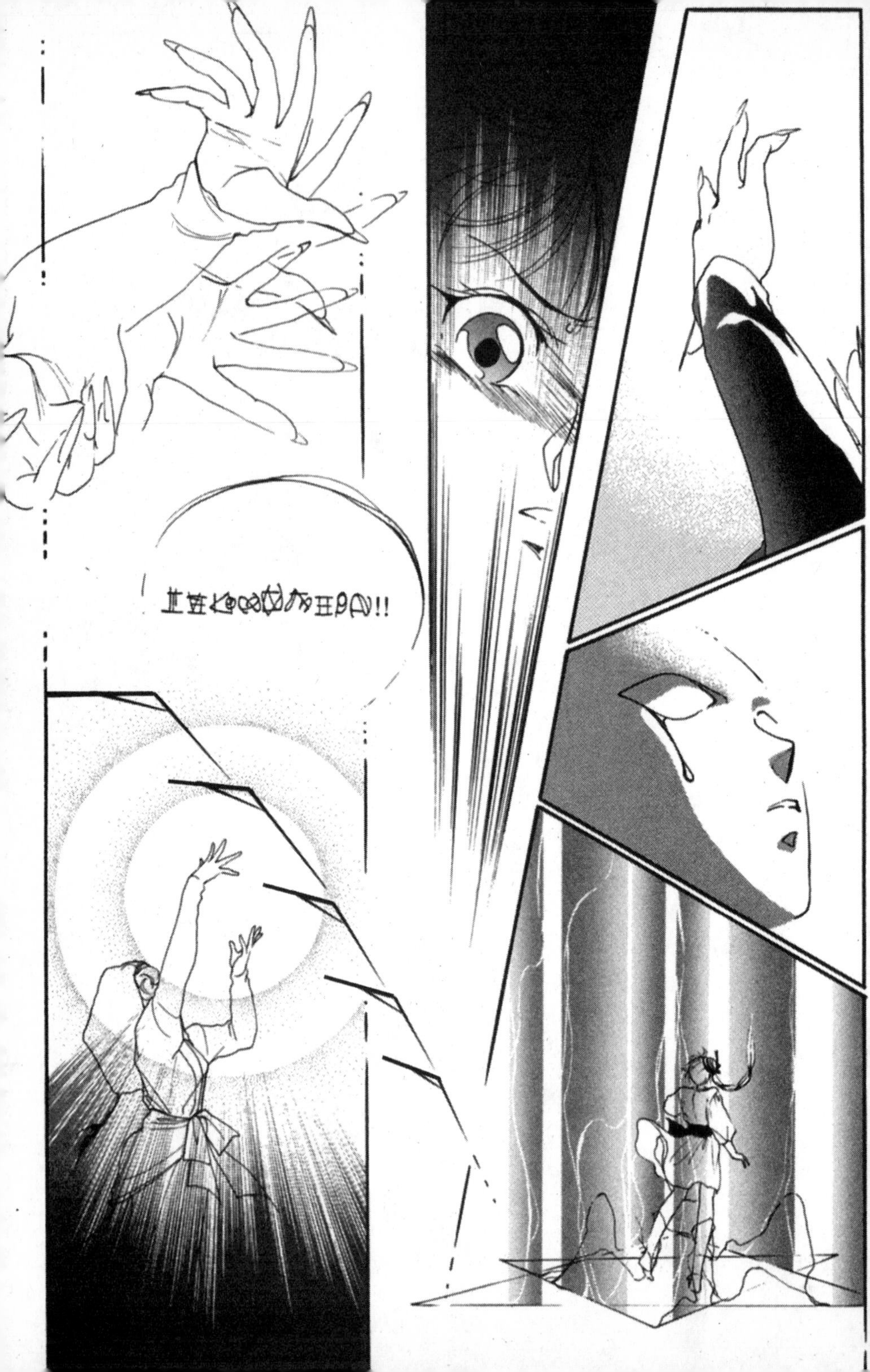

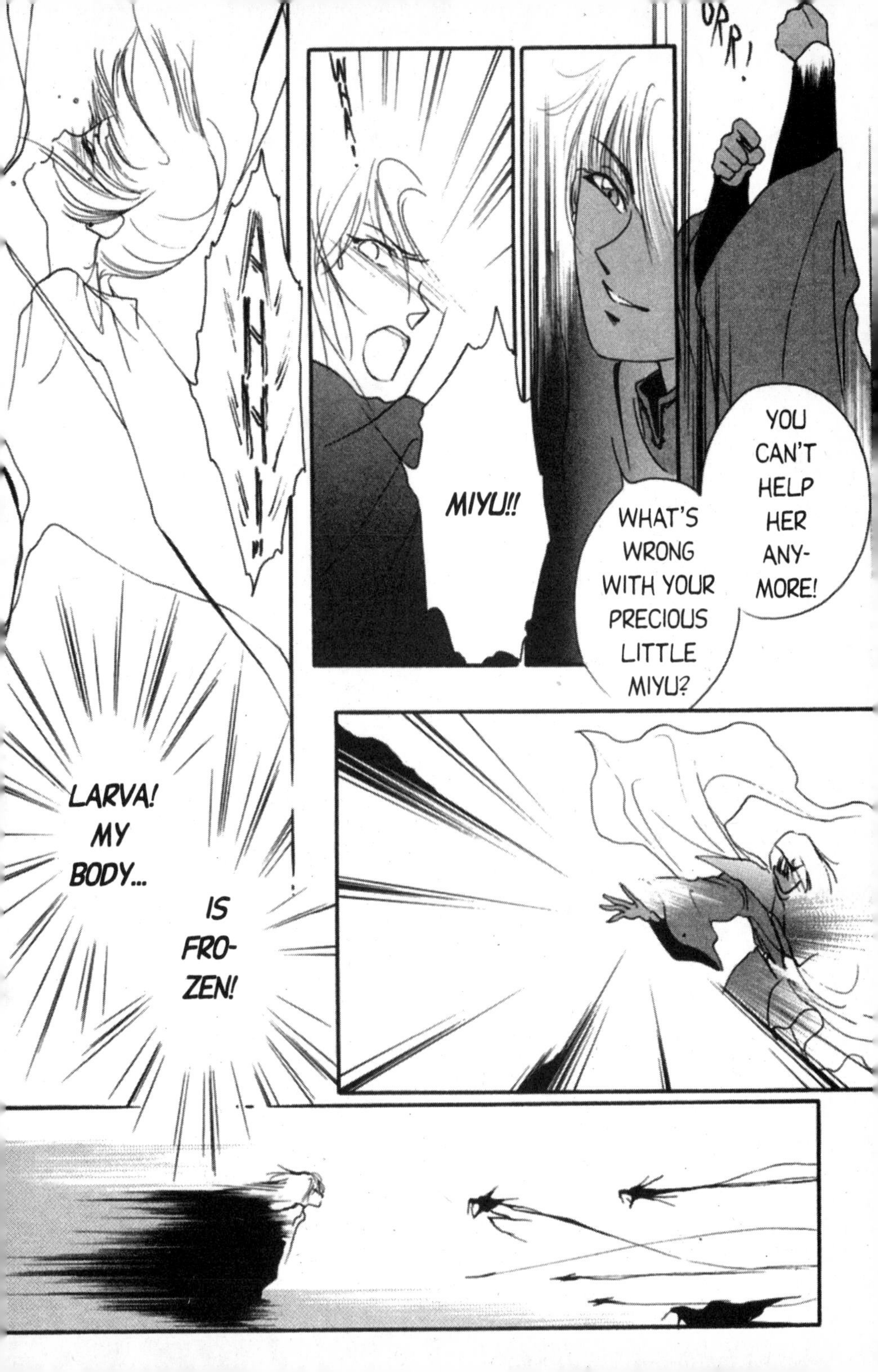
YOU CAN'T HELP HER ANY-MORE!
WHAT'S WRONG WITH YOUR PRECIOUS LITTLE MIYU?
MIYU!!
LARVA! MY BODY...
IS FRO-ZEN!

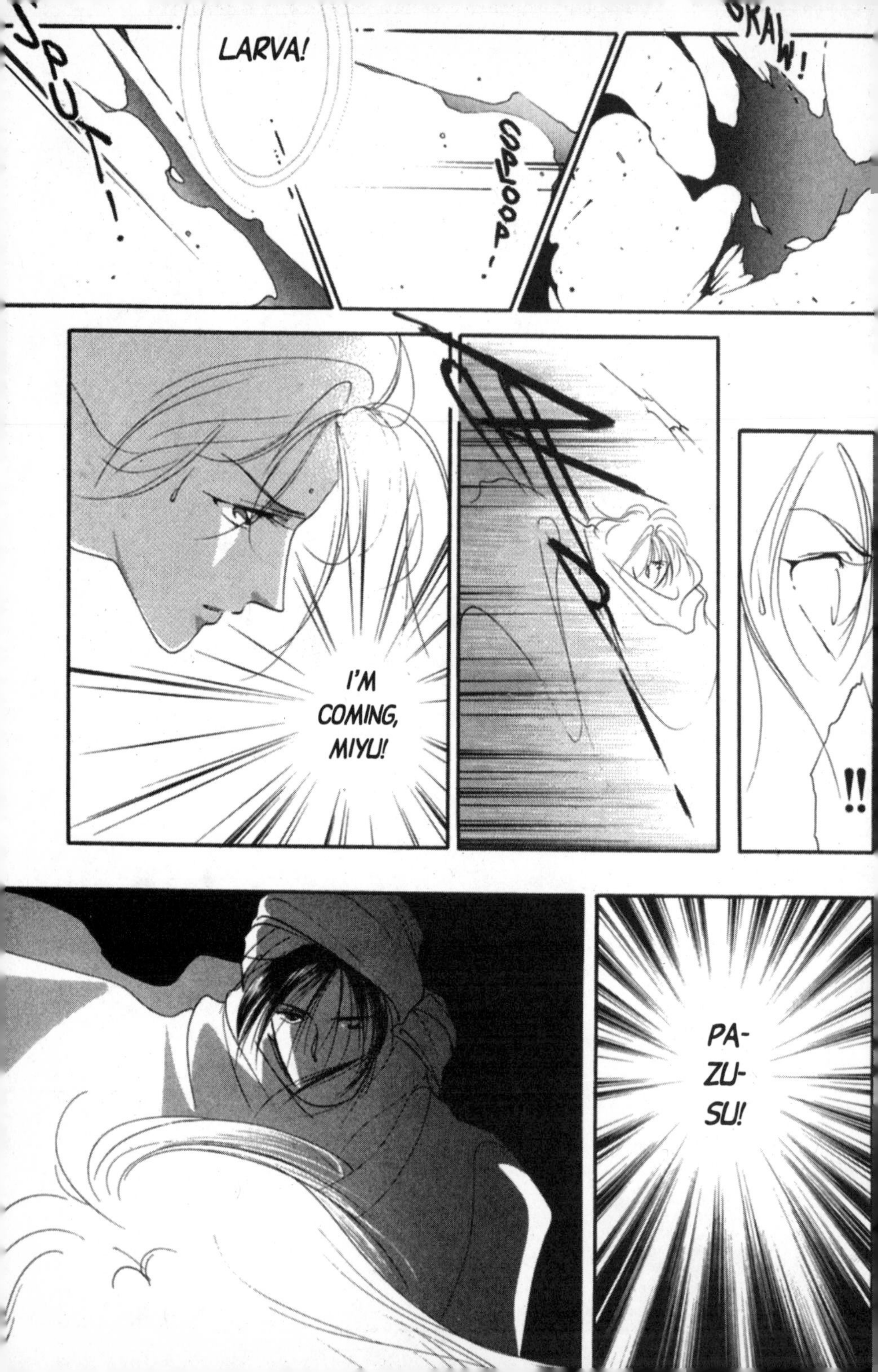
SKRAW!
GOBLOOP...
LARVA!
SPRUK...
!!
I'M COMING, MIYU!
PA-ZU-SU!

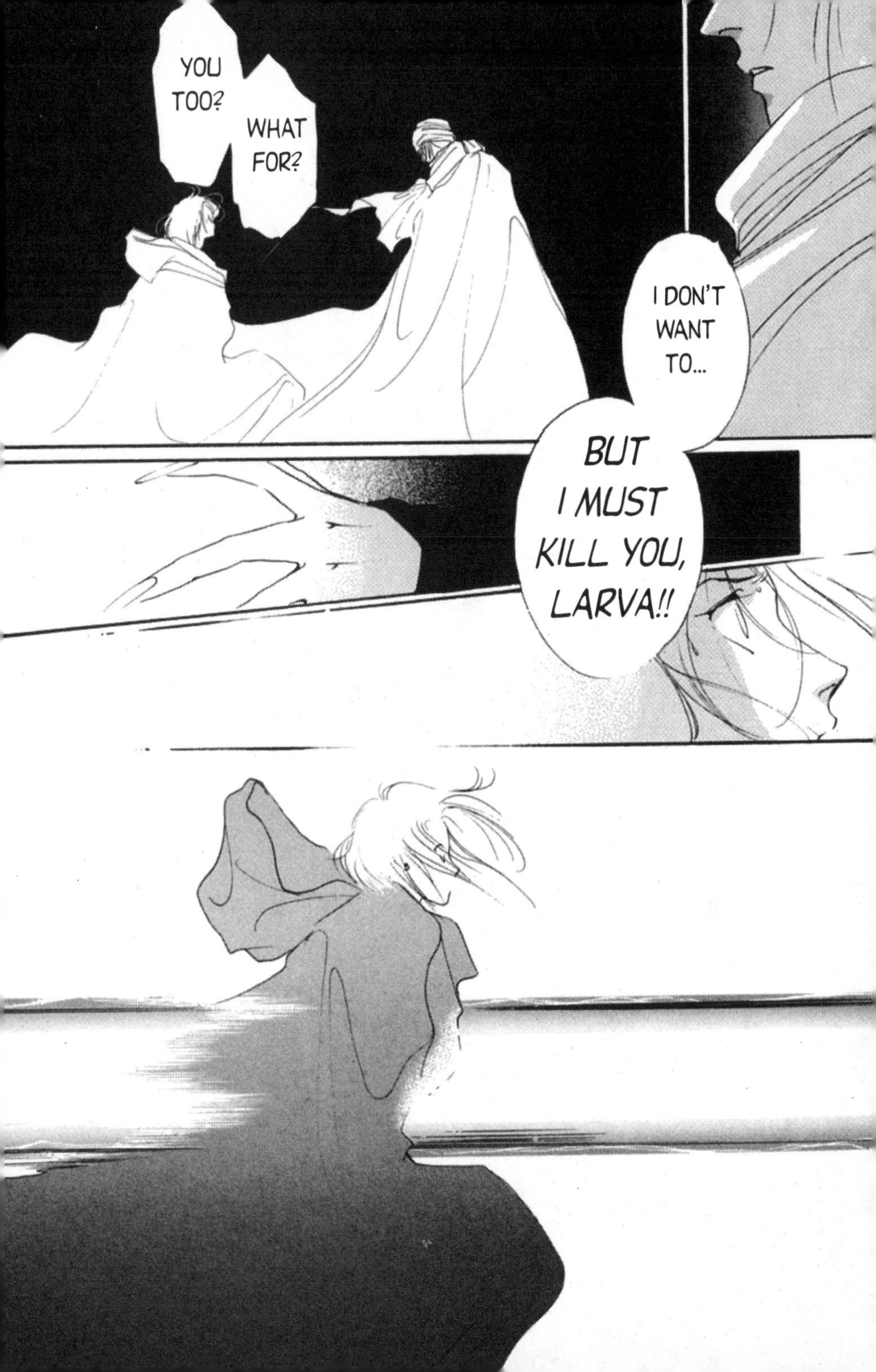
I DON'T WANT TO...
BUT I MUST KILL YOU, LARVA!!
YOU TOO?
WHAT FOR?

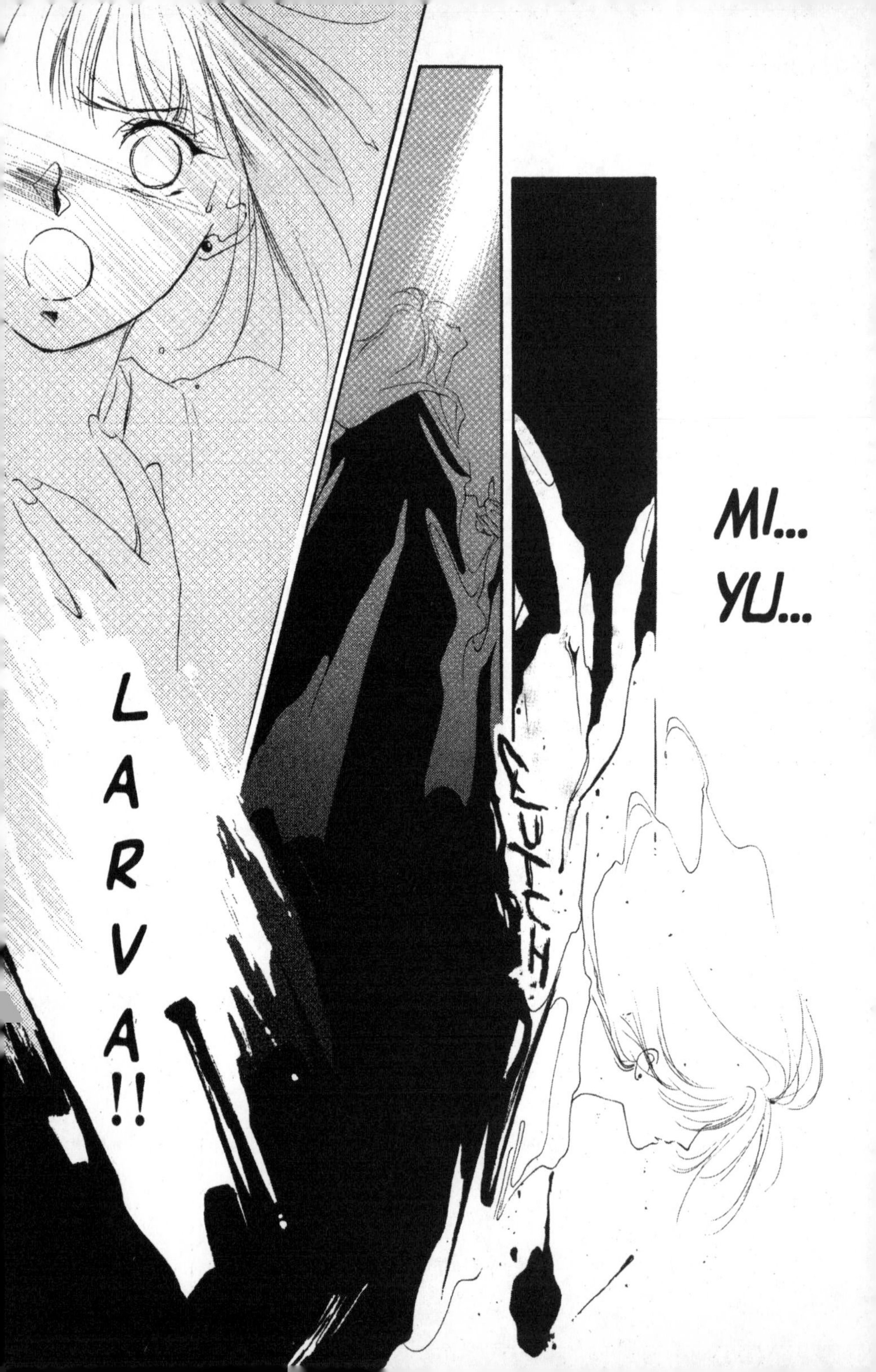
MI...
YU...
LARVA!!

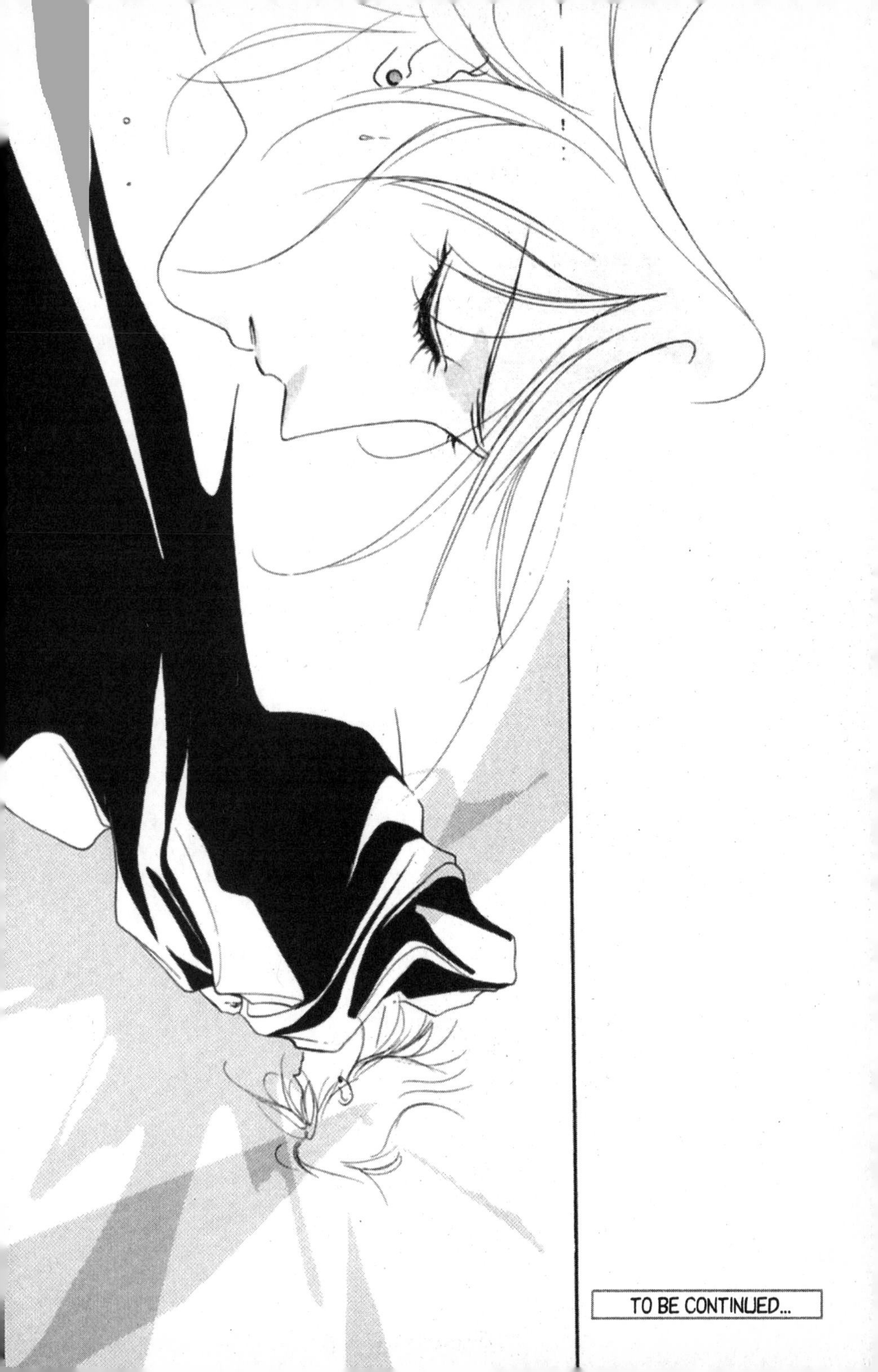
TO BE CONTINUED...

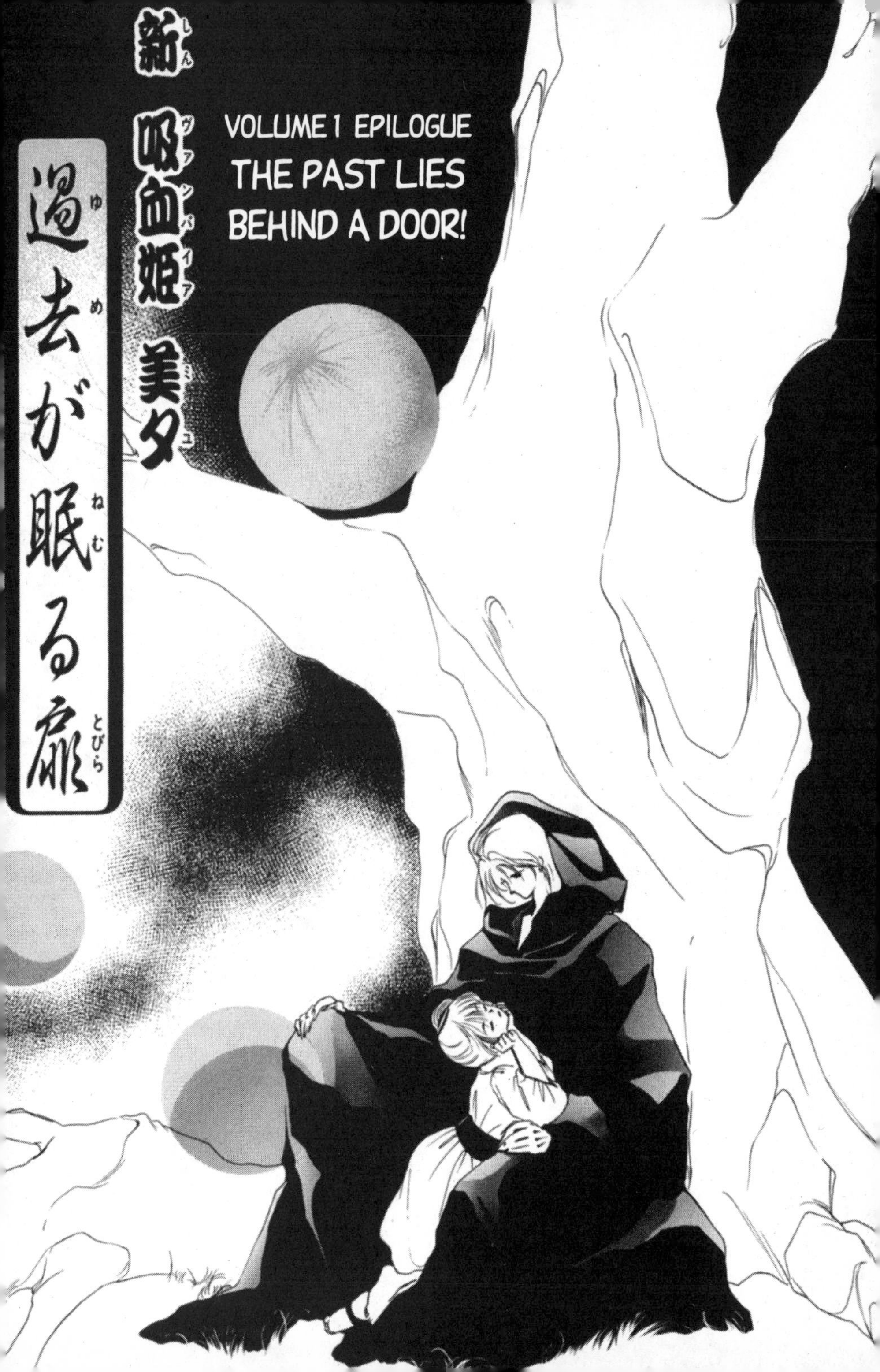
VOLUME 1 EPILOGUE
THE PAST LIES
BEHIND A DOOR!
新吸血姫美夕
過去が眠る扉

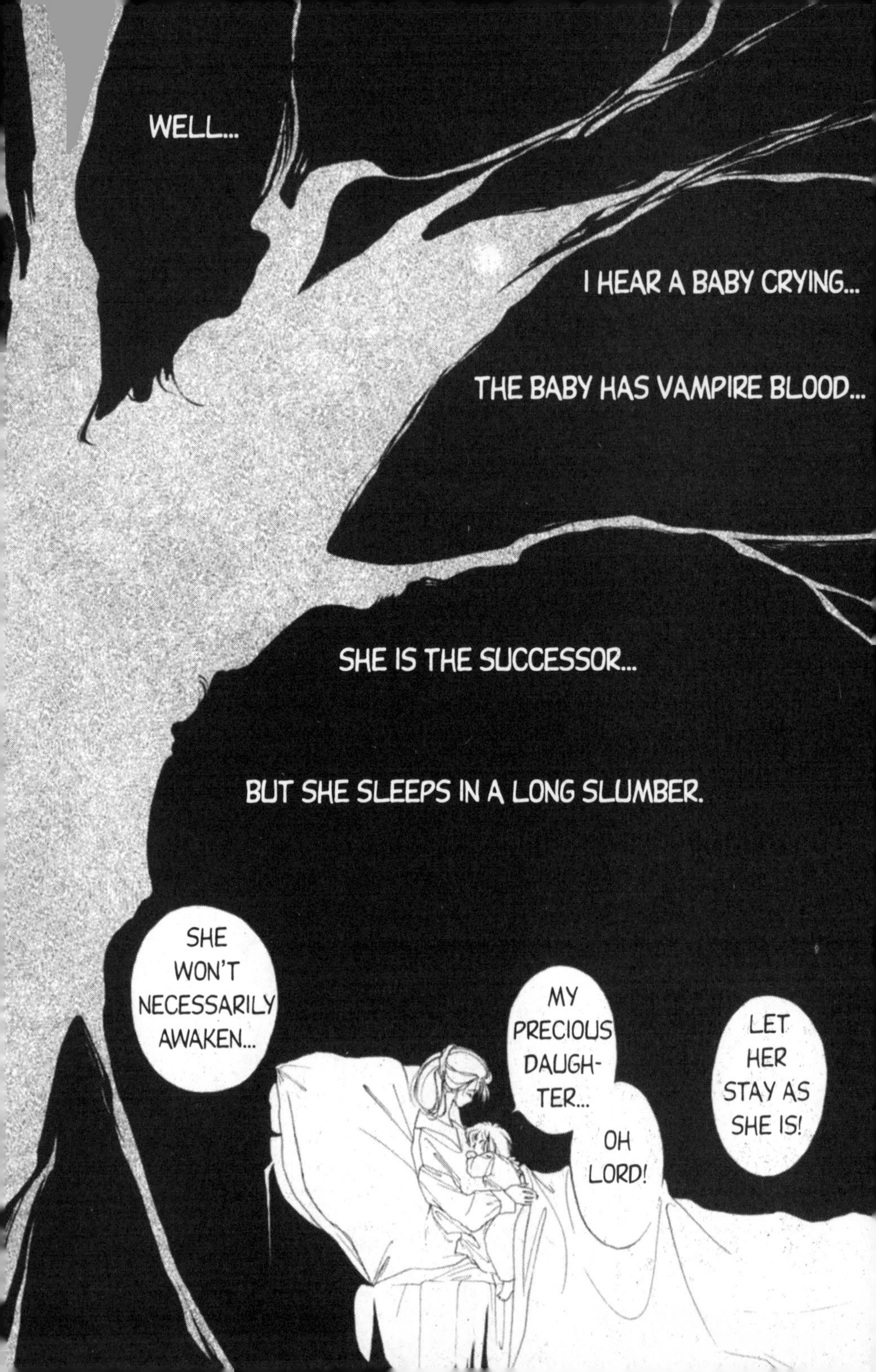
WELL...
I HEAR A BABY CRYING...
THE BABY HAS VAMPIRE BLOOD...
SHE IS THE SUCCESSOR...
BUT SHE SLEEPS IN A LONG SLUMBER.
LET HER STAY AS SHE IS!
MY PRECIOUS DAUGH-TER...
OH LORD!
SHE WON'T NECESSARILY AWAKEN...

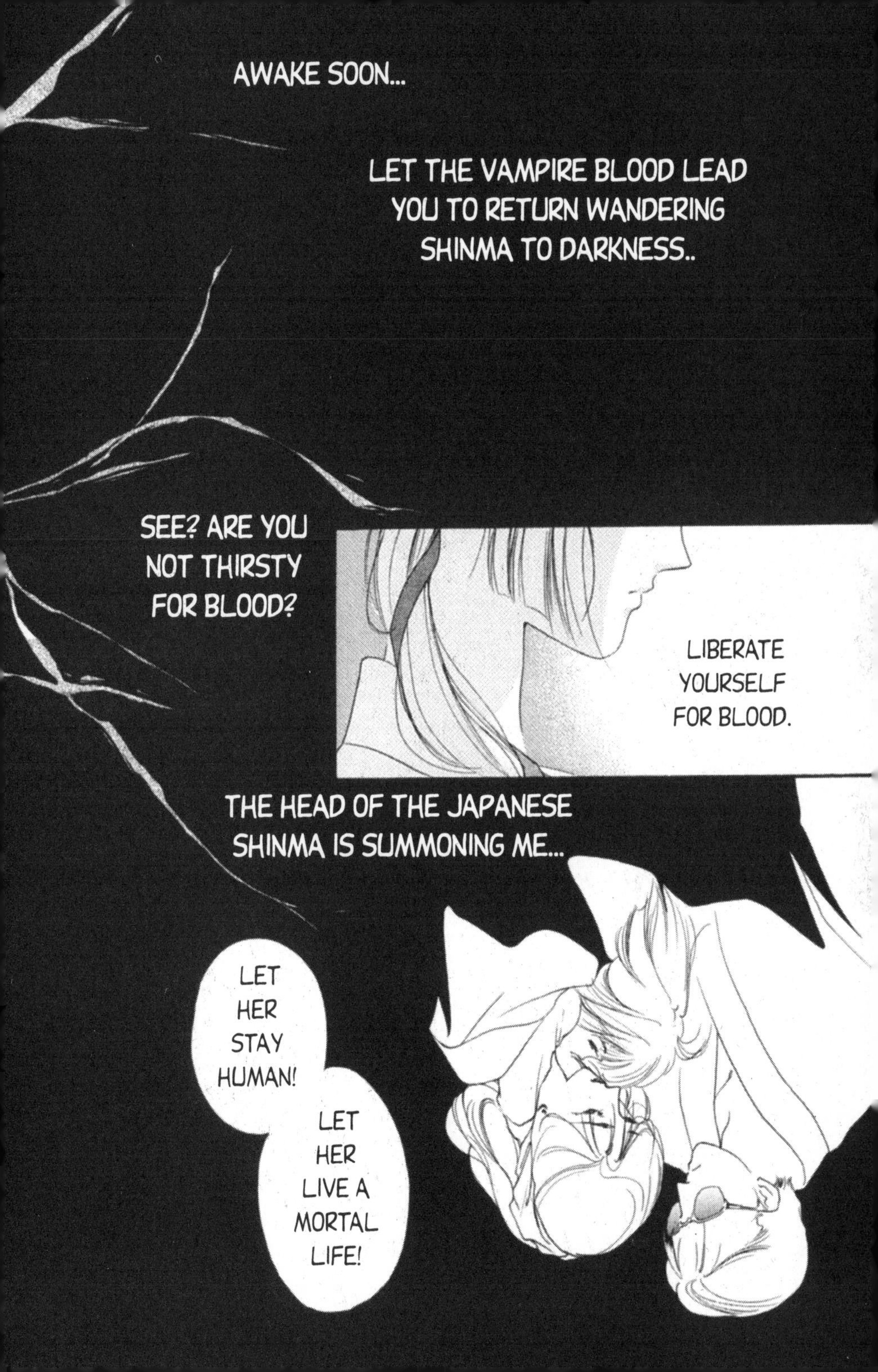

AWAKE SOON...
LET THE VAMPIRE BLOOD LEAD YOU TO RETURN WANDERING SHINMA TO DARKNESS..
SEE? ARE YOU NOT THIRSTY FOR BLOOD?
LIBERATE YOURSELF FOR BLOOD.
THE HEAD OF THE JAPANESE SHINMA IS SUMMONING ME...
LET HER STAY HUMAN!
LET HER LIVE A MORTAL LIFE!

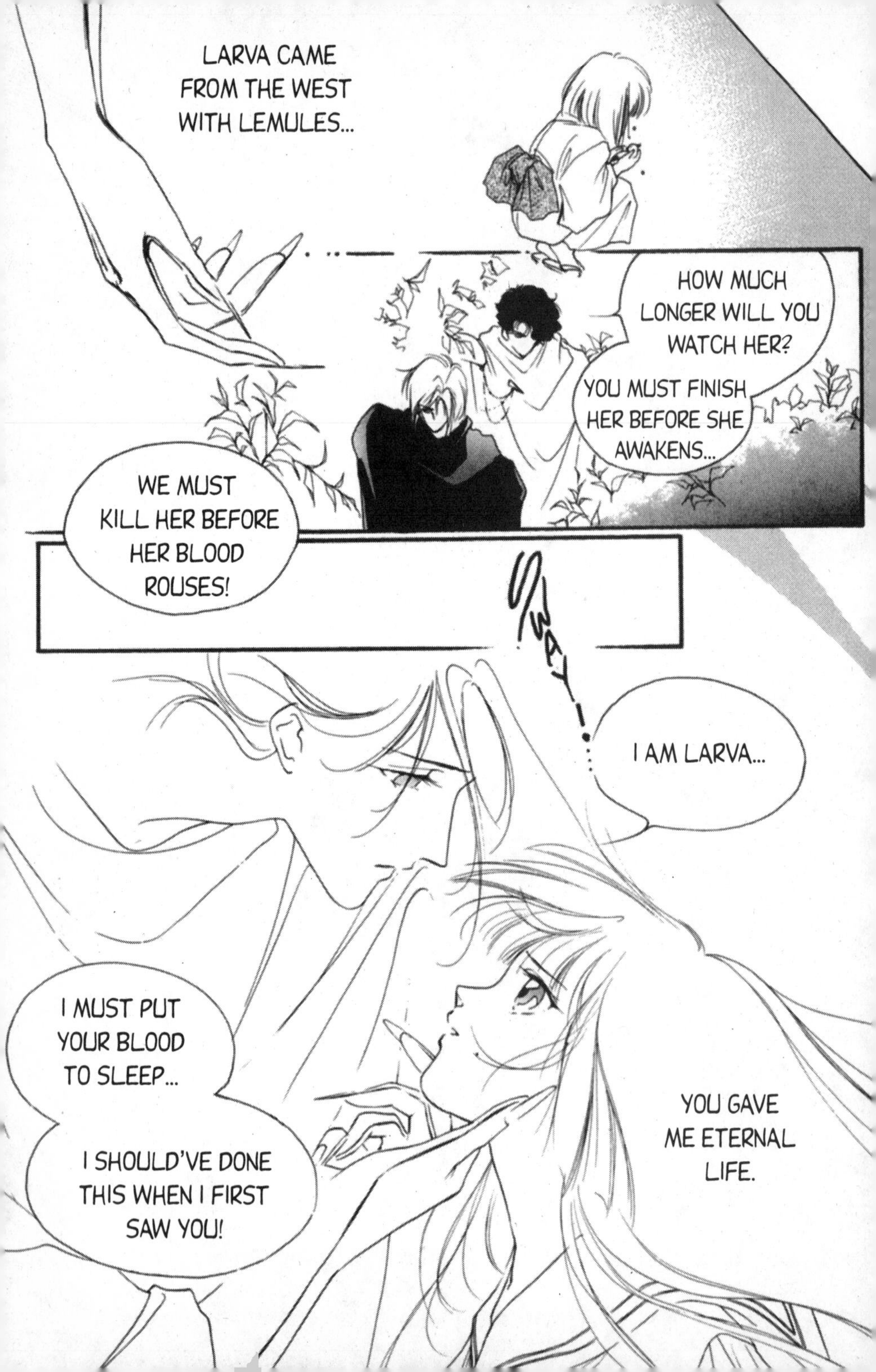
LARVA CAME FROM THE WEST WITH LEMULES...
HOW MUCH LONGER WILL YOU WATCH HER?
YOU MUST FINISH HER BEFORE SHE AWAKENS...
WE MUST KILL HER BEFORE HER BLOOD ROUSES!
SWAY...
I AM LARVA...
I MUST PUT YOUR BLOOD TO SLEEP...
I SHOULD'VE DONE THIS WHEN I FIRST SAW YOU!
YOU GAVE ME ETERNAL LIFE.

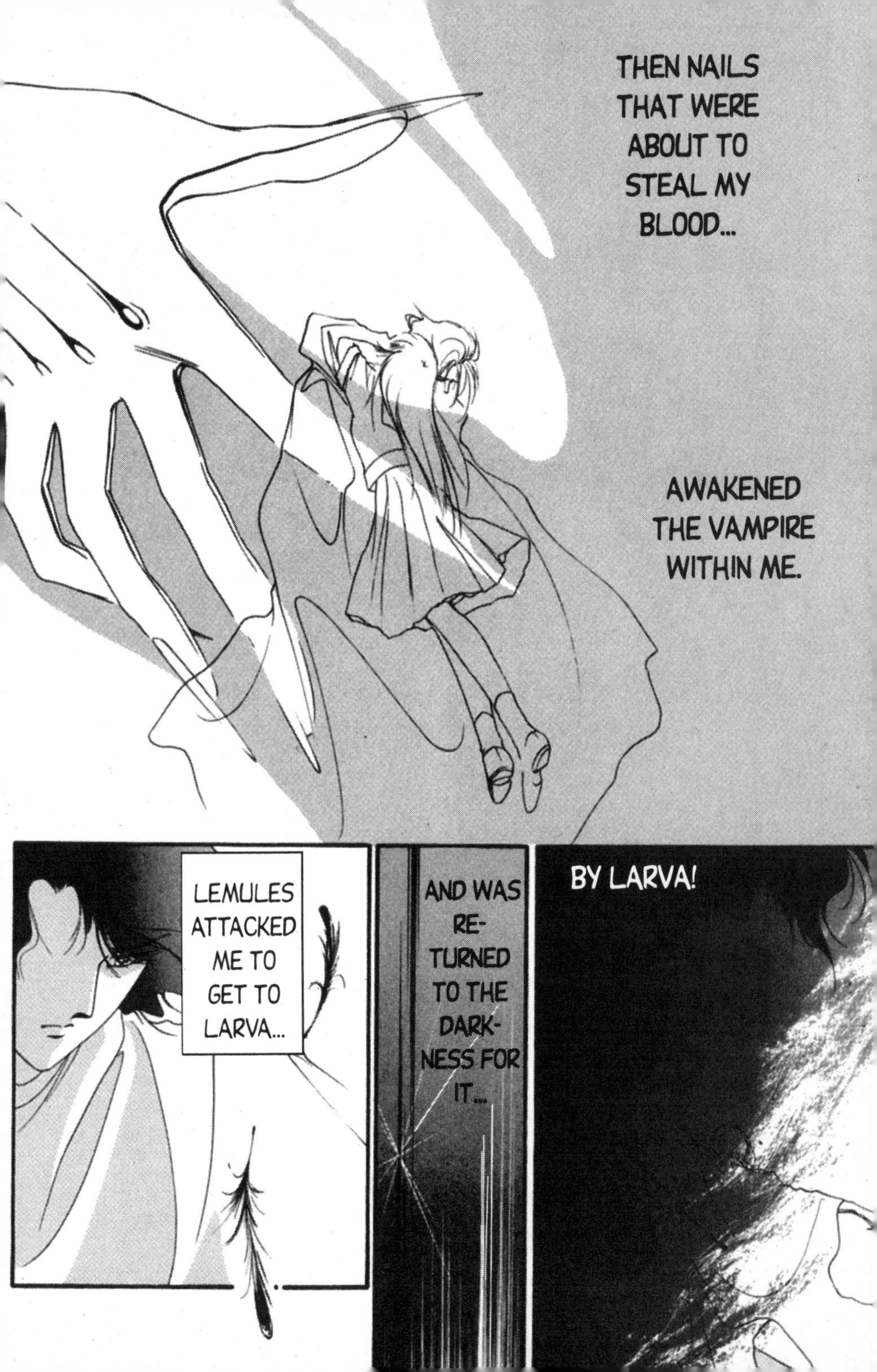
THEN NAILS THAT WERE ABOUT TO STEAL MY BLOOD...
AWAKENED THE VAMPIRE WITHIN ME.
LEMULES ATTACKED ME TO GET TO LARVA...
AND WAS RE-TURNED TO THE DARK-NESS FOR IT...
BY LARVA!

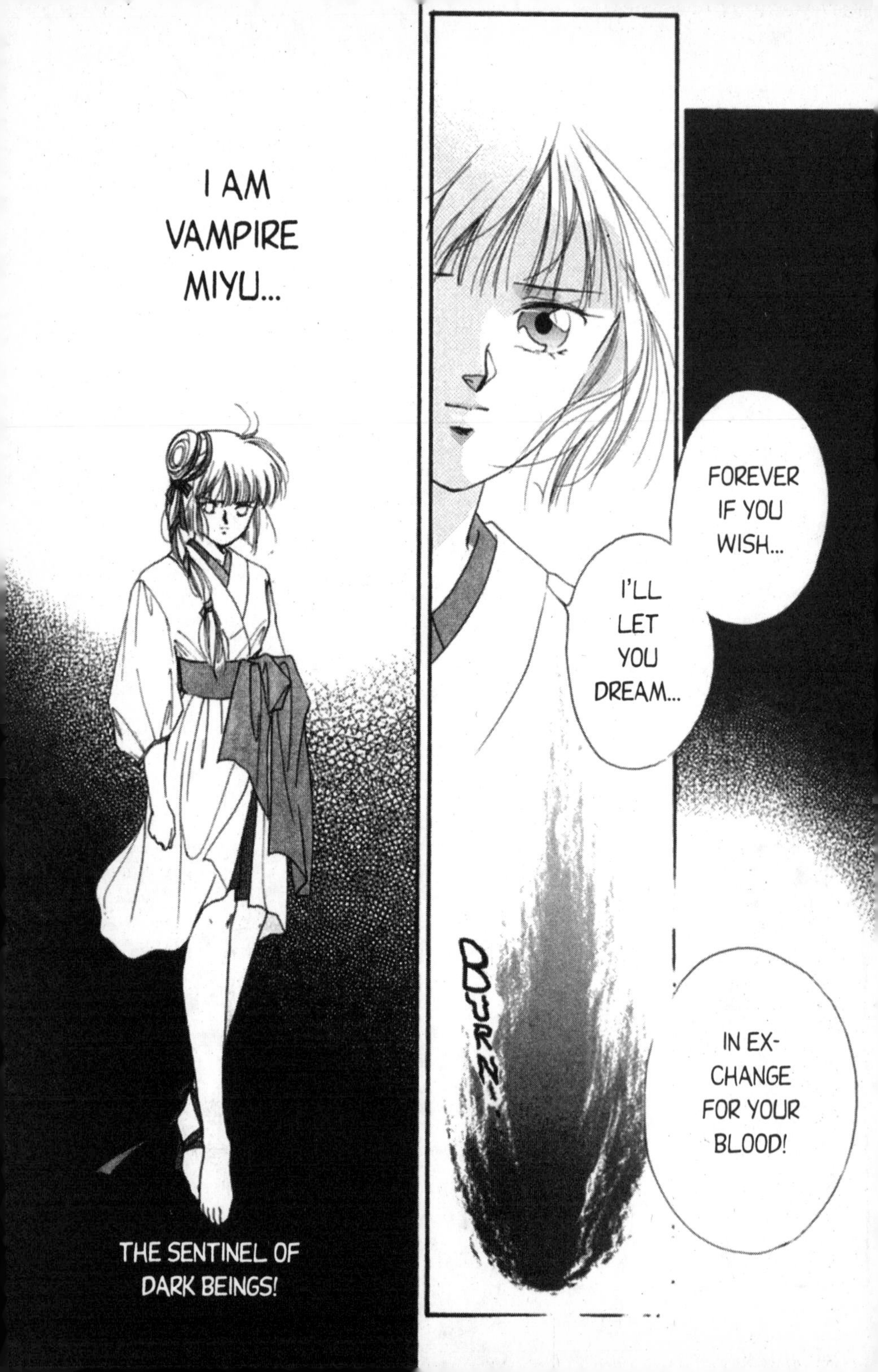
FOREVER IF YOU WISH...
I'LL LET YOU DREAM...
IN EX-CHANGE FOR YOUR BLOOD!
BURN!
I AM VAMPIRE MIYU...
THE SENTINEL OF DARK BEINGS!

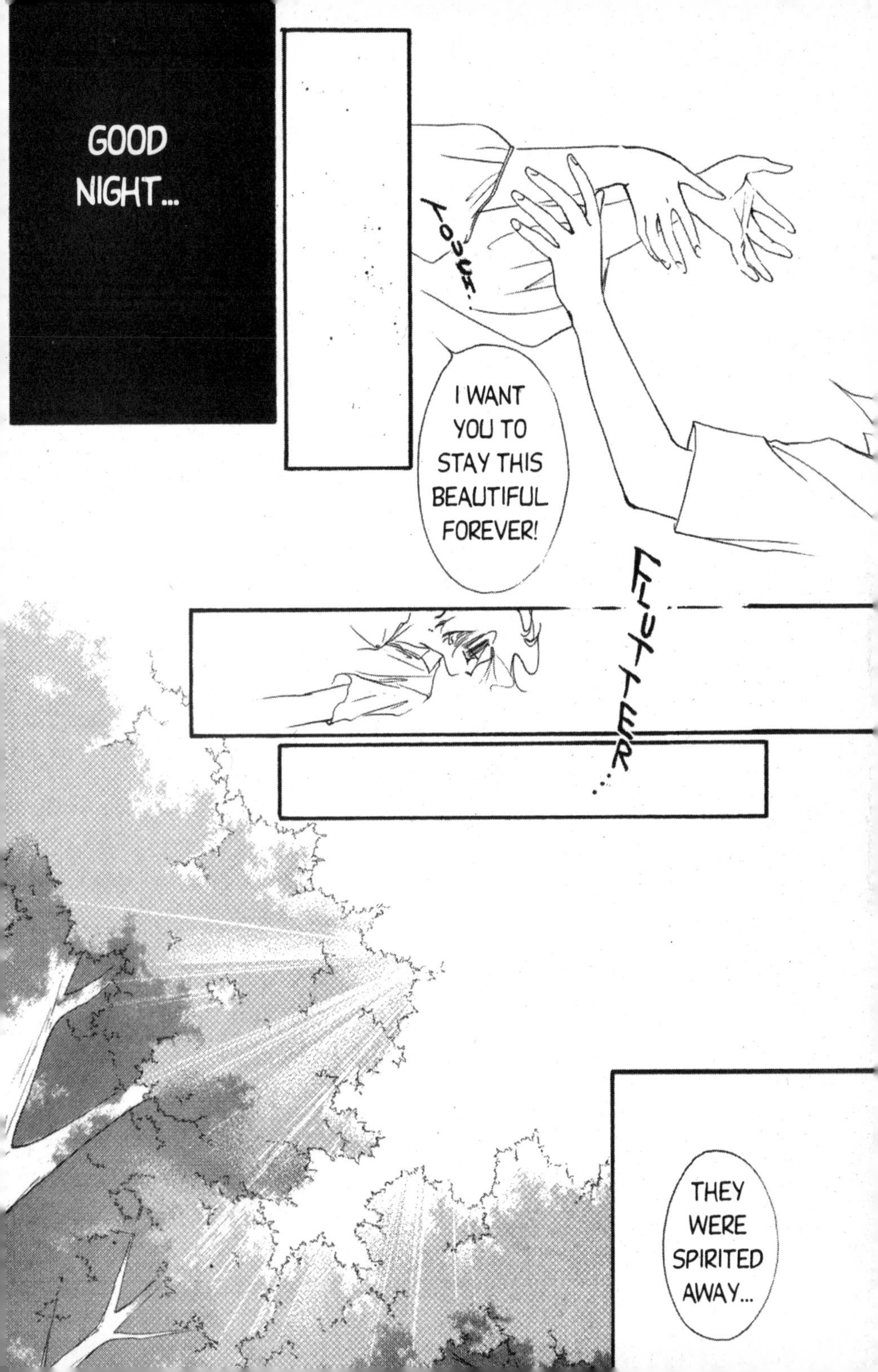
GOOD NIGHT...
TOUCH.
I WANT YOU TO STAY THIS BEAUTIFUL FOREVER!
FLUTTER...
THEY WERE SPIRITED AWAY...

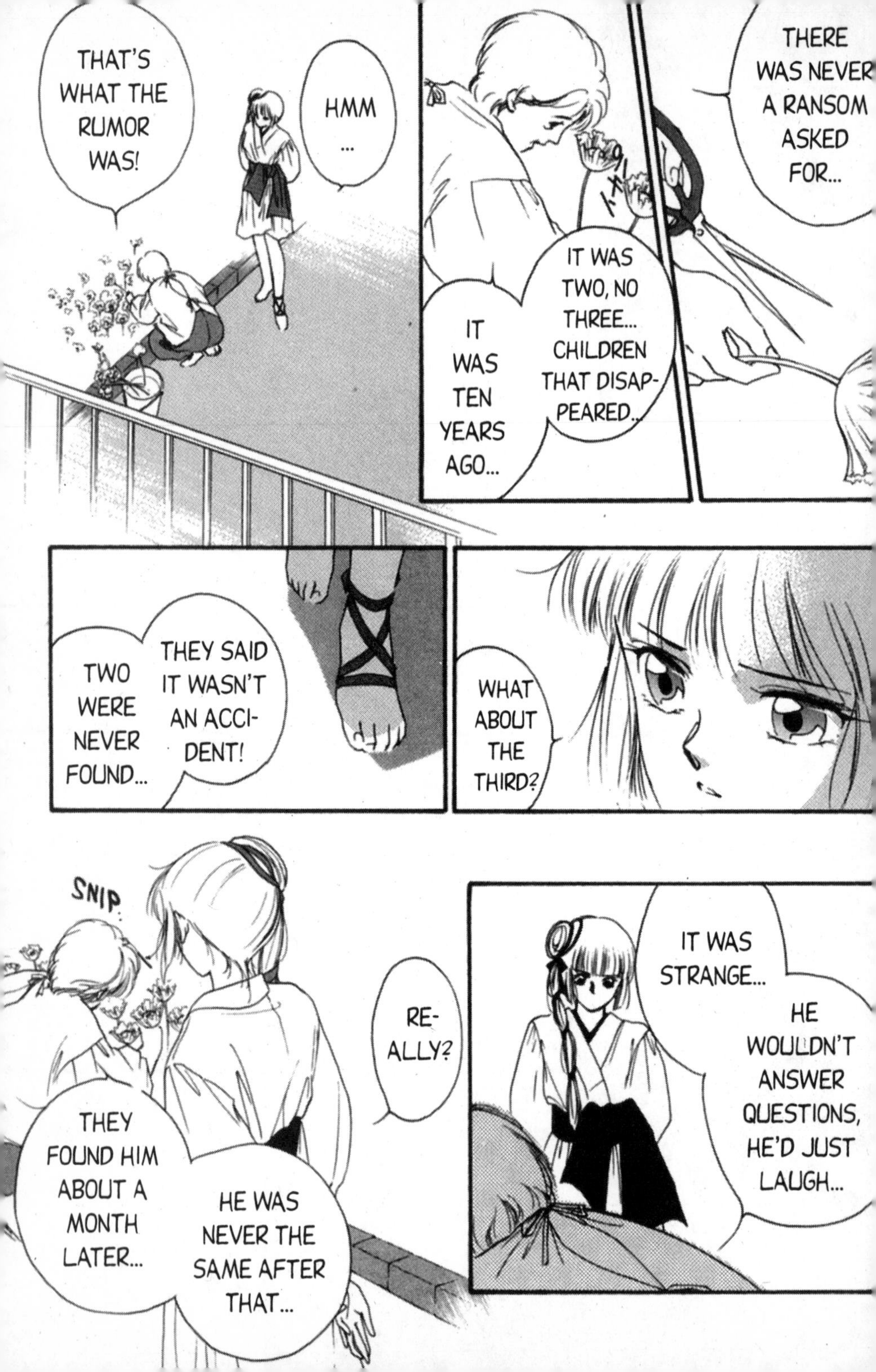
THAT'S WHAT THE RUMOR WAS!
HMM ...
IT WAS TEN YEARS AGO...
IT WAS TWO, NO THREE... CHILDREN THAT DISAPPEARED...
THERE WAS NEVER A RANSOM ASKED FOR...
THEY SAID IT WASN'T AN ACCIDENT!
TWO WERE NEVER FOUND...
WHAT ABOUT THE THIRD?
SNIP
THEY FOUND HIM ABOUT A MONTH LATER...
HE WAS NEVER THE SAME AFTER THAT...
RE-ALLY?
IT WAS STRANGE...
HE WOULDN'T ANSWER QUESTIONS, HE'D JUST LAUGH...

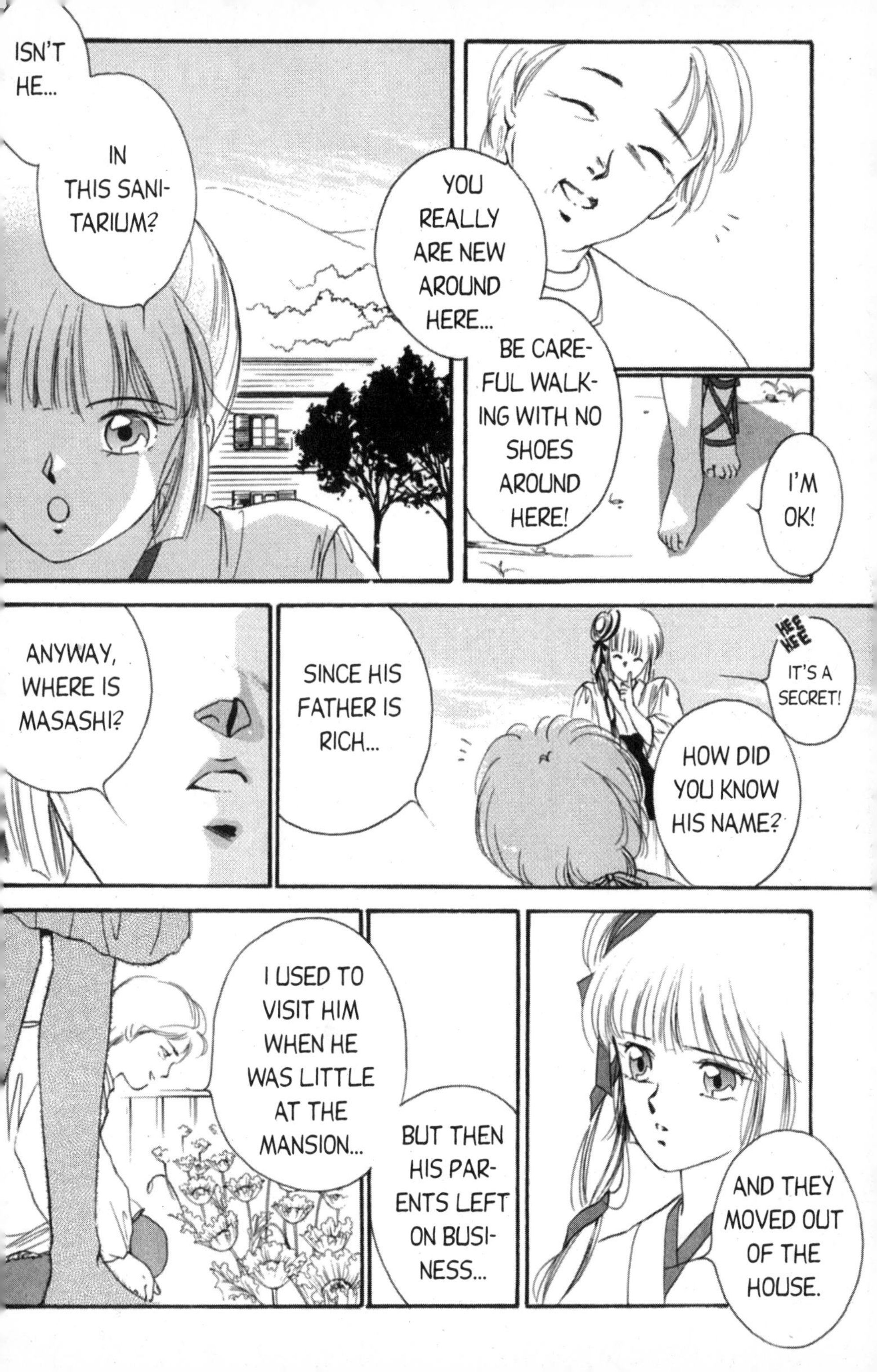
ISN'T HE...
IN THIS SANI-TARIUM?
YOU REALLY ARE NEW AROUND HERE...
BE CARE-FUL WALK-ING WITH NO SHOES AROUND HERE!
I'M OK!
ANYWAY, WHERE IS MASASHI?
SINCE HIS FATHER IS RICH...
HOW DID YOU KNOW HIS NAME?
HEE HEE
IT'S A SECRET!
I USED TO VISIT HIM WHEN HE WAS LITTLE AT THE MANSION...
BUT THEN HIS PAR-ENTS LEFT ON BUSI-NESS...
AND THEY MOVED OUT OF THE HOUSE.

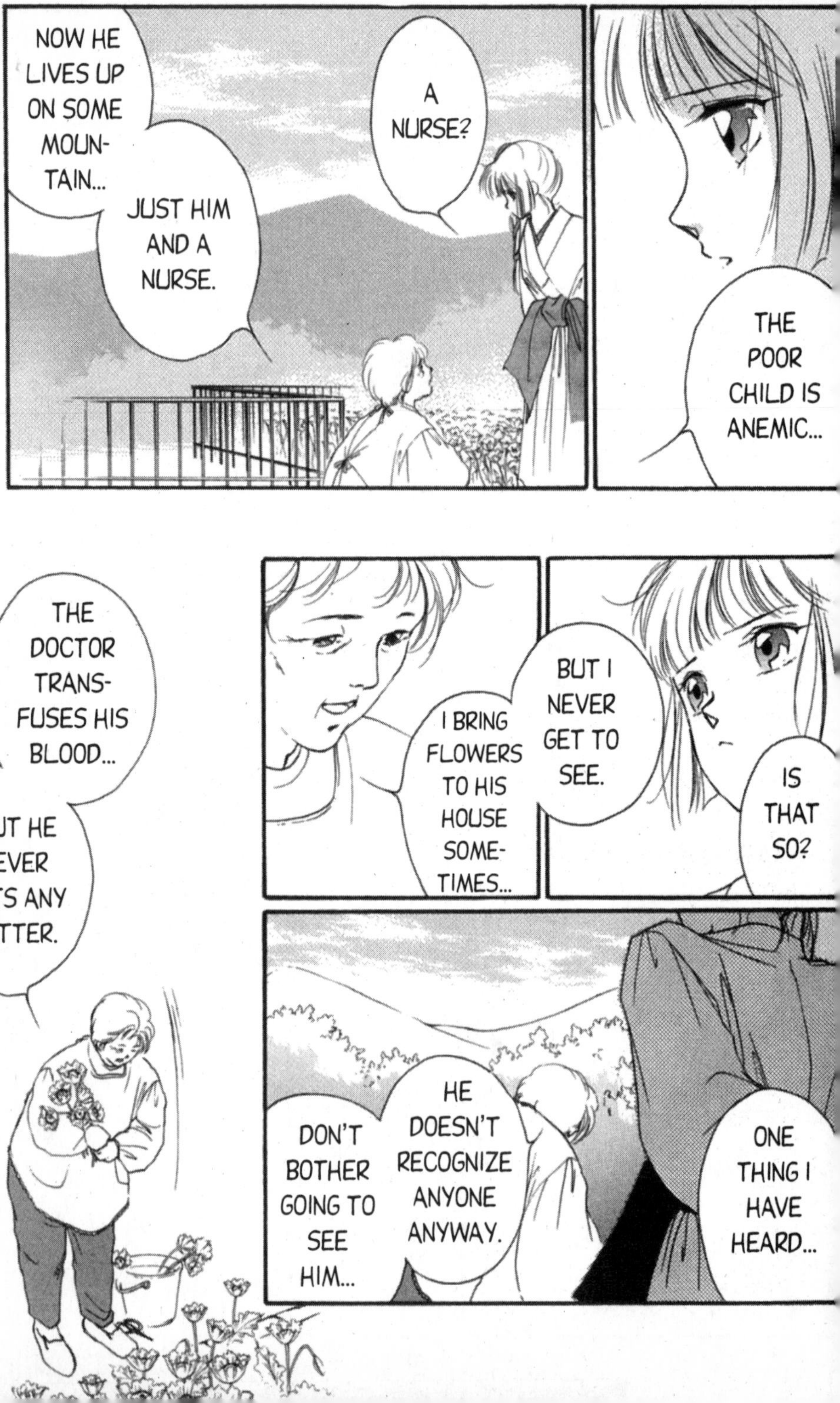
NOW HE LIVES UP ON SOME MOUN-TAIN...
JUST HIM AND A NURSE.
A NURSE?
THE POOR CHILD IS ANEMIC...
THE DOCTOR TRANS-FUSES HIS BLOOD...
BUT HE NEVER GETS ANY BETTER.
I BRING FLOWERS TO HIS HOUSE SOME-TIMES...
BUT I NEVER GET TO SEE.
IS THAT SO?
DON'T BOTHER GOING TO SEE HIM...
HE DOESN'T RECOGNIZE ANYONE ANYWAY.
ONE THING I HAVE HEARD...

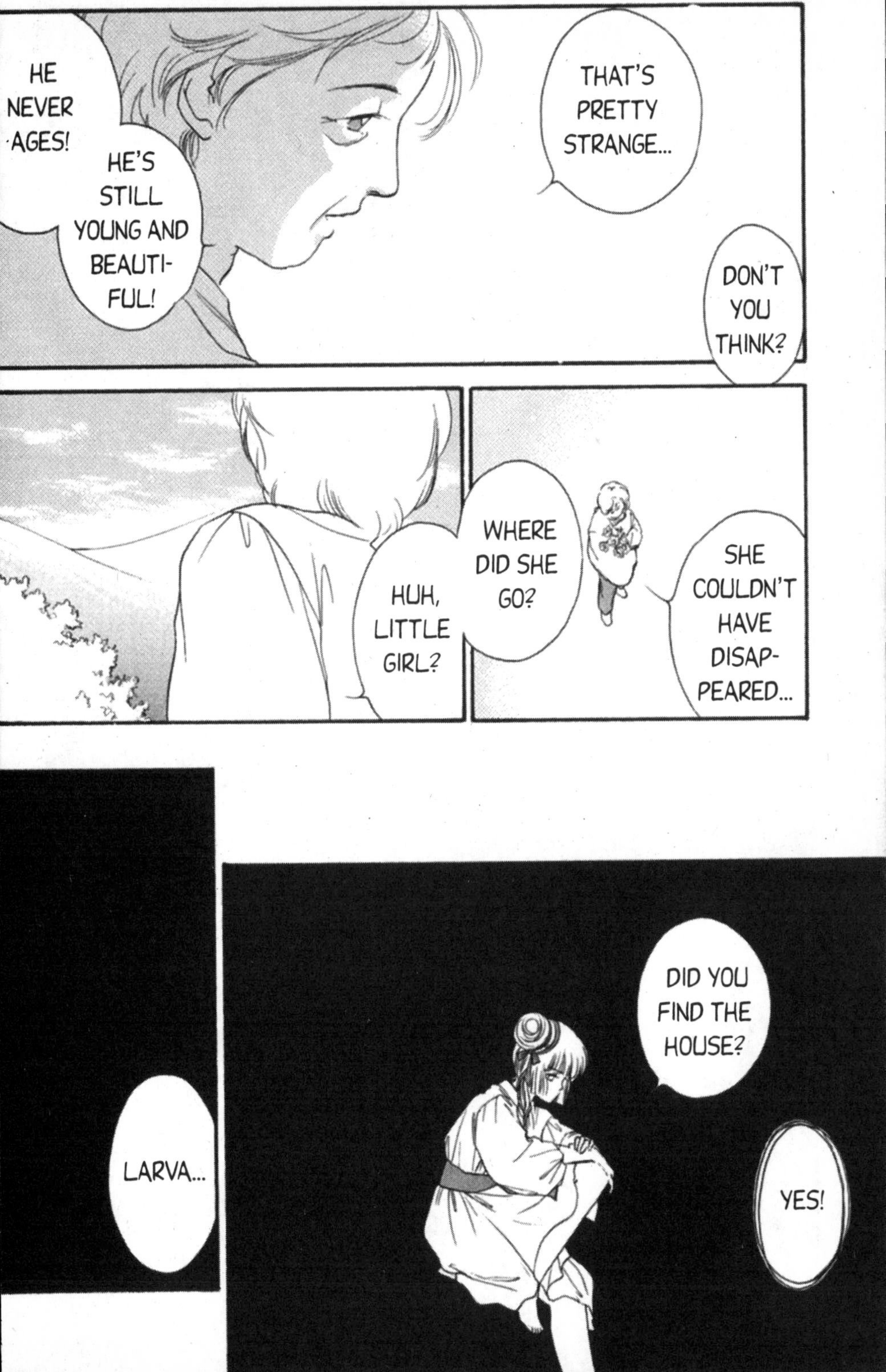
HE NEVER AGES!
HE'S STILL YOUNG AND BEAUTI-FUL!
THAT'S PRETTY STRANGE...
DON'T YOU THINK?
HUH, LITTLE GIRL?
WHERE DID SHE GO?
SHE COULDN'T HAVE DISAP-PEARED...
LARVA...
DID YOU FIND THE HOUSE?
YES!

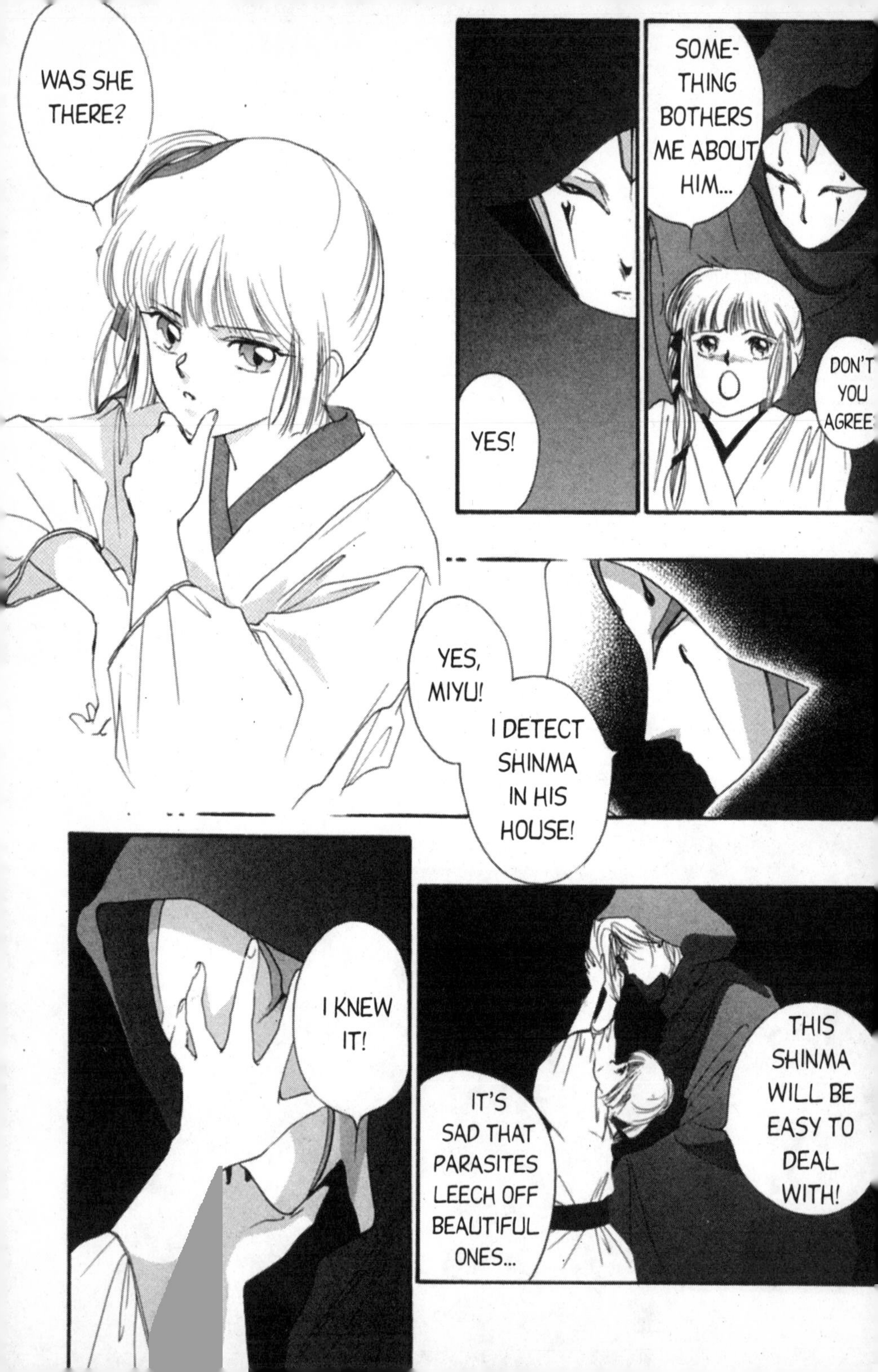
WAS SHE THERE?
YES!
SOME-THING BOTHERS ME ABOUT HIM...
DON'T YOU AGREE
YES, MIYU!
I DETECT SHINMA IN HIS HOUSE!
I KNEW IT!
IT'S SAD THAT PARASITES LEECH OFF BEAUTIFUL ONES...
THIS SHINMA WILL BE EASY TO DEAL WITH!

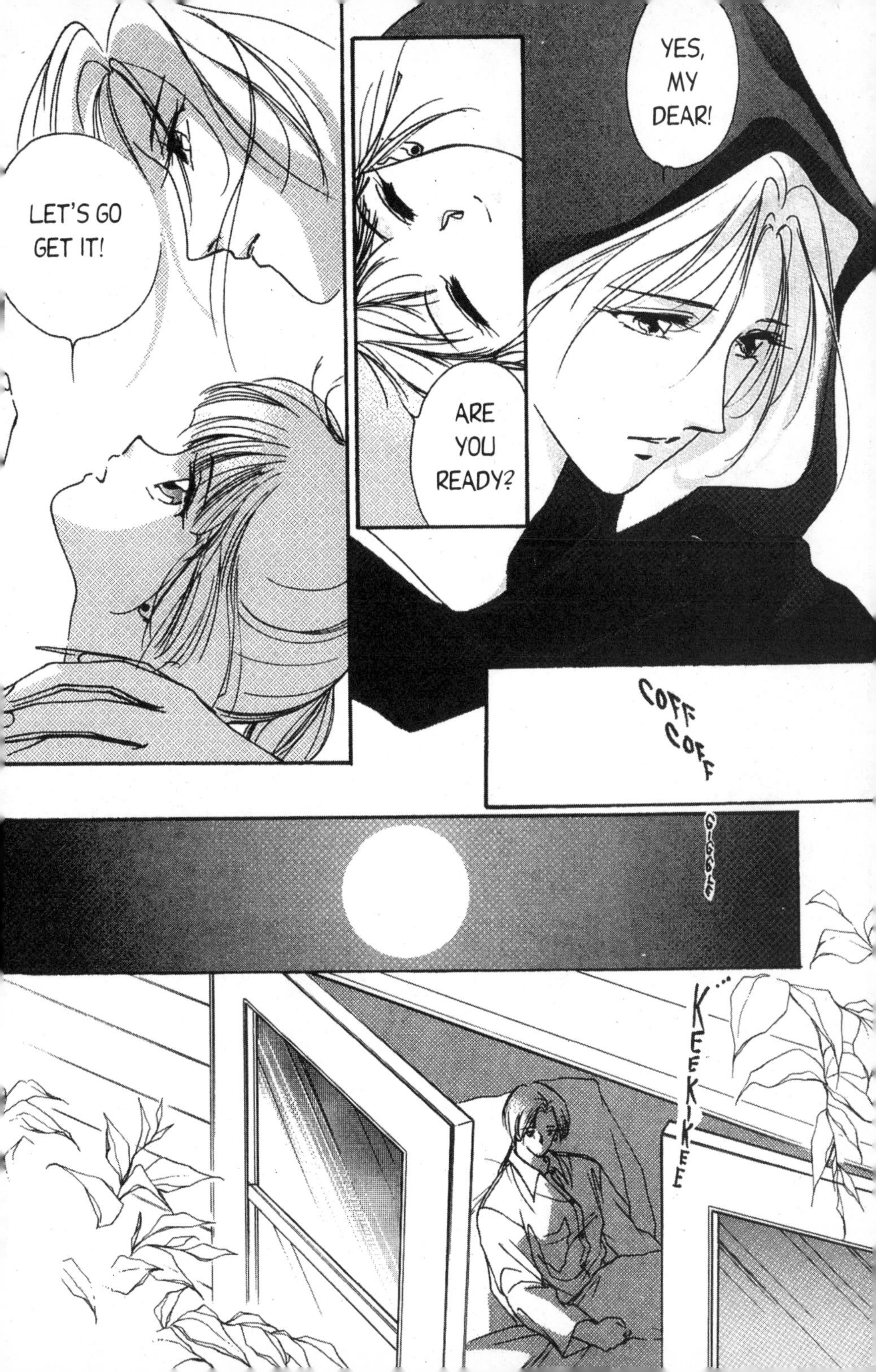
YES, MY DEAR!
ARE YOU READY?
LET'S GO GET IT!
COFF COFF
GIGGLE
KEEKIKEE...

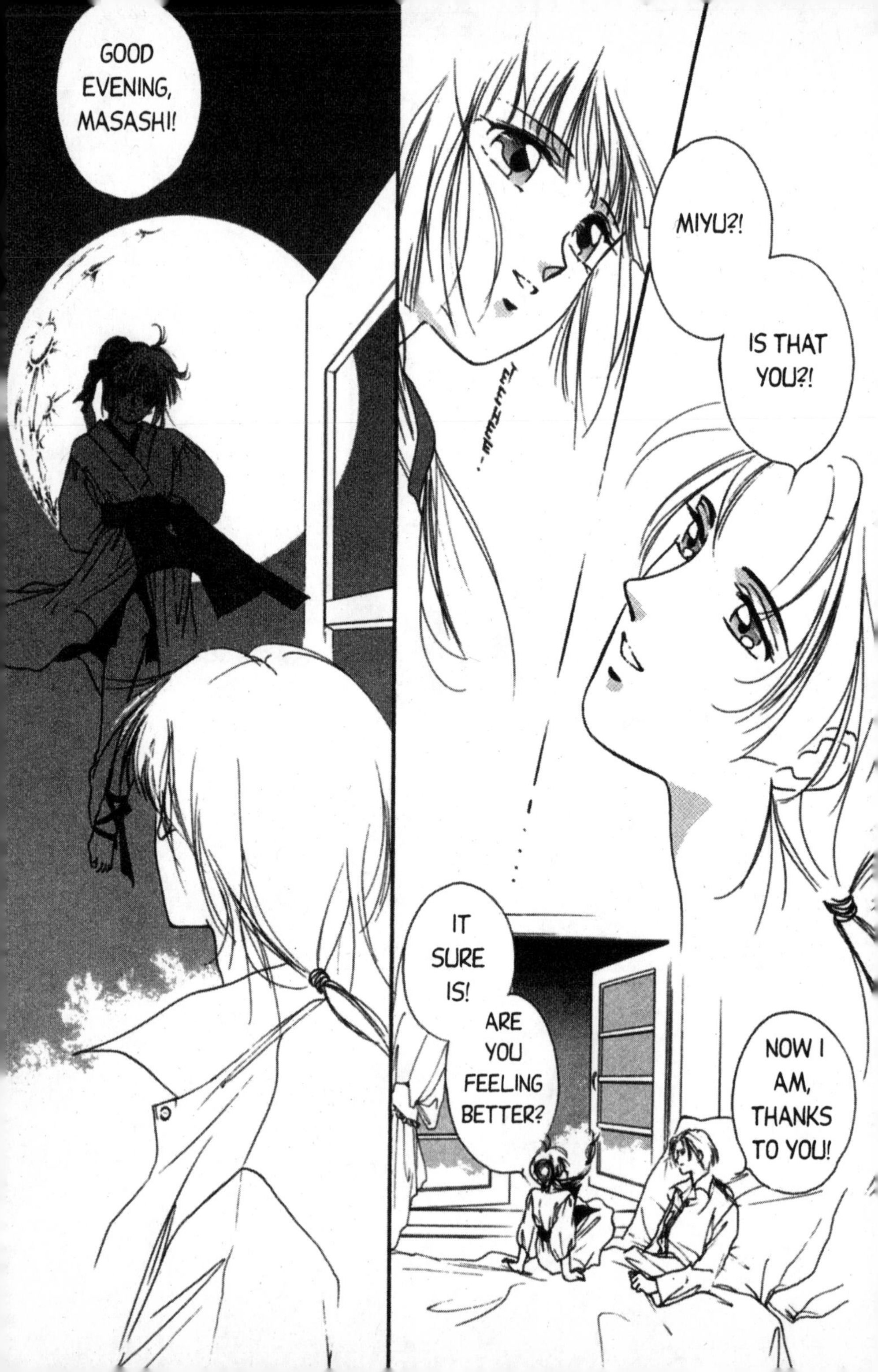
GOOD EVENING, MASASHI!
MIYU?!
IS THAT YOU?!
IT SURE IS!
ARE YOU FEELING BETTER?
NOW I AM, THANKS TO YOU!

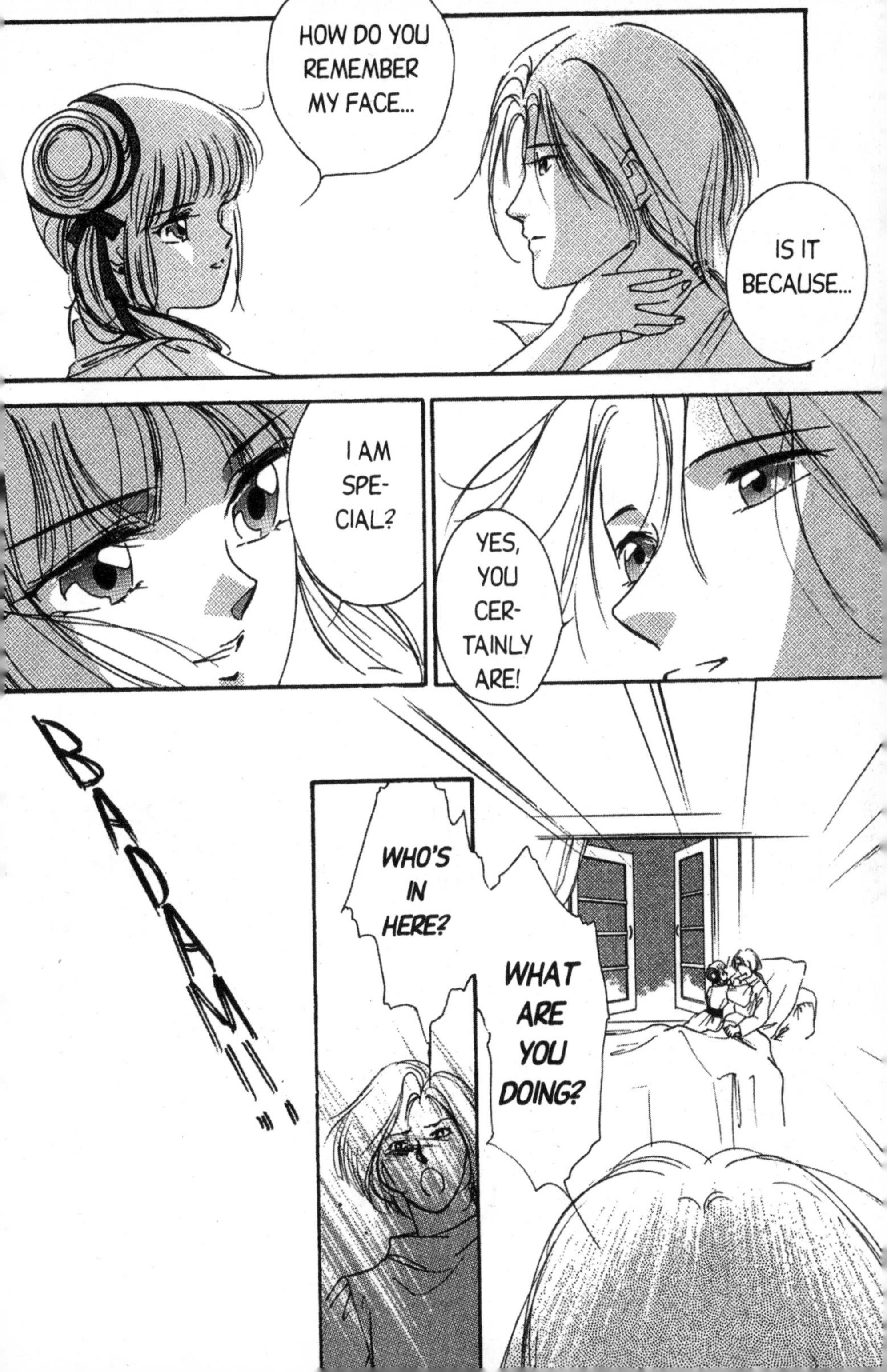
HOW DO YOU REMEMBER MY FACE...
IS IT BECAUSE...
I AM SPE-CIAL?
YES, YOU CER-TAINLY ARE!
BADAM!!
WHO'S IN HERE?
WHAT ARE YOU DOING?

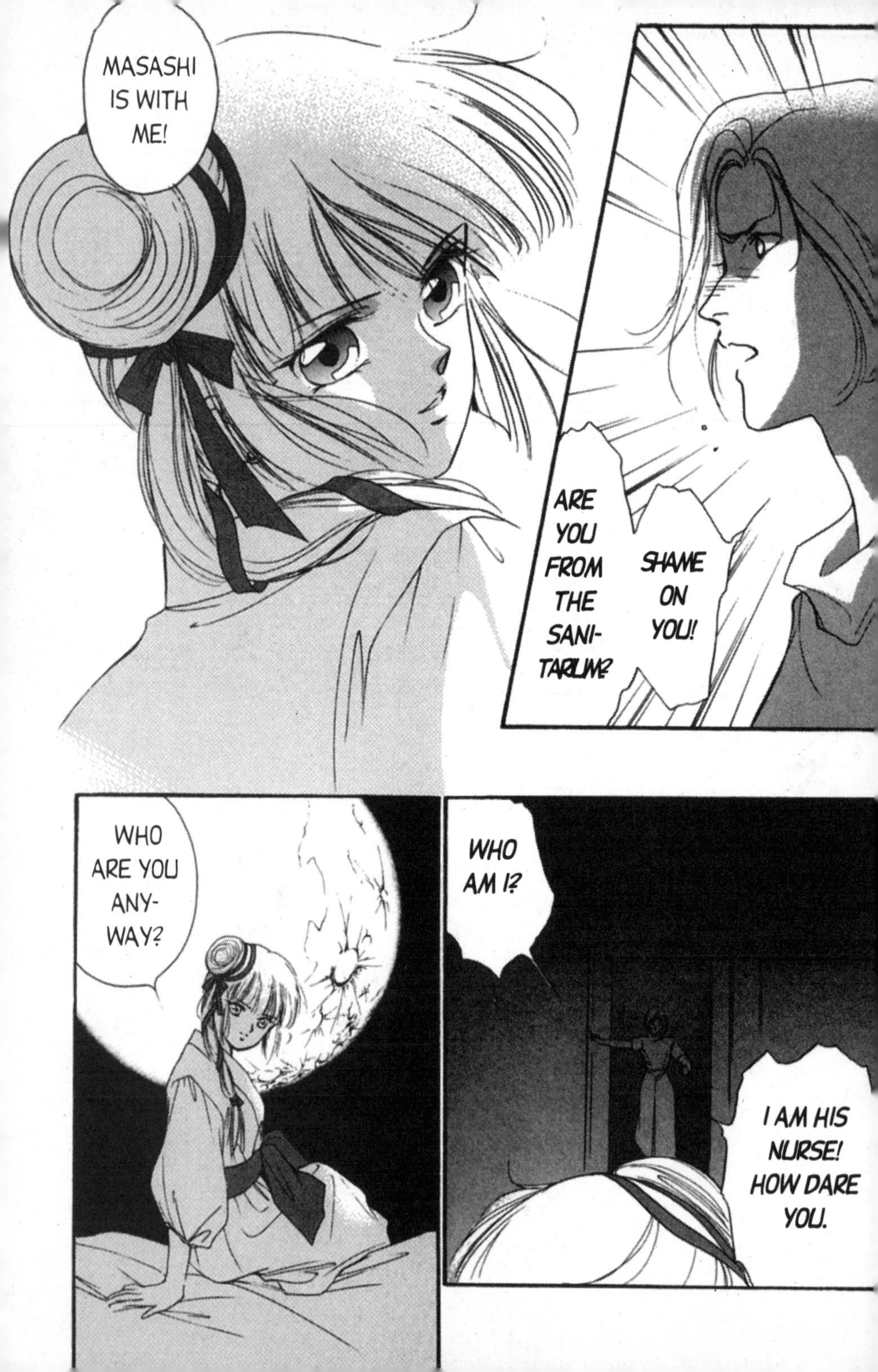
SHAME ON YOU!
ARE YOU FROM THE SANI-TARIUM?
MASASHI IS WITH ME!
WHO ARE YOU ANY-WAY?
WHO AM I?
I AM HIS NURSE! HOW DARE YOU.

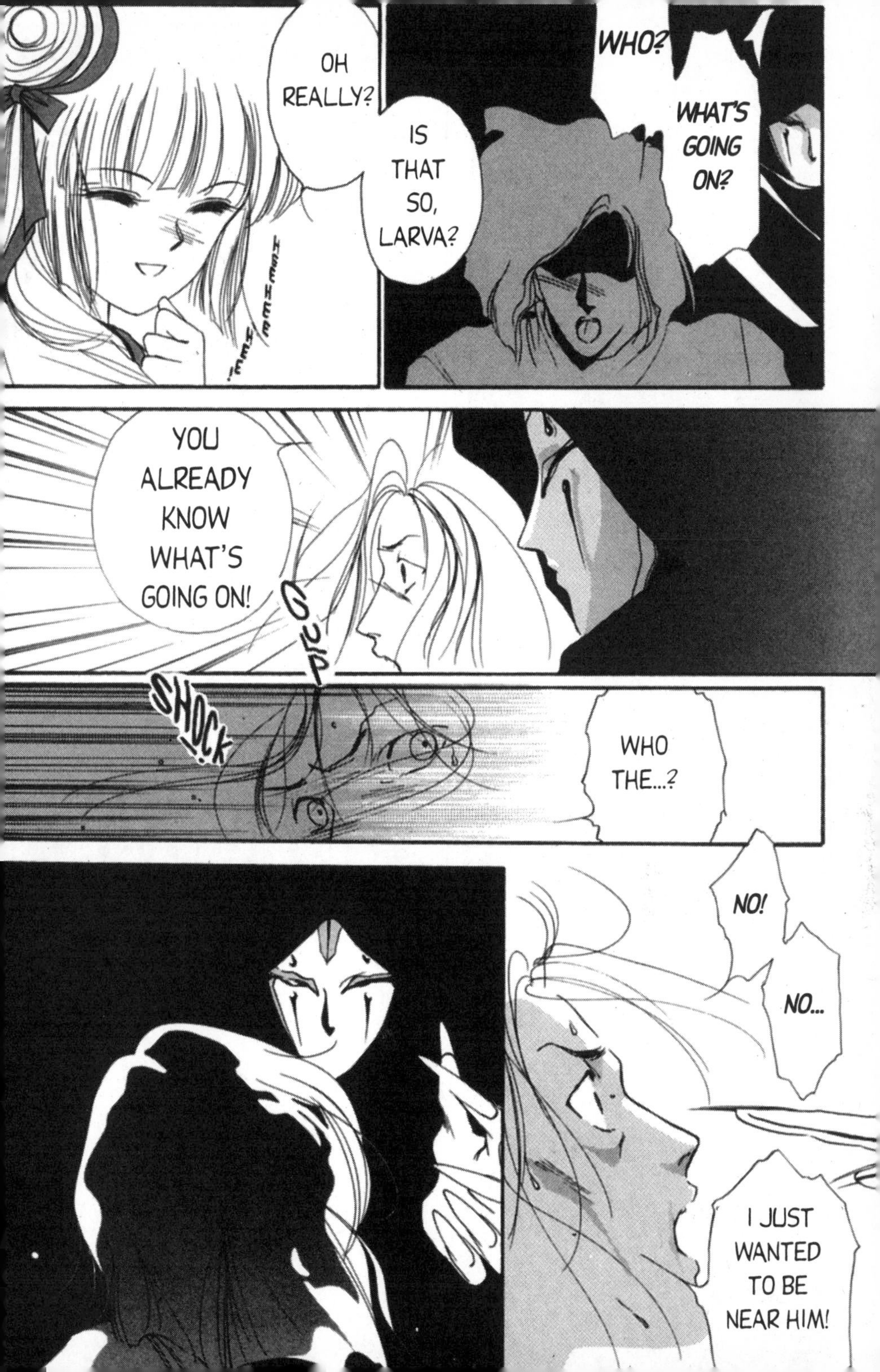
OH REALLY?
IS THAT SO, LARVA?
WHO?
WHAT'S GOING ON?
YOU ALREADY KNOW WHAT'S GOING ON!
GULP
SHOCK
WHO THE...?
NO!
NO...
I JUST WANTED TO BE NEAR HIM!

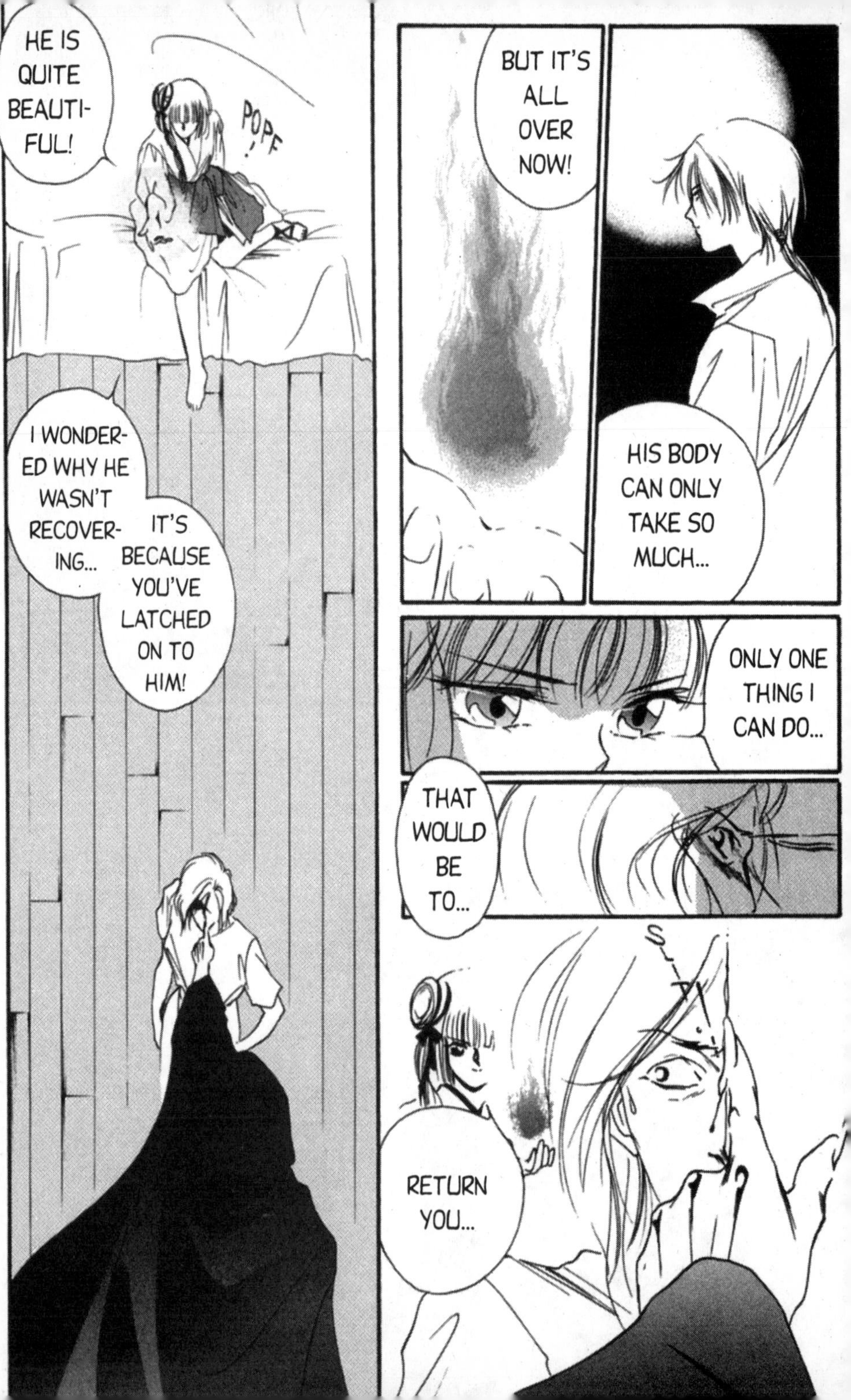
BUT IT'S ALL OVER NOW!
HIS BODY CAN ONLY TAKE SO MUCH...
ONLY ONE THING I CAN DO...
THAT WOULD BE TO...
RETURN YOU...
HE IS QUITE BEAUTI-FUL!
POPF
I WONDER-ED WHY HE WASN'T RECOVER-ING...
IT'S BECAUSE YOU'VE LATCHED ON TO HIM!

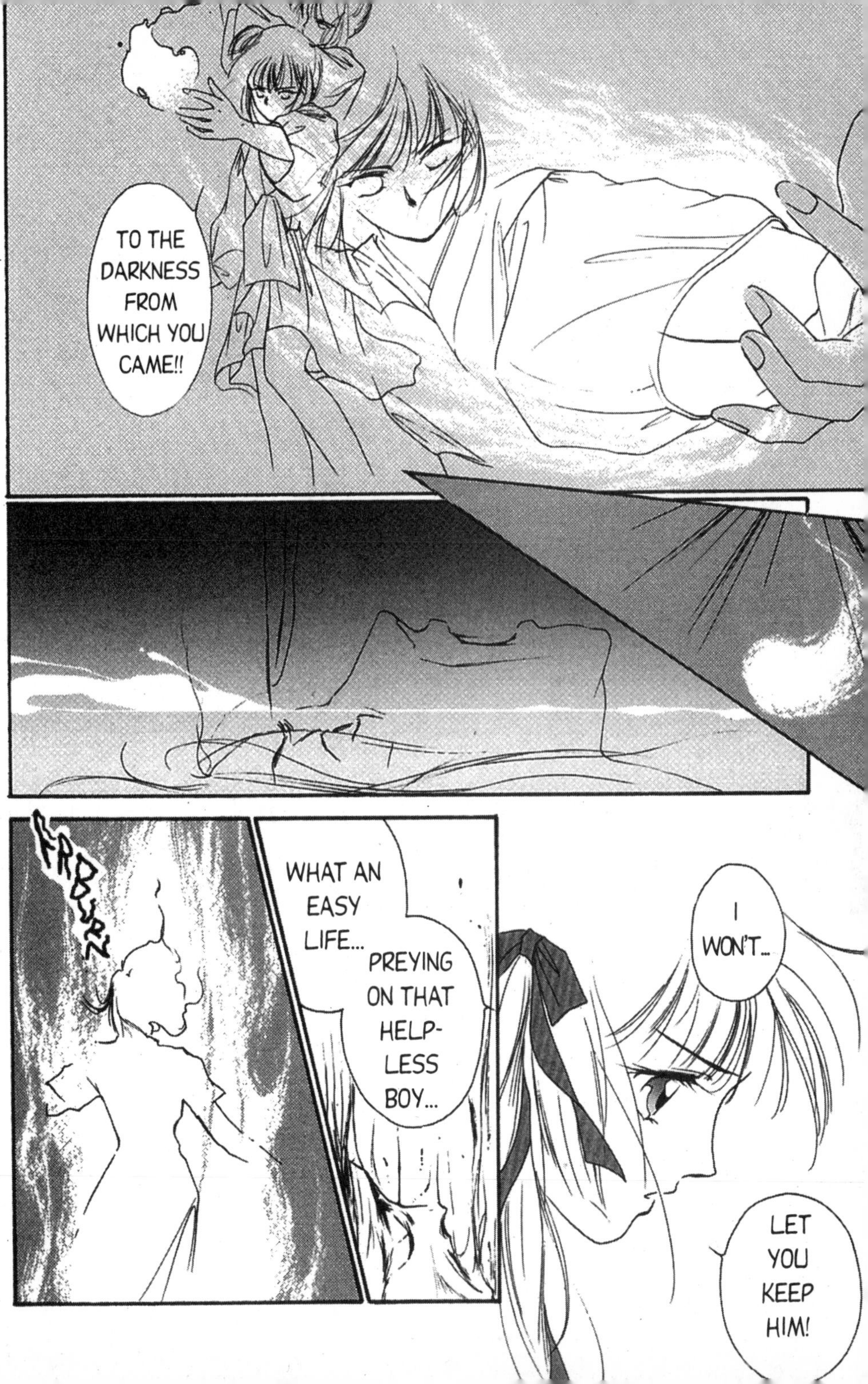
TO THE DARKNESS FROM WHICH YOU CAME!!
I WON'T...
LET YOU KEEP HIM!
WHAT AN EASY LIFE...
PREYING ON THAT HELP-LESS BOY...
FRBURN

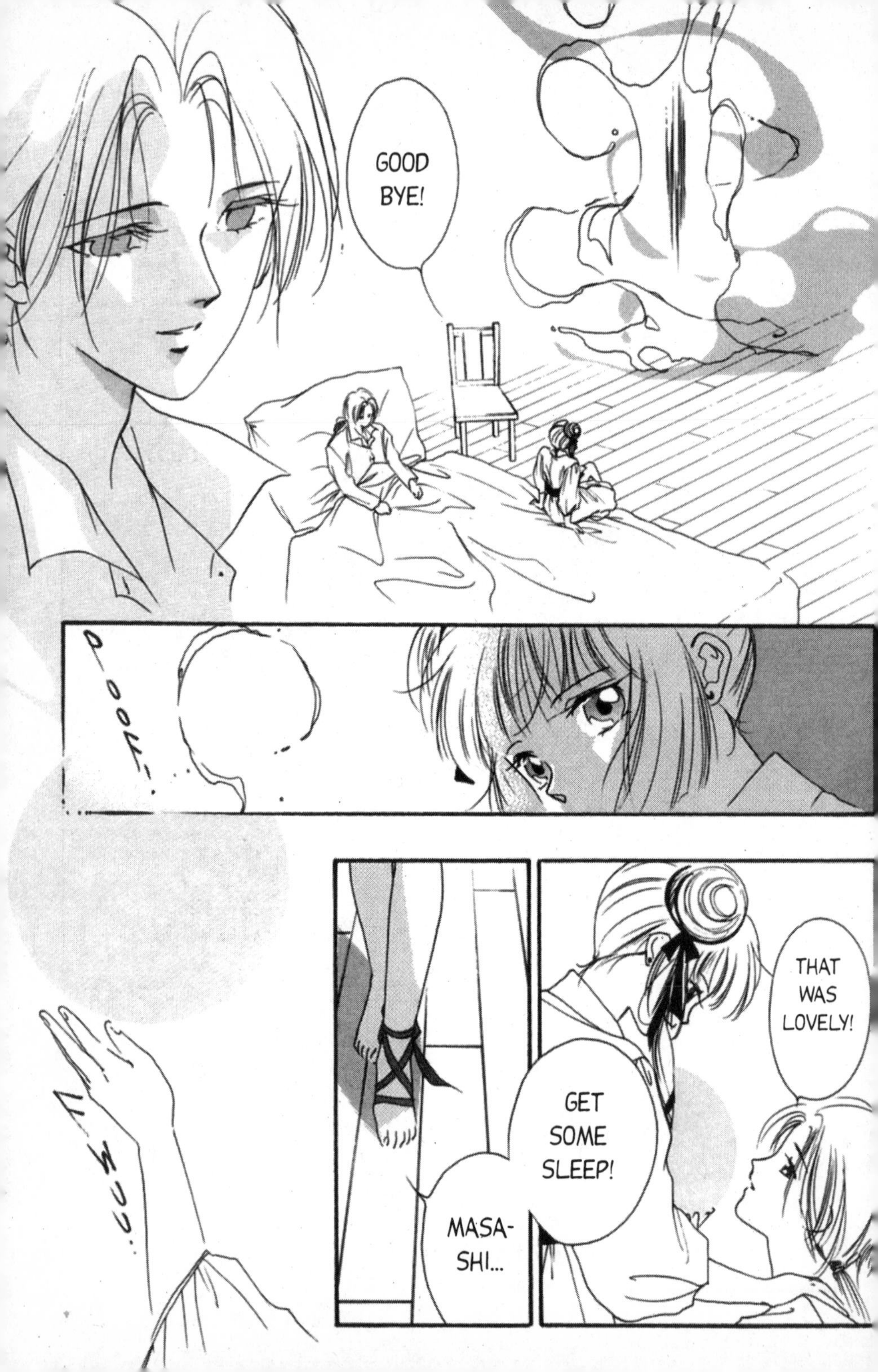
GOOD BYE!
THAT WAS LOVELY!
GET SOME SLEEP!
MASA-SHI...

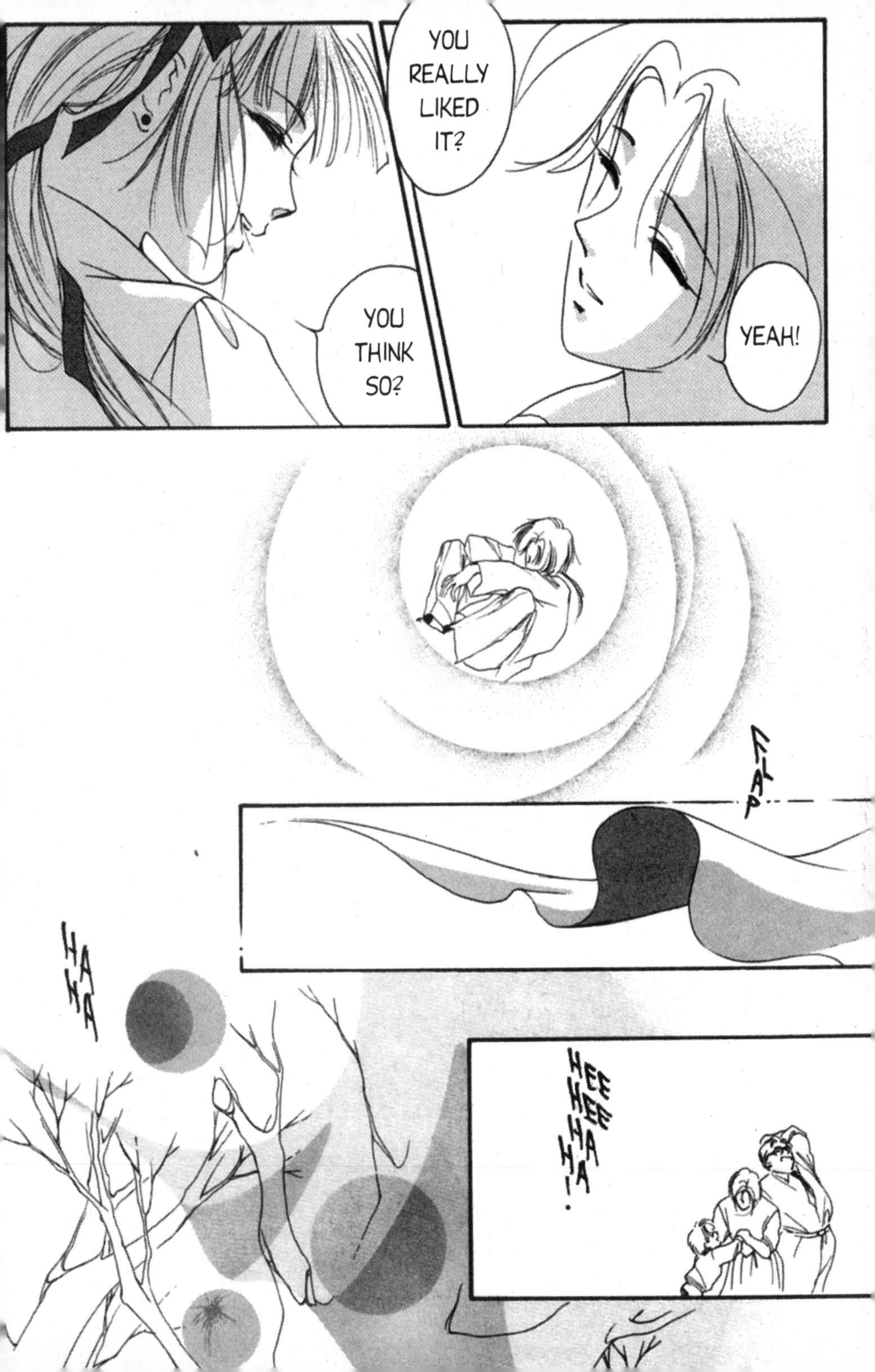
YOU REALLY LIKED IT?
YOU THINK SO?
YEAH!
FLAP
HA HA
HEE HEE HA HA!

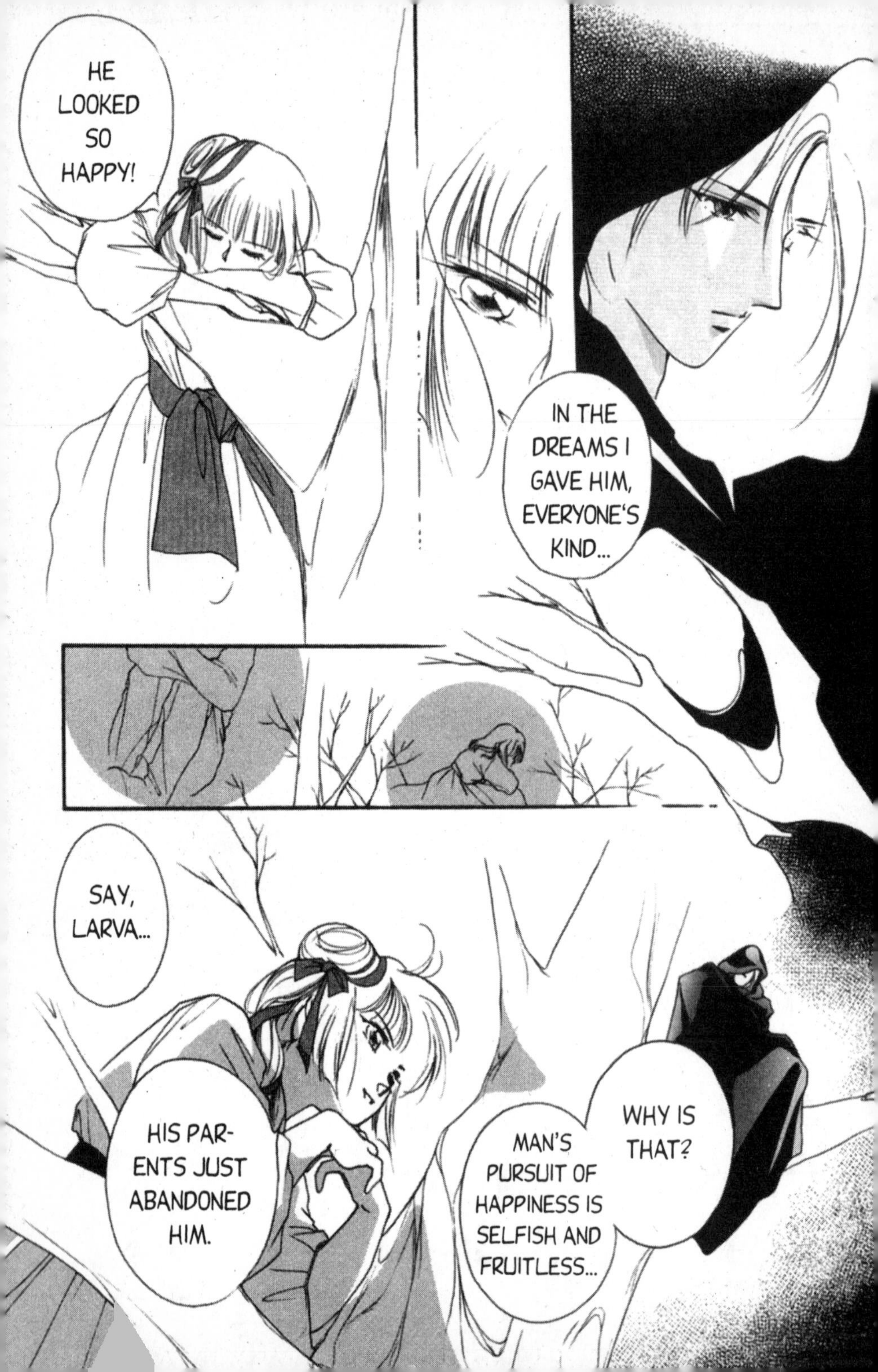
HE LOOKED SO HAPPY!
IN THE DREAMS I GAVE HIM, EVERYONE'S KIND...
SAY, LARVA...
HIS PAR-ENTS JUST ABANDONED HIM.
WHY IS THAT?
MAN'S PURSUIT OF HAPPINESS IS SELFISH AND FRUITLESS...

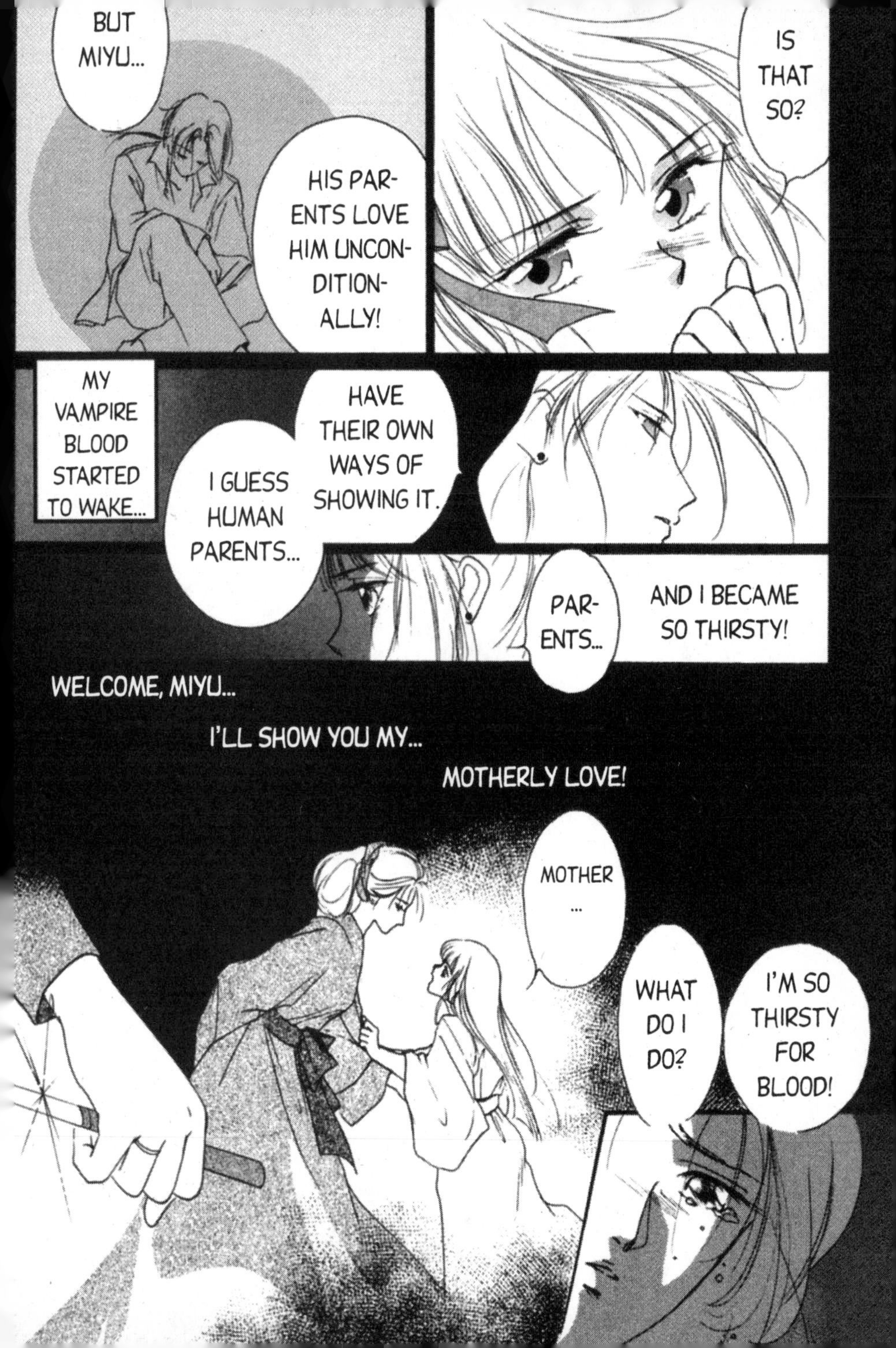
BUT MIYU...
HIS PARENTS LOVE HIM UNCONDITIONALLY!
IS THAT SO?
MY VAMPIRE BLOOD STARTED TO WAKE...
I GUESS HUMAN PARENTS...
HAVE THEIR OWN WAYS OF SHOWING IT.
PARENTS...
AND I BECAME SO THIRSTY!
WELCOME, MIYU...
I'LL SHOW YOU MY...
MOTHERLY LOVE!
MOTHER...
WHAT DO I DO?
I'M SO THIRSTY FOR BLOOD!

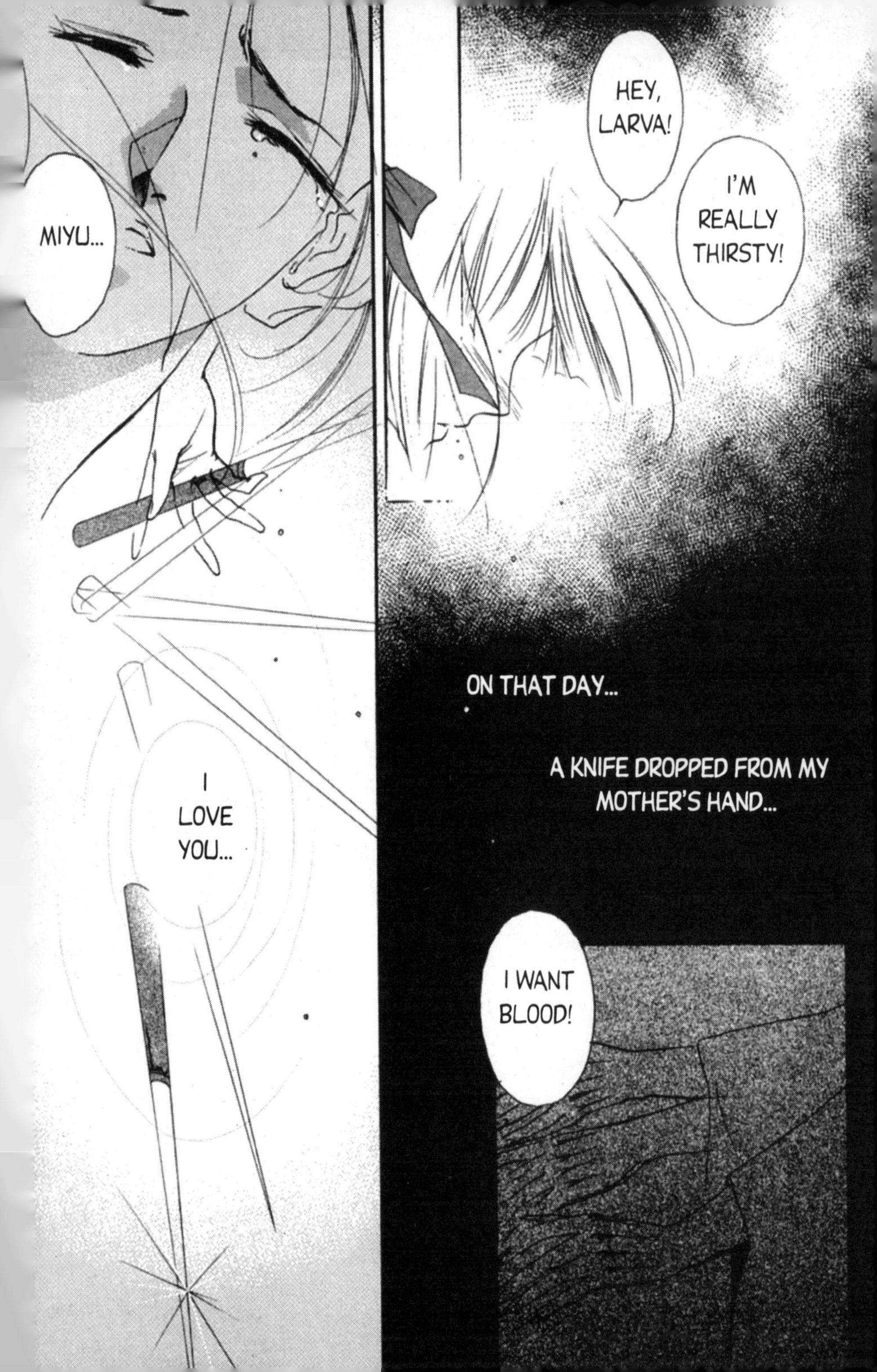
HEY, LARVA!
I'M REALLY THIRSTY!
ON THAT DAY...
A KNIFE DROPPED FROM MY MOTHER'S HAND...
I WANT BLOOD!
MIYU...
I LOVE YOU...

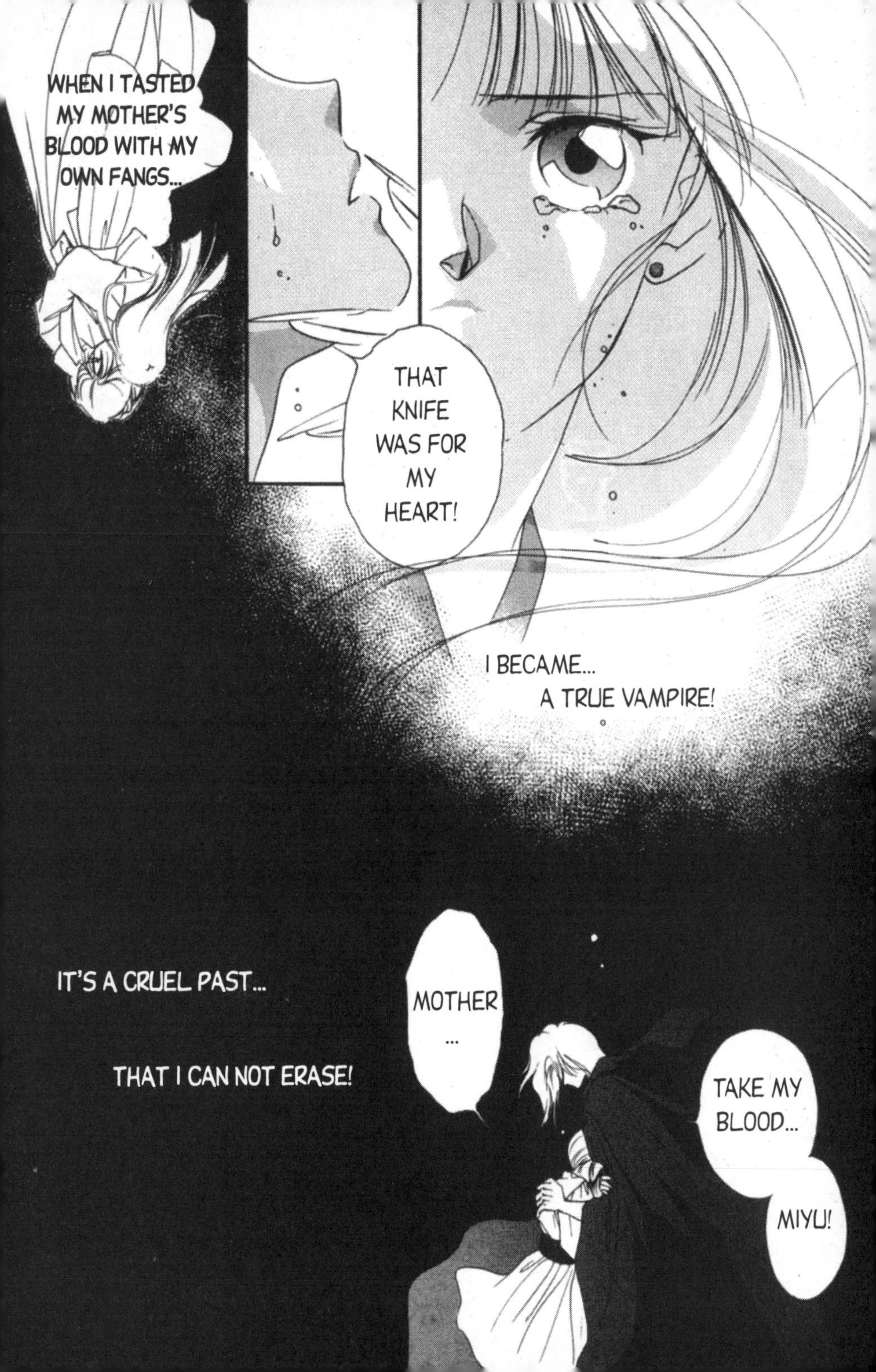
WHEN I TASTED MY MOTHER'S BLOOD WITH MY OWN FANGS...
THAT KNIFE WAS FOR MY HEART!
I BECAME... A TRUE VAMPIRE!
TAKE MY BLOOD...
MIYU!
MOTHER ...
IT'S A CRUEL PAST...
THAT I CAN NOT ERASE!

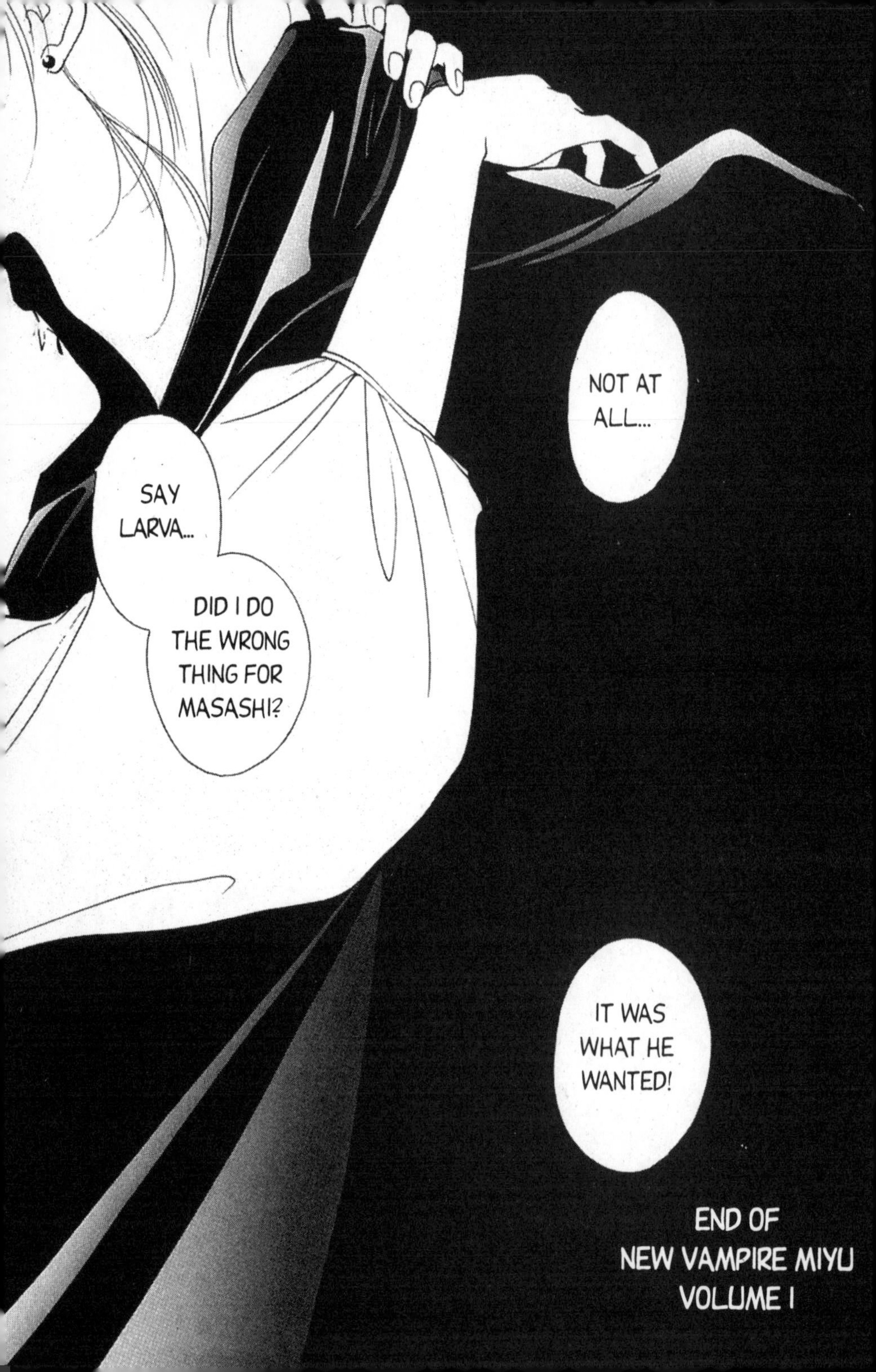
NOT AT ALL...
SAY LARVA...
DID I DO THE WRONG THING FOR MASASHI!?
IT WAS WHAT HE WANTED!
END OF NEW VAMPIRE MIYU VOLUME I

New Vampire Miyu
Illustration Gallery

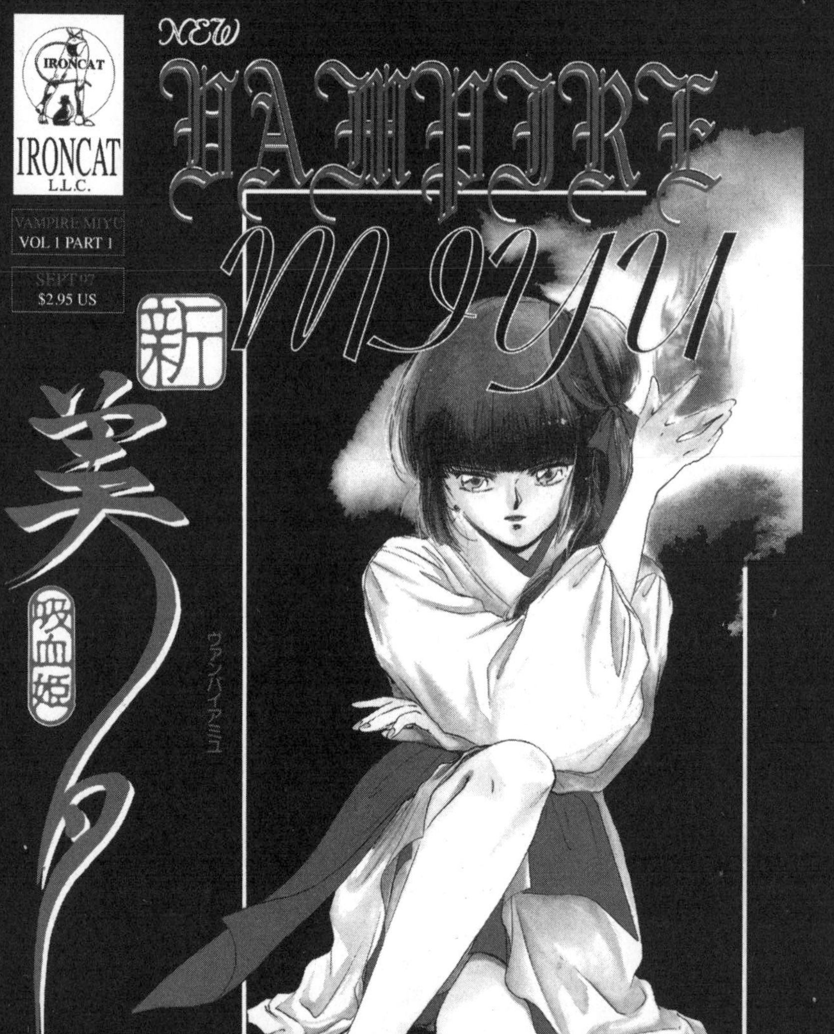
IRONCAT
IRONCAT
L.L.C.
VAMPIRE MIYU
VOL 1 PART 1
SEPT 97
$2.95 US
NEW
VAMPIRE
MIYU
新
美夕
吸血姫
ヴァンパイアミユ
Toshihiro Hirano & Narumi Kakinouchi

NEW VAMPIRE MIYU VOL. 1 ISSUE 1 COVER
RELEASED IN SEPTEMBER 1997

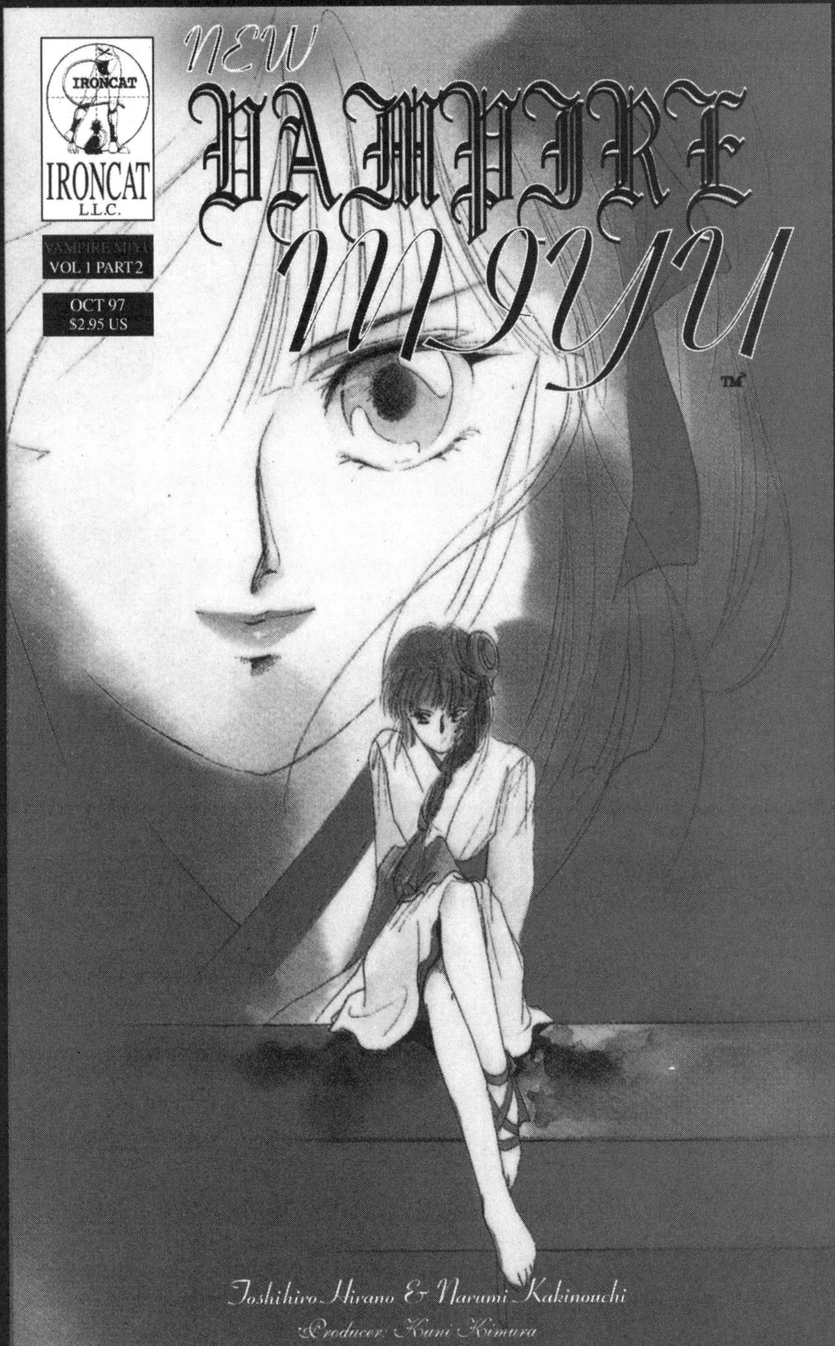
IRONCAT
IRONCAT
L.L.C.
NEW
VAMPIRE
MIYU
TM
VAMPIRE MIYU
VOL 1 PART 2
OCT 97
$2.95 US
Toshihiro Hirano & Narumi Kakinouchi
Producer: Kuni Kimura

NEW VAMPIRE MIYU VOL. 1 ISSUE 2 COVER
RELEASED IN OCTOBER 1997

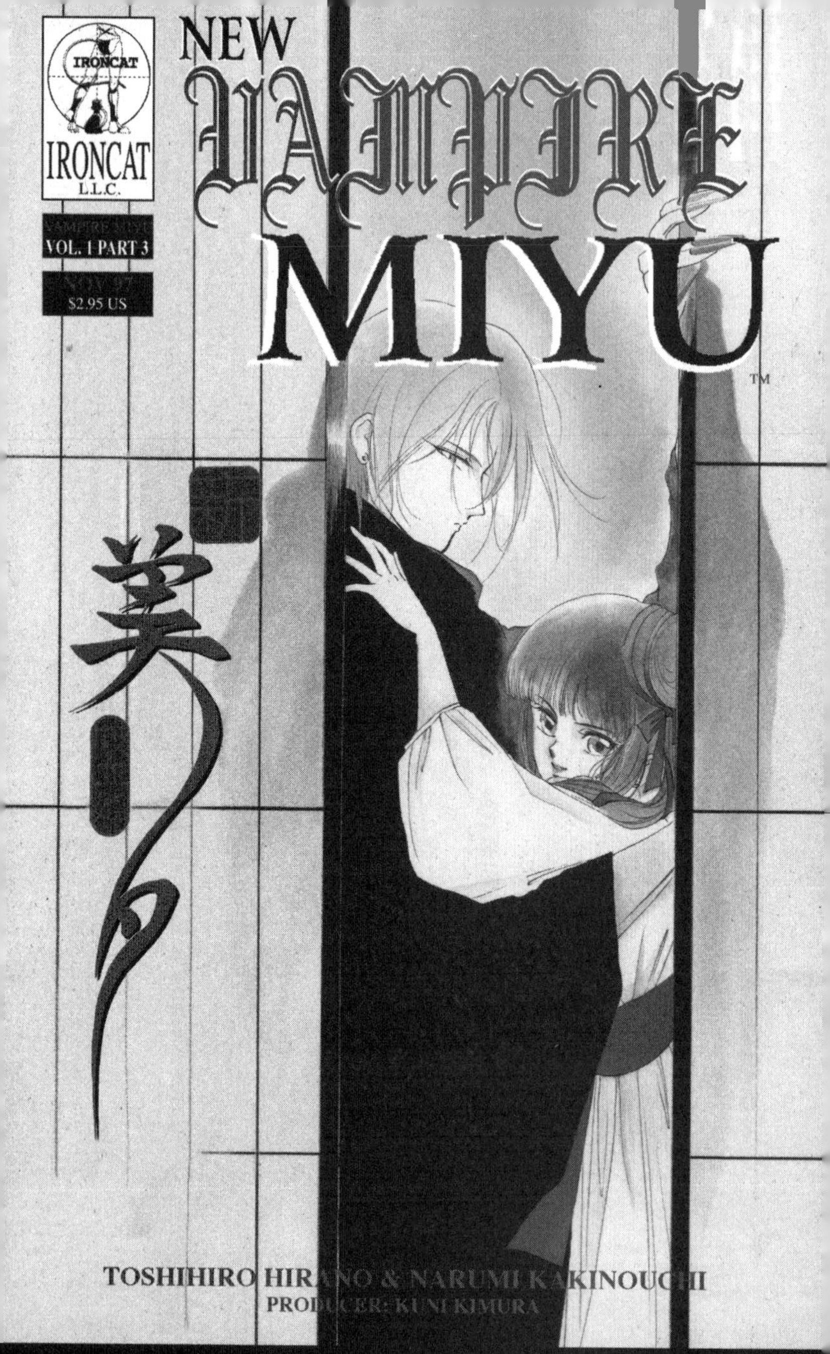
IRONCAT
IRONCAT L.L.C.
VOL. 1 PART 3
NOV 97
$2.95 US
NEW VAMPIRE MIYU
TM
美夕
TOSHIHIRO HIRANO & NARUMI KAKINOUCHI
PRODUCER: KUNI KIMURA

NEW VAMPIRE MIYU VOL. 1 ISSUE 3 COVER

IRONCAT L.L.C.

VAMPIRE MIYU
VOL 1 PART 4

DEC 97
$2.95 US
$4.10 CAN

NEW VAMPIRE MIYU

TOSHIHIRO HIRANO & NARUMI KAKINOUCHI
PRODUCER: KUNI KIMURA

NEW VAMPIRE MIYU VOL. I ISSUE 4 COVER
RELEASED IN DECEMBER 1997

IRONCAT
L.L.C.

VAMPIRE MIYU
VOL 1 PART 5

JAN 98
$2.95 US
$4.10 CAN

NEW VAMPIRE MIYU

TOSHIHIRO HIRANO & NARUMI KAKINOUCHI
PRODUCED KUNI KIMURA

NEW VAMPIRE MIYU VOL. I ISSUE 5 COVER
RELEASED IN JANUARY 1998

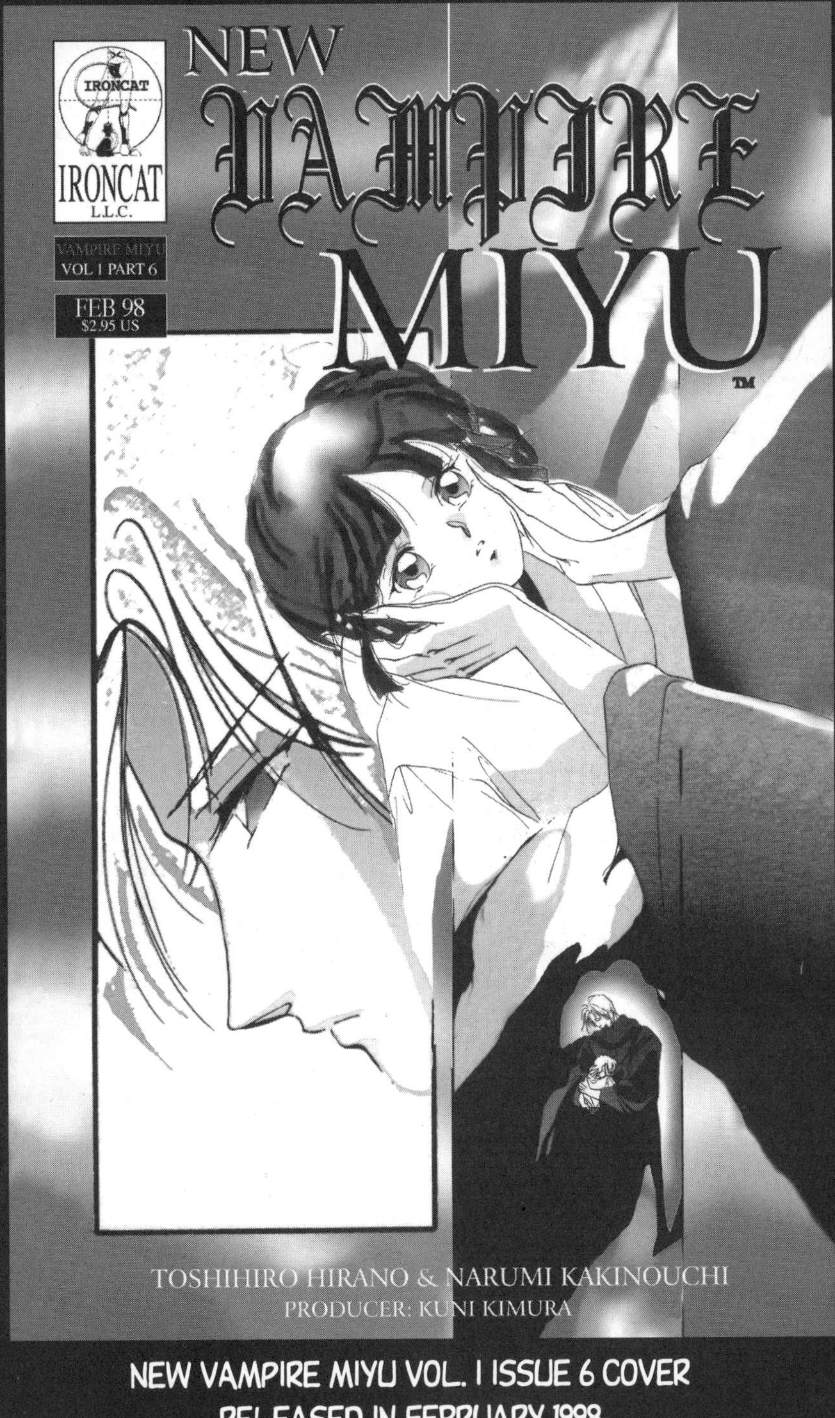
IRONCAT
IRONCAT
L.L.C.
NEW
VAMPIRE
MIYU
™
VAMPIRE MIYU
VOL 1 PART 6
FEB 98
$2.95 US
TOSHIHIRO HIRANO & NARUMI KAKINOUCHI
PRODUCER: KUNI KIMURA

NEW VAMPIRE MIYU VOL. 1 ISSUE 6 COVER
RELEASED IN FEBRUARY 1998

IRONCAT
L.L.C.

VAMPIRE MIYU
VOL 1 PART 7

MAR 98
$2.95 US

NEW VAMPIRE MIYU

TOSHIHIRO HIRANO & NARUMI KAKINOUCHI
PRODUCER: KUNI KIMURA

NEW VAMPIRE MIYU VOL. I ISSUE 7 COVER
RELEASED IN MARCH

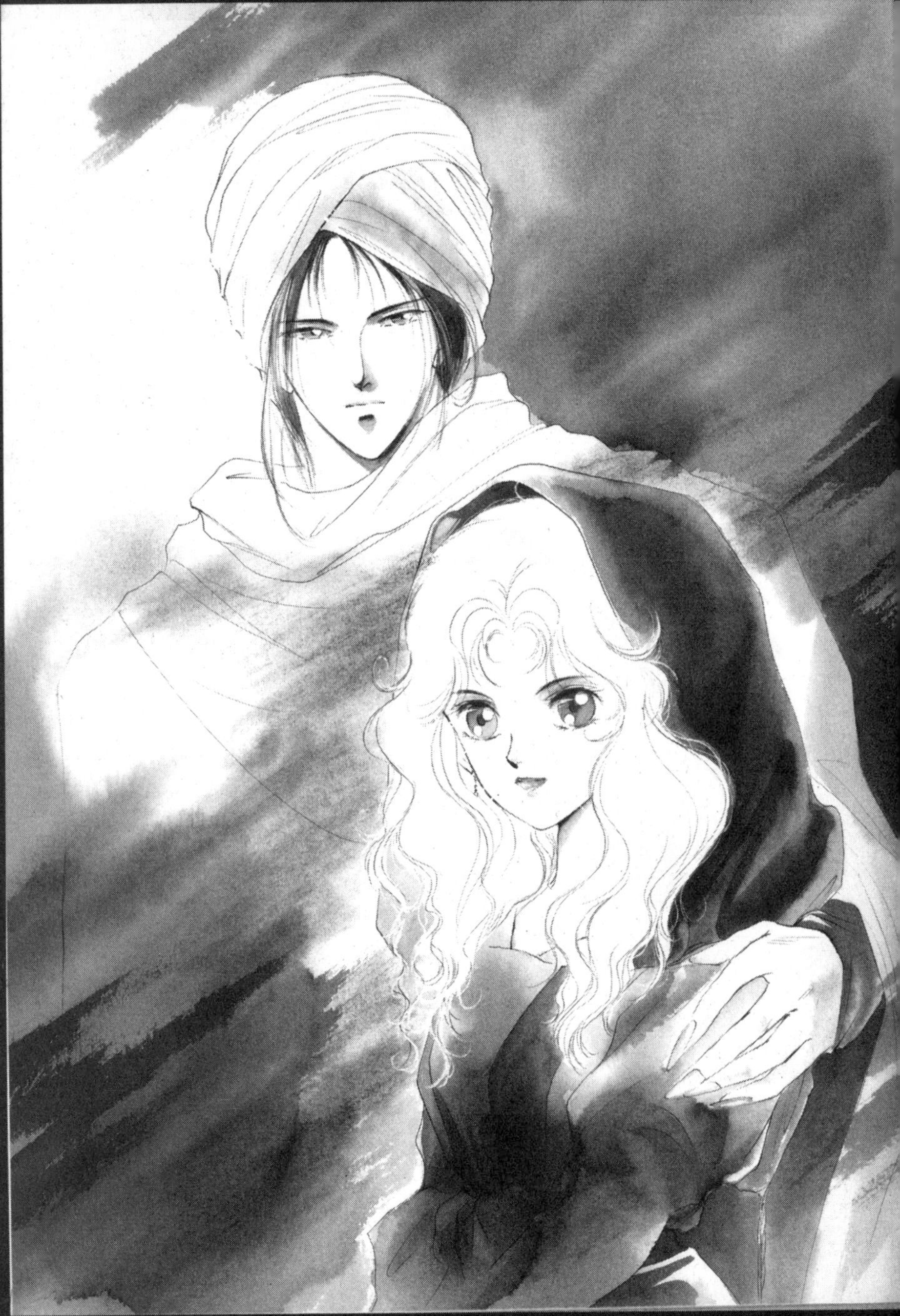

Pazusu & Carlua
“Susperia” Magazine cover.
February ‘93

The Western Shinma

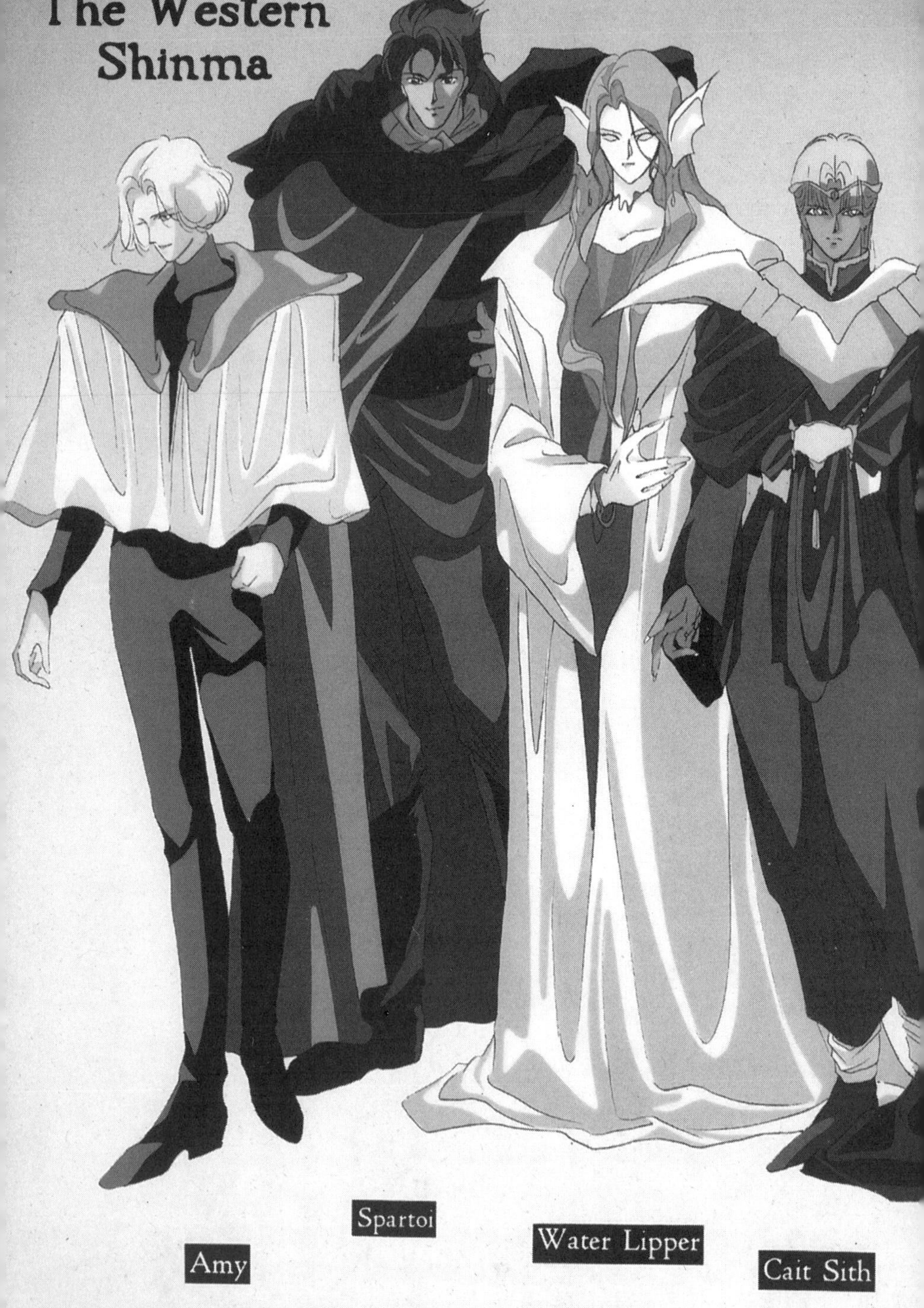

Spartoi
Amy
Water Lipper
Cait Sith

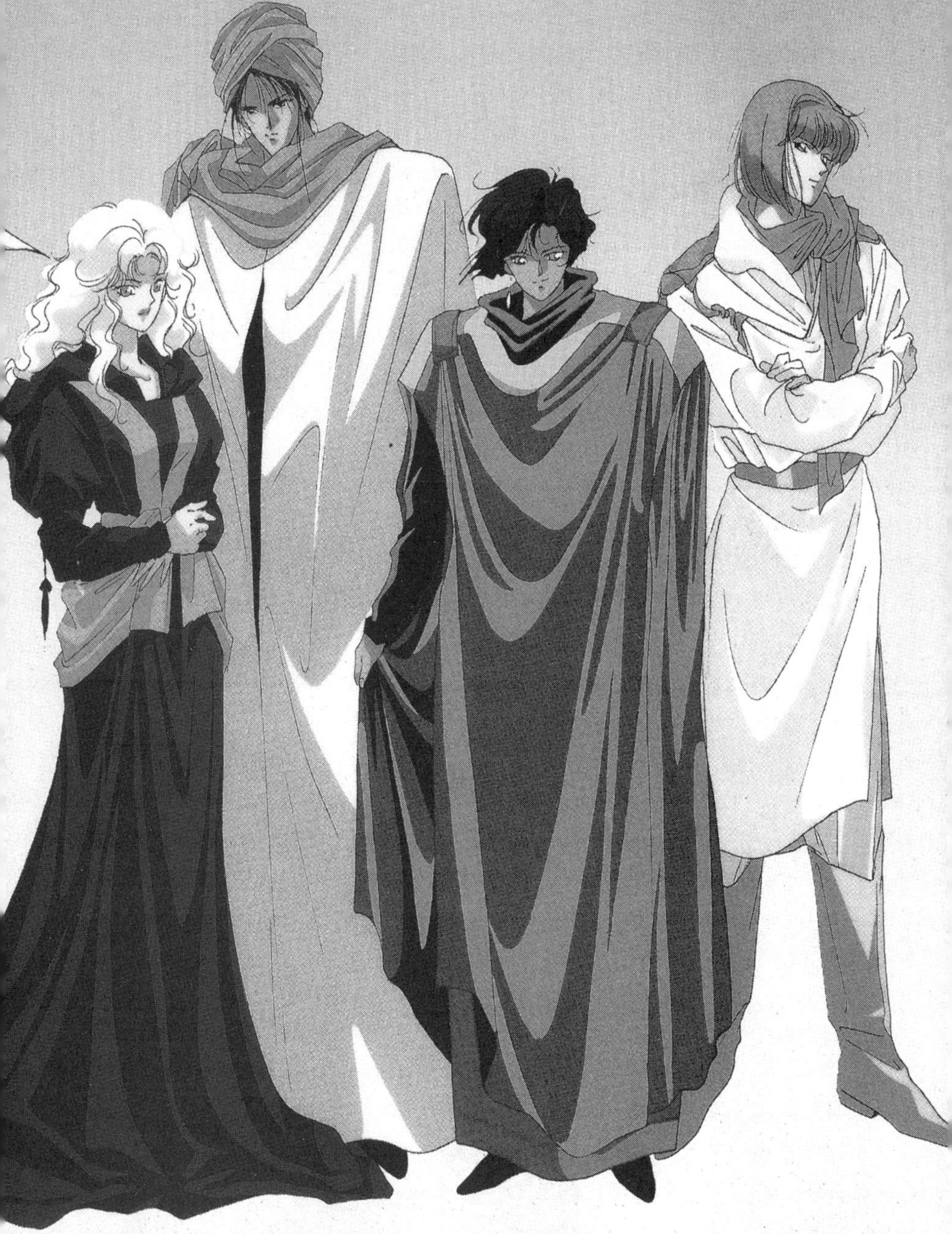

Carlua Pazusu Lemunia Night Gia

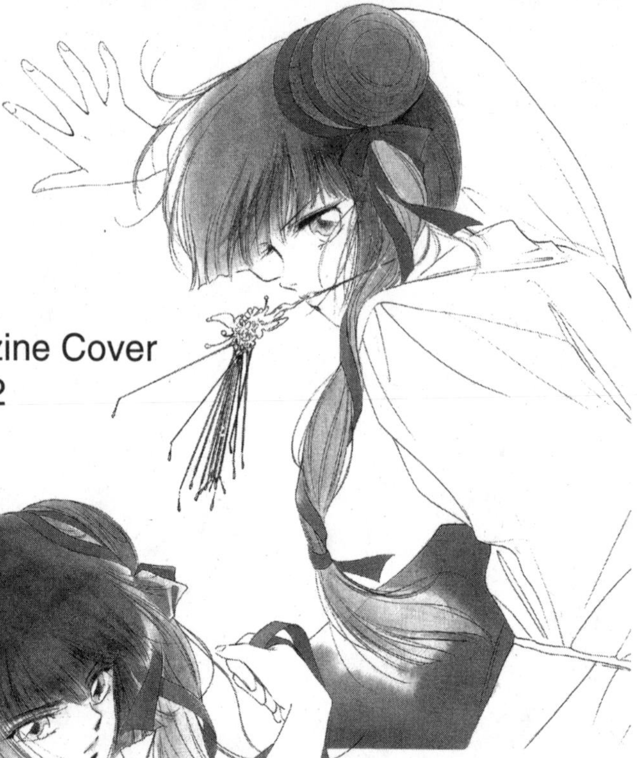

Miyu

"Susperia" Magazine Cover
June '92

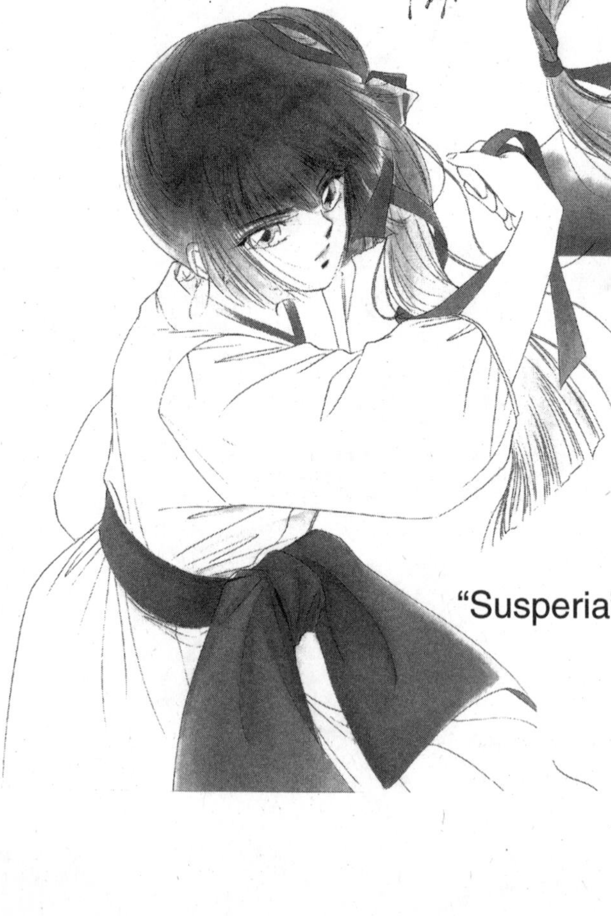

Miyu

"Susperia" Magazine Cove
May '92

新

美

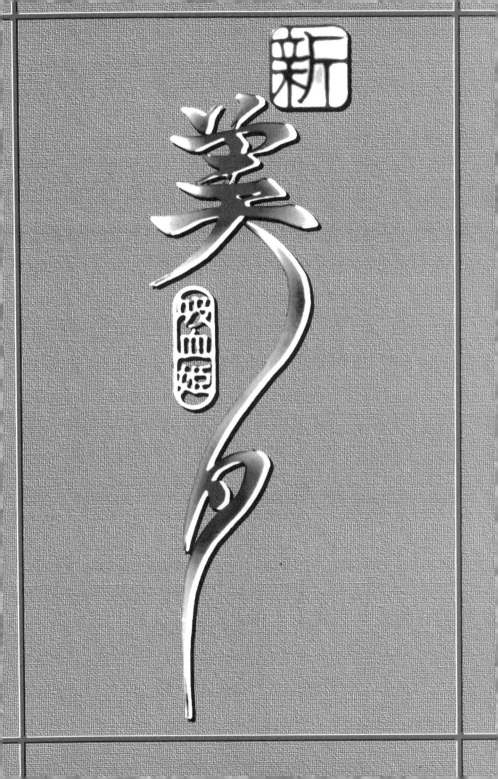

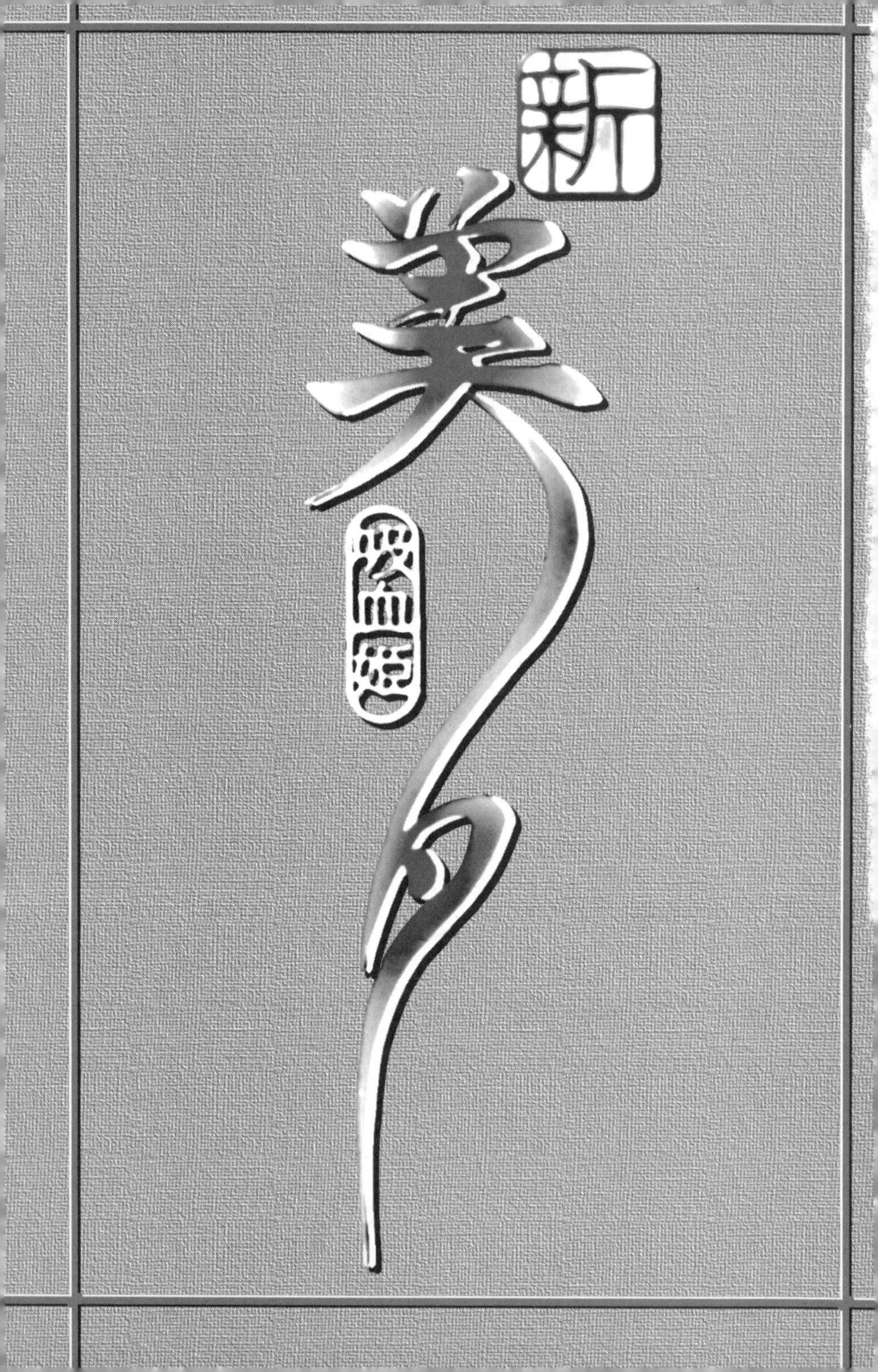
新
美